ƒP

Lapdogs

HOW THE PRESS ROLLED OVER FOR BUSH

Eric Boehlert

FREE PRESS

New York   London   Toronto   Sydney

FREE PRESS
A Division of Simon & Schuster, Inc.
1230 Avenue of the Americas
New York, NY 10020

Copyright © 2006 by Eric Boehlert

Manufactured in the United States of America

1   3   5   7   9   10   8   6   4   2

Library of Congress Cataloging-in-Publication Data is available

ISBN-13: 978-0-7432-8931-3
ISBN-10:   0-7432-8931-5

For information regarding special discounts for bulk purchases,
please contact Simon & Schuster Special Sales at
1-800-456-6798 or business@simonandschuster.com

To my friend, the late,
great Timothy White,
who inspired me to be a journalist.

Contents

Preface and Acknowledgments

Thanks go out to many people for helping make this book possible. I'll start with my agent Richard Abate whom I've known since the eighth grade back at Baldwin Middle School in Guilford, Connecticut. He really made this book happen. Thanks to my Free Press editor Dominick Anfuso, I appreciate his support.

Special thanks to Sidney Blumenthal for his guidance throughout the writing and editing process. Also a special thanks to Eric Alterman, whose 2003 book *What Liberal Media?* I clearly use as a blueprint for my own book, and whose daily Altercation blog on MSNBC.com has been an invaluable resource. Alterman also offered me the single best piece of advice for writing *Lapdogs*. I want to thank Mark Hertsgaard for writing *On Bended Knee: The Press and the Reagan Presidency* and to Gene Lyons for writing *Fools for Scandal: How the Media Invented Whitewater*, two momentous books that meant a lot to me years before I ever contemplated writing a book about the press and politics myself.

Of course, I want to thank my family (brothers, sister, parents, cousins, aunts, uncles) for their endless support, and especially my wife Tracy who has always believed in me. Thanks to my good friend Ted Dawson for designing the book cover. And to Bob Breslin, thanks for the suspenders.

Over the years lots of people, places, and things have influenced me in my personal and professional pursuits (perhaps unbeknownst to them), and I'd like to take this opportunity to express my appreciation to Mr. B., Joe Maher, Donnie Kaufman, Mary Beth McQueeney, Marty Musket, Adnar Haydar, *The Daily Collegian*, WOZA, CD Hotline, Steve Morse, Gary Hoenig, John Motavalli, Chuck Ross, Phyllis Stark, Keith Moerer, Jim DeRogatis, Bill Wyman, Russ Smith, Jonathan Alter, Katrina Vanden Heuvel, and, of course, the Condors.

The goal of *Lapdogs* is to cut through incessant rhetoric about a liberal media bias, and to show, factually, just how the mainstream media has tipped the scales in President Bush's favor for going on six years. The proof for that is all in the public record; in the voluminous pages of the *New York Times, Washington Post, Newsweek,* and *Time,* just to name a few, as well as in the mountain of transcripts produced by network and cable news programs. *Lapdogs* simply corrals as much of the information as possible and lays it out in a way I think makes the conclusion—that the press rolled over for Bush—inescapable.

The foundation of *Lapdogs* rests on the dozens of news articles and essays I wrote about the media for *Salon* between 2000 and 2005, as well as later contributions on the Huffington Post. While I relied on that work, and I'm grateful to *Salon* and the Huffington Post for letting me reproduce portions of them in *Lapdogs,* I also significantly expanded the research and reporting to give as vivid a picture of today's mainstream media as possible.

Indeed, I've been fortunate, amidst rampant media consolidation, to be associated with three of the few remaining national, independent outlets, which welcomed my work. Thanks to *Salon, Rolling Stone,* and the Huffington Post. And specifically, thanks to David Talbot and Joan Walsh, Jann Wenner and Arianna Huffington.

The explosion of online political commentary, and specifically the close eye being kept on the press, has made a book like *Lapdogs* all the more easy to research and write. Thanks to the army of often amateur writers and researchers on the Web who have injected their savvy passion into the debate over the American media.

A special note about two online resources whose work I relied on extensively: Media Matters for America and The Daily Howler. Media Matters for America was founded by David Brock as a way to monitor the press in real time and to pinpoint factual inaccuracies as well as instances where the mainstream media simply adopt Republican spin as their narrative of choice. The group's voluminous research is not only meticulous, but has already had a substantial impact on the public dialogue about the American press.

As for The Daily Howler, I'm not sure I can recall the first time I read Bob Somerby's website (it was sometime in the late 1990s), but I do know over the years his writing has been extraordinarily influential in how I think about the press. Somerby's daily critiques are fearless, exhaustive, and brilliant (as well as often hilarious), which is why I lean so heavily on his work in this book. Throughout *Lapdogs* I try to credit both Media Matters for America and The Daily Howler as often as possible. But just so there is no doubt, I want to be clear: if it weren't for the tireless work of Media Matters for America and The Daily Howler, *Lapdogs* would not have been possible.

Two other notes about research. The main tools I used to navigate my way through all those print stories and television newscasts were Nexis and TVEyes. Nexis is widely regarded as the definitive news research database, allowing users to search through the libraries of virtually every major American news outlet. And it's Nexis that I relied upon to determine with specificity, for instance, which stories were and were not covered. The same with TVEyes. For instance, in chapter 9 I write definitively that, "Between May 1 and June 6, the Downing Street memo story received approximately twenty mentions on CNN, Fox News, MSNBC, ABC, CBS, NBC, and PBS *combined.*" That is based on my use of the extraordinary research tools available at TVEyes, the around-the-clock digital television monitoring service which captures virtually every word uttered on the major networks, cable channels, and leading radio stations. Thanks to Larry Gallo at TVEyes.

As for the book's formatting, some of the chapters focus intently on specific events or news stories and dissect how they were covered, or not covered, by the press. Those include detailed looks at the Downing Street memo, Bush's time in the Texas Air National Guard, the Swift Boat Veterans for Truth attacks against John Kerry in 2004, and the media's prewar reporting. Other chapters are more thematic, such as chapter 1, which examines Bush's press coverage over the turbulent twelve-month period between September 2004 and September 2005, as well as chapter 2, which addresses the Beltway culture that allowed both the media's timidity to flourish and the administration's effort to push back against the press to proceed nearly unchecked.

By its very nature, media criticism requires picking and choosing which news dispatches to focus on and which ones to ignore. Some might argue *Lapdogs* cherry-picks press offerings in order to paint a tainted picture of the news media, and that for every example I give of the press's timidity there are scores of news reports and articles that highlight the news media's aggressiveness. Having monitored the Beltway press for the last five years, I'm confident *Lapdogs* presents a fair and accurate reflection of the press's work. But I'd also note that just because an article or television report seems on the surface to be asking sharp questions of the administration does not necessarily mean it disproves the basis of my book. For instance, on February 12, 2006, CBS's *60 Minutes* aired two reports that were tough on the Bush administration. One examined the Iraq reconstruction boondoggle, in which nearly $8 billion in U.S. funds earmarked for rebuilding Iraq had gone missing, unaccounted for. Another report that evening examined the oddity of having 400,000 embryonic cells stored away in liquid nitrogen tanks at fertility clinics, yet off limits to stem cell researchers because Bush, citing his pro-life beliefs, does not want them destroyed in the name of science. That, despite the fact unwanted embryos were being destroyed—thawed, and then destroyed—all the time at fertility clinics after patients decide they no longer wanted to pay to keep their unused embryos on ice. So the *60 Minutes* reports were proof that the press was getting tough on Bush, right? Not quite, because I'd argue both stories arrived about two years after the fact; two years after it became obvious that politically connected contractors were ripping off the U.S. government in Iraq while the Pentagon simply looked the other way, and at least two years after scientists made plain that Bush's controversial stance on embryonic stem cell research, which bans federal funds from being used to work on stem cells, was going to have a long-lasting and damaging effect in key research areas.

Rather than vindicating the press, I'd suggest the February 12th *60 Minutes* simply reinforced my argument that the press under Bush had lost a step, or more likely two.

Lapdogs

Afraid of the Facts

It was must have been an awkward encounter when Bob Woodward sat down for two hours at his Washington, D.C., attorney's M Street office on November 14, 2005, to answer questions, under oath, posed by special prosecutor Patrick Fitzgerald. Woodward, of Watergate and *Washington Post* fame, was the most famous reporter of his generation, and Fitzpatrick, by the fall of 2005, was the most talked-about investigator in America. Appointed to uncover who inside the Bush administration had leaked the identity of Valerie Plame, a CIA operative married to a prominent war critic, Fitzgerald's media-centric investigation had already put one *New York Times* reporter, Judith Miller, behind bars. His probe had also issued subpoenas to half a dozen influential Beltway reporters as well as most members of Bush's inner circle. Fitzgerald's pursuit had become the most fevered Beltway whodunit of the Bush presidency.

The sit-down between Woodward and Fitzgerald must have been awkward for a variety of reasons. Awkward because Woodward had made a handsome living starring in the role as the capitol's velvet-gloved inquisitor of people in power. For decades the soft-spoken Woodward had asked the questions. Now he was told to answer them. Awkward because Woodward, through his various television appearances during the previous months, had made it quite clear that he thought little of Fitzgerald's investigation, that it was "disgraceful," that Fitzgerald was a "junkyard prosecutor," and that the Plame leak had caused the CIA no harm. And awkward also because just weeks after Fitzgerald issued indictments in the case, targeting Vice President Dick Cheney's chief of staff I. Lewis "Scooter" Libby for obstructing justice and lying to Fitzgerald's grand jury, a source of Woodward's came forward and told Fitzgerald that he'd actually told the star reporter about Plame's identity long before Libby started chatting up reporters in 2003. In other words, Woodward had been sitting on the scoop for more than two years. Woodward insisted the information he had received about Plame was insignificant; not newsworthy. But if his scoop had been revealed months earlier—let alone years earlier—it would have created enormous political and legal problems for the Bush White House. That Woodward, who in 1972 famously kept digging into a story of White House corruption while much of the mainstream media waved off Watergate as a second-rate burglary, was now serving as the media elite's unofficial ambassador—trying to wave off the Fitzgerald investigation and trying to keep crucial information under wraps—only hinted at the larger ironies in play.

It was ironic that a federal prosecutor was quizzing a journalist, trying to pry out of him sensitive information that was damaging to the Bush White House and information the investigate reporter had *refused to share* with the public, let alone his editors. The strange truth was that, at least in regards to the Plame investigation, the special prosecutor had supplanted the timid D.C. press corps and become the fact finder of record. It was Fitzgerald and his team of G-men—not journalists—who were running down leads, asking tough questions and, in the end, helping inform the American people about possible criminal activity inside the White House. For two years, the press had shown little interest in that touchy task and if it hadn't been for Fitzgerald's work, the Plame story would have quietly faded away like so many other disturbing suggestions of Bush administration misdeeds. (Lots of frustrated news consumers must have been wondering where was the special prosecutor for Enron, Halliburton, and prewar intelligence?) As conservative blogger Glenn Reynolds noted in the wake of Woodward's embarrassing revelation about his nonaction, "This is Watergate in reverse. The press is engaged in the cover-up here. If everybody in the press simply published everything they knew about this, we would have gotten to the bottom of this in a week instead of dragging it out for two or three years."

Woodward's decision to sit on the Plame scoop seemed to confirm that Beltway access had trumped news reporting. (At the time, Woodward was hard at work on his third Bush book, which required continued entrée to administration sources.) But the puzzling inaction, which could have extended indefinitely had Woodward's source not contacted Fitzgerald himself, highlighted a much more pervasive problem: how the mainstream news media completely lost their bearings during the Bush years and abdicated their Fourth Estate responsibility to report without fear or favor and to ask uncomfortable questions to people in power. And how, most dramatically, the press came to fear the facts and the consequences of reporting them. Morphing into a status quo–loving group, the mainstream media became trapped in a dysfunctional hate/love relationship; the Republican White House hated the press, but the press loved the White House. Or at least feared it. Yes, there were exceptions, and some within the mainstream media during the Bush years produced shining examples of industrious reporting and refused to adopt the telltale timidity. Many of those examples are cited in this book. But taken as a whole, the mainstream media's political reporting during Bush's first five years in office was infected with unfortunate nervousness. The mainstream media filter favored Bush. (For the sake of brevity, mainstream media will hereafter be referred to as MSM.)

Abandoning their traditional role of public watchdog, the MSM for years meekly adopted a gentlemanly tone more reminiscent of the Eisenhower era than what was to be expected at the dawn of the twenty-first century when the press's investigate zeal, displayed during the Clinton era, appeared unmatched. The forces behind the news media's dramatic mood swing, which conveniently coincided with Bush's first presidential run, were many. Key factors included the consolidated media landscape in which owners were increasingly—almost exclusively—multinational corporations; the same corporations anxious to win approval from the Republican-controlled federal government to allow for even further ownership consolidation. The press timidity was also fueled by the Republicans' tight grip on Congress and the White House, mixed with the GOP's love of hardball, and the MSM's natural tendency to revere Beltway power. Not to mention the deep-pocketed Republican media noise machine, created decades ago in an effort to denounce and distract the MSM. The timidity was also driven by Beltway careerism; by media insiders who understood that despite the cliché about the liberal media, advancement to senior positions was actually made doubly difficult for anyone with a reputation for being too far left, or too caustic toward Republicans. On the flip side, that same Beltway career path rewarded journalists who showed a willingness to be openly contemptuous of Democrats. And there are many eager to do so.

Part of that seemed to be visceral. News gathering is not supposed to be a popularity contest, but it was obvious journalists simply don't like or respect prominent Democrats such as Al Gore, John Kerry, Howard Dean, and Nancy Pelosi, and the coverage reflected that. And while the MSM might have respected President Bill Clinton's legendary political skills, much of the D.C. press flashed an odd, personal contempt for him, even before the Monica Lewinsky scandal came to light. The stunning stick-to-itiveness the press displayed in flogging the phony Whitewater real estate scandal, for example, illustrated a deep desire among journalists to try to find wrongdoing—real or imagined—inside the White House. It was a desire that evaporated upon Bush's arrival in Washington, D.C.

And even when the press periodically awoke from its slumber to cover one of the Bush administration's high-profile blunders, reporters inevitably retreated back into their shell, nervous that their questions to the White House had been too rude. A perfect example came in February 2006 when, in one of the most absurd events in recent White House history, Cheney shot a man during a hunting accident and then failed to inform the public or the press for nearly twenty-four hours. Even White House aides privately conceded Cheney and his office had completely mismanaged the situation. The White House's uncommunicative spokesman Scott McClellan came under days' worth of attacks from reporters who were trying to get to the bottom of the strange, inconsistent, and secretive tale. By midweek, Bush loyalists in the conservative press, like Fox News's Bill O'Reilly, right-wing syndicated columnist Robert Novak, and press-hating blogger Michelle Malkin, began their predictable attacks on the MSM, insisting journalists were blowing the story out of proportion and unfairly attacking the White House. Instead of dismissing those barbs as obvious attempts at damage control, journalists by week's end gathered on CNN's *Reliable Source* to fret about how the news media had been "whining" about the Cheney story, and guilty of "overkill." It was the type of nervous hand wringing that rarely took place within the Beltway press corps during the 1990s.

Fearful of being tagged with the liberal Scarlet L by an army of conservative press activists who, having codified their institutional rage against the MSM, stood determined to strip the press of its long-held influence, Beltway journalists throttled way back, and made a mockery out of the right-wing chestnut about the MSM pushing a progressive agenda. And in November 2005, Bob Woodward, the former star sleuth, came to symbolize the press's stunning U-turn from attack dog to lapdog.

The purpose of "outing" Valerie Plame was to undermine the operative's husband, Joseph Wilson, a former U.S. diplomat whose public critique of Bush's war rationale had struck a nerve inside the White House. It is a federal crime to intentionally reveal the identity of an undercover intelligence agent. Beyond that, Wilson had been the U.S. ambassador to Iraq under the first Bush presidency, and during the first Gulf War. His wife was a CIA analyst working on weapons of mass destruction. Both, in other words, had devoted their adult lives—at no small risk—to their country's safety. In September 2003 the *Washington Post* reported there had been a concerted effort by White House officials to spread the word to reporters that Wilson's wife worked at the CIA. Twenty-five months later Libby was indicted, not for blowing her cover but for obstructing justice and lying to federal investigators. Woodward, who enjoys access to sources at the very highest levels of the administration, received his tip about Plame in mid-June, 2003.

According to Woodward's account, he only sprang into action—his "aggressive reporting mode"—after Fitzgerald held his October 2005 press conference announcing the indictments of Libby. Fitzgerald mentioned Libby was the first known government official to pass along to reporters information about Wilson's CIA wife. That's when Woodward said "whoa"—as he later put it—and decided he had to act because he realized Libby was not the first official to leak the Plame info; Woodward's source was. Woodward contacted the source who decided to tell all to the prosecutor. The prosecutor then called Woodward in to testify. That it took Woodward more than two years to get into his "aggressive reporting mode" was puzzling. The famed reporter had countless opportunities to become engaged in the story:

- July 2003, when Wilson published an op-ed in the *New York Times* questioning Bush's State of the Union Address claim that Iraq had sought to purchase uranium from Niger.
- Later that month when conservative columnist Robert Novak outed Wilson's wife in his own newspaper column.
- September 2003, when the *Post* broke the story about the criminal probe, or when White House spokesman Scott McClellan told reporters categorically, and falsely, that nobody from the White House was involved in the leak.
- December 2003, when Attorney General John Ashcroft unexpectedly recused himself from the case and appointed Fitzgerald as special prosecutor.
- June 2004, when Bush met with a private attorney who advised the president on the investigation.
- February 2005, when a federal appeals court in Washington ruled the *Times*'s Judith Miller and *Time* magazine's Matthew Cooper had to cooperate with Fitzgerald's grand jury investigation.
- June 2005, when the United States Supreme Court refused to hear Miller's and Cooper's appeal.
- July 2005, when Miller began to serve her contempt sentence in jail or when Cooper revealed Karl Rove first told him about Wilson's wife working at the CIA.

At any point along the way if Woodward had come forward with his information about the Plame leak it would have been damaging for the White House. And Woodward's bombshell would have been especially devastating for Bush had it come in the summer of 2005, just as it was becoming clear the White House had lied about its involvement in the leak, or had it come right before Fitzgerald's indictment was announced in October, when public attention was at its highest level. Instead, Woodward remained mum about the facts while publicly mocking Fitzgerald's investigation. It seemed as though Woodward, like the Bush White House, was hoping the Fitzgerald cloud would simply go away.

When finally forced to discuss his leak, Woodward, like lots of politicians, was cagey with his explanation, which evolved over time.

For instance, Woodward at first said he didn't come forward with the vital information because he feared being subpoenaed by Fitzgerald. But Woodward received his tip in June 2003 and Fitzgerald wasn't assigned the case until December of that year, and his first subpoenas were not issued until May 2004, so there was no reason for Woodward to be concerned about subpoenas.

When Woodward finally met with Fitzgerald, he did so because he received a waiver from his source which allowed Woodward to lift the confidentiality agreement that existed when their off-the-record conversation took place in 2003. The source gave Woodward permission to reveal his identity to Fitzgerald and to Woodward's editor at the *Washington Post*, but not to the *Post*'s readers, which seemed too cute by half. Months earlier when *Time* magazine's Cooper received a waiver from his source—Karl Rove—and cooperated with Fitzgerald, Cooper immediately wrote about his testimony and informed the public who the source was. When the *Times*'s Miller received a waiver from her source—Libby—she, albeit reluctantly, wrote about her testimony and informed the public who her source was. Woodward though, refused to talk publicly about the details of his testimony and refused to reveal the identity of his source, who appeared to be part of a widespread administration effort to discredit a war critic.

Meanwhile, Woodward claimed he tried twice, once in 2004 and once in 2005, to get his source to lift his confidentiality restriction so Woodward could "put something in the newspaper or a book." The source, prior to November 2005, refused. But if Woodward thought the Plame tip was a "casual offhand remark," as he stressed it was, why did he bother going back not once but twice in an effort to break the confidentiality bond? And if Woodward was simply going to use the source's information for his book, he wouldn't have needed to ask his source to waive confidentiality because, as nearly every reviewer has noted, the bulk of Woodward's books are based on background, or off-the-record, conversations. The only reason Woodward would have approached his source in 2004 and 2005 asking that their confidentiality pact be lifted was because Woodward wanted to report the leak in the *Washington Post*, which meant Woodward recognized it was news. So why, when he was finally forced to go public with his leak information, did he pretend it was *not* news?

Woodward claimed he told Walter Pincus, a *Post* colleague, about the

Plame tip right when it occurred in June 2003. But Pincus says Woodward did no such thing. Besides, if Woodward felt comfortable telling Pincus, why didn't Woodward tell the paper's editor? And if Woodward was concerned that telling people about the leak would lead to a subpoena, than why did he supposedly share the information with his colleague?

As part of his testimony, Woodward relayed to Fitzgerald that he met with another Bush official on June 27, 2003, precisely at "5:10 p.m." and that the reporter produced four typed pages of notes from the meeting. (Woodward is famous for his meticulous note-taking.) Yet when it came to recalling his meeting with his CIA leak source, Woodward, at least publicly, went fuzzy, explaining that the conversation took place sometime in "mid-June."

Asked by CNN's Larry King whether his source had mentioned whether Plame worked undercover at the CIA (if the source had, that could have meant legal troubles for the source), Woodward insisted the source had not, and Woodward even recalled the exact language the source used to describe Plame's job; a WMD analyst, not necessarily undercover. Woodward's total recall for the language used simply highlighted the oddity of his inability to even recall the date when the conversation took place. And again, if the leaked information was given to Woodward in a casual, offhanded manner, why, two and a half years later, was Woodward able to recall parts of the discussion verbatim (i.e., that Plame was a WMD analyst) in a way that was pleasing for the White House?

Woodward suggested—falsely—that the Plame controversy was really about the use of anonymous sources and noted his most famous Watergate source, Deep Throat, had also been anonymous. The key difference, of course, was Woodward *used* the information provided to him by Deep Throat, but sat on the information provided to him by his secret Bush administration source.

Woodward's wandering explanations, most of which were aired during the interview with King on CNN, represented a kaleidoscope of half answers and misinformation.

(Following Woodward's head-scratching appearance, one blogger quipped, "This is the guy who brought down Nixon?") Toward the end of the *Larry King Live* interview, Woodward assured viewers he was suddenly in hot pursuit of the story he'd ignored for twenty-nine months: "We'll keep chipping at it and running at it. And people will write things, and there will be controversy. And welcome to American journalism."

If that's the state of American journalism, then there is something seriously wrong. The press enjoys extraordinary freedom within the United States, and with that freedom comes the serious responsibility of informing the citizens, of providing unvarnished reporting to the day's events. And perhaps in no area is that duty more important than in the political arena, where the press is supposed to act as a neutral observer, helping Americans make informed decisions about the day's most pressing matters, whether it's to support a war or support reelection. A democracy literally cannot function without a fair, robust press corps. During the Bush years, though, the press too often failed to provide its most important service.

The MSM itself is back on its heels, grappling with a changing media landscape where more and more news organizations are owned by fewer entities (which narrows career choices for journalists), while their collective clout is usurped by new online players. The newspaper industry, losing millions of readers each year, is contracting at an unprecedented rate, with deep cutbacks hitting virtually every major newsroom in the country. Meanwhile, television news teams are under intense pressure to turn a profit, which has driven some of the decision-making process into the ground. That's particularly true of the twenty-four-hour cable news channels, where pointless high-speed car chases are occasionally broadcast live under the guise of "breaking news." Widespread economic uncertainty gripping the news business means authentic job security has become scarce, which in turn feeds an urge to follow the pack. All of that has added to the Beltway media's tentativeness, on display since 2000.

Yet to hear Bush's former flak Ari Fleischer tell it, the durable D.C. press corps is "one of the toughest, sharpest, most skeptical groups anyone will encounter." Fleischer insists newsrooms feed off conflict: "Conflict is juicy, conflict sells, the public is interested in conflict, and the White House press corps respond by providing it."

There was a time the D.C. press corps mostly lived up to the hype— skeptical scribes at the top of their game. But in covering the Bush White

House, too many journalists walked away from their traditional role as referee, freeing the Bush administration up to tackle all sorts of extraordinary press initiatives, like producing phony, look-alike newscasts to run on local television stations, paying pundits to hype White House initiatives, severely restricting the government's public flow of information, sponsoring a partisan crusade against public television, prosecuting journalists, and giving special White House press privileges to a former GOP male escort who was waved into the Bush White House—minus the FBI background check—while volunteering for a right-wing propaganda website. All of it was designed to undercut the Fourth Estate. But who could blame the White House for adopting such a radical media agenda? In five-plus years the press failed again and again to assert itself and hold the administration accountable.

The MSM's unique brand of journalism, unveiled just for Bush, represented precisely the kind of clubby, get-along reporting that would have been roundly mocked by journalists themselves just a few years earlier. During the Clinton years, *the* D.C. newsroom sin was to be seen as soft on Democrats—"a Clinton apologist"—and journalists went to extraordinary lengths to prove their mettle by staying up late chasing Whitewater rumors and trying to prove the White House gave away weapons secrets to the Chinese in exchange for campaign contributions. The phrase "double standard" barely begins to describe the titanic shift that occurred in how Bush and his Republican administration were covered by the suddenly timorous press corps. It's hard to believe the Bush-era slumbering press was the same one that a decade earlier shifted into overdrive when bogus allegations flew that President Clinton caused commercial airplanes to back up at Los Angeles International Airport while he received a $200 haircut from a celebrity stylist aboard Air Force One in 1993. Federal Aviation Administration records later showed no such delays occurred, but that didn't stop the *Washington Post* from referencing the silly incident fifty-plus times in less than thirty days, treating the hoax as a serious political story. (The *Post* staff managed to squeeze in nearly one hundred Clinton haircut references during the 1993 calendar year.) Then again, just four months into his first term, the *Post* published a lengthy, mocking feature on Clinton's soft approval ratings. ("The Failed Clinton Presidency. It has a certain ring to it.") Yet in 2005 when Bush's job approval rating plunged into the 30s, the *Post* refused to print the phrase "failed presidency" to describe Bush's second term. To do so would simply invite conservative scorn; something the newsroom seemed to go to extraordinarily lengths to avoid.

It's all part of the double standard adopted for Bush and Republicans that became the unfortunate news norm and that produced endless, head-scratching anomalies. It's why, despite the avalanche of Iraq coverage between 2002 and 2005, not one major news outlet went back and highlighted this incriminating August 27, 2000, quote from Vice President Dick Cheney, uttered on network television, regarding the wisdom of U.S. forces taking over Iraq:

> I think it would be a mistake for us to go on to Baghdad [during the first Gulf War]. I think it would have sundered the coalition. None of our Arab allies was prepared to do that. We would have been all alone in Baghdad and we would have switched from being the international organizer of this coalition that defeated aggression, to a situation in which we were sort of a colonialist power—an imperialist power coming in taking down governments and replacing them. That would have been a very big mistake for us.

It's why in the fall of 2003 *Time* printed the White House's insistence that Karl Rove was not involved in the CIA leak of Valerie Plame, despite the fact at least three *Time* reporters working on the article knew that denial was a lie because they had firsthand knowledge that Rove *was* the source. As blogger Jane Hamsher asked, "Under what journalistic principle is a magazine obligated to print bold, outright lies perpetuated by Administration spokesmen that it knows for a fact are untrue?"

It's why amid the 2004 national nominating conventions, Bush's interview blunder when he told NBC's Matt Lauer the War on Terror might not be winnable received a fraction of the coverage lavished on Teresa Heinz Kerry's trivial, caught-on-tape "shove it" barb tossed toward a reporter.

It's why an obvious bulge seen under Bush's suit jacket during the first presidential debate was deemed to be not worth serious attention from mainstream reporters.

It's why during the Terri Schiavo right-to-die debate, ABC News released a poll on the morning of March 21, 2005, showing 67 percent of Americans thought politicians, including Bush, intervening in the case were doing so simply "for political advantage." Yet that night's *ABC World News Tonight*, which led with a Schiavo story and aired four separate reports on the issue, made no mention of its own bad-news-for-Bush poll results.

It's why in 2005, despite the fact well-known national pollster John Zogby had found that 53 percent of Americans were in favor of Congress considering impeachment proceedings against Bush if he lied about the reasons for taking the nation to war, the *Washington Post* refused even to poll on the issue of impeachment because the question was "biased" and "not a serious option."

"Accommodating passivity" is how Mark Hertsgaard described the media in his landmark 1988 book, *On Bended Knee: The Press and the Reagan Presidency.* Despite the incessant chatter even then about the "liberal media," that Reagan, the so-called Teflon President, received fawning press coverage was common knowledge among his top aides, such as former communications director David Gergen. "A lot of the Teflon came from the press. They didn't want to go after him that toughly," Gergen told Hertsgaard. Today's crop of pundits and reporters passed the accommodating passivity marker a long time ago—Bush's Teflon coating grew much thicker than any press protection Reagan ever enjoyed.

The stakes during the Bush years couldn't have been higher for the press and the public. With the Republicans' one-party rule in Washington, D.C., and the GOP's decision to end Congressional oversight of the executive branch, the press's watchdog role was all the more vital, and especially pronounced during the run-up to the U.S.-led invasion of Iraq, Bush's unique war of choice, where credible information and an honest, vigorous debate would have helped Americans make informed decisions. The country needed the press to report aggressively and clearly, to be unafraid of the facts and to be unafraid of being unpopular. Instead, the press ceded to Bush, while at the same time treating his opponents, be it Democrats or antiwar activists, with open disdain. Or, as Daniel Okrent, the former public editor, or ombudsman, of the *New York Times*, described it, "The general rolling over on the part of the American press allowed the war to happen." It's hard to imagine a news media failure more grave than that.

The press's rampant timidity towards Bush was not simply a reflection of the flag-waving patriotism that surrounded a wartime culture either, because some of Bush's most supine and pleasing coverage came between the fall of 2004 and the fall of 2005, long after the national shock of 9/11 had worn off and long after television anchors removed the American flag lapel pins that were donned during the 2003 invasion of Iraq.

That Bush would receive pleasing press coverage as president from faithful courtesans came as no great shock. The MSM signaled their affection for Bush during the 2000 campaign, showering him with accolades for being authentic and fun to be around, while at the same time mocking and ridiculing his opponent Al Gore at nearly every turn. (Just ask conservative cable TV talker Joe Scarborough: "In the 2000 elections, I think [the media] were fairly brutal towards Al Gore.") And the MSM's personal affection for Bush remained strong for years, even after the president's popularity plummeted during his second term. On the November 28, 2005 telecast of MSNBC's *Hardball*, host Chris Matthews insisted "Everybody sort of likes the president, except for the real whack-jobs, maybe on the left." Matthews's thinking likely reflected a simple yet firmly held belief inside the Beltway among the courteous press corps: Bush, good; his critics, bad. But as the watchdog group Media Matters for America noted, polling data at the time of Matthews's comment showed a clear majority of Americans not only didn't approve of the job Bush was doing as president, but they did not like him personally and they did not think he was honest. Sobering results, but at least Bush could count on celebrity pundits to vouch for him while insulting his critics as "whack-jobs."

The MSM flip-flop was duly noted. "The press is missing in action, with all due respect," complained Senator Hillary Rodham Clinton in 2004. "Where are the investigative reporters today? Why aren't they asking the hard questions? I mean, c'mon, toughen up, guys, it's only our Constitution and country at stake." Thin-skinned Beltway pundits quickly derided Clinton's comments, but members of the MSM had heard that same complaint loud and clear. Note this exchange between *Washington Post* political reporter Jim VandeHei and a reader during a newspaper-sponsored online chat:

Reader: Why is the national media easy on Bush and his boys? It doesn't seem that the media goes after Bush and his boys like they used to go after Clinton and his boys!

VandeHei: If I had a dollar for every time I get asked that question, I could retire.

The newsroom retreat did not occur in a vacuum. It was fueled by the fact that America's consolidated MSM had "their ears cocked to the right," as historian Todd Gitlin put it in 2005. "They know where political power lies." Conservative activists have perfected the art of media intimidation through its deep-pocketed noise machine (Matt Drudge, Fox News, Rush Limbaugh, and an army of bloggers) that wields extraordinary power in its ability to keep press attention fixed on whatever given story the right deems urgent or vaguely newsworthy. When the right yelled jump, as in the right-to-die saga of Terri Schiavo or the bogus GOP-fed Swift Boat Veterans for Truth attacks, the press asked how high? Alternately, when the right begged silence, as in the bizarre tale of conservative White House correspondent/male escort Jeff Gannon, or the embarrassing prewar revelations from the Downing Street memo, the MSM whispered how soft?

The press bullying from the right is not new, but the ferocity is. (Fox News anchor: "Is the liberal media taking up the defense of Saddam Hussein?") The tough talk has worked. Journalists have acknowledged the intimidation at play. At a 2004 media panel held at Harvard University, NBC anchor Tom Brokaw discussed how conservative activists "feel they have to go to war against the networks every day." The late Peter Jennings of ABC News added, "I hear more about conservative concerns than I have in the past. This wave of resentment rushes at our advertisers, rushes at our corporate suites. I feel the presence of anger all the time." And CBS's Dan Rather, describing the toxic atmosphere, noted the press haters are "all over your telephones, all over your e-mail, all over your mail," creating "an undertow in which you say to yourself, 'You know, I think we're right on this story. I think we've got it in the right context, I think we've got it in the right perspective, but we better pick another day.' " And that was before he became the target of right-wing rage following CBS's botched use of memos in its 2004 report on Bush's Texas Air National Guard service.

On the eve of the first presidential debates during the 2004 campaign, influential conservative blogger, and former Nixon Library director, Hugh Hewitt wrote a preemptive threat against moderator Jim Lehrer of PBS, warning him that if activists thought he went easy on Kerry (i.e., if they saw "any detectable bias on Lehrer's part") the results would be "a cyber-tsunami headed towards PBS affiliates across the country," with activists "canceling their pledges to local PBS affiliates." Taking their cue from the White House, which regularly attacked news organizations by name, and whose chief of staff Andy Card once announced the press corps was nothing more than another special interest group seeking access, the press haters during the Bush years—buoyed by a wartime culture that rendered reporters unusually docile—moved in for the kill.

"You have to be prepared before you go up against these guys," warned Chris Satullo, editorial page editor of the *Philadelphia Inquirer*, who became the target of a Republican attack campaign following the paper's endorsement of Kerry in October 2004. "It was a tough month, trying to deal with the storm they created," said Satullo.

"This particular anti-press campaign is not about Journalism 101," wrote *Washington Post* columnist E. J. Dionne. "It is about Power 101. It is a sophisticated effort to demolish the idea of a press independent of political parties by way of discouraging scrutiny of conservative politicians in power." The "new postmodernists" on the right want to "shift attention away from the truth or falsity of specific facts and allegations—and move the discussion to the motives of the journalists and media organizations putting them forward," wrote Dionne. In other words, the goal is to create a news culture where there are few if any agreed upon facts, thereby making serious debate impossible.

Bring back the Ben Bradlee of 1978, the hard-charging editor of the *Washington Post*, who fired off a letter to Accuracy in Media founder Reed Irvine, a conservative press critic who pioneered the art of intimidation-meets-fabrication. In his missive to Irvine, Bradlee referred to him as a "miserable, carping retromingent vigilante." As Bradlee's correspondence illustrates, coordinated conservative efforts to undermine the press have been underway for decades. (Accusing the MSM of having a liberal bias is like referring to Social Security as the third rail of American politics; it's become the ultimate cliché.)

The press's accelerated retreat under Bush not only manifested itself in the soft coverage, but in a lot of other disturbing ways. Determined not to offend Republicans, reporters began to worship at the altar of "balance." Not necessarily "fairness," which is a prerequisite for all serious journalism, but the manufactured need to be balanced, which when it came to political reporting translated into a he-said/he-said recitation of accusations, while too often tentatively refusing to inform news consumers which set of facts were accurate. "It used to be we, as the press, would adjudicate the facts of the battle," said Scott Shepard, a political correspondent for the Cox newspaper chain who covered his fifth presidential election in 2004. "We don't do that anymore. Now we present attacks. That's troublesome to me. We've gotten the idea if we say something is 'fact' than somehow we're biased. The attacks have worked. People are intimidated."

After seeing his 2004 campaign reporting on Republican efforts to suppress voter turnout in Missouri appear as part of a larger, watered down, everybody-does-it campaign dispatch, *Los Angeles Times* investigative reporter Ken Silverstein complained to his editors in an email: "I am completely exasperated by this approach to the news. The idea seems to be that we go out to report but when it comes time to write we turn our brains off and repeat the spin from both sides. God forbid we should . . . attempt to fairly assess what we see with our own eyes."

That fear of conservative press critics—and the desire to mollify them—also explains why right-wing extremists are treated like serious commentators by the MSM and so rarely challenged. Interviewing Fox News's chronic fabricator Bill O'Reilly, ABC's *Good Morning America* co-host Charlie Gibson cooed, "I always have a good time talking to him." Previewing a November 2005 speech Bush was giving on Iraq's future, NBC's *Today* show invited O'Reilly on the program to comment on world affairs, despite the fact O'Reilly announced he had no intention of listening to Bush's Iraq speech. O'Reilly did, though, compare Democrats to Hitler sympathizers on *Today*, a tasteless attack that host Katie Couric let pass without comment. (It was left to a late-night comedian, David Letterman, weeks later, to actually press O'Reilly on his hateful rhetoric when O'Reilly appeared on CBS's *The Late Show*.) In November 2005, CNN turned to esteemed military strategist Ann Coulter to discuss troop withdrawal proposals for Iraq.

Weeks later CNN entered into discussions with former Reagan education secretary Bill Bennett to become an on-air political analyst. A self-styled values czar who had to admit to a monstrous gambling addiction, Bennett's CNN deal came just months after he told radio listeners that, hypothetically, aborting "every black baby in this country" would help reduce the crime rate. CNN welcomed Bennett within weeks of announcing it had hired former GOP congressman J. C. Watts to be yet another right-wing pundit in the CNN stable. Meanwhile, in January 2006, CNN *Headline News* signed right-wing radio talker Glenn Beck to a nightly hour-long talk show. Announcing the new hire, *Headline News* president Ken Jautz, trying to take the edge off Beck's fringe past, described the host as "cordial" and "not confrontational." Yet the previous year, when not fantasizing about killing filmmaker Michael Moore ("I'm wondering if I could kill him myself, or if I would need to hire somebody to do it") Beck told his listeners that Hurricane Katrina survivors trapped in New Orleans were "scumbags," and that he hated "9/11 victims' families." He also labled antiwar protester Cindy Sheehan a "pretty big prostitute."

So much for being "cordial."

It's not just the name-calling that journalists fear from the right, it's the career track implications the "liberal bias" allegations carry. "When I covered the White House I had the unlimited backing of the late [ABC News president] Roone Arledge," recalled Sam Donaldson, who famously shouted some of the few tough questions posed to Reagan during his term. "One time I got a raise because of what he considered to be unwarranted criticism of my work. Today, not all the bosses support their reporters. So if you're a reporter at the White House and you're thinking about further successes in the business and you're nervous about your boss getting a call, maybe you pull your punches because of the career track." Conversely, those in the MSM who play nice with the White House are compensated. Noted *New York Times* columnist Paul Krugman: "Let's be frank: the Bush administration has made brilliant use of journalistic careerism. Those who wrote puff pieces about Mr. Bush and those around him have been rewarded with career-boosting access."

Whatever the specific motives, the timidity became entrenched and the results plain to see. And that's what *Lapdogs* documents in detail.

CHAPTER 1

From the Big Apple to the Big Easy

On the night of September 2, 2004, standing at the podium on a cus-
tom-made, theater-in-the-round stage in Madison Square Garden,
President George Bush accepted his party's nomination for a second
term. Following a videotaped introduction that replayed 9/11-related
images of Bush standing amidst the Twin Towers rubble, Bush, speaking just fifty blocks from Ground Zero, announced, "I will never relent
in defending America—whatever it takes," which unleashed chants of
"U-S-A! U-S-A!" among the loyal delegates. The sixty-two-minute
speech won rave reviews from the MSM, which praised Bush, "The
tough-talking 58-year-old Texan" (*Boston Herald*), for his "lofty" (*Washington Post*) and "powerful" (*Chicago Tribune*)" address. Within hours of
the speech, the *New York Times*, relying on GOP sources, declared on
page one that "Republican strategists have succeeded, at the moment,
in setting the terms of the debate." On September 2, 2004, Bush was
right where he wanted to be, defining his presidency through the prism
of defeating terrorism, while GOP operatives offstage raised doubts
about his Democratic opponents' ability, and willingness, to defend
America.

Fast-forward 365 days and Bush was where he did not want to be—
standing alongside Michael Brown, the beleaguered director of the
Federal Emergency Management Agency. The two men had been
thrown together by the monstrous winds of Hurricane Katrina, which
three days earlier had blown ashore along the Gulf Coast as a massive
category-four storm, killing more than 1,300 people and effectively
drowning the city of New Orleans. After days of delay (aides had to put
together a DVD of newscast images to impress upon the president the
severity of the situation), Bush finally arrived in the decimated region
for a damage assessment tour. One year after standing tall in New

York City, Bush, now slouching through the Southeast, turned to "Brownie" and announced to the assembled reporters that the FEMA director was doing "one heckuva job" providing comfort to victims in the region. The ringing "heckuva job" endorsement, coming against the grim backdrop of the federal government's utterly botched emergency relief response, gained instant fame. (It was later tapped Bush's most memorable phrase of 2005.) Within weeks Brown was out as FEMA chief and Bush's approval ratings, already soft by second-term standards, were cratering.

What happened to Bush's presidency between the Big Apple in 2004 and the Big Easy in 2005 will likely to by dissected by historians for years to come. The two dates—September 2, 2004 and September 2, 2005—serve as a convenient prism through which to view not only Bush, but also the MSM and their coverage of his September-to-September collapse. And by all indications it was a collapse the MSM never saw coming, having spent so many of the previous twelve months in palace court mode, presenting the news with a Bush-friendly spin. From the closing months of the presidential campaign to the rush to announce Bush's reelection "mandate," to refusing to acknowledge his historically low Inauguration Day approval ratings, politely ignoring the White House press room Jeff Gannon controversy, obediently presenting the Terri Schiavo right-to-die story as a "national debate," looking the other way as Bush declared—falsely—that Social Security would be "bankrupt" in 2040, pretending the prewar intelligence revelations found in the Downing Street memo were old news (see Chapter 8), and initially downplaying the confirmation that Karl Rove was implicated in the CIA leak investigation, the MSM for twelve months refused to puncture the White House façade.

Conventional wisdom held that the press's timid coverage of Bush (and only the most avid of partisans would deny it occurred) grew out of the traumatic events of September 11, and that in a time of national crisis, particularly when the nation is attacked, journalists traditionally back off aggressive coverage and quiet their critiques of the administration. "The news media have been operating under a loose kind of 9/11 syndrome," conceded NBC anchor Brian Williams, echoing the point *New York Times* columnist Thomas Friedman made, suggesting 9/11 had created a "halo over the presidency" which in turn ushered in the media's "deference" towards Bush. But the soft coverage between September 2004 and September 2005, three-plus years removed from the trauma of Al Qaeda's guided bombers, cuts through that 9/11 myth and illustrates that the MSM's timidity toward Bush was adopted by choice. Indeed, it seemed the press's deference actually *increased* over time—morphing into reverence—as the stark memories of 9/11 slowly faded a bit with each passing year.

During the closing months of the 2004 election campaign Bush could do little wrong in the eyes of the MSM. When he made the odd campaign trail suggestion that perhaps America should scrap its current tax system in favor of instituting a national sales tax, when he suggested the United States might not be able to win the war on terror, and when he allowed the popular assault rifle weapon ban to expire, the newsworthy events represented mere blips on the media's supposedly fine-tuned, election-year radar.

The media questions from the campaign still persist: What if the press, and especially TV news, had not turned its attention away from the chaos in Iraq during the summer and fall of 2004, or had pulled the curtain back on the Swift Boat Veterans for Truth smear campaign that clipped Senator John Kerry? What if the press uncovered which White House aides played central roles in the CIA leak, or drilled to the bottom of the story behind Bush's missing years from the Texas Air National Guard? And what if the *New York Times* hadn't held for a year its exclusive about Bush authorizing the government to wiretap phones without getting proper court approval? Instead of facing those hurdles, the Bush campaign through the late months of the election season was blessed with supine news coverage.

Following Bush's narrow win in November, former *National Review* editor John O'Sullivan celebrated the victory, toasting Bush's reelection over "a hostile press corps." "Try as they might," O'Sullivan boasted, "they couldn't put Kerry over the top." O'Sullivan must have been monitoring a different campaign. It's true that a study conducted by the Project for Excellence in Journalism analyzing the "tone" of the coverage for both Bush and Kerry late in the campaign concluded "More than half of all Bush stories studied were decidedly negative in tone. By contrast, only a quarter of all Kerry stories were clearly negative." The survey received a fair amount of publicity and helped reinforce the stereotype of a liberal press corps giving the Republican candidate a harder time. But the study focused its attention on the first two weeks of October when the three presidential debates were held. Polls showed Bush lost every one of the debates, so it was natural that during that small window of time the tone of his coverage was going to be more critical. The survey, though, in no way proved that Kerry received better press than Bush.

For instance, if anything the press was reserved in how it depicted Kerry's debate sweep. At the time of the first debate on September 30, the Democrat was trailing badly in terms of momentum, and noticeably in some of the national polls. But few pundits thought Kerry would find relief in the debates since Bush entered the final stretch season with an unblemished career debate record. And yet Kerry went three-for-three, with instant poll after poll declaring him the winner of every debate. Kerry threw a shutout; a startling and completely unforeseen achievement. Yet by the night of the final debate the pundits' reaction seemed to be, "Ho-hum, just a Kerry sweep." It's hard to imagine that if an array of polls spread over three debates and two weeks revealed Kerry had failed to win a single survey—let alone a single debate—that the MSM would have been as similarly restrained reporting on a stunning Bush sweep.

Poll results weren't the only things pundits played down following the third debate. During the telecast Kerry charged, "Six months after he said Osama bin Laden must be caught dead or alive, this president was asked, 'Where is Osama bin Laden?' He said, 'I don't know. I don't really think about him very much. I'm not that concerned.' " Bush shot back: "Gosh, I just don't think I ever said I'm not worried about Osama bin Laden. It's kind of one of those exaggerations." But Kerry wasn't exaggerating. Bush had said precisely what Kerry claimed he had. It was just the kind of factual misstep that the press corps seized upon when uttered by Vice President Gore during the 2000 debates. The MSM, goaded on by Bush campaign talking points, quickly turned Gore's so-called exaggerations into a damaging, and defining, narrative during the final months of the campaign. In 2004, though, the MSM didn't care much about factual debate gaffes, at least not ones made by Bush about capturing Public Enemy No. 1.

That MSM timidity toward Republicans was extended to the October 5 vice presidential debate, and specifically how the press treated Cheney's glaring misstep when, criticizing Senator John Edwards as being too inexperienced for the job, Cheney insisted, "The first time I ever met you was when you walked on the stage tonight." In fact, the two men had met publicly at least three times prior to that. On February 1, 2001, Cheney thanked Edwards by name at a Senate prayer breakfast and sat beside him during the event. On April 8, 2001, Cheney and Edwards shook hands when they met off-camera during a taping of NBC's *Meet the Press*. And on January 8, 2003, the two met when Edwards accompanied fellow North Carolinian Elizabeth Dole to her swearing-in on the Senate floor, which was overseen by Cheney. Within hours, if not minutes, of the debate's conclusion Democratic aides informed reporters that Cheney's claim was false. The gaffe had the potential of overshadowing the rest of his debate performance, just as Gore's stumble did in 2000.

But the next morning many major newspapers published their fact-checking stories about the debate and completely ignored the biggest blunder of the night: Cheney's claim that he'd never met Edwards. For instance, the Knight Ridder Newspapers' Service produced a story headlined, "Cheney, Edwards stretch facts, figures to make points," and the *Washington Post* produced, "Misleading Assertions Cover Iraq War and Voting Records," yet neither article made any mention of Cheney's whopper. The *New York Times* produced, "When Points Weren't Personal, Liberties Were Taken with the Truth," and the twenty-seventh paragraph of a twenty-eight-paragraph story included a single reference to Cheney's bold misstatement.

Worse than ignoring the Cheney misstep, some within the MSM went to great lengths to pretend it was true. Nobody clung more tightly to that notion that MSNBC's Chris Matthews who, in post-debate mode, announced Cheney had trounced Edwards, insisting the Democrat looked stunned, as if he'd been "slapped" by Cheney's devastating debating technique, that Edwards even looked like he was "crying." Matthews demanded to know if the "liberal press" would admit "Cheney won." (Why would it? A CBS poll of undecided viewers showed Edwards easily won the debate, by a margin of 13 points.) What was more peculiar was the fact that Matthews cheered Cheney's fictitious claim about having never met Edwards before. For Matthews it was the right hook that staggered the Democrat. That it was not true seemed to be of little concern.

The next morning, appearing on NBC's *Today* show, Matthews belatedly acknowledged Cheney's error: "It turns out that the vice president was wrong in saying he'd never met John Edwards before. That's an established fact now." But then things got really strange. In a segment that aired on MSNBC later that afternoon, Matthews flip-flopped and once again insisted Cheney had succeeded in damaging Edwards by claiming he'd never even met Edwards before. "The message was that Dick Cheney is a heavyweight and this new kid on the block hasn't made a name for himself to the point [Cheney] hasn't even met him yet. Now that was a powerful swipe and I think it was the most powerful swipe of the night," Matthews announced. The fact that "the most powerful swipe of the night" was false didn't seem to stop Matthews. By the time his evening *Hardball* program aired that night, Matthews was convinced Cheney's *fictional* accusation was the high point of the debate. "I thought Edwards got slammed on the issue of, 'I've never met this man before,' " he announced. Later he called Cheney's charge "a thunderous blow against a new arrival on the scene."

And Matthews's wasn't the only strange performance put in by the NBC family of pundits on the night of the VP debate. *Meet the Press* moderator Tim Russert appeared on MSNBC and, like everyone else, was chattering about Cheney's put-down of Edwards, which the pundit thought was effective. But Russert, perhaps better than anyone, immediately recognized Cheney's I've-never-met-you charge wasn't true because Russert was *there* when Cheney and Edwards were guests on *Meet the Press* on April 8, 2001. Appearing the next day on the *Today* show, Russert, discussing the debate's pivotal moment, said, "I thought that John Edwards would call him on it right at that very moment," suggesting Russert knew, "at that very moment" that Cheney's claim was false. And yet following the debate, as Russert analyzed the event on live television, he remained mum about the uncomfortable fact that the two vice presidential candidates had met on his program. Instead of deflating Cheney's attack with some relevant facts, Russert, who enjoyed a series of exclusive Sunday morning talk show interviews with Cheney since 2001, simply sat on the facts.

Again and again through the fall of 2004 the MSM turned away from potentially troublesome revelations for Cheney and Bush. Out of the first debate sprang a peculiar story that had all the makings of a juicy, gotcha-type of media favorite, the kind pundits could chew on night after night on the cable shows while avoiding more serious topics such as tax cuts and foreign affairs. The story was hatched when some careful viewers went back and watched the debate again and noticed, with the aid of a video freeze frame, the outlines of a bulge protruding out of the back of Bush's suit jacket, between his shoulder blades. Suspicious observers noted Bush's debate advance team had insisted that no cameras be positioned behind Bush or Kerry during the debate. But Fox News ignored the request and one of its cameras caught an image of Bush as he stood at the debate lectern, capturing the clear bulge under his jacket. Online, the issue became a frenzied topic of debate and speculation, with some even wondering if Bush had been wired during the debate and had answers transmitted to him.

When Bush aides were pressed for a serious response to the bulge question (the TV image did not lie; a shadowy bulge was obvious), they alternatively insisted the controversial image had been "doctored," then that it was merely a "badly tailored suit," a "poorly tailored shirt," and that the presidential tailor responsible had been fired. Asked specifically by the *New York Times* whether the bulge was a bulletproof vest, a Bush aide insisted it was not; the president was not wearing one the night of the debate. It turned out none of those public pronouncements were true.

Intrigued by the debate unfolding online, Robert Nelson, a thirty-year Jet Propulsion Laboratory scientist who works on photo imaging for NASA's various space probes and is an international authority on image analysis, began to do some at-home research on the bulge image. Nelson, with no partisan ties, took a video image of Bush's back captured from the first debate and, using the same methods used to analyze images taken from spacecrafts, greatly sharpened the details, and specifically the shadows.

Nelson quickly concluded the bulge was real. And the enhanced image Nelson created of Bush from the debate ended any speculation. It was irrefutable that Bush was wearing some sort of device across his back; something that looked like a wire snaking down his back. The image resembled a large flyswatter stuffed underneath the president's suit jacket. Disturbed by the misleading explanations he had read from Bush aides in the press, Nelson forwarded his information to a *New York Times* science reporter, who was interested. Eventually, three reporters were assigned to the story.

According to the reporting of David Lindorff, writing for Fairness and Accuracy in Reporting's *Extra!*, Nelson was told by a *Times* reporter that the bulge article, complete with his compelling imagery, would run October 28, one week before the election. Instead, on the night of October 27 the story was killed. In an email the next day, one of the *Times* reporters apologized to Nelson: "Sorry to have been a source of disappointment and frustration to you." Two months later, executive editor Bill Keller explained, "In the end, nobody, including the scientist who brought it up, could take the story beyond speculation. In the crush of election-finale stories, it died a quiet, unlamented death." In other words, while the *Times* article would have easily proven there was a bulge underneath Bush's jacket during the debate, which would have undercut his campaign's public denials, because the story could not authoritatively say *what* the bulge was (and because Bush aides still refused to acknowledge its existence), the article was not worth printing. As for Keller's insistence the story died a "quiet, unlamented death," that was not true. At least one of the reporters assigned to the article, Andrew Revkin, publicly expressed his frustration with the decision to kill the story, noting the oddity of accepting the Bush campaign's flimsy explanation about a tailor's mistake over the word of an esteemed scientist who produced images that were impossible to ignore. The *Times*'s public editor later said he also thought the paper should have run the bulge story.

Some background: Two days before the bulge story was killed the *Times* published a controversial and hard-hitting article claiming that U.S. forces had failed to protect a large Iraqi ammunition dump containing 400 tons of high-density explosives. The dump was secured right after the invasion in 2003 but in the ensuing months it was left unmonitored as tons of ammunition went missing just as insurgents increased their attacks on U.S. troops. The Bush campaign immediately denounced the story as false, and the right-wing media unleashed days-worth of attacks on the *Times*, claiming its late-breaking story was not only wrong, but was a naked attempt by the paper to tilt the election in

Kerry's favor. Rush Limbaugh railed that the story represented "another attack by the media on our election process," and compared it to Pearl Harbor and 9/11. (The *Times*'s ammunition reporting was quickly vindicated when video shot by a Minnesota television station, KSTP, whose news crew had been embedded with U.S. troops, was uncovered in the wake of the *Times* article. It showed troops at the ammunition site immediately following the invasion and the explosives sealed in containers; months later the explosives were gone and unaccounted for.) Also, prior to the ammunition article, Vice President Dick Cheney had kicked the *Times* reporter off Air Force Two, Bush had mocked the paper in his prime-time convention speech, and Republican National Committee chairman Ed Gillespie had publicly attacked one *Times* campaign article as "Kitty Kelley journalism," referring to the controversial biographer of the stars. Also, on October 22 Rove had met with Keller for cocktails to personally and emphatically detail his "long litany of complaints" about the paper's coverage of the Bush campaign. It was against that tense backdrop that the bulge story was shelved on October 27.

Having had no luck with the *New York Times*, Nelson was soon in touch with *Washington Post* assistant managing editor and famed investigative reporter Bob Woodward. But after being told by Woodward that he'd have to go through a lot of hoops to get this story published, Nelson finally got his article published in *Salon* on October 29. "I am willing to stake my scientific reputation to the statement that Bush was wearing something under his jacket during the debate," he told *Salon*. "This is not about a bad suit. And there's no way the bulge can be described as a wrinkled shirt." Despite Nelson's esteemed background and his stunning image, which was not disputed, the MSM uniformly looked the other way when the *Salon* article was published. ABC ignored Nelson's work, so did CBS and NBC and CNN and Fox and MSNBC and NPR and *every* major newspaper in America. For reporters, Nelson simply did not exist. The same news organizations that had spent hundreds, if not thousands, of man-hours detailing the CBS's botched memo story regarding Bush and the National Guard during the autumn of 2004, refused to even acknowledge the bulge story as confirmed by Nelson.

A postscript: Two days after the election the Congressional magazine, *The Hill*, relying on anonymous sources and adopting the MSM's dismissive tone, announced that "conspiracy freaks" could relax, Bush's bulge was in fact a strap holding his bulletproof vest in place. So in the end, Bush's aides lied about the bulge being a "badly tailored suit." They lied about Bush's tailor being fired. They lied about photos being "doctored." And if indeed the bulge was a bulletproof vest, than they lied about that as well, having told the *New York Times* categorically in October that Bush was not wearing a vest the night of the debate. The palace court press corps thought none of that was of interest, let alone newsworthy.

The *Times* was joined by other MSM outlets engaged in self-censorship, picking and choosing what to report on the basis of how it would affect Bush's reelection chances. Over at CBS, in the wake of the embarrassing Memogate scandal, the network announced that a thirty-minute report by veteran *60 Minutes* correspondent Ed Bradley examining the administration's faulty claims about Saddam Hussein's nuclear weapons capabilities was being pushed back until after the election. CBS News president Andrew Heyward, under fire from conservative critics for the network's allegedly liberal ways, announced it would have been "inappropriate to broadcast the WMD report *so close* to the presidential election." [Emphasis added.] The election was six weeks away at the time of the announcement. Even after the election, Bradley's report, which took months to prepare, never aired. (Bradley refused to comment publicly on CBS's decision to shelve his story.)

In 2004 *Time* magazine's Matthew Cooper got caught up in the special prosecutor's CIA leak investigation. Patrick Fitzgerald's grand jury subpoenaed Cooper to find out who leaked the Plame identity to him. He and *Time* initially refused to cooperate. Eventually Cooper agreed to testify during the summer of 2005 after receiving a waiver from his source, Karl Rove, assuring him it was okay to disclose their confidential conversation. Of course, Cooper could have asked for that same waiver in 2004, which would have quickened the pace of the investigation significantly. But Cooper did not, according to a *Los Angeles Times* report, because "*Time* editors were concerned about becoming part of such an explosive story in an election year." They preferred he wait until 2005, after the ballots had been safely counted, to reveal that the White House had lied repeatedly about Rove's role in the scandal. Announcing the indictment of Libby on October 29, 2005, Fitzgerald stressed that his two-year investigation could have been over twelve months earlier if reporters had cooperated. "We would have been here *in October 2004* instead of October 2005," said Fitzgerald. [Emphasis added.] What the implications for Bush would have been of an indictment being handed down the month prior to the presidential election will remain an unknown.

Meanwhile, more pressing issues, like deadly battles in Iraq, were also postponed until after the election by the MSM. On November 4, two days after the nationwide vote, *NBC Nightly News* anchor Tom Brokaw reported. "In Iraq, the American forces have been poised to make a major assault on Fallujah. We all anticipate that that could happen at any moment." He asked Pentagon correspondent Jim Miklaszewski, "What about other strategic and tactical changes in Iraq *now that the election is over?*" (Emphasis added.) Said Miklaszewski, "U.S. military officials have said for some time that they were putting off any kind of major offensive operation in [Fallujah] until after the U.S. elections, for obvious political reasons."

According to NBC, military planners had been telling reporters "for some time" that, in what appeared to be a blatant attempt to boost Bush's domestic fortunes, the bloody offensive to try to retake Fallujah was going to be postponed "for obvious political reasons" until after the U.S. Election Day. The problem was that prior to November 2, nobody at NBC—not Brokaw, not Miklaszewski—actually reported that fact to viewers as they pondered their presidential pick. (The go-slow approach to Fallujah proved to be a wise public relations move for Republicans—November 2004 became the single deadliest month for U.S. servicemen and women serving in Iraq; 137 dead.)

The actions of NBC or CBS's *60 Minutes* hardly stood out as unique, as television reporters and producers seemed to adopt a completely new, lax standard for the Bush campaign during the autumn of his reelection run. The president's aides knew it and they took advantage of it constantly. For instance, on the morning of October 6, the Bush team easily duped the twenty-four-hour news channels, resulting in the president grabbing fifty minutes of free, uninterrupted TV airtime less than one month before the election. News outlets were told in advance that Bush's speech that day from Wilkes-Barre, Pennsylvania, would be a

substantive one addressing the war on terror and the economy, which is
why CNN, Fox, and MSNBC all agreed to carry it live. That's certainly
how they hyped it that morning:

- "President Bush heads to Michigan for what is billed as a major
  speech."—MSNBC
- "President Bush heading to Pennsylvania for what's called a signif-
  icant speech on the economy and the war on terror."—CNN
- "President Bush is making what's being called a significant speech on
  Iraq and the economy."—Fox News

Instead, the address turned out to be nothing more than a raucous
pep rally staged in front of handpicked partisans who booed each mention of John Kerry's name. As all three news channels went live, Bush
unleashed his most sustained and personal attacks against Kerry, portraying him as an out-of-touch liberal who could not be trusted to
defend America. Throughout the duration of the fall campaign the
news channels occasionally cut away to air stump speeches from both
candidates for ten minutes at a time, but certainly never the full fifty
minutes they allotted Bush. And when it became apparent that Bush's
policy speech was nothing more than an attack on Kerry, clearly it no
longer constituted news. Reached for comment that day, an MSNBC
spokesperson insisted the speech, "was compelling enough and interesting enough to merit" the coverage.

Just how badly the MSM allowed themselves to be used was made
clear later that day when Bush delivered the same speech, this time in
Farmington Hills, Michigan. When the White House posted the full
text of the Farmington Hills speech on its website, the address was
accurately titled "George W. Bush delivers remarks at *Victory 2004
Rally.*" [Emphasis added.] It was just another stump speech, but when it
was delivered in Wilkes-Barre, Pennsylvania, the cable outlets treated
it as news.

Riding a slim electoral victory in Ohio to reelection, Bush's win set
off a torrent of MSM chatter about the president's impressive "mandate" from the people. In fact, Bush's final margin of the popular vote,
51–48, was almost identical to Jimmy Carter's win over Gerald Ford in
1976, when there was very little discussion of a mandate for the Dem-

ocrat. In its November 4 editorial, the *Columbus Dispatch* stated that "President Bush won reelection decisively in the Electoral College tally." Decisively? In the previous eighty years, only three times had presidents been elected with fewer than 300 electoral votes. Bush accounted for two of the three anomalies; in 2000 he won 271 electoral votes, and in 2004 he captured 286. (Carter was the third, with 297 electoral votes.) In a tangled ode to Bush, the *Washington Post* congratulated him for being able, amid "the polarized atmosphere of a 50-50 nation," to win *51* percent of the vote.

Bush supporters and some members of the press pointed to the fact that in raw numbers Bush won more votes than any other president— 62 million—as proof of his clear and decisive victory. But as Greg Mitchell of *Editor & Publisher* accurately noted amid the mandate talk, "President Bush . . . also had more people voting against him than any winning candidate for president in history." Indeed, 59 million Americans million voted *against* Bush—a new high-water mark. Bush's reelection win of just 51 percent represented the worst showing among modern presidents winning second terms in two-candidate races; Ronald Reagan won reelection with 59 percent of the popular vote, Richard Nixon won with 61, Lyndon Johnson with 61, and Dwight Eisenhower with 57 percent. In truth, Bush's victory was the narrowest win for a sitting president since Woodrow Wilson in 1916. Yet the mandate talk, uninitiated by the White House, was relentless:

- Bush had secured "a narrow but unmistakable mandate." (*Washington Post*, November 3)
- Bush is "going to say he's got a mandate from the American people, and by all accounts he does." (CNN's Wolf Blitzer, November 3)
- Bush's victory grants him "a clear mandate to advance a conservative agenda over the next four years." (*Boston Globe*, November 4)
- "Clear Mandate Will Boost Bush's Authority, Reach" (*USA Today* headline, November 4)
- "I think he does have a mandate." (CNBC's Gloria Bogler, November 4)
- "Bush can claim a solid mandate of 51 percent of the vote." (*Los Angeles Times*, November 5)
- "But Mr. Bush no longer has to pretend that he possesses a clear

electoral mandate. Because for the first time in his presidency, he can argue that he has the real thing." (*New York Times*, November 5)

Note that in 1996 when Clinton waltzed to reelection, grabbing nearly 90 more electoral votes than Bush did in 2004, the *New York Times*'s news pages announced, "There was no ringing mandate for President Clinton."

Following his reelection, the MSM stood in awe of Bush, overly impressed that a conservative Republican president, who one year prior to the campaign boasted job approval ratings in the 70s, was able to narrowly defeat a liberal from Massachusetts during a wartime environment. Nearly a year later when the wheels began to fall off Bush's second term, the *Wall Street Journal* suggested "Mr. Bush overestimated his postelection capital." But who could blame him? Reading those press clippings, which obediently reflected White House spin, Bush was feted as immensely poplar and powerful, a Ronald Reagan–like iconic figure.

Time magazine devoted seven articles, nineteen photos, and 16,000 words to toasting Bush—his "discipline, secrecy and nerve"—as its 2004 Man of the Year. A decade earlier when *Time* tapped Bill Clinton as its Man of the Year, the magazine devoted half as many articles and half as many words to toasting the Democrat. Playing catch-up, *Newsweek*'s cover story on the eve of Bush's second inauguration was equally fawning, insisting that contrary to what readers may have read or suspected, Bush was "hands-on, [is] detail-oriented and hates 'yes' men." He's a commander in chief who "masters details and reads avidly, who chews over his mistakes" and who "digs deep into his briefing books." According to whom? Bush's closest "aides" and "friends," of course.

It was not surprising that awed reporters and pundits, carrying on about Bush's mandate and his lofty stature were so slow to acknowledge that Bush at the time of his second swearing-in stood as an historically unpopular president. On January 20, a *New York Times*/CBS poll revealed Bush's job approval rating was just 49 percent, marking the worst Inauguration Day approval rating for any president since modern day polling began nearly eighty years earlier. On the day of Bush's swearing-in, even as they searched for topics to discuss during the all-day coverage, television pundits politely avoided mentions of Bush's poor standing. Over the course of four hours of continuous inauguration coverage from 8 a.m. to noon (collectively, that's twenty-four hours among the three networks and three all-news cable channels), the topic of the president's (historically poor) approval ratings came up exactly four times. Perhaps that's because on Inauguration Day, the all-news cable channels dissed Democrats and liberals. According to a tally conducted by Media Matters for America, Republican and conservative guests that day outnumbered Democrats and progressives 42 to 10 on CNN, Fox News, and MSNBC.

That sort of imbalance was common. For instance, just two days after Bush's reelection CNN's *Wolf Blitzer Reports* welcomed two in-studio experts to discuss the issue of Social Security. One expert was from the conservative American Enterprise Institute and one was from the very conservative Heritage Foundation. Both supported Bush's unprecedented plan to privatize Social Security. So began the nation's media-driven debate about Social Security, in which the press often let Bush say whatever he wanted, regardless of the facts. For instance, at an April 2005 appearance in Fairfax, Virginia, before handpicked supporters, Bush, talking up the need to radically reform Social Security, declared, "And if you're a younger worker and you start paying into the payroll system today and 2041 is about the time you start retiring, I'm telling you, the system's going to be bankrupt unless we do something about it. . . . By the time it comes for you to get ready to retire, there's nothing there."

He once told a twenty-seven-year-old diary farmer from Utah, "If nothing happens, at your age, [Social Security] will be bust by the time it comes time for you to retire. By the time Josh gets to retirement age, the system will be flat broke. After all, the system will be bankrupt by the year 2040."

He made the same pronouncement at a White House forum: "If you're twenty years old, in your mid-twenties, and you're beginning to work, I want you to think about a Social Security system that will be flat bust."

The following day the dire prediction was made by Bush to a group of students in Falls Church, Virginia: "We will not be able to look at the high school seniors of today and say we have done our duty in protecting Social Security for you; for after all, the system will be bankrupt by the year 2040."

Bush hyped the same warning again and again as he crisscrossed the country—Social Security would go "bankrupt" in 2040. It was, according to an internal White House memo, all part of a strategy to convince the public "the current system is heading for an iceberg." But the assertion, a central plank to Bush's sales pitch, was categorically false, and every serious reporter covering the Social Security debate knew it was false, yet remained cautious about informing news consumers. Set aside the simple fact Social Security cannot go "bankrupt" since technically it has no creditors. More important, according to the Congressional Budget Office estimate from which Bush was working, Social Security's reserves will be exhausted by 2040, but payroll taxes will still be rolling in which means the system will not be "flat broke" in 2040, but will instead by paying out benefits at 74 percent of the promised amount. Despite Bush's claim, no independent projection existed in which Social Security went "bankrupt" in 2040. So why did so many reporters politely avoid calling Bush out on his rather bold decision to misinform Americans about a very serious public policy issue? On ABC, Peter Jennings introduced a January 11 report, coming in the wake of the White House Social Security forum, by noting, "At the White House today, Mr. Bush warned that Social Security would go bankrupt unless Congress steps in. There is, of course, *some argument* about that." [Emphasis added.] The argument, as it was, was rather simple; Bush was making up facts about Social Security that in no way could be substantiated. That was the "argument."

NBC Nightly News took a similarly passive stance following the White House forum. Its January 11 report included a video clip of Bush making the phony claim that Social Security would be "flat broke." But NBC never noted the assertion was untrue. Instead, it mentioned in passing unnamed "criticism" that Bush was "exaggerating" the need for reform.

But in early 2005 that was simply how the MSM functioned—tough, uncomfortable questions were not the norm. Take the peculiar tale of journalist Jeff Gannon (aka Jeff Guckert) which unfolded right inside the White House briefing room and how, nearly to a person, MSM journalists refused to acknowledge the news story or its significance. A story, that if it had emerged during the Clinton years, would have been a staple on the cable talk shows for days, even weeks, on end.

The story was hatched during Bush's January 26 news conference when the president bypassed dozens of eager reporters from nationally and internationally recognized news outlets and selected Gannon to pose a question. Bush's nod bestowed instant credibility on the apparently novice reporter, as well as the little-known conservative organization he worked for at the time, called Talon News. That attention only intensified when Gannon asked Bush a loaded, partisan question that mocked Democrats for having, "divorced themselves from reality."

Rush Limbaugh told listeners he loved the query, but Gannon's star turn piqued the interest of online sleuths who wondered how an obvious Republican operative had been granted access to daily White House press briefings normally reserved for accredited journalists working for legitimate, independent news organizations. Left-leaning bloggers soon discovered Talon was created by a Texas-based conservative activist organization called GOPUSA, that Talon's "news" staff consisted largely of volunteer Republican activists with no journalism experience but lots of GOP campaign practice, that Gannon on occasion simply rewrote GOP press releases when filing his Talon dispatches, that Gannon was not his real name, and that just months before arriving at the White House as a would-be reporter Gannon was offering himself up online as a $200 an-hour gay male escort on sites like MaleCorps.com, WorkingBoys.net, and Meetlocalmen.com.

Clearly Gannon was a partisan who fell outside the normal boundaries for White House reporters. Posting on the right-wing forum, FreeRepublic.com, Gannon once urged fellow conservatives to stage a demonstration outside Senator John Kerry's headquarters and chant Jane Fonda's name and throw DNC medals, a reference to the Vietnam ribbons of honor Kerry threw away during an antiwar demonstration in the early 1970s. Gannon was more of a GOP prankster than a conservative journalist. Nonetheless, according to Secret Service records Gannon made more than 200 appearances at the White House, attending more than 150 press briefings.

And it was that issue of access that should have attracted the interest of MSM reporters. The vast majority of journalists covering the White House have what's called a "hard," or permanent, pass. To obtain one they have to verify they work for a recognized news organization with job responsibilities covering the White House. They have to submit to a lengthy security background check conducted by the FBI, which can take months to complete and requires being photographed and finger-printed. Journalists also must verify to the White House that they already have credentials to cover Capitol Hill. Without them, the White House won't complete a hard pass application. In late 2003, having arrived in Washington, D.C., from eastern Pennsylvania where he worked in an auto-body repair shop, Gannon applied for a Capitol Hill pass but was denied because Talon, which enjoyed close ties to GOPUSA.com, was not deemed to be a legitimate news outlet. That in and of itself should have been a red flag for the White House press office. Yet for nearly two years, it allowed Gannon to circumvent the hard pass system by using what's called a day pass whenever he needed White House access. The day pass requires just a minimal background check.

Asked how Talon qualified as a legitimate news organization, White House spokesman Scott McClellan said staffers confirmed that the site "published regularly," an extraordinarily low threshold for admittance. After all, the *National Inquirer* gets "published regularly." That explanation didn't hold up when it was discovered Gannon had been granted White House access as early as February 2003, two months *before* Talon started publishing. Instead, Gannon was being waved into the White House while volunteering for GOPUSA, a site devoted entirely to the advancement of Republican issues. Asked how GOPUSA qualified as a legitimate news organization, McClellan said staffers confirmed that the site "existed." In a White House obsessed, at least publicly, with security in the post-9/11 world and where journalists could not even move between the White House and the nearby Old Executive Building without a personal escort, Gannon's lenient White House requirement in early 2004—he had no standing whatsoever as a working journalist—was unprecedented.

It's likely that if during the Clinton years it was discovered that a former male escort was using an alias while volunteering for a left-wing news outlet run by Arkansas activists, and he had managed to land instant access to White House briefings without having to submit to a full background check, the MSM would have treated that story as newsworthy.

Yet early on, the MSM completely ignored Gannon, leaving the story to unfold almost exclusively online at Media Matters for America and *Salon*, as well as blogs such as RawStory, AmericaBlog, Mediaciti-zen, Daily Kos, and Eschaton.

On February 17, at a time when all the bizarre facts of the Gannon story were publicly known, Bush met with reporters for a press briefing and took nearly twenty questions. None of them were about Gannon. That night *NBC Nightly News* did air a report on Gannon, with Brian Williams accurately informing viewers that the unlikely saga was "the talk of Washington." (And the country; for the week ending February 21, the online search of "Jeff Gannon" ranked among the fast-rising queries on Google.) But NBC was among the few MSM outlets willing to report on it. As of February 17, ABC News had not reported one word about what was by then a three-week-running scandal. Neither had CBS News. During that three-week span, ABC and CBS news divisions aired nearly forty hours of news programming combined, yet found *no time* to discuss the Gannan imbroglio. Also, as of February 17, well after Gannon was outed and questions were raised about his access, there had been no meaningful coverage in *USA Today* or in the *Los Angeles Times, Miami Herald, St. Louis Post-Dispatch, Detroit Free Press, Cleveland Plain Dealer, San Francisco Chronicle, Indianapolis Star, Denver Post, Oakland Tribune*, or *Philadelphia Inquirer*, to name just a few.

Of all the facts uncovered about Gannon during January and Febru-ary, the MSM was responsible for almost none of them—they watched silently while the bloggers did most of the real work. ABC's White House correspondent Terry Moran, who successfully ignored the saga for weeks as it played out right in front of him in the press room, later defended Gannon's presence, in part, suggesting his briefing questions were "valuable and necessary," while *Washington Post* reporter Mike Allen cautioned it was "super naive" to think the White House officials had anything to do with getting Gannon whisked inside the press room. But was it super naive? The Gannon story arrived just weeks after it was revealed the administration had been paying D.C. pundits, such as Armstrong Williams, large sums of taxpayer money to say and write nice things about White House initiatives, an unprecedented practice the Government Accountability Office later concluded was akin to "covert propaganda."

The irony of that initiative was, why did the administration feel it had to pay pundits when the MSM seemed so willing to reproduce White

House–friendly reports for free? The press had proven time and again how amenable it was to present events through the prism of Republican talking points, and at times to present conflicts from solely the Republican perspective. There was no better example of that phenomenon between September 2004 and September 2005 than the Terri Schiavo right-to-die legal battle that pitted Schiavo's husband, Michael, against Terri's parents. The two sides were at odds over who had the final say over removing Terri from the feeding tube that had been delivering liquid meals to her for fifteen years, ever since she became severely brain damaged and incapacitated. Michael insisted Terri had told him she would never want to be kept alive artificially and he was determined to have the tube removed. The parents fought Michael for seven years in the courts. Scores of judges who heard the case over the years all agreed: the husband had the final say in the case.

A touchstone issue for conservative pro-life Christians who rallied to the parents' side as the case wound its way through state and federal courts, as well as the Florida legislature, the Schiavo story exploded nationally in March when Republicans signaled their intent, with the White House's backing, to pass unprecedented emergency legislation on behalf of the parents. Republicans went so far as to subpoena Terri and Michael Schiavo and planned to hold a pseudo House Government Reform Committee hearing inside Schiavo's hospice room in Pinellas Park, Florida. (A local judge quickly quashed that motion.)

The story became *the* dominant news event as the MSM allowed the far right to highjack the nation's news agenda for two weeks running. At the height of the frenzy, Media Matters for America counted "81 [Schiavo] articles in the past seven days . . . in *The New York Times* alone." The Schiavo saga was written, produced, and directed by conservatives. Convinced the Schiavo story was hugely important, the MSM lavished it with extravagant attention. During the two weeks of Schiavo mania in late March, the cable news channels and networks mentioned "Schiavo" more than 15,000 times, according to a search of TVEyes, the around-the-clock digital television monitoring service. That was *five times* as many TV references than were made during that time to "Iraq," where eighteen American servicemen died in late March.

The Schiavo coverage began with a strikingly deferential tone with the MSM clearly awed by the Republicans' culture-of-life strategy.

Indeed, *radical* was a word the MSM all but refused to use when reporting any part of the Schiavo story, despite the fact it was being fueled by rampant far-right extremism. The controversy highlighted not only how far to the right the GOP had lunged—a 2003 Fox News poll found just *2 percent* of Americans thought the government should decide the right-to-die issue—but it also illustrated how paralyzed the MSM had become in pointing out the obvious: that the GOP leadership often operated well outside the mainstream of American politics. Reporters, fearful of being tagged as liberal or anti-religion, politely ignored the salient fact.

That press's telltale timidity was illustrated by its odd reluctance to report on the Schiavo polling results that reflected so poorly on Republicans. The decision to sit on the polling data was critical because publicizing the results would have extended the debate from one that focused exclusively on a complicated moral and ethical dilemma, to one that examined just how far a radical and powerful group of religious conservatives were willing to go to push their political beliefs on the public. The MSM absolutely refused to examine that part of the Schiavo story.

Even as the Schiavo story first emerged nationally in mid-March 2005, there was already plenty of polling data available for reporters to reference. Just as every judge who ever heard the Schiavo case had ruled in the husband's favor, every poll taken showed an unmistakable majority supporting the husband's position. In survey after survey dating between 2003 and 2005 (when the Schiavo case was making headlines in Florida), asked who should have the final right-to-die decision, the majority of Americans answered, the spouse. From national polls (ABC News/*Washington Post*, 65–25; and Fox News, 50–31) to statewide polls (*St. Petersburg Times* in Florida, 75–13) to unscientific, interactive polls (CNN, 65–26; and MSNBC, 63–37), the response had always been the same. Yet the poll results were routinely downplayed in 2005. During the first week of its 2005 Schiavo coverage the *Los Angeles Times* published ten stories on the unfolding controversy and none of them mentioned any poll results. The same was true of the *Chicago Tribune* (eleven initial Schiavo stories, but no mention of polls) and the *New York Times* (ten stories, also with no specific mention of poll results). The *Baltimore Sun* deserved credit for its story March 20 that, right in the fifth paragraph, made a clear reference to poll results regarding Schiavo, while the *St. Petersburg Times* published an extensive breakdown of the available polling data. But those papers were virtually alone among major dailies in highlighting the issue.

Early on, ABC News was in the best position to put the unfolding events in context because it had foreseen the story's potential and ordered up a nationwide survey, which was conducted March 10–13. Asked about the Schiavo scenario, the survey found 65 percent of Americans thought a spouse should have the final decision, and that just 25 percent said the parents should have the final say. Asked if they would want to be kept alive under conditions similar to Schiavo's, 87 percent said no. Yet on March 17, ABC's *World News Tonight* aired a report on the unfolding controversy and made no mention of its own polling data. In fact, *World News Tonight* aired Schiavo reports—often the top story of the night—on March 20, 21, 23, 24, 25, 27, 28, and 30. None of the segments ever mentioned the fact that ABC's own polling showed a strong bipartisan coalition of Americans opposed the notion that Terri's parents should have the final say in right-to-die case. For ABC reporters, anchors, and producers, it seemed their own Schiavo polling results did not exist. And it wasn't just the March 10–13 poll that ABC staffers ignored. The network ordered up another round of polling conducted on March 20. Those results were even more telling; 67 percent thought elected officials were acting for political advantage rather than for the principles involved; a stunning public rebuke for the administration. Those data were released March 21. Once again that night on *World News Tonight* the top story was the unfolding Schiavo controversy, and once again ABC completely ignored its new polling results.

Television coverage was barren regarding the polls. NBC's *Meet the Press* on March 20 featured its weekly rountable of journalists, who discussed the Schiavo issue. Yet neither host Tim Russert nor guests Ron Brownstein (*Los Angeles Times*), David Broder (*Washington Post*), John Harwood (*Wall Street Journal*), or Gwen Ifill (PBS) ever mentioned any polls on the Schiavo case. That show was the model for coverage across the dial that crucial Schiavo weekend: Avoid the polls and—indirectly—any suggestion that Congress and Bush were acting in a radical manner. By initially refusing to acknowledge the very strong opposition to the Republican intervention, not only were the journalists able to avoid having to criticize conservatives, but the MSM was allowed to stick to its preferred narrative that the Schiavo story had sparked a divisive "debate" about the right-to-die issue:

- "Strong divided opinions across the country." (CNN)
- "These images [of Schiavo] have sparked a bitter national debate about." (CBS)
- "A furious debate." (Newsweek.com)
- "There is a huge national debate over Terri Schiavo." (ABC)
- Terri Schiavo [is] at the center of what's becoming a national debate." (NBC)
- "Schiavo Debate Grips Nation." (*Chicago Tribune* headline)

No doubt Republicans and White House officials appreciated the "national debate" talk, as it helped frame the Schiavo story as a gripping, lofty struggle of conscience. The MSM liked the angle itself, since it helped justify the absurd amount of coverage the story was given. The problem was, the "national debate" slant was completely manufactured. How could there be a "huge national debate" if 60, 70, and 80 percent of Americans were in heated agreement over the very issue the MSM insisted we were so feverishly debating?

As summer rolled into July perhaps no headline caused more problems for the White House than the revelation that Bush's top political aide, Karl Rove, was at the center of the two-year running criminal investigation into who leaked the name of an undercover CIA operative, Valerie Plame in 2003 in an effort to discredit Plame's husband, war critic Joseph Wilson who traveled to Niger in 2002 at the behest of the CIA to investigate reports that Iraq had purchased yellowcake uranium (a lightly processed form of uranium ore) from Niger. Wilson concluded that no such sale had taken place, and reported his findings to the CIA. After President Bush referred to the uranium deal in his 2003 State of the Union address as justification to fear Iraq's growing arsenal, Wilson detailed the findings of his Niger trip in a July 6, 2003, *New York Times* op-ed. Eight days later columnist Robert Novak identified Plame as "an Agency operative on weapons of mass destruction," and wrote: "Two senior administration officials told me Wilson's wife suggested sending him to Niger." The White House, through an orchestrated campaign, attempted to discredit Wilson by suggesting that Plame recommended him for the mission to Niger, or the "boon-doggle," as one administration source put it. Special prosecutor Patrick Fitzgerald was appointed to investigate whether any laws were violated in connection with the leak of Plame's identity.

By October 2005 Fitzgerald's grand jury indicted not Rove, but Vice President Dick Cheney's chief of staff Scooter Libby on five charges, including perjury, obstruction of justice, and making false statements. Libby became the first senior White House official in 135 years to be indicted while serving the president. The revelation set off a MSM firestorm as the investigation engulfed the Bush presidency. But it's telling to look at how the press handled the story first when it broke during the summer of 2003 and then again when it took its dramatic turn directly toward two of Bush's closest aides during the summer of 2005, and note how at both crucial junctures the press's signature timidity under Bush was on clear display.

For nearly two years the Plame investigation was the best-running whodunit in D.C., with the MSM collectively announcing they were officially stumped as to who was behind the Plame leaks that set events into motion. As late as July 12, 2005, ABC's *Nightline* reported that, "For two years, it's been unknown who told reporters the identity of Valerie Plame." But that was not true. It was well established that a handful of high-profile journalists working at the nation's largest and most influential news organizations (*New York Times*, *Washington Post*, *Time*, etc.), had been personally contacted by senior officials about Plame. That handful of reporters did nothing, though. In a company town like Washington, D.C., built on professional gossip and where information doubles as currency, it's almost certain that word of the leaker's identity spread, at least among the media elites and their cocktail circuit. Yet almost nobody acted on the coveted details. Here's a partial list of the MSM D.C. reporters who could have broken the story about the Plame leak, or at least advanced the story in real time: Novak, NBC's Tim Russert and Andrea Mitchell, MSNBC's Chris Matthews, *Time*'s Matthew Cooper, along with Michael Duffy, John Dickerson, and Vivica Novak (no relation to Bob), the *New York Times*'s Miller, and the *Post*'s Woodward. They could have, but none of them did. Instead, there was an unspoken Beltway race *away* from the Bush scandal story, a collective retreat that's likely unprecedented in modern day Beltway journalism. Like the White House, journalists seemed more interested in keeping the dark secret hidden.

Yes, reporters with firsthand knowledge of the leak were bound to maintain the confidentiality that they promised their sources, which explained the reporters' initial reluctance to come forward. But off-the-record pacts are by no means absolute. The question instead should have been: What about sources who hid behind their confidentiality agreements and misled reporters to score political points via the press? What about sources who lied or endangered covert agents with their disclosures? When considering whether to maintain agreements of confidentiality, "reporters should at least take into consideration if they've been badly used," noted Geneva Overholser, former ombudsman for the *Washington Post.* "If they've been lied to, are they still going to protect their source? That's an odd ethical bond. Why protect somebody who spun you and endangered somebody's livelihood."

Yet even after White House spokesman Scott McClellan announced categorically, and repeatedly, in September and October 2003, that Rove was not part of the orchestrated leak, stressing the suggestion was "totally ridiculous" (McClellan later added Libby to that blanket denial), reporters who received the leak and who knew the White House was spreading rampant misinformation about a criminal case did nothing.

Like Bush, who expressed public doubt that "we'll find out who the leaker is," it's likely most reporters never thought the Plame case would be cracked. Those kinds of leak inquiries were historically futile, in part because there was no precedent for journalists cooperating with criminal prosecutors, which would be a must to solve the Plame riddle. And so if the leakers weren't going to be found out, what, from the MSM's perspective, was the point of prying into the story and angering the White House, and especially powerful sources like Rove and Libby? The administration had already established a habit for making life professionally unpleasant for reporters who pressed too hard, and with a president who at that time still boasted lofty approval ratings, most journalists shied away from the conflict. Instead, it fell to a special prosecutor to do the watchdog work traditionally overseen by the D.C. press corps. If it weren't for Fitzgerald, it's doubtful the press ever would have fully reported the leak story on its own, even though scores of reporters, editors, and producers were sitting on the key facts of the case. Perhaps in no other time in recent U.S. history had such a serious White House scandal unfolded with such little input from the MSM.

The contrast between the MSM's go-slow approach to the CIA leak investigation and the media's obsession for digging during the Clinton years was stunning. For instance, when it was alleged in 1998 that senior members of Clinton's staff had privately contacted reporters to smear Monica Lewinksy's reputation for political gain following news of her affair with the president, that news angle was covered with wild abandon. (The smear campaign was later proved to be nonexistent.) A search of the Nexis electronic database for articles and television reports between 1998 and 2000 regarding the Lewinsky saga that also contain mention of the White House and "smear campaign" retrieves approximately 850 matches. But a Nexis search for news accounts between September 2003 and October 2005 on the Plame investigation that mention the White House and a "smear campaign" found just 150 matches.

Interestingly, in the days and weeks before the indictments were announced, it was so-called liberal media elite columnists who urged criminal charges *not* be filed. The *New York Times*'s Nicholas Kristof didn't want people to "exaggerate" the leaking of Plame's identity, arguing White House insiders probably didn't know she was under-cover. ("Negligence rather than vengeance.") The *Washington Post*'s Richard Cohen dismissed the criminal investigation as trivial. "The best thing Patrick Fitzgerald could do for his country is get out of Washington, return to Chicago and prosecute some real criminals," he wrote. And *Slate*'s Jacob Weisberg, belittling the entire investigation, didn't want any "creative crap charges." The establishment pundits all tapped into a feeling within parts of the MSM that the Plame investigation, while tolerated, was never fully embraced like previous White House scandals. In fact it was occasionally mocked: *Newsweek*'s Charlie Gasparino went on TV and equated Plame to a janitor working at the CIA. What was more telling was the palpable sense of pure indifference much of the MSM showed toward the Plame case. That was especially true watching the signature, long-form news programs at network television—they couldn't care less about the Plame story.

On the eve of the indictments in October 2005, a search of Nexis revealed that since September 28, 2003, when the *Washington Post* first revealed there had been a concerted effort from inside the White House to try to discredit Joseph Wilson, CBS's award-winning investigative series *60 Minutes*, as well as its spin-off *60 Minutes II*, aired approximately 180 episodes during that time frame. Zero of them examined the Plame case. Over at NBC it was the same story with the network's prime-time news magazine, *Dateline*. Between September 28, 2003 and October 28, 2005, *Dateline* aired approximately one hundred episodes. Zero of them examined the Plame case. More of the same at ABC's *Primetime Live*, which also aired approximately one hundred episodes. None addressed the Plame case. That meant in the twenty-four months after the Plame story broke, there were nearly nearly four hundred broadcasts of ABC, CBS, and NBC's signature long-form news programs and none reported on the leak investigation that reached into the most senior levels of the White House. It was worse if added into the equation was the fact that shows like *60 Minutes* and *60 Minutes II* include multiple topics within each broadcast. That meant between September 2003 and October 2005, the network news magazines aired at least 750 reports. None were about the most talked-about criminal investigation of the Bush presidency.

Fact: During the twenty-four months between September 2003 and September 2005, ABC's *Nightline* devoted just three full programs to the unfolding Plame investigation, for which a special assistant to the president was eventually indicted. On the night of the Libby indictments, *Nightline* devoted just five percent of its program to that topic. In the week following the criminal charges, *Nightline* never revisted the issue. Compare that to the fact that during the twenty-four months between January 1994 and January 1996, when ABC's *Nightline* devoted *nineteen* programs to the then-unfolding Whitewater scandal. The MSM's stunning apathy on the Plame scandal did not reflect mainstream Americans, 79 percent of whom said the indictment of Libby was a matter of importance to the nation; a greater percentage than who said the same thing about 1998 charges that Clinton had lied under oath about his affair with Lewinsky.

Outside of prime-time television, most of the MSM was much more aggressive on the story, particularly as it became clear the Fitzgerald investigation was focusing its attention on the most senior members of the Bush staff and that indictments were imminent. That's a blockbuster story by any Beltway standards. And yet, if you look back to the first days in July when the story took its telling turn toward Rove, the press corps, as usual, seemed timid and unsure of how to proceed. On July 6, *Time*'s Cooper, on the verge to being sent to prison for refusing to cooperate with the investigation, received a last-minute waiver from his confidential White House source, allowing him to speak freely about the conversations he had had on July 11, 2003, about Wilson and his wife.

But on the night of July 1, 2005, respected pundit and former Beltway insider Lawrence O'Donnell, taping an episode of the roundtable talk show *The McLaughlin Group*, announced Cooper's secret source had been Rove. O'Donnell made the same authoritative claim the next day with an entry online at the Huffington Post. That Sunday, July 3, *Newsweek* confirmed the story, reporting that internal emails between Cooper and his *Time* editors revealed that Cooper's source was indeed White House deputy chief of staff Rove. At that point it was the single most important development of the Plame investigation, signaling both the serious legal peril senior White House staffers might face, as well as a gathering political storm for the White House, which in 2003 had emphatically denied Rove was involved in any way in the leak. Despite that, the Beltway press yawned. Returning from the long Independence Day holiday weekend, White House spokesman Scott McClellan met with reporters on July 5 and took thirty-one questions. None were about Rove or the Plame investigation. McClellan met with reporters three more times that week and took twenty-six more questions. None were about Rove or the Plame investigation. The Rove story continued to hide in plain sight. It was not until the following week, after Cooper penned a first-person account for *Time*, reconfirming that Rove was his source, that McClellan started to hear from reporters about the topic.

When the Plame story took another startling turn in late September and began to plainly focus on Rove and Libby, the *Washington Post* felt the need to tiptoe around the obvious fact that the White House had been caught in a lie. In an October 1 article the *Post* noted that Libby and Rove both played central roles in the Plame controversy conflicted with the strong, plain denials administration officials offered on behalf of the men when the scandal first broke in 2003. But note the language of the *Post*'s payoff passage: "Their testimony *seems* to contradict what the White House was saying a few months after Plame's CIA job became public." [Emphasis added.]

Of course, a more accurate *Post* description for its article would have been. "Their testimony *completely* contradicts what the White House was saying a few months after Plame's CIA job became public." Or "flatly," or "fully," or just plain "contradicts." But "seems"? That made no sense. Here, for example, is how White House spokesman McClellan handled a Plame leak question at a September 29, 2003, briefing: "I've made it very clear that [Rove] was not involved, that there's no truth to the suggestion that he was." How does that "seem" to contradict the fact that Rove actually played a *central role* in the leak?

Even after the Libby indictments were filed on October 28, *Newsweek* rushed to assure readers, in the second paragraph of its cover story, that Libby and Cheney likely never meant any harm by their Plame whispering campaign. Instead, relying on a hunch, the magazine reported, "It is much more likely they believed that they were somehow *safeguarding the republic.*" [Emphasis added.] Elsewhere, the same article compared Libby to "Roman centurions and Plato's Men of Silver." White House officials couldn't have said it better themselves.

Libby's soft-edge coverage was telegraphed in the weeks before. As legal trouble loomed for the VP's chief of staff in the fall, the MSM played nice as they introduced the Washington insider to readers and viewers with profiles detailing Libby's resume, from his college days right through his time in the White House. It was telling how many of those features forgot to mention that during the 1990s Libby pocketed $2 million in fees working as the American attorney and chief advocate for Marc Rich, the disgraced billionaire fugitive. It was Libby who helped construct the sales pitch used to try to secure Rich a presidential pardon. The pardon was finally granted by President Clinton during his last days in office, which ignited one last freewheeling Clinton press scandal. (Libby called Rich to congratulate him when he heard the good news of the pardon.) Prior to the indictments, it was the only real stain on Libby's impressive resume and cast some doubt on Libby's lofty, Man for All Seasons persona pushed in the press. And it certainly seemed worth at least a passing mention. But the MSM politely demurred.

On television, there was complete amnesia about Libby's work for Rich during the week when the Libby indictments were announced and the story was treated as very big news (except, still, at the long-form network news programs). The investigation generated constant chatter on CNN, CNN Headline News, Fox, MSNBC, NPR, ABC, CBS, and NBC. In fact, the name Libby was mentioned more than 3,200 times that week according to TVEyes. The name of Marc Rich, though, was mentioned just eight times.

In an October 21 feature published online at *Slate*, titled "Who Is Scooter Libby?" the magazine painted a detailed portrait of Libby's professional life—"Lewis Libby is a graduate of Yale University and Columbia University School of Law"—but did not think the Rich/pardon angle needed to be included. Neither did the Knight Ridder News Service, which touched all the Libby bases in a 1,000-word profile and forgot to mention the Rich scandal. Ditto for a detailed page-one biography of Libby in the *Baltimore Sun*—no Rich mention. *Newsweek* set aside seven full pages for its fawning Libby feature (he boasted "a heroic, romantic sense of his boss and his own role in history"), but there was no mention of Rich. Meanwhile, on October 23, the *Washington Post* published a gentle, page-one Libby portrait, told exclusively through the eyes—and quotes—of his conservative, partisan friends William Kristol, Paul Wolfowitz, and Mary Matalin. There was not a discouraging word to be found in the 2,400-word valentine, in which readers learned Libby has a "sense of humor," was an "audacious novelist" who boasted "animated conviction," yet rarely lost sight of "the grandeur of his mission." (A reference to Rich's pardon was tucked into the twenty-eighth paragraph.) One week later the *Post* published *another* fawning Libby profile ("a self-effacing public servant, more interested in service than power"), which politely omitted any mention of Libby's $2 million payday courtesy of the billionaire fugitive.

Perhaps the most telling tidbit about Libby found in that *Post* profile, though, was this: "He is diligent about returning reporters' calls." In other words, inside a White House that was notoriously closemouthed, reporters liked Libby and found him to be a useful source, which may have been another reason so many journalists seemed allergic to the idea of aggressively uncovering the two-year whodunnit in which Libby had become entangled.

Despite the July revelations about the Plume inquiry, along with the fact that gas prices began their summer-long march through the roof that month, that Bush's honesty ratings hit an all-time low, and Congressional Republicans in droves abandoned Bush's position on stem cell research, despite all that, the *New York Times* announced, as the month came to a close, that Bush had had a "pretty good July." (The *Times* was overly impressed by the July passage of an energy bill and transportation bill.) And *Newsweek* assured readers that Bush's laundry list of woes was merely a "summer slump." That kind of collective, rampant see-no-evil mind-set set the stage for the startling events that unfolded in New Orleans over Labor Day weekend, as the wrath of Hurricane Katrina breached two flood levee walls and quickly submerged the city, stranding tens of thousands of people and ushering in a Third World–like drama of failed rescue and relief that was televised internationally over an entire week. (Republican Congressional investigators, in a rare public rebuke of the administration, later concluded the White House had completely botched the relief response.) Then, and only then, did the MSM rediscover their backbone. The press, for one of the few times during the Bush presidency, pushed back hard against scripted White House rhetoric and demanded, with a real urgency, a fuller accounting.

Frustrated news consumers were supposed to be cheering that the national press corps had finally awoken from its self-induced slumber, opting to play hardball with the Bush administration by actually holding officials accountable in the wake of the Katrina catastrophe. Stunned by what they witnessed firsthand in the Big Easy cesspool, reporters, especially television news correspondents, were leading the sense of outrage and bringing back some welcome passion to their trade. Indeed, there was CNN's Anderson Cooper interrupting a Louisiana pol on live TV. There was ABC's Ted Koppel grilling Michael Brown, the chief of the Federal Emergency Management Agency. There was NBC's Tim Russert barking, "How could the president be so wrong, so misinformed?" There was the White House press corps undressing White House spokesman Scott McClellan in a series of bare-knuckled press briefings. And there was CBS's Bob Schieffer telling Homeland Security Secretary Michael Chertoff, "It seems to me this has just been a total failure."

The press wrote at length about its public reawaking. "After a couple of years on the run from the government, public skepticism and self-inflicted wounds, the press corps felt its toes touch bottom in the Gulf Coast and came up big," noted the *New York Times*. Yet the fact that the MSM's aggressive questioning of people in power during times of crisis suddenly passed as news only highlighted just how timid the mainstream press corps had become during the Bush years. Imagine if the press had shown a glimmer of its newfound truth-telling fervor while pursuing the WMD story or uncovering the Swift Boat Veterans for Truth hoax in 2004, or half a dozen lesser episodes in which the Bush White House shaded the truth and the press knew it but then looked away.

The consensus among Katrina observers was that reporters in the besieged city of New Orleans experienced such a huge disconnect between what they were seeing up close and what they were hearing from government officials that they couldn't help boiling over on the air. No doubt that's true. But for how many months (years?) had reporters in Iraq been witnessing firsthand the disconnect between the often burgeoning, bloody insurgency and rhetoric from White House officials, such as Cheney's 2005 proclamation that insurgency was in its "final throes"? Why did so little anger and passion about Iraq ever appear on TV screens? Why didn't CBS's Schieffer ever turn to guest Secretary of Defense Donald Rumsfeld when discussing Iraq and say, "It seems to me this has just been a total failure"? One likely reason: There was a powerful, organized conservative push-back against the press whenever it hit hard on Iraq, but there was no such campaign with regards to Katrina reporting, which meant the press could do its job without having to look over its shoulder.

Despite the media's eventual get-tough brand of reporting, early on in the Katrina crisis the MSM displayed its patented hands-off approach when faced with the possibility of criticizing the Bush administration. In a September 1st editorial that the *Washington Post*'s editors would probably like to have back, the paper insisted, "So far, the federal government's immediate response to the destruction of one of the nation's most historic cities does seem commensurate with the scale of the disaster." Three days later David Broder, the dean of the D.C. press corps, also came to Bush's aid, suggesting that the turmoil in New Orleans represented "an advantageous setting" for the president and that his handling of the situation would open "new opportunities for him to regain his standing with the public." (Broder later conceded his Katrina column had been "wildly off target.") Meanwhile, swept up in damage control mode and out to shift the blame to local New Orleans officials, one anonymous Bush aide got the *Washington Post* to report that five days after Katrina hit, Louisiana's Democratic governor still hadn't declared a state of emergency. Wrong—she declared an SOS three days *before* Katrina slammed ashore. Assessing the possible long-term political fallout from the botched relief effort, the *Washington Post* reported it was "incumbents" (as in Republicans *and* Democrats) who might catch voters' wrath. The timid analysis was curious since there probably was not another example from modern American history in which voters unleashed disdain in response to the federal government's handling of a specific crisis, and the *party out of power* suffered the political consequences.

Eventually, though, the pictures from New Orleans became too ghastly to ignore and reporters turned angry. Better late than never. Only after the Katrina debacle did *Time* and *Newsweek*, for instance, feel confident enough to detail for readers how Bush operated in a "bubble" and an "echo chamber," and that he's an "oddly self-congratulatory," "cold," "snappish," "petulant" chief executive who prefers yes men at the ready. Too bad Americans weren't clued into that in 2003, before Bush ordered the invasion of Iraq.

For years, some frustrated news consumers had wondered what it would take to for the press—at least temporarily—to awaken from its perpetual slumber. In early September 2005 they got their answer: One ravaged American city and one thousand dead civilians.

CHAPTER 2

Watching the White House Play Hardball

When Vice President Dick Cheney sat down for a generous, thirty-five-minute television interview on December 15, 2003, the conversation turned to two favorite administration themes: a threat from without and a threat from within. The first danger was "The possibility of that group of terrorists acquiring deadlier weapons to use against us—a biological weapon of some kind, or even a nuclear weapon," Cheney warned. The second was that the American press too often engaged in "cheap shot journalism," with the vice president complaining about reporters who "don't check the facts." The topics may have been predictable but two things were unusual about the interview. The first was how easy and utterly nonconfrontational the questions posed to Cheney were (i.e., "Why do you think the media is so obsessed in trying to tie you to Halliburton?"). Even against the backdrop of the MSM's signature soft handling of Bush administration officials, the questions stood out as especially deferential, serving less as avenues of serious inquiry and more as verbal prompters for Cheney to unfurl time-honored White House talking points.

The other curiosity was the second-tier media outlet that scored the exclusive time with the normally press-shy vice president—a "rare interview" as NPR called it at the time. The host was the then little-known Sinclair Broadcasting, operators of sixty-plus television stations in thirty-nine mostly medium-sized American markets. At the time of Cheney's December 2003 interview, Sinclair had not yet made national headlines for its openly partisan practices. That came the following spring when the broadcast company refused to allow its ABC affiliates to air *Nightline* when anchor Ted Koppel read aloud the names of U.S. soldiers killed in Iraq; the company denounced the unique memorial as antiwar propaganda. Months later, on the eve of Election Day, Sinclair, breaking with a long-standing tradition among broadcasters to cover presidential campaigns without partisan favor, pushed its affiliates to preempt their regular programming in order to air a one-sided, anti–John Kerry documentary, *Stolen Honor: Wounds that Never Heal,* which attacked the Democrat's antiwar activism following his return from Vietnam.

It's likely the comfortable confines of Sinclair, combined with its national audience reach, prompted Cheney to agree to the interview. But there was perhaps another reason why the vice president gave the green light—his soft-edged host was pundit Armstrong Williams who, aside from being a dependable member of the conservative media echo chamber and a Sinclair political analyst, was, like Cheney, on the Bush administration payroll. Unlike Cheney though, viewers didn't know Williams was cashing Uncle Sam's checks.

Specifically, thirteen days before his exclusive sit-down with Cheney, Williams, in an unprecedented media move, formalized a $240,000 contract to become essentially a paid propagandist hired to hype administration initiatives, but to do so under the guise of a public commentator. The payday came courtesy of the Department of Education which, trying to build support among black families for its education policies, paid Williams and his public relations firm six figures to promote Bush's controversial "No Child Left Behind" law on Armstrong's nationally syndicated television show and through his newspaper column, and to urge other black journalists to do the same. Armstrong, a friend of Clarence Thomas, a self-described "opportunist," and one of the best-known black conservative pundits in the country, never informed his viewers or readers about the unprecedented pay scheme.

The revelations in January 2005 about Williams's pact prompted one former Sinclair producer to think back to an earlier interview Williams had done with Secretary of Education Rod Paige, the very man who approved Williams's lucrative $240,000 deal. The Sinclair producer called the Williams-Paige Q&A the "single worst interview I've seen in my career. It was nothing but softball questions." It was so unprofessional the producer urged his Sinclair bosses not to air the interview. (They did.)

Williams wasn't the only conservative pundit cashing Bush administration checks, though. Michael McManus, a conservative marriage advocate whose syndicated column, "Ethics & Religion," appeared in fifty newspapers, was hired to foster a Bush-approved marriage initiative. Also, the Department of Health and Human Services paid syndicated columnist and conservative marriage advocate Maggie Gallagher $21,000 to write brochures and essays and to brief government employees on the president's marriage initiative. Gallagher later wrote she would have revealed the $21,000 payment to readers had she recalled receiving it. Federal investigators later determined the administration had disseminated "covert propaganda" inside the United States by essentially purchasing positive news coverage, which is against the law.

The administration's misinformation campaign first came to light in 2004 when the *New York Times* reported television stations (some unwittingly) had aired in full a pro-Medicare-reform video news release (VNR) created by the Department of Health and Human Services. Seamlessly produced to look like a news report and beamed to local television stations that are often looking for ways to fill their time with professional looking segments, the agency's VNR was a bit too realistic. When the tape aired in its entirely in nearly forty local television markets between January 22 and February 12, 2004, viewers were never told the ninety-second package had been created by the government. Adding to the confusion was the use of a hired narrator, who, after saying Bush's reform program "gets an A-plus," ended the segment with the sign-off: "In Washington, I'm Karen Ryan reporting." In other words, Ryan was hired by the government to read from a script and made to appear as though she was engaged in actual news gathering. De facto propaganda, the video release went far beyond the usual government goal of distributing information electronically and crossed over the line into government-manufactured news. (Federal agencies had used VNRs for years, but never before in an obvious attempt to camouflage them as independent news.)

The Bush administration's soft spot for propaganda was not restricted to the United States. During the summer of 2005 the Pentagon was caught ginning up fake news by typing up phony quotes from everyday Iraqis for U.S. press releases. That kind of monkeying around paled in comparison to the November 2005 revelation from the *Los Angeles Times* that the military had been busy "secretly paying Iraqi newspapers to publish stories written by American troops in an effort to burnish the image of the U.S. mission in Iraq." Penned by U.S. "information operations" troops, the Pentagon puff pieces were handed over to a Beltway public relations firm which translated them and then paid off Iraqi newspapers to run them.

Government-sponsored contempt for the press doesn't get much more pronounced than paying off journalists and creating fake news stories, both at home and abroad. Then again the Bush White House never tried to hide its disdain for the MSM.

Bush himself often bragged about not reading newspapers and administration officials were not shy about pushing the press around. After *Houston Chronicle* reporter Bennett Roth's May 10, 2001, question to Ari Fleischer about underage drinking by the president's daughter, the White House spokesman later called Roth and ominously informed him that his question had been "noted in the building." ABC News anchor Peter Jennings recalled to *The New Yorker* that he "did a story on a senior figure in the Bush White House and was told in advance, 'It better be good.' " And during the 2004 campaign election, Vice President Dick Cheney kicked *New York Times* reporters off his campaign plane.

The White House's almost metaphysical chutzpah regarding the press was best captured in an October 2004 article for the *New York Times Magazine*, in which a senior Bush advisor dismissed journalists for living in the "the reality-based community." The advisor said, "That's not the way the world really works anymore. We're an empire now, and when we act, we create our own reality." Separately, discussing the role of journalists, White House chief of staff Andy Card famously insisted, "They don't represent the public any more than other people do. In our democracy, the people who represent the public stood for election. I don't believe [journalists] have a check-and-balance function."

Curbing access, bullying reporters, paying off pundits, and producing fake newsreels. It was all part of an audacious White House press plan. And thanks to the passive MSM, too timid to push back, the plan was deftly implemented. The MSM's get-along culture during the Bush years, their rush to embrace conservative talking points while mocking Democrats, was solidified by friendships between prominent journalists and senior administration officials. Indeed, rather than resent the administration's brickbats, the press stood back respectfully, openly admiring the signature brand of hardball the White House was playing with the press. "I believe the press is in awe of the Bush juggernaut," said Jay Rosen, former chairman of New York University's journalism department. "Journalists respect a winner and those they think of as savvy and effective. Besides, what's a worse crime according to journalists, shading the truth or being naive about the way the world really works? It's definitely the latter." The White House's attacks on the press were part of a larger agenda to undermine the MSM, or "decertify" the press, as Rosen called it; to unseat the idea that journalists play a legitimate role in the public debate over politics.

"Republicans have a clear, agreed-upon plan how to diminish the mainstream press," said Ron Suskind, a former *Wall Street Journal* reporter who was granted unique access inside the White House in 2002 to report on the administration's communication strategy. "For them, essentially the way to handle the press is the same as how to handle the federal government; you starve the beast. When it's in a weakened and undernourished condition, then you're able to affect a variety of subtle partisan and political attacks. Armstrong Williams and others are examples of that."

Journalists were being actively undermined but seemed mesmerized by the takedown. CBS's veteran White House correspondent Bill Plante told the *American Journalism Review* that despite being frustrated by the administration's closed approach to the media, he was "fascinated by how well they've been able to manage" the press.

Despite administration attempts to undermine the press, a soothing, nonconfrontational culture became the MSM hallmark during the Bush years, particularly inside television newsrooms as producers, anchors, and reporters celebrated Republican icons, embraced conservative cultural issues, and packaged discussions in a way that ensured liberals had little say in the national debates. The irony was that while the press was being belittled and undercut by the Republican White House, the MSM took their collective frustration out on Democrats who became the knee-jerk targets of contempt. It's why in 2002 a *New York Times* television writer effortlessly, and without the slightest fear of pushback, referred to Al Gore as a "high-level laughingstock."

Heading into 2005, TV pundits were certain that the party worth watching, the party whose demise was going to dominate the political calendar, was the Democratic Party. In June, *Time* columnist Joe Klein, often booked by TV producers to fill the slot of a Democrat, pronounced on MSNBC, "At this point the Democrats are a party with absolutely no redeeming social value. They're doing nothing. It's a really boring and flat party." Yet months later it was the Democrats who had opened up a fourteen-point lead over Republicans in a Pew Research poll that asked which party was doing a better job handling the nation's top problems. No matter, Klein was still belittling the Democratic leadership. Specifically, in a December 10, 2005 Time.com column he targeted party chair Howard Dean for his defeatist comments about Iraq. Here's what Klein wrote (note Klein's use of the ellipses):

> The party chairman, Howard Dean, was not inaccurate when he said, "The idea that we are going to win this war . . . is just plain wrong." If Dean had added the word militarily, most generals would agree with him. The trouble is, Dean—as always—seemed downright gleeful about the bad news. He seemed to be rooting for defeat.

Here's what Dean actually said: "The idea that we're going win this war is an idea that *unfortunately* is just plain wrong. [Emphasis added.] As Greg Sargent at *American Prospect* noted, how could Dean be "gleeful" about bad news from Iraq when he himself suggested it was "unfortunate"? Klein, in an effort to embarrass the head of the Democratic Party, simply molded the quote for effect. (Three weeks later Klein, once again teeing off on Democrats, accused the party's leadership of "a small but cheesy bit of deception"; the same could be said of Klein himself.)

For the MSM's culture of Democratic derision, though, it was hard to beat the display put on by ABC's Ted Koppel the night of December 9, 2003, when he co-moderated a debate among the party's presidential hopefuls. Determined to take the level of discourse down a notch, Koppel persisted for the first thirty minutes of the debate in focusing not on national issues of importance, but on process questions about endorsements, polling, and fund-raising. Koppel treated the assembled Democrats like children—actually asking for a show of hands in response to his first question—and then displayed an odd obsession with scolding them for inattentive clock management: "Ambassador, I'm afraid we're out of time"; "You're out of time, Congressman"; "You're out of time, Senator"; "You're out of time"; "We're out of time, General"; "You're out of time." By night's end, Koppel was openly lecturing the candidates: "And to all of you, if I may make the observation, what you need every once in a while is someone up here who ticks you off a little bit. You're much better when you're angry."

Early on in the evening Representative Dennis Kucinich protested to Koppel, suggesting there were more pressing issues at hand: "To begin this kind of a forum with a question about an endorsement, no matter by who, I think actually trivializes the issues that are before us. For example, at this moment there are 130,000 troops in Iraq. I mean, I would like to hear you ask during this event what the plan for getting out is. I hope we have a substantive discussion tonight."

After yet another round of slights disguised as questions ("Ambassador Braun, Reverend Sharpton, Congressman Kucinich: You don't have any money, or at least not much"), Kucinich punched back again: "I want the American people to see where the media takes politics in this country. We start talking about endorsements, now we're talking about polls, and then we're talking about money. Well, you know, when you do that, you don't have to talk about what's important to the American people." But Koppel still would not relent; eying Senator Edwards he noted, "You're not doing terrific in the polls, either." Then to Kerry, a question about Dean's poll numbers. Like Kucinich, Kerry's patience was gone: "Ted, I'll tell you, there's something to be learned from your question. And if I were an impolite person, I'd tell you where you could take your polls. You know, this has got to stop." The audience roared in approval.

It was telling that sitting alongside Koppel that night was his co-moderator, Scott Spradling from ABC's local New Hampshire affiliate WMUR. Unaware that the night's agenda was supposed to revolve around demeaning, inside-baseball queries about fund-raising and polling, Spradling used his early questions to ask the Democratic candidates respectful, yet substantive questions about issues New Hampshire voters might actually care about, such as U.S. troop levels in

Iraq, religion's role in politics, abortion, and national security. And not once did Spradling warn anyone they were "out of time."

Even before Koppel's appearance at the Democratic debate, then-front-runner Howard Dean had already been educated in the ways of the so-called liberal media and its double standard for Democrats. Specifically, he got schooled on the June 22, 2003, telecast of *Meet the Press*. During the hour-long sit-down, Dean faced off against a clearly combative host, Tim Russert, who prepared for the interview in part by asking the Bush Treasury Department to produce what the *Washington Post* later called a "highly selective" analysis of the Democratic candidate's proposed tax program. The GOP-friendly analysis prompted Russert to ask incredulously of Dean, "Can you honestly go across the country and say, 'I'm going to raise your taxes 4,000 percent or 107 percent and be elected?' " That was Russert's second substantive question of the interview. His *first* was about the then-recent arrest of Dean's son for helping steal beer from a country club. Russert though, famed for his pre-show prep, botched the facts and erroneously informed viewers that Dean's teenage son had been "indicted." Deep into the interview Russert asked how many men and women were serving in the U.S. military, a gotcha-style question designed solely to put Dean on the spot. When Dean said he didn't know the exact number, Russert lectured the candidate, "As commander in chief, you should know that." Dean answered the question by saying there were between one and two million men and women in active duty; according to the Pentagon, there were in fact 1.4 million.

Following the telecast the D.C. conventional wisdom was clear: Dean had failed the Russert Primary, a sort of sixty-minute, on-air boot camp all serious candidates must endure. Russert, the MSM agreed, had cleaned Dean's clock and showed how unprepared the candidate was to go heads-up against Bush. "Mr. Dean's *Meet the Press* performance was, to put it charitably, less than impressive," tsk-tsked a condescending *Post* editorial.

But travel back in time to November 1999, when Russert had a far more civil sit-down with then-candidate Bush. (Russert: "Can kids avoid sex?" Bush: "I hope so. I think so.") Russert, in a rare move, even agreed to leave his NBC studio and to travel to Bush's home turf in Texas to conduct the interview, thereby giving the Texas governor a sort of homefield advantage. In fact, Russert first flew down to Austin in April 1999 to "get to know the governor of Texas," as the moderator put it, and to begin lobbying Bush for a *Meet the Press* appearance. (There's no indication Russert ever traveled up to Vermont in 2003 to "get to know" Dean or to persuade him to appear on the Sunday talk show.) For nearly sixty minutes Bush and Russert talked about key issues, but Russert never tried to pin the Republican candidate down the way he did Dean. When the host did spring a specific policy question on Bush, asking how many missiles would still be in place if a new START II nuclear weapons treaty were signed, a stumped Bush simply answered: "I can't remember the exact number." But unlike his session with Dean, Russert never lectured Bush that "as commander in chief, you should know that." Note also that in his 2003 interview with the Democrat, Russert pressed Dean about the details of the medical deferment that kept him from having to serve during the Vietnam War. Back in 1999 though, Russert never asked Bush about how he was able to land a coveted spot in the Texas National Guard during the height of the war. That issue had come up time and again during Bush's previous Texas campaigns, but Russert was not interested.

For Democrats, the Bush era often meant either being mocked by the MSM or just plain ignored, as reporters, enthralled by Republicans, simply stopped asking Democrats for their input. The examples are nearly endless, but just look at two articles that appeared on the same day—November 20, 2005—in the *New York Times*. Both addressed political troubles facing the Republican Party and both relied solely on Republicans and independent, or nonpartisan, sources to tell the story. The Democratic or liberal perspective was of no interest to *Times* reporters. The first example was a reported piece from the "Week in Review" section that addressed the Bush administration's hardball practices, specifically its "politicization of the government." The article quoted a Congressional Republican as well as one former Bush administration official and four academics, one of whom worked for a conservative think tank. None of the other three academics was identified as left-leaning, which meant the *Times* gathered quotes from three Republican partisan observers and three independent observers while completely excluding Democrats and liberals from a lengthy dissection of the administration governing style.

That same day the *Times* ran a news report on Representative Jean Schmidt, a Republican from Ohio who made news two days earlier when, during a heated House of Representatives debate on withdrawing troops from Iraq, she used the word "coward" when talking about comments made by Democrat John Murtha from Pennsylvania, a respected Vietnam veteran. Her comments set off an embarrassing firestorm for Republicans and Schmidt was forced to apologize. The *Times* typed up the story quoting one independent analyst of Ohio politics and four conservative Schmidt defenders. Once again, Democrats were completely ignored. And that was just from *one day* at the *Times*. It goes without saying that during the 1990s it would have been unthinkable for the *New York Times*, or any other MSM outlet, to write up reports detailing Clinton White House troubles without including large dollops of quotes from Republicans or conservatives.

The problem of sourcing was even more pronounced on the television talk shows, where panel discussions between liberals and conservatives often failed to actually include a liberal. Part of the problem was that producers pretended that neutral news reporters who appeared on TV chat shows were de facto liberals. But most respected MSM news outlets have strict guidelines that prohibit reporters from delving into partisan opinion during television appearances. In a 2005 memo to his staff, *Times* executive Keller reiterated that point: "When we go on television, we are bound by the same rules of impartiality that govern our work in the news pages: we do not opine, we do not predict." So a reporter from the *Times* or *Post*, or *Boston Globe* or *Dallas Morning News* appearing on *Meet the Press*, for instance, is not going to forcefully advocate the liberal position, or any position for that matter. But television producers, buying into the conservative canard that all journalists are liberal, pretend the presence of reporters on a program balances the discussion against open partisans. It's a Beltway shell game that's been going on for years and simply highlights how allergic the MSM is to potent liberal voices. But the currents of the trend became rampant during the Bush years to the point where true liberals were consistently banned from the televised debates taking place.

The set-up created a typical "balanced" discussion like the one on the January 2, 2005, telecast of *Meet the Press*, when in the program's final segment, journalists David Broder (*Washington Post*), Kate O'Beirne

(*National Review*), William Safire (*New York Times*), and Evan Thomas (*Newsweek*) discussed Bush's unfolding second term. Safire and O'Beirne appeared as Bush cheerleaders (Safire: "I think you'll see a strong, activist presidency, at least for the first two years."), while Broder and Evans reflected the Beltway conventional wisdoms. No Bush critics were invited to the discussion.

In fact, during the first ten months of 2005, *Meet the Press* producers invited journalists and media pundits to appear on the show for round table discussions fifty-six times. Of those fifty-six slots, twelve were filled by media guests who pushed obvious conservative agendas, such the *Weekly Standard*'s Stephen Hayes, *National Review*'s Byron York, and *Chicago Sun-Times*'s Robert Novak. But just four of those fifty-six slots were filled by scribes with strong liberal voices: the *Times*'s Frank Rich and Paul Krugman, as well as the *Post*'s E. J. Dionne, who appeared twice that year. The remaining slots were filled either by MSM centrists who did not adhere to an agenda per se, such as NBC's Andrea Mitchell or CNN's Judy Woodruff, or bipartisan critics such as the *Times*'s Maureen Dowd, who hit Clinton just as hard as she hit Bush. During all of 2004 the gap at *Meet the Press* was even more pronounced. Of the sixty-two journalist slots, just one was filled by a liberal advocate: Dionne from the *Post*, while thirteen slots were filled by obvious Republican partisans.

Even at C-Span, which prides itself on its meticulous policy of balancing out guests for its call-in shows, the network's flagship political program, the weekday morning *Washington Journal*, slants way to the right while giving liberals the short shrift. According to a study conducted by Fairness and Accuracy in Reporting, of the guests booked on *Washington Journal* between November 1, 2004 and April 30, 2005, Republicans outnumbered Democrats nearly two to one (134 to 70). And specifically, of the opinion journalists booked on the program, conservatives outnumbered liberals nearly two to one (32 to 19).

Those kinds of pro-Republican media markers on television were set down nearly from the dawn of the Bush presidency. On the night of August 9, 2001, Bush made his first major policy address to the nation when, in a much-hyped prime-time speech, he announced his carefully choreographed decision about federal funding for stem cell research. Following his speech, CNN spent the next two hours parading Republicans—and Republicans only—on the air to discuss the controversial policy: Bush advisor Karen Hughes, conservative Republican senators Orrin Hatch and Sam Brownback, Dr. James Dobson, founder of the conservative group Focus on the Family, Bush Cabinet member Tommy Thompson, Republican pollster Frank Luntz, conservative commentator Tony Blankley, conservative Republican presidential candidate Alan Keyes, and the conservative deputy director of the U.S. Conference of Catholic Bishops. Not only did no Democratic elected officials appear on-camera at CNN that night, but neither did a single Democratic-leaning pollster, consultant, or columnist.

That media's warm embrace of Republicans perfectly reflected what blogger Joshua Marshall tagged "the right-leaning dinner-party centrism of establishment Washington," where Republican politicians and MSM journalists mingle comfortably together. Many news celebrities in fact occupy a rarified world, both socially and economically, which makes bucking the Establishment somewhat uncomfortable. There's certainly nothing wrong with journalists reaching the upper echelons of the tax bracket. (In 2004 MSNBC's Matthews purchased a $4.4 million vacation home on the exclusive island of Nantucket; Ted Koppel's Maryland neighbors have publicly complained about his massive river-front estate home being a "Taj Mahal.") But the paydays do offer a hint into the timid, get-along mind-set that's dominated the Beltway elite since the pro-business, pro-tax cut Republican administration arrived in power in 2001. Given that MSM perspective, perhaps it was not surprising to hear the reaction, in April 2004, when Bush spoke to a ballroom full of senior newspaper executives gathered for an annual convention. The assembled editors and publishers sat passively as the president spoke about job training, energy preservation, and free trade, among other issues. Journalists only broke into spontaneous applause when Bush finally touched on a topic apparently dear to their hearts—abolishing the death tax. The 37 percent death tax applies to gifts passed on at death that are in excess of $625,000; that sum will increase to $1 million in 2006. *That's* what sparked applause among the editors and publishers.

That right-leaning dinner-party centrism of establishment Washington includes some close friendships between journalists and Bush administration players. Of course journalists have been befriending Washington, D.C., politicians and officials for generations. Former

Washington Post editor Ben Bradlee was not only John F. Kennedy's Washington, D.C., neighbor during the 1950s, but remained his good friend and confidant until Kennedy's death. Ethically, is it smart for reporters or television anchors, people who do not trade in opinion, to befriend the same people they're supposed to report on? "Just say no," warned Jonathan Yardley in the *Washington Post.* Yet odds are most editors and producers wouldn't mind their reporters having that kind of inside access or establishing close bonds with key sources. In theory it can lead to a better flow of information. What happened during the Bush years, though, was the opposite; journalists apparently nervous of upsetting their White House friends and sources, sat on embarrassing information or downplayed it rather than report it forthrightly. Certainly some high-profile journalists befriended Clinton aides, mingled at their parties, and formed close social ties. (Journalist Sidney Blumenthal even became a senior Clinton aide.) But the MSM was so relentlessly aggressive in covering Clinton, launching overexcited investigation after investigation, that the notion reporters were covering for the Clintons in order to avoid any social awkwardness was laughable. If anything, Beltway journalists risked being ostracized if they *didn't* attack the Clintons for a living. But with members of the same press corps suddenly turning so timid and groggy covering the Bush White House, the close social ties offer a clue into some of the press's shrieking passivity.

Most news consumers probably don't know ABC's Koppel and Bush's former Secretary of State Colin Powell are good friends. Consumers might also think that's odd considering Koppel, in theory, was supposed to cover Powell independently during two wars under Bush's guidance. News consumers might think journalists kept appropriate personal, professional distance between themselves and their sources. But inside Washington, D.C., the fact that they do not is common knowledge. (Koppel had a habit of forming close relationships with Republican secretaries of state. "We are lucky to have had you," Koppel phoned to tell Henry Kissinger as he prepared to leave office following the GOP election loss in 1976, and just years after Kissinger helped oversee the U.S. bombing of Laos and Cambodia which killed nearly one million civilians.) During an October 2004 Washington, D.C., gala, after having been roasted good naturedly by Koppel, Powell told one of his favorite stories about his ABC pal. It's worth reading in full, just to get a sense of the cozy, backstage culture among the Beltway elite during the Bush years:

> Every couple of years, Ted will come by my house on the spur of the moment and we'll sit in the backyard and have a cup of coffee. And he's usually driving one of his hot cars. He always has a fast car of some kind. And so about, oh, four or five years ago, he came by the house and he had this real muscle car, and after we had a cup of coffee and chatted for a while, he says, "You've got to take it out and drive it, Colin. You've just got to drive this thing. I want you to feel that power."
>
> I said, "Okay, Ted. You want to go with me?"
>
> "No, you go. I'll just wait right here in front of the house."
>
> And so I go out and up 123 in McLean. I will not tell anyone how fast I was going by the time I hit the CIA turnoff, but it didn't take me long to get there. And I came back around, pulled up in front of my driveway, and felt something go boom. And I got out of the car and the right rear tire was flat. There must have been about two inches of air left in it.
>
> I said, "Oh, my gosh, Ted. I'm so sorry. I messed up your car."
>
> And he comes back, "Oh, it's okay, it's okay. I've got to go now."
>
> So I went to the back of the car and I looked at the tire. There was no tread on it. The wires were coming through. This guy had sent me out to speed up and down 123 with this car that had no tires on it. And I said, "Ted, how much are they paying you at ABC, man? Surely you can do better than this."

Powell's back slapping, which elicited loud laughs, took place in October 2004. Go back to February 5, 2003, when Powell, in perhaps his single most memorable act as Bush's secretary of state, traveled to the United Nations to address the skeptical Security Council and spell out the reasons for war in Iraq. Known as a "reluctant warrior," and one of the few members of Bush's senior inner circle who had actually experienced combat, Powell was not only the most popular member of Bush's cabinet, but also the most trusted by the public. His soldier-diplomat presentation, broadcast live around the word, carried with it his stamp of approval on the war. The next day liberal *Washington Post* columnist Mary McGrory cheered Powell and famously wrote, "I can only say that he persuaded me, and I was as tough as France to convince."

That night, ABC's Koppel announced Powell's brief was "a litany of Iraqi deception, evasion, brutality, and noncompliance." Within days though, the powerful presentation was dinged with some embarrassing dents. The top-notch British intelligence dossier Powell cited as an up-to-the-minute, nineteen-page catalog "which describes in exquisite detail Iraqi deception activities," turned out to have been obviously plagiarized, with parts lifted (typo-for-typo) right off the Internet. Within weeks documents that Powell insisted represented strong evidence that Iraq was developing nuclear weapons—that Saddam had tried to buy 500 tons of uranium from Niger—were dismissed as forgeries, obvious fakes, by U.N. weapons inspectors. Within months, after the invasion of Iraq produced no nuclear, biological, or chemical weapons, questions swirled around the guts of Powell's laundry list of evidentiary proof. Two years later, as the truth began to tumble out about the administration's widespread bungling of prewar intelligence, the consensus was that Powell's address, as an actual intelligence briefing, was a worthless embarrassment. In 2005, Powell conceded as much, saying his speech at the U.N. was a "blot" on his record: "I'm the one who presented it to the world, and [it] will always be a part of my record. It was painful. It is painful now."

But how, in the months that followed his critical U.N. address, did Powell's friend Koppel at ABC handle the unfolding story of botched U.S. intelligence, and specifically how did he deal with the secretary of state's central role in selling that flawed intelligence? The answer is Koppel basically ignored the unpleasantness. In the thirteen months following the March 2003 invasion Powell was unusually generous with *Nightline*, agreeing to sit for three in-depth interviews with Koppel. (On-air, the friends occasionally chatted about Powell's health as well as the health of the NFL's Washington Redskins.) During Powell's first *Nightline* interview, October 31, 2003, he was not asked one question about his U.N. performance despite the fact that observers had already detailed the obvious errors in Powell's presentation. In fact it took the international press just *one week* to detail the holes in Powell's speech. But eight months later on *Nightline*, Koppel paid no attention to that fact.

On January 7, 2004 Powell returned for another *Nightline* interview and brought up the topic of the U.N. presentation himself. Powell insisted his discredited briefing was "a balanced presentation" and also claimed "the president had a powerful case" to launch a preemptive war. Koppel did not question either dubious assertion. On April 23, Powell received the same soft *Nightline* treatment; no questions about his infamous and erroneous Security Council presentation for war. Over the course of three *Nightlines*, Koppel posed approximately sixty questions to Powell. Just one question—and it was in passing—was about the uncomfortable topic of Powell's flawed pro-war presentation at the United Nations; Powell's most public contribution to the prewar effort. Just one. It's bad enough that the press lay down during the tense times before the war, nervous about appearing unpatriotic or not enthusiastic enough for war. But after the fact, after it had been established that the White House, and in this case Powell specifically, had told a string of blatant untruths in an effort to convince the country to go to war, if the press won't do its job then, really, what's the point?

Koppel was hardly alone among celebrity Beltway journalists who considered Powell, or other senior Bush officials, a friend. NBC's national security correspondent Andrea Mitchell conceded that when Powell returned to government as Bush's secretary of state it was a bit awkward ("a difficult balancing act") for her as a reporter because Powell and his wife were guests at Mitchell's wedding. (Mitchell is married to Alan Greenspan, the former chairman of the Federal Reserve Board.) Also, in her memoir, Mitchell described this 2003 inside-the-Beltway holiday scene, as cabinet members and celebrity journalists socialized: "At the Rumsfelds', everyone seemed especially jolly. The defense secretary was almost bouncing on his heels. The vice president and my husband huddled in a corner. George Tenet was cracking jokes. At one point, Tim Russert told the CIA director that he'd dreamed Saddam had been captured."

In his own book, Russert wrote fondly of the day in 2001 when he and his son were invited to the White House for a ceremony honoring Hall of Fame baseball players. Once inside, Bush whisked the Russerts, along with Cheney, into the Oval Office for a private sports chat. After the visit Russert's son decided when he grew up he wanted to be in the Hall of Fame and the White House. "The next time I saw the president, I told him about my son's ambitious plans," wrote Russert. "His

response was beautiful: 'Never get between a boy and his dreams.' "
Bush's sentimental quote actually doubled as the subtitle to a chapter on
fatherhood in Russert's book. (There were no similarly heartwarming
tales involving Russert and president Clinton in the book; in fact there
was virtually no mention of Clinton at all.)

Interestingly, no Sunday morning talk show enjoyed closer relations with the Bush White House than *Meet the Press*, as Russert landed
a string of exclusive interviews, particularly with Vice President Cheney
who appreciated the forum. For instance, on September 8, 2002, with
the first anniversary of 9/11 looming, and, more importantly from the
administration's perspective, a war with Iraq just months away, Cheney,
out "marketing" the war effort, as the White House put it, walked
Russert through various doomsday scenarios the United States might
face if Iraq were not immediately dealt with. Note Russert's anxious
responses:

> **Cheney:** "This just isn't a guy who's now back trying once again to
> build nuclear weapons. It's the fact that we've also seen him in these
> other areas, in chemicals, but also especially in biological weapons,
> increase his capacity to produce and deliver these weapons upon,
> upon his enemies.
>
> **Russert:** But if he ever did that, would we not wipe him off the face of
> the Earth?
>
> **Cheney:** Who did the anthrax attack last fall, Tim? We don't know.
>
> **Russert:** Could it have been Saddam?

Meanwhile, PBS's Gwen Ifill made friends with Secretary of State
Condoleezza Rice. Appearing onstage together at the National Association of Black Journalists Convention in August 2003, Rice publicly
thanked Ifill for inviting her over for dinner and complimented her for
being such "an excellent cook." Again, that sort of after-dinner outreach
to top government officials has been a cornerstone of the capitol's
social fabric for decades. But it's been the media's own supine performance during the Bush years that raised questions about impropriety.

Because around the same time Rice was complimenting Ifill's home
cooking, Bush's top adviser was coming under increasing pressure to
explain why, as then–national security adviser, she hadn't kept out of the

2003 State of the Union Address the questionable allegation that Saddam had sought to boost his nuclear weapons capabilities by purchasing uranium from Africa. It was later revealed there were sharp differences within the administration, at both the State Department and the CIA, as to whether the allegation was true. The State Department, in fact, labeled the uranium charge "highly dubious." The White House eventually apologized for including the uranium portion in the address. But questions persisted as to whether Bush's team, led by Rice, knowingly included false allegations in the State of the Union Address in order to scare Americans into war.

On July 20, the *Washington Post* reported the rather startling fact that, according to a White House briefer speaking on behalf of the administration, the reason Rice did not know about the uranium debate was, in part, because she did not read the ninety-page National Intelligence Estimate on Iraq in its entirety. (Neither did Bush, claimed the source.) The NIE, created by the CIA in October 2002, was touted as the most definitive look at Iraq's weapons capabilities and was used by the administration to justify the invasion. But Rice didn't read it all. If she had, she would have learned about the doubts expressed regarding the uranium allegations. In some administrations, Rice's dereliction of duty might be considered grounds for dismissal. At the very least the press would hold Rice accountable for her odd work habits, right? In the ten days that followed the embarrassing revelation Rice kept a low media profile, not sitting for any extended interviews. Then on July 31, Rice emerged for a Q&A with her former dinner host Ifill on PBS's *NewsHour with Jim Lehrer*. The topic was prewar intelligence and the NIE was mentioned by name. But, as the Daily Howler noted, Rice never had to answer the awkward question about why she did not read the critical CIA report in full because Ifill *never asked about it*. That unpleasant fact went unmentioned.

One month later, sitting for another Ifill interview at the Black Journalist Convention, Rice completely changed her story about the NIE. In response to a question from an audience member about the dubious uranium claim, Rice suddenly insisted she had read the NIE "cover to cover a couple of times." Ifill ignored the discrepancy and never asked Rice to explain why, if she read the report "cover to cover," did the White House tell reporters she had not? Like Koppel with Powell, Ifill let a senior administration official who was personally responsible for serious intelligence blunders tiptoe her way from having to face truly pressing questions about competency.

Meanwhile, over at CBS, news anchor Bob Schieffer enjoyed the ultimate friendship—he used to play golf and go to baseball's spring training with the president. Schieffer's brother, Tom Schieffer, is a former business partner of Bush's—he served as team president of the Texas Rangers. Both Schieffer and Bush made millions of dollars thanks to their relatively modest 1989 investments in the baseball team that was later sold for $250 million. Bush subsequently appointed Tom Schieffer ambassador to Australia, and then later Japan. Bush's goodwill extended to Schieffer's brother at CBS. Immediately following his reelection as governor of Texas in 1996, Bush was inundated with interview requests from the national media, curious about his political ambitions. Bush turned them all down, but one. "I told them all no," said Bush at the time. "The only TV show I've done was *Face the Nation* with Bob Schieffer. I know him and I feel comfortable with him."

Schieffer clearly felt comfortable with Bush as well. In his 2004 book about the history of *Face the Nation*, which Schieffer moderates, he recalled an interview with Bush on the eve of the 2000 New Hampshire primary. Schieffer was bursting with pride—for Bush. "I thought it was one of the best interviews Bush had given. As he left our headquarters I congratulated him on what I though had been a fine interview. I thought he had said exactly what needed to be said." By contrast, in the book Schieffer recalled his Gore interview from the same period, insisting it "went nowhere." Schieffer mocked Gore's clothes and his mannerisms and complained Gore's "answers were clearly rehearsed," as if that were somehow unusual for a presidential candidate.

Four years later, in the wake of CBS's Memogate scandal during the 2004 campaign, Schieffer replaced Dan Rather as *CBS Nightly News* anchorman. The company's chairman Les Moonves breathed a sigh of relief, telling reporters, "The White House doesn't hate CBS anymore with Schieffer in the [anchor] chair." Moonves noted Schieffer was looked upon kindly by 1600 Pennsylvania Ave. And why not? Following the first presidential debate in 2004, after which every poll by overwhelming margins showed Americans crowned John Kerry the winner, Schieffer told CBS viewers that the debate had essentially been a tie. In fact, CBS proved to be a pro-Bush oasis that night: Even *after* CBS's instant poll showed Kerry winning the debate 44–26, CBS's John Roberts called the face-off "as close to a draw as you could possibly come." (Three days after the debate CBS owner and Viacom chairman Sumner Redstone announced he was voting for Bush, insisting that from a Viacom standpoint, "the election of a Republican administration is a better deal.")

In October 2005, in the wake of Republican Majority Leader Tom DeLay's indictment in Texas on conspiracy charges, Schieffer's *Face the Nation* took a unique approach to covering the GOP scandal—it banned Democrats. The program invited a Republican-only panel of guests to discuss the issue because it was a "Republican problem," as Schieffer put it. CBS could not point to a single instance during the Clinton impeachment when *Face the Nation* devoted a Sunday morning to a Democratic-only discussion of the scandal because it was a "Democratic problem."

The next month saw more of Schieffer's goodwill toward the White House on display. Despite a mountain of evidence that the administration had misled the country into war with reams of dubious allegations, as well as scores of polls that had shown a majority of Americans no longer believed the reasons Bush gave for the invasion, Schieffer, discussing the war with radio host Don Imus, stood by the president and his closest aides: "I still give them the benefit of the doubt. I don't think they deliberately misled people." In January 2006, when Osama bin Laden released a new audiotape in which he condemned U.S. troops, Schieffer made the intemperate suggestion that the terrorist's rhetoric simply echoed previous statements made by Senator John Kerry.

Two days after Schieffer compared bin Laden to a prominent Democrat, CBS News announced a big scoop: "Bob Schieffer will have an exclusive interview with President Bush—his only television interview prior to the State of the Union message."

CHAPTER 3

Noted at ABC

The telltale timidity that distinguished so much of the MSM's coverage of Bush would have stood out as strange in any era. The lack of curiosity, the professional hesitancy; those are not the normal traits of the modern day Beltway press corps. The fact that passivity blanketed the Bush coverage just years after the press had gone to war with the Democratic White House only highlighted how dramatically the pendulum had swung between the Clinton and Bush presidencies—how the arrival of a Republican swept in with it dramatic new rules of conduct for the MSM, whose gotcha bug was miraculously cured just in time for Bush 43.

But for those itching for the old Clinton-chasing days, there was an inkling of déjà vu during the spring of 2005. A Clinton-flavored scandal was brewing and the press, seamlessly reflecting the hopes and wishes of Republicans, thought the story might have legs. In May, Senator Hillary Rodham Clinton's former campaign finance director, David Rosen, went on trial for his handling of a 2000 fundraiser staged in Hollywood to benefit Clinton's campaign for New York senator. Rosen was accused of hiding, or underreporting, $800,000 worth of costs. At the time, CNN political editor John Mercurio suggested Rosen's funny money trial "reminds people of Whitewater" and the "sleazy side of the Clinton administration that [Hillary] and the president are both trying to forget." Undeniably the story brought with it a sense of nostalgia for the time when MSM, confronted with speculative charges surrounding the Clintons, routinely hyped doomsday scenarios. Then when the outcome inevitably paled in comparison to the dire predictions, the MSM quietly turned away. It had been more than fifty months since the Clintons left the White House, but the Rosen trial in 2005 showed that the press corps hadn't lost its touch.

Taking the lead in trumpeting the Rosen trial was ABC's The Note. An inside baseball–type daily tip sheet for the so-called "Gang of 500" (politicians, lobbyists, consultants, and journalists who help shape the Beltway's public agenda), The Note began as an internal rundown of the day's must-read stories for staffers at ABC's political news team. In January 2002, ABC began posting The Note every weekday morning online, including not only links to that day's top reports for political junkies, but offering up dollops of rumor, spin, reported innuendo, and prognostications. Thanks to its exhaustive lineup (the Note can run up to ten printed pages each day), as well as its wit and its creepy, incessant stroking of Beltway reporters and pundits, The Note quickly established itself as *the* agenda-setting morning round-up for the political class. And at The Note, the Rosen trial was a big deal. The Note wrote about and linked to news stories about the unfolding trial on May 2, 9, 10, 11, 12, 13, 18, 19, 20, 23, 24, 25, 26, and 27. In all, The Note posted nearly forty links to Rosen-related articles. A typical Note entry came on May 10, which highlighted "The opening and closing paragraphs in Dick Morris' *New York Post* column—perfectly explaining why the David Rosen story is going to be with us for a while."

Here's what Morris wrote and what The Note found so insightful: "The Justice Department case against David Rosen, national finance chairman of Hillary Clinton's 2000 Senate race, is getting stronger, increasing the odds the aide will start cooperating with the government—which could be disastrous for the senator's ambitions."

Three weeks later Morris's analysis became suspect when a federal jury acquitted Rosen of any wrongdoing.

So how did The Note handle that news about the trial it hyped? The Note simply ignored the verdict. Despite the fact that on May 26 The Note listed the number one priority among the Gang of 500 as "Waiting for the Rosen verdict," when the anticlimatic acquittal was announced the next day the story tumbled down the memory hole. It's true the verdict came on the eve of the Memorial Day weekend when most D.C. journalists were off. But the following Tuesday morning The Note, acknowledging the long weekend, published a round-up of "must-read efforts from Saturday through Monday." Rosen's not guilty verdict—good news for Clinton and Democrats—was not included. The Note linked to forty-four must-reads, but not one had to do with the Rosen acquittal.

Perhaps close readers of The Note were not surprised by the glaring oversight since The Note seemed to operate from a very simple premise: if Beltway Republicans were chattering about something (i.e., the opening of the Rosen trial), then it was news. But if Beltway Republicans were not chattering about it (i.e., the close of the Rosen trial), then it was not news. The Note prides itself with being plugged in, but it only appears to be really plugged into one of the two major parties—the Republicans.

It's impossible to overstate the behind-the-scenes influence of The Note. Whereas ten or even five years ago a serious examination of the Beltway press might put the work of the *New York Times*'s D.C. bureau under a microscope and dissect it for clues to media trends and emphasis, today it's The Note that most succinctly speaks for the political press elite, and whose body of work deserves close attention. (The Note's prominence in part reflects the shift in the political media landscape, which in recent years saw online voices gain extraordinary influence, and often at the expense of the traditional media outlets.) Mary Matalin, the longtime GOP operative and one of Dick Cheney's most trusted first-term advisors, compared the readership of The Note to a kind of "Skull and Bones for the political class." CNN *Crossfire* host Paul Begala likened The Note to the Presidential Daily Briefing, the CIA update that marks the beginning of each presidential day. "For everyone else in Washington The Note [is] our version of the P.D.B," said Begala. When *The New Yorker* in a lengthy, laudatory 2004 feature labeled The Note "the most influential tip sheet in Washington," there was no argument, and the Note's influence has only grown since then. The Note remains the birthing place for serious D.C. buzz, where cable news producers turn to help select the day's top political stories as well as to determine which guests to book, and it's what MSM reporters, editors, and columnists use as a benchmark for what's hot and what's not.

As Mark Halperin, ABC's political director and founder of The Note, once explained, "We try to channel what the chattering class is chattering about, and to capture the sensibility, ethos, and rituals of the Gang of 500, which still largely sets the political agenda for the country." The Gang of 500 may set the nation's political agenda. But who helps set the agenda for the Gang of 500? The Note.

Industrious, well-written, often witty, and purposefully sprinkled with Beltway lingo and some hard-to-decipher references that only add to its allure and well manicured sense of insiderdom, The Note, worshipping at the altar of conventional wisdom, reflects, in pitch-perfect tone, the Beltway media's rightward tilt. (Or, the Beltway media reflect the tone of The Note. Either way it's an impressive accomplishment.) Star-struck by Republicans, The Note is dismissive of Democrats (it thinks party boss Howard Dean is a fool and former party boss Terry McAuliffe is a "Cliché-Meister"), it frets about being tagged as liberal, it was reluctant to dwell on Bush's fifth-year collapse, it overhyped the Terri Schiavo story, it didn't think much of Cindy Sheehan, it mocked the Downing Street memo, it lost interest in Iraq approximately eighth months after the invasion, it was nostalgic for Clinton-era scandals, and it remained in awe of the Bush White House and its galaxy of all-stars. (According to The Note, Mike Gerson may just be the "greatest presidential speechwriter of all time.") In its role as an overly influential player, The Note has served as a prime engine in driving a consistently timid press narrative about the Bush White House. "To read ABC News's 'The Note'—which has developed into a kind of *Pravda* for the 'Gang of 500' who cover national politics every day—is to enter a world in which the President and his advisers are treated in a manner not unlike the way *US Weekly* treats 'Brad and Jen,' " wrote *The Nation*'s Eric Alterman.

The Note represents an anthropological document of Bush's Washington, reflecting the weakness of journalism that echoes the sources of the dominant party but lacks its own independent notion of news. The Note also reflects the weakness of purely political reporting that cares only about the game but cannot distinguish the actual significance of the plays, that doesn't want to offend any members of the beloved home team.

To suggest The Note is enamored with GOP talking points is not an exaggeration. It's literal. From July 15, 2005: "Who wrote (and edited) the latest very awesome Republican talking points defending Rove that address the Novak situation and much more?" The Note is in love with the Bush White House and it's not afraid to say so: "Hats off to the White House communication team for handling the run-up and staging of this so well," The Note wrote glowingly of the White House decision to stage a meeting between members of the 9/11 Commission and Bush. As for a White House–led public relations blitz designed to improve the tattered image of Saudi Arabia, The Note cheered, "The scheme you came up with is so clever, we think it should be used as a case study in political campaign management schools."

That the GOP-friendly Note springs from inside ABC's political unit should not be surprising. Despite the fact right-wingers regularly ridiculed ABC's late anchor Peter Jennings for being too liberal, ABC during the Clinton years proved anxious to assist Republicans in their conspiracy pursuits. Specifically, ABC, led by reporter Jackie Judd and producer Chris Vlasto, served as an overeager outlet for, and staunch defender of, Kenneth Starr's investigation. Indeed, ABC occupied a unique role amid the seven-year, $70 million media feeding frenzy surrounding Starr's probes. For instance, on January 25, 1998, Judd appeared on ABC's *This Week* and reported, "Several sources have told us that in the spring of 1996, the president and Lewinsky were caught in an intimate encounter in a private area of the White House." The revelation set off a month's worth of cable TV chatter, but the report that Clinton and Lewinsky had been found out proved to be fictitious. As the *Los Angeles Times* later noted, "Judd did not say who her sources were, how many sources she had or what the sources' affiliations or allegiances were. She had not spoken to the alleged eyewitness herself and didn't know who the eyewitness was or even, as she conceded on the air, whether the alleged witness was a Secret Service agent or a member of the White House staff."

Later that year *Salon*'s Joe Conason wrote, "After Murray Waas and I published an article in the *Nation* about Starr's conflicts of interest . . . [a]mong the most hostile responses was a telephone call from ABC producer Chris Vlasto, who has worked the Clinton scandal beat at the network for several years. After swiftly dismissing our story, Vlasto proceeded to berate me for criticizing Starr, and condescended to inform me that the corrupt liars were in the White House, not the independent counsel's office. The possibility that Clinton and Starr both might need skeptical interrogation evidently didn't occur to Vlasto."

As for Bush, when not cheering his White House, The Note often ran interference for it. During the Swift Boat Veterans for Truth smear campaign during the 2004 election The Note breathlessly detailed every development, posting nearly one hundred links during one seven-day stretch, and scolding journalists who pointed out the obvious holes in the Swift Boat accusations. For instance, William Rood served alongside Kerry in Vietnam and was one of just three officers present for the events of February 28, 1969 when Kerry won a Silver Star. The Swift Boat Veterans called the award a fraud because Kerry faced no enemy fire. Rood, after breaking thirty-five years of silence, confirmed Kerry did face enemy fire and labeled the Swift Boat allegations lies. (Or more politely, "stories I know to be untrue.") The revelation was a direct hit against the Swift Boat Veterans and their already shaky credibility and came at a crucial juncture for the larger Swift Boat story; if Rood's truth-telling struck a nerve with the MSM it could have signaled an end to the controversy that had dogged Kerry. But here's how The Note played the Rood story the next day: "Undermining ONE of the Swift Boat Veterans for Truth charges—such as William Rood did—does not undermine them all. The reporting on Rood by many news organizations over the weekend—painting him as repudiating all the charges being made after 'dramatically breaking his silence'—was embarrassing."

Around the same time, the *New York Times* published a lengthy and admirable investigation into which Republican players were behind the Swift Boat attack campaign. The article also detailed many of the veterans' obvious contradictions. The Note, in part, mocked the *Times* article, suggesting sections of it "read more like something from *The Nation* or *Salon*." The reference to the two left-leaning publications was clear Beltway code for a *Times* story that veered a bit too close to the fringe, too aggressive for the MSM's polite tastes. For The Note, clear, independent reporting on the GOP-funded Swift Boat attacks was either "embarrassing" or fringe.

And look at how The Note sprang into action for the GOP-presented Schiavo saga. During that conservative-driven story The Note was all hands on deck, linking to twenty Schiavo stories . . . in *one day*. It also thought Republicans had themselves a winning issue with the right-to-die story: "The Republican leadership seems to have succeeded in framing the discourse around a moral question," wrote The Note, convinced the controversy served as "a prism to examine the health of the two major American political parties." And yes, The Note was convinced the Schiavo story showed the Democrats as the weaker of the two major American political parties. Listening too closely to GOP spins The Note insisted the Democrats' "lack of clarity and weakness are the orders of the day."

On March 21, The Note's parent, ABC News, released the findings from a Schiavo poll which found 67 percent thought elected officials were acting for political advantage rather than for the principles involved. The Note did its best to spin the results in favor of the White House, writing the Republican intervention in the Schiavo matter had been met with "some public opposition." Only in 2005 Beltway media environment, where the Republican administration was consistently coddled, could a controversial GOP initiative that was rejected by by a broad cross-section of Americans—including 58 percent of self-identified *conservative Republicans*—been described as having been met with "some public opposition." But that is how The Note presented it.

Two days later, detecting widesread mainstream criticism of the Republicans' heavy-handed intervention, The Note reported it was "perhaps the beginning of a *media* backlash." [Emphasis added.] Published polls had already shown more than 80 percent of Americans sympathized with the position of Schiavo's husband, but The Note sensed the tide was turning because of a "media backlash." When Bush's own poll numbers began an immediate decline in the wake of the Schiavo intervention—dropping seven points in seven days according to one national survey—editors at The Note scratched their heads as well, declaring it was impossible to figure out "what exactly accounts for the President's droopy poll numbers."

That confusion over Bush's sagging poll numbers was not surprising since the Note, as a rule, routinely feigned indifference to developments that embarrassed the administration in 2005. For instance, The Note dutifully stayed away from the saga of Jeff Gannon, the former male escort and wannabe right-wing journalist who was, for unexplained reasons, whisked into White House press briefings. During the month of February, as the media story unfolded for weeks, The Note posted links to nearly seven hundred must-read articles; approximately ten were about Gannon. (The Note seemed more upset with liberals for digging into Gannon's past than with White House officials for handing out press passes to strangers.)

In April, as legal and ethical troubles began to mount for the GOP leadership, The Note, again channeling GOP talking points, announced:

1. There is an iron triangle of liberal interest groups, Democratic congressional staffers, and media jackals (both investigatively minded and liberally oriented) who have never identified with or liked Tom DeLay (and what he stands for) and are enjoying every minute of their conspiring to bring him down.
2. Almost every accusation swirling around DeLay involves actions by him that have exact analogues among other members of Congress of both parties.

On May 11, two confused, lost, and uncommunicative pilots of a small aircraft wandered into the capitol's no flight zone and seemed headed for a collision with the White House. The terror warning code was immediately raised to red, which sent 35,000 people running and screaming out of the Capitol building. While the First Lady was ushered into a bunker underneath the White House, the vice president was rushed to an undisclosed location, and the Pentagon was minutes away from giving orders to shoot down the airborne intruder. The whole time, Bush was oblivious, calmly riding his bike in a Maryland state park. Secret Service agents riding along with Bush were notified about the unfolding crisis, but waited forty-seven minutes—until the bike ride was over—before telling the president about the terrorist scare. The almost comical way in which the commander in chief was purposely kept uninformed while people inside the White House ran for their lives raised thorny questions for an administration that advertised Bush as a decisive leader in times of crisis. Some media outlets addressed the issue (one former Bush security official told a reporter "It's a very big deal") and even Laura Bush later said it was mistake to keep the president in the dark. The Note, though, signaled to the larger Beltway press corps that that embarrassing incident was of no interest. Between May 12 and 13, The Note linked to more than 110 stories; not one was about the White House's bizarre don't tell–don't tell policy for Bush regarding terror-related evacuations inside the nation's capital.

The Note also ignored the Downing Street memo, which revealed the impression among senior British officials that the Bush administration, eight months before the start of the Iraq war, had already decided to invade, that intelligence was being "fixed" to support the invasion, and that the U.S. justification for war was "thin." The *Sunday Times* of London first published the memo on May 1, 2005. For weeks the American MSM looked the other way, refusing to give the story the news attention it deserved. For The Note, the Downing Street memo definitely did not matter. From May 1 until June 20, when the American media had finally, and begrudgingly, addressed the memo in-depth, The Note linked to more than 1,700 stories. Approximately ten, or 1 percent, were links to stories about the Downing Street memo. (On June 14, The Note, reading the minds of Republicans, announced dismissively that the "The Left is unappeasable" on the issue of the Downing Street memo.)

In early July, when it was revealed Karl Rove, the president's closest political adviser, had a starring role in the CIA leak investigation, The Note shrugged. On the morning of July 11, returning from a one week summer hiatus, The Note announced which two stories were "consuming" the Gang of 500—the breaking Rove controversy was not among them. In fact, The Note didn't bother referencing the scandal story until the forty-eighth paragraph of that day's post, committing just a couple sentences to the fact that the president's most powerful aide was suddenly front-and-center in an escalating criminal investigation.

In September, amid the crisis of Hurricane Katrina, which plunged Bush's job approval ratings to new lows, The Note actually thought the White House was winning the spin war: "Mr. Bush still hasn't found his footing or his voice on this story, but his side clearly won the last news cycle in raw political terms," in part because "The President's poll numbers are mostly holding so far." That same day, though, pollster John Zogby reported Bush's job approval rating had just hit the lowest mark of his entire presidency. The following week, belatedly acknowledging the administration's spin failure, The Note reported, "living with [approval] ratings in the *40s* is White House reality for now." [Emphasis added.] The truth was, based on ABC's own polling, the White House had been living with approval ratings in the 40s for five months. The post-Katrina news was that Bush had tumbled into the 30s. The Note was oblivious.

It was also oblivious to the October 6 CBS poll that reported Bush's approval rating hitting yet another new low. Between the 6th and October 7 The Note linked to nearly one hundred must-reads, but the CBS report, available at the network's website, was not mentioned. When an October poll from NBC revealed that just *2 percent* of African-Americans approved of Bush's job performance, The Note ignored that stunning development. (That, despite the fact that months earlier The Note announced that MSM conventional wisdom was the Republican outreach effort to minority voters "will probably bear fruit.") On November 17, a new Harris poll, written up in the *Wall Street Journal* among other places, showed Bush's approval tumbling all the way down to 34 percent; The Note, which prides itself on casting a wide net and collecting the day's most important political developments, ignored the news.

That same month the *Washington Post* reported its latest polling data, showing that the political advantages the Republican Party had built up since 9/11 regarding a whole host of issues—Iraq, Social Security, taxes, spending, ethics, etc.—had completely evaporated as the party's standing with voters had collapsed. The poll also found Democrats had opened a gaping 17-point lead in a poll that asked Americans which party they intended to vote for during the 2006 Congressional elections. The Note, whose only real editorial mission is to chronicle the ups and down of the two major parties, completely ignored the *Post*'s unpleasant-for-Republicans report. That day The Note linked to seventy-plus articles and even included a separate "2006" category for must-read stories about the upcoming Congressional elections. But for The Note, the *Post*'s in-depth look at Bush's floundering GOP did not exist.

On December 6, while surveying the Republican's weakened political state, The Note, once more channeling angry conservative bloggers, identified the reason behind "all of the Republican Party's problems." It wasn't because of botched policies or ethical shortcomings, but rather it "boiled down" to the fact that the press was rooting against the GOP.

The Note, for one, was certainly not rooting against Republicans. Just the opposite, which was why Bush's second term collapse in 2005 was *not* the story the Note was busy chronicling—The Note completely missed the story of the year. (Or did everybody just assume that twelve months after reelection Bush's job ratings would be down nearly 20 points, one of the worst fifth-year presidential slides in modern history?) It was not until January 2006 that The Note finally figured out the previous year for Bush had been "disastrous and defensive." In real time, The Note refused to clearly and consistently document the obvious. Instead, through much of 2005 The Note was preoccupied with mocking Democratic leaders. Despite the fact it was Republican chiefs like Representative Tom DeLay and Senator Bill Frist who were hiring lawyers to fend off campaign indictments and to deal with insider trading subpoenas, The Note again and again emphasized how Democratic leaders were the ones floundering. A couple of examples:

- "Does the Democratic Party have anything real going for it at this point? It appears not." (August 4, 2005)
- "Leader Pelosi and Leader Reid are 'in charge' of the Democratic political 'strategy' on Katrina." (September 7, 2005; note the mocking quotation marks)

Not only is The Note openly hostile toward Democrats, but more important, considering its role as an influential distribution point for ideas, spin, and information, it almost uniformly ignores the political left. The Note often fails to include among its daily links of must-reads articles and essays offerings from *American Prospect, Salon, Washington Monthly,* or *The Nation,* for instance. Too fringe. Yet The Note routinely reaches out for entries from the radical right and presents them as thoughtful. "At National Review Online, lawyer Andrew McCarthy suggests prosecuting Michael Schiavo *for torture*" [emphasis added] read one Note link from March 2005, as the right-to-die case proceeded. That is the prism through which The Note views American politics. And indirectly, that's how the Beltway press corps views the battle of ideas as well—the far, far right is part of the daily discussion while the left is ignored.

Hard-core partisans on the right, like syndicated columnist Bob Novak and the *Weekly Standard*'s Bill Kristol and Fred Barnes are hailed by The Note as wise men whose work should not be missed, while their liberal counterparts are either ignored or mocked. *New York Times* columnist Paul Krugman, among Bush's sharpest and most articulate critics, is routinely shunned by The Note. And when it does link to a Krugman column, it's not accompanied by The Note's usual praise, but instead with dismissive put-downs: Krugman's work is "apocalyptic and apoplectic." (In late 2004, previewing the coming Social Security initiative, The Note warned readers, "Like it or not, Krugman is going to be part of this national debate.") The *Times's* Frank Rich, arguably the most influential liberal columnist in the country, essentially does not exist from perspective of The Note. And the *Washington Post's* E. J. Dionne, another potent and powerful voice on the left, should be read, according to The Note, simply to get "a window into what anti-Bush liberals are now all thinking inside their brains."

Given that standard, does The Note present conservative columnists as anti-Democratic and apocalyptic? No. The Note presents them as reasoned, savvy, and powerful. According to The Note, the best way to get a read on Democrats is to pay attention to what *conservative* columnists are saying about them. Columnists like John Podhoretz at the *New York Post* (who labeled DNC boss Dean a "lunatic leftist") and the "must-readable" *New York Times's* David Brooks, crowned by The Note as "the best columnist today writing about the Democratic Party." In a piece recommended by The Note, Brooks wrote a nasty column that made fun of Senator Kerry ("Senator Ahab") for criticizing Bush in the wake of the deadly Katrina relief fiasco. (Brooks couldn't understand why people were so *angry* at Bush following Katrina.) At The Note, Brooks's name-calling passed as valuable insight into the Democratic Party. Back on December 9, 2003, The Note highlighted "David Brooks' must-read New York Times column" about then-Democratic front-runner Dean. Built around more name calling, the column insisted Dean was "incoherent" and not "normal." The Note cheered the analysis. In other words, when the *Times's* Brooks got angry and mocked a Democrat (Dean) as "incoherent," The Note applauded. And when Brooks mocked a Democrat (Kerry) for being too angry, The Note applauded. Double standards don't come much more obvious than that.

What also distinguishes The Note, besides its open crush on the GOP, is the unique voice it's written in. Cutesy, creepy, and relentlessly effusive towards the media elite, The Note confirms the old adage that life really is like high school, with The Note filling the role of cheerleader-meets-yearbook editor, taking notes on where the cool kids are eating lunch, what they're wearing, and who's having the big party this weekend. To The Note's eyes, the MSM can do no wrong. Beltway reporters are wonderfully talented, and everyone deserves a raise (i.e., "Will *New York Times* management recognize how great [reporter] Anne Kornblut is and act accordingly?").

No doubt The Note's incestuous and over-the-top backslapping is meant to be taken somewhat tongue in cheek. (The Note does boast a wry sense of humor.) But after a while the compliments—the egregious stroking of the press—become so pervasive that readers suspect The Note actually believes the press valentines, that CNN's Judy Woodruff really is "one of the greatest political journalists of her generation," that *New York Times*'s John Tierney is "successful and dashing," his colleague Adam Nagourney is a "poet/historian," that *US News & World Report*'s Roger Simon flashes "brilliance, elan, and grace," that the work of *Time*'s Mike Allen is "indescribably delicious," that *Newsday*'s Glenn Thrush is "super savvy and smart" and that "*Time*'s [managing editor] Jim Kelly is more powerful than all but 23 United States Senators."

In The Note's world, the media players themselves, their promotions and their preening, rank right up with the policy makers they're covering. Journalists are part of the show and their savvy fabulousness should not—cannot!—be overlooked or ignored, no matter how pressing the national affairs may be.

And how do Beltway reporters respond to the cooing? They tell other reporters how The Note "is the arbiter of who is on the cutting edge," that "it has certain intelligence to it," it's "often ahead of the news," and "sets out concepts for stories and ways to look at the world." As Halperin himself once put it, explaining one of The Note's obvious formulas for success: "Reporters really like to see their names in The Note." And make no mistake, getting an article plugged by The Note represents a big deal inside MSM newsrooms, a badge of honor and one that bosses notice.

In fact, there appears to be only one way for reporters to earn the scorn of The Note, and that's to ask tough questions about the Bush White House or be nice to Democrats. Do that, and reporters run the risk of being tagged Democratic lackeys—the equivalent of the Beltway

Scarlet letter. For instance, in August 2005 when Republican Senator Frist broke with Bush over his conservative stance on stem cell research, embracing more a Democratic Party position on the science issue, Frist won some good press, specifically from the *Boston Globe*. The Note, however, quickly admonished the *Globe* reporter for "slobber[ing] so effusively on the Dr./Sen./Leader that we hope that they are both wearing doctor's coats (or lobster bibs)." Good luck trying to find The Note's references to reporters whose fawning coverage of the Bush administration was mocked as "slobbering." For The Note, that sin does not exist. Instead, that's considered being "smart" and "super savvy."

Again, during the 2005 debate over the faulty war intelligence used by the White House for the invasion of Iraq, the New York *Daily News* correctly shed light on the internal group of senior officials at the center of the misinformation campaign prior to the war. The Note was dismissive, suggesting the *Daily News* was doing "just as the DNC would want." For The Note, there is no more bruising insult than to suggest a reporter is doing the work of Democrats.

It should be noted that ABC's Halperin, who guides The Note, did spark a frenzied outcry from conservative press critics who shouted liberal bias late in the 2004 campaign. It came in the wake of an October 8 memo Halperin wrote to the ABC staff, urging everyone, in the closing weeks of the campaign, to hold both Kerry and Bush accountable for their misstatements, and saying that ABC should not feel constrained, in the name of balance, to simply report they're both doing it. Halperin suggested, correctly, that Bush's campaign was using misstatements about Kerry as a cornerstone to its reelection push.

The conservative media echo chamber immediately set upon Halperin. At the right-wing website FreeRepublic.com, a member demanded "Halperin's head should roll," while Laura Ingraham quoted from the memo on her syndicated radio show and announced it was a blatant "expression of partisanship on the part of ABC News," Conservative commentators pretended that orders from an editor to accurately report on the presidential campaign somehow pulled back the curtain on the MSM's liberal bias.

Some on the radical right took the attacks even further. In the wake of the memo, FrontPage.com, an archconservative site perpetually on the hunt for unpatriotic journalists, printed a lengthy feature on

Halperin and noted his father, Morton, once worked for Henry Kissinger on the National Security Council (and as President Richard Nixon's assistant for national security affairs), but quit in 1970 to protest the U.S.'s invasion of Cambodia. Twenty-two years later when President Clinton nominated Halperin to the new position of Assistant Secretary of Defense for Democracy and Peacekeeping, conservatives, still angry about the Vietnam War, orchestrated a nasty, personal campaign to defeat Halperin's appointment and to ruin his reputation, suggesting the CIA had a secret dossier on Halperin and hinting he was a traitor. FrontPage, channeling Senator Joseph McCarthy, saw a connection between The Note's Halperin and his dad: "Mark Halperin's idea of what is right may be what is Left. He was born in 1965 in Bethesda, Maryland, the red-diaper baby of hard-Left-connected controversial foreign policy specialist Morton Halperin. This fact reveals an entire Left-spin universe in which Mark grew up exposed to his father's comrades and radical ideas." (In 2004, Halperin told the *New Yorker* the rule he learned from his father regarding the role of media was "to hold powerful interests accountable to the public interest." Reading The Note though, there is virtually no evidence of that.)

The conservatives' nasty attack campaign against The Note in 2004 appeared to work, especially since it came in the wake of the CBS Memogate scandal when critics shouting "Liberal bias!" quickened Dan Rather's retirement. Halperin refused to publicly defend the logical contents of his campaign memo, an ABC spokesman nervously defended Halperin as being unbiased, and The Note quickly lurched even further to the right, adopting an openly Republican-pleasing perspective heading into 2005. That did not stop all the attacks on the right, though. Rush Limbaugh, forever on the hunt for ammunition to use in his profitable battle to reveal liberal media bias, would on occasion charge The Note with being unfair to Bush. How did The Note respond to phony attacks from the right? It tiptoed around Limbaugh and asked for his understanding and forgiveness.

- "The last thing we want is for Rush Limbaugh to quote from The Note for the third straight day."
- "Note to Rush Limbaugh: out of professional courtesy, before you attack us (wrongly) for being liberally biased or anti-Bush, we would

ask you to do three things: [1] consider each item one-by-one and ask yourself if you really think what we wrote is wrong; [2] ask the White House if they disagree with any of this—except that Pelosi item; [3] call us to discuss it. Then: trash us." (Halperin himself remains a faithful Limbaugh listener. "Twelve o'clock for a normal person might be 'Let's think about having lunch,' but for me it's 'Rush Limbaugh is on,' " he once told a reporter.)

By contrast, look at how The Note dealt with the more sustained and serious allegations about bias that came from the left. From July 20, 2005: "Judge John Roberts is by all accounts smart, nice, smooth, experienced, genial, a 'good man,' and—let's face it—a pretty darn good looking guy. (We wrote that sentence to simultaneously give you major insight into the President's mind, and to get a lot of angry left-wing blogs to link to today's Note, to boost our traffic.)" Faced with liberal critics, The Note mocked them. Faced with conservative critics, The Note begged understanding. Once again, The Note perfectly mirrored the MSM spirit.

Just the way The Note mirrored the MSM's gentle handling of Iraq as an ongoing political news story: On July 14, 2004, The Note, addressing the connection between headlines from Iraq and the president's reelection chances, stressed "The Bush campaign is counting on the continued absence of a drumbeat of bad news out of Iraq to improve right track/wrong track" polling numbers.

But had there really an "absence of bad news from Iraq" in July 2004? No. Nearly three dozen G.I.s were killed during the first two weeks of July—a sizeable jump over the previous month. On the same July 14 that The Note wrote about the absence of bad news, Iraq erupted in a new wave of violence when a suicide attacker detonated a massive car bomb near the British Embassy, killing eleven and wounding forty. An insurgent group, likely led by Abu Musab al-Zarqawi, announced it had beheaded a Bulgarian hostage. Five Iraqis were killed and twenty-one insurgents were wounded in fierce fighting in the Iraqi city of Ramadi. Insurgents assassinated the governor of Mosul as he was driving in a convoy of vehicles. A gunman assassinated the director general of Iraq's Industry Ministry as he left his Baghdad home. Meanwhile, two G.I.s were killed when their vehicle rolled over. That was all in *one day*. The next day, canvassing the media landscape for stories that might affect the November election, The Note made no reference to the carnage in Iraq. That was often the case in 2004, as The Note, much to the relief of the White House, steered political reporters' attention away from Iraq.

Fast forward to February 28, 2005, when insurgents set off a mega-blast in Baghdad, killing more than one hundred people. That morning, in an unintentionally revealing post, The Note wrote that even though the story was "sure to dominate cable and network news all day" (it did not), the fact that the White House had nothing to fear from any kind of fallout from the deadly blasts simply highlighted "how politically strong President Bush is right now." The Note stood in awe of the White House's good fortune and its media message dicipline, and how nearly two years after the invasion, with, at times, hundreds of Iraqis being killed on a weekly basis, Bush was able to swat away bad news and fear no repercussions. The Note was amazed how unsettling events that would "have brought hailstorms down on past presidents (say: Bill Clinton) don't seem to be seen as 'political' problems for this adminis-tration right now." The notion that the MSM, with its often supine cov-erage of Bush's war, had anything to do with insolating the president from negative fallout from Iraq seemed completely foreign to The Note, as it was with most inside the Beltway. To them, Bush stood res-olute, rising above the Iraq obstacle by his stick-to-itiveness and the sheer power of his reelection "mandate." Being blessed with a consis-tently docile and incurious press corps had nothing to do with it.

In May, The Note explained why the war, which it accurately described as "hands down the biggest story every day in the world," no longer qualified as big news among the MSM:

"We say with all the genuine apolitical and non-partisan human concern that we can muster that the death and carnage in Iraq is truly staggering. And/but we are sort of resigned to the Notion that it simply isn't going to break through to American news organizations, or, for the most part, Americans."

The Note even assigned blame for Iraq's no-news status—it was the Democrats' fault. Because Democrats were not, according to The Note, complaining vociferously about the war it was impossible for reporters to continue to play the story big. "No conflict at home = no coverage," The Note wrote. At least The Note was consistent. In the one week prior to announcing why Iraq was no longer considered newsworthy, The Note itself had linked to approximately 270 stories; none of them was about Iraq. The truth was that The Note months (years?) earlier had stopped paying attention to the war, signaling to the Beltway Gang of 500 that, particularly in 2004 and early 2005, the story was increasingly irrelevant to covering—let alone grading—the Bush administration, which is just how the White House liked it.

The ABC online team, supposedly scouring the media landscape with a team of "Googling monkeys" (Note-speak for young staffers who manically surfed the net each morning for news), simply could not uncover news stories about Iraq that were "must-readable" or might shape the domestic political landscape, which is what The Note really cares about. When it came to Iraq, The Note had adopted a modified don't ask, don't tell policy regarding bad news. For instance, on June 13, 2005, Knight Ridder newspapers, including the *Philadelphia Inquirer* and *Miami Herald*, published a unsettling piece of page-one analysis, reporting, "A growing number of senior American military officers in Iraq have concluded that there is no long-term military solution to an insurgency that has killed thousands of Iraqis and more than 1,300 U.S. troops during the past two years." That day, The Note linked to more than forty-five must-reads, but the Knight Ridder story did not make the cut.

Later that month while previewing yet another one of Bush's prime-time addresses about Iraq, The Note sounded like a cross between RNC boss Ken Mehlman and Fox News chief Roger Ailes, who offered free advice to Bush following 9/11: it urged the president to use the wartime speech to ignore Democrats and to rally his conservative base:

> The nation is at war and you are the Commander-in-Chief. Events on the ground matter, of course—but so do your words. Democrats and left-leaning independents matter, of course—okay, maybe they don't all that much in this context. Tonight is about winning back the base, and turning some of those 55-45-against poll numbers back around.

"Events on the ground matter," wrote The Note. But no, not really, because the day of the Iraq speech and the day after it, The Note linked to nearly one hundred stories and not one had to do with what was actually happening inside Iraq. On and on it went.

- On August 3, 2005, a roadside bombing, the the deadliest single attack on U.S. forces of the entire war, claimed the lives of fourteen Marines. The next day The Note made no reference to the historic fatalities, or any political implications they might carry.
- During the summer of 2005, while Bush vacationed in Crawford, Texas, antiwar mom Cindy Sheehan staged a vigil outside Bush's ranch that mushroomed into a phenomenon; but The Note, like the White House, was unimpressed. Between August 8 and August 16, as the Sheehan story swelled with the arrivals of hundreds of fellow protesters, The Note linked to approximately 270 stories covering a wide range of topics; fewer than ten were about Sheehan. Halfway through August, and two weeks into Sheehan's vigil, The Note theorized on which news events might fill the "vacuum" with Congress being in recess and Bush being on vacation. The Note listed eight possibilities. Sheehan, who clearly *did* fill the vacuum, was not among the listed options. Because for The Note, like the White House, Sheehan was of little interest.
- On Sunday, September 25, 2005, Sheehan helped lead a massive antiwar rally in Washington, which drew between 100,000 and 200,000 participants, making it the largest United States demonstration since the war began. That Monday, ABC's The Note linked to nearly seventy stories, covering nineteen separate news categories, but not one that simply detailed the peace rally.
- When the 2,000th U.S. service member was killed in Iraq on October 25, The Note the next day linked to thirty-one stories covering fourteen different news topics, but none was about the Iraq milestone or what the political implications might be. The Note's silence mirrored the day's Republican spin that, as Fox News anchor Brit Hume put it, the two-thousandth casualty figure was "negligible." (That day's Note arrived with the fittingly blissful headline, "Yada, Yada, Yada—and So We Go.")
- On November 2 the *Washington Post* published this page one exclusive: In a move that skirted laws banning torture, the CIA had been maintaining secret facilities in Eastern Europe where it was holding

suspected terrorists; facilities, dubbed "black sites" that not even members of Congress were told about. That day The Note high-lighted fifty-three stories, and found space to tip readers off to the fact that "At 11:30 am ET, Attorney General Gonzales gives the keynote speech at the Latino Leaders Luncheon Series in Washing-ton, DC." But there was no mention of the *Post* exclusive unmasking a network of secret, and likely illegal, jails being run by the CIA.

- On November 6 and 7 scores of major news organizations reported that newly released classified documents showed that the White House had been warned as early as 2002 by the hawkish Defense Intelligence Agency not to trust an al-Qaida informant in custody who claimed he had received training for biological and chemical weapons inside Iraq. The man "was intentionally misleading the debriefers," the administration was told. Bush's lieutenants ignored the warning and hyped the informants' phony allegations anyway. The Note paid no attention to a story that went straight to the heart of the ongoing political controversy over the administration's mis-leading use of prewar intelligence.
- During a chaotic, four-day stretch in January 2006, twenty-nine U.S. service members were killed in Iraq. Bad news politically for Bush at home, but The Note no made mention of the bloodshed.

Meanwhile, The Note's almost complete dependence on Republican staffers for its political insight was on clear display on November 18, 2005, when Republicans in the House of Representatives, wrestling with how to battle the growing chorus of concern about the war in Iraq, opted to introduce a resolution, hours before Congress broke for a hol-iday recess, calling for the immediate withdrawal of U.S. troops from Iraq. The resolution, an I-dare-you move by the GOP, came after Representative John Murtha, a hawkish Democrat from Pennsylva-nia, made headlines the day before when he called for U.S. troops to be withdrawn from Iraq over the next six months. News of the Republi-can's last-minute Congressional ploy broke late in the day and the GOP, sensing an opening, was clearly excited at the prospects of the showdown with Democrats over troop strength.

The AfterNote, a sort of P.M. cousin to the morning Note, breath-lessly reported the Republican majority had "decided to call Rep. John

Murtha's bluff," adding Republicans were "basically daring the Democrats to vote to withdraw American troops." The political pros at ABC, having just consulted with their GOP sources on the Hill, were convinced Murtha and Democrats had walked into a trap: "It will be interesting to see how the party keeps other liberal Congressmen who have expressed similar viewpoints to Murtha from joining him, a vote the Republican will no doubt point to as a Democratic chorus of weak-kneed liberals."

If anyone at The Note had bothered to check with Democrats they would have learned that the resolution the Republicans were introducing that night was not the same one Murtha put forward the day before, which meant few if any Democrats were going to vote for it, which meant the Republican bluff would be a failure, which it was. Things only got worse for the GOP when all hell broke loose on the House floor during the troop withdrawal debate when a freshman Republican from Ohio used the word "coward" in conjunction with Murtha, a Vietnam veteran who won two Purple Hearts. In the end, all the clumsy Republican maneuver did was give Murtha more television exposure; his address to Congress that night was carried live, in part, by CNN in primetime. Thanks to the Republicans, Democrats, at least momentarily, had a conservative, pro-military member as their most high-profile antiwar critic.

The team at The Note, though, thought the maneuver was a sure thing for the GOP.

CHAPTER 4

The Press Haters

It was April 1, 2005, and syndicated columnist, Fox News analyst, and influential conservative blogger Michelle Malkin was furious—again—with the MSM. Ever since the Terri Schiavo right-to-die story had emerged as a national phenomenon two weeks earlier, Malkin and her band of online combatants had become obsessed with the subplot surrounding a Republican talking points memo that had circulated among some in the U.S. Senate. The partisan outline urged GOP members to support Schiavo's pro-life parents, noting their crusade represented "a great political issue" for Republicans, would excite "the pro-life base," and be "a tough issue for Democrats."

News of the memo, first reported by ABC and the *Washington Post*, became a source of embarrassment for Republicans who had insisted moral and ethical considerations—not opportunistic political positioning—were the reasons they undertook unprecedented action on behalf of Schiavo's parents who were nearing the end of their seven-year legal battle to artificially keep their severely brain damaged daughter alive.

Conservative bloggers, however, thought they smelled a rat and in an effort to connect nonexistent dots they set off on an "investigation," quickly concluding the Schiavo memo was likely a farce from the get-go. Based on nothing more than their vivid, partisan imaginations, they surmised that a wily, unknown Democratic dirty trickster had typed up the memo and gotten the willing press corps to report that the fake memo came from the Republican side. Charging into battle along-side Power Line, a Minnesota-based conservative blog run by three attorneys who posted over a dozen conspiratorial reports about the Schiavo memo, bloggers seized on misspellings in the memo as proof of deception and, relying on anonymous GOP staffers on the Hill for tips, became more certain in their pursuit of the "political dirty trick." The fearless sleuths whipped themselves into a tizzy, with one right-wing blogger even sponsoring a contest to name the "scandal." ("Schiavo-Quiddick" was crowned the winner.) For two weeks conservative media cops ticketed the MSM for bias infractions:

- "[The memo] does not sound like something written by a conservative; it sounds like a liberal fantasy of how conservatives talk." (Power Line, March 21)
- "Talking Points Story Imploding?" (Power Line, March 22)
- "There is no evidence that this memo came from the Republicans at all." (Power Line, March 24)
- "Will ABC News officials continue to stonewall? Or will they come clean and promptly issue a correction?" (MichelleMalkin.com, March 24)
- "There is not a bit of evidence connecting the memo to any Republican, and, for all of the reasons we have repeatedly spelled out on this site, there are excellent reasons to believe it is a hoax perpetrated by still-unidentified Democrats." (Power Line, March 26)
- "I still believe the [MSM] has no basis for implying over and over again that the memo was distributed by Republicans." (Michelle-Malkin.com, March 26)
- "ABCNews.com still hasn't retracted its unsubstantiated characterization of the memo as 'GOP Talking Points.' " (Michelle-Malkin.com, March 30)

In her April 1 post belittling the "Schiavo talking points memo mess," Malkin continued her attack on the *Washington Post* and demanded the daily start publishing a laundry list of retractions for its fraudulent coverage of the Schiavo memo. It was fitting that Malkin's indignant blog entry appeared on April Fools' Day, because just five days later the author of the infamous memo reluctantly stepped forward and the joke was on Malkin—the mystery man was the legal counsel for Mel Martinez, the Republican senator from Florida, which meant, of course, the memo *was* written by Republicans, it *was* used for talking point purposes, and it *was* distributed by a Republican.

It was another off balance swing at the liberal media and another embarrassing miss. The press critics, though, refused to acknowledge their colossal blunder; they actually congratulated themselves for helping get to the bottom of the memo story—a story that they stitched together out of whole cloth in the first place. Prominent bloggers like Malkin and the ones at Power Line (both sites ranked among *New York* magazine's "Top 50" in terms of the most influential blogs) helped blaze a new path as they launched loaded, personal, and conspiratorial attacks against the press, often armed with little more than guesswork, as with the Schiavo story. Their arrogant, ask-questions-later approach to media criticism has become the hallmark for angry assaults on the press; assaults that helped foster a culture of fear inside MSM newsrooms during the Bush years. Call them the press haters. The term is not meant to be flippant or used casually. It's simply the most accurate way to describe the critics and the relentless, 24/7 war they wage on the MSM. As the Schiavo memo charade proved, they don't often allow the facts to get in their way. Indeed, they prefer to peddle misinformation, purposefully muddying the waters and scuttling any chance for serious debate about media bias and responsibility.

That's not to suggest all allegations that the MSM tilts left should simply be dismissed. The *Los Angeles Times*'s late media critic David Shaw, in his thoughtful media analysis from the 1990s, showed convincingly that "the news media consistently use language and images that frame the entire abortion debate in terms that implicitly favor abortion-rights advocates." But the press haters, by and large, aren't interested in thoughtful analysis or improving the craft of journalism. The new breed of conservative critic flashes a minimal understanding about how journalism works, and certainly shows no interest in actually enhancing it. The new generation wants to dismantle journalism, leaving one less independent institution to question the conservative agenda.

Press haters treat journalism the way their predecessors fixated on communism decades ago; as if it were a virus. During a private New York City screening in October 2005, area Power Line readers were invited to watch George Clooney's new movie *Good Night, and Good Luck*, which documented legendary 1950s newsman Edward R. Murrow's showdown with crusading Red baiter Senator Joseph

McCarthy. When the movie was over some Power Line readers, apparently rooting for McCarthy, booed and hissed, highlighting the press haters' telltale distaste for journalists, even iconic ones like Murrow. Note that when former CBS anchor Dan Rather warned, in a September 2005 speech, that a climate of fear was permeating inside newsrooms, a Power Line blogger cheered, "I certainly hope that this is so."

The truth is, the new school of right-wing pundits—and especially those online—simply double as Republican Party activists as they attack MSM in a never-ending goal to not only spook newsrooms, but to de-legitimize the press. The press haters specialize in creating smokescreens. They scurry around feverishly trying to undercut news reports that might pose a problem for the administration by shifting attention away from official misdeeds and onto the media's role in reporting the facts. In other words, the press haters play kill the messenger. They want to create confusion about facts, while simultaneously undermining news consumers' confidence in the MSM.

For them, the MSM represent *the* enemy, the only real interesting point of attack. The new generation, often peddling questionable "evidence" of liberal bias and with disregard for the facts, has no interest in simply "working the refs"; trying to get journalists to think twice next time they have to make a tough newsroom call on a sensitive political story. Press haters want to mug the refs, to drag them in the alley and pummel them. Al Gore called the haters "digital brownshirts," on orders "to harass and hector any journalist who is critical of the President." Indeed, the press haters don't simply portray offending journalists as misguided or deceitful. They hold up MSM members as objects of scorn and vilify them as unpatriotic, or even treasonous. "Which side is the NYTimes on?" sneered Malkin on the eve of the 2005 Iraq election, suggesting the daily might be rooting for insurgents who were killing U.S. troops.

The reason the press haters are so important and deserve close attention is because their ferocious, ongoing attacks against the so-called liberal media have dramatically altered the playing field; too many journalists are cowed. For instance, on June 28, 2005, Bush delivered a prime-time speech about Iraq, another in a string of pep talks designed to stem the tide of public disapproval of the war. That afternoon, officials at CBS and NBC signaled they would not carry the event live, correctly assuming the Bush update was not going to be newsworthy. By 8 p.m. though, something changed and Bush was given complete access to the networks. The next morning the *Washington Post*'s Tom Shales spelled out one likely reason behind the collective change of heart: "The managements of the networks may have feared hostile reaction if they didn't air the speech live. Refusing to air the speech probably would have led to unpleasantness—or at the least given the new subculture of bellicose bloggers another alleged media conspiracy to shriek about." Those shrieks are being heard—and fretted over—at the highest levels of the MSM.

Journalists are being actively undermined, yet reporters and editors won't even put up a fight. Rather than pushing back by pointing out the absurdity of the conservative press attacks (most MSM members politely ignored the Schiavo memo blunder, for instance), or at least ignoring the haters' endless stream of baseless accusations, MSM journalists, anxious to prove they are not liberal, toast the press haters' tenacity, gloss over their radical rhetoric, and pretend they're adding something to the public dialogue.

The new generation of the press haters, idolizing the toxic rhetoric of Rush Limbaugh and Ann Coulter, has been blessed with good timing. Along with a wartime backdrop which heightened newsroom anxiety about charges of not being sufficiently patriotic, MSM outlets suffered self-inflicted wounds with newsroom scandals revealing bold fabricators, such as Jayson Blair at the *New York Times* and Jack Kelley at *USA Today*. (A devout Christian, Kelley once declared, "God has called me to proclaim truth.") Then in September 2004, CBS's *60 Minutes II* was unable to authenticate memos it used to report on Bush's National Guard duty, an embarrassing failure that most observers agree led to Rather's early retirement. In truth, even if the discredited CBS memos were tossed out—even if CBS never reported on them—they changed nothing in regards to the central allegation that Bush had walked away from his Texas Air National Guard duty for more than a year during the Vietnam War. But spooked by the press haters' bloodthirsty attacks on CBS, the press quickly dropped the National Guard story, pretending CBS's gaffe had rendered it obsolete. (*Time* honored Power Line as its Blog of the Year in 2004 for its role in Memogate.)

Of course, the press outlets that occasionally stumbled during the Bush years were the same ones that made colossal errors of judgment while covering the Clinton White House; Whitewater was a media-driven hoax that thrived for nearly six years. But back then the Beltway media establishment was rarely held accountable for its sins of excess, and it certainly never fretted over attacks made from the left the way it does now about arrows coming from the right; arrows that have ushered in an age of timidity, which in turn has driven down the level of public trust. The press haters can be proud. "Thanks to their tireless efforts, the American people have lost faith in a cowed media that finds itself constantly trying to deflect charges that have no basis in reality," wrote *The Nation*'s Eric Alterman.

And make no mistake, press haters often take extended breaks from reality when launching their excited broadsides against the MSM. Take, as just one example, their December 2004 crusade against the Associated Press after one of its freelance photographers in Baghdad snapped dramatic pictures of Iraqi election workers being executed by insurgents in broad daylight amid stopped traffic on Haifa Street. Going on nothing more than an angry, anti-media hunch—the photos were a jarring reminder of how badly the U.S.-led reconstruction of Iraq was going—the bloggers, anointing themselves experts in wartime photojournalism, concluded the AP freelancer could only have captured the images if he'd been tipped off by terrorists who wanted the executions publicized. Read: The AP was in bed with terrorists. As Malkin put it, the bloggers were "raising troubling questions" about the photographs.

The right-wing critics worked off the novel and misguided assumption that when covering a war, journalists were supposed to root for the good guys, and that for every photo they snapped and article they published that did not portray the U.S. occupation as victorious, journalists had to answer to the press haters. And their questions for the AP regarding the Haifa Street photos were:

1. How did the photographer stumble across the execution scene?
2. How did he get so close. (Power Line theorized he was "within a few yards" from the scene of the murder.)
3. Why wasn't he afraid the insurgents would kill him?

The established facts were as follows:

1. Haifa Street was a hotbed for insurgents and on the day of the execution the AP freelancer had been tipped by another journalist that "something happened on Haifa Street."
2. He used a 400 mm zoom lens from *55 yards away.*
3. He was indeed afraid. The photographer's name was never released publicly out of concern about possible retribution from Iraqi insurgents.

So much for that controversy. And like so many of the press haters' hollow attacks, it faded away with a whimper and certainly without any acknowledgment that any false accusations had been made. But then four months later, when the AP captured a Pulitzer Prize for "its stunning series of photographs of bloody year-long combat inside Iraqi cities," including the Haifa Street execution photos, the press haters went nuts, again. With even less proof of a terrorist connection, the war supporters went all in on a bluff. "Pulitzer Prize for felony murder," shrieked Power Line, indicting the AP photographers "with complicity with murderers and enemies of the United States." Power Line's soul mate at Little Green Footballs blared "The media establishment puts their thumb in the eye of the blogosphere, awarding a Pulitzer Prize for photography to the Associated Press's anonymous and very possibly staged photographs of terrorists committing murder on Baghdad's Haifa Street." Malkin, whose 2005 book was appropriately titled *Unhinged,* demanded to know whether Pulitzer Prize judges had studied the bloggers' conspiratorial claims before passing out the award. (They had not.)

Power Line soon posted extensive analysis of the photo, concluding it was taken from approximately 16 yards away (wrong), was captured with a 150 mm lens (wrong), which meant "the assassination picture has all the earmarks of a planned image" (wrong). Keep in mind, this came from the same press-hating website that once lectured the MSM, "If you're going to serve up a conspiracy theory—without any evidence, of course—shouldn't the theory at least make some kind of sense?"

The truth is, the controversy over the award-winning images had nothing to do with how they came to be, and everything to do with the images that were captured. And from the press hater perspective, they were the *wrong* images. The manufactured controversy over the photographs was an end run at censorship, plain and simple. It was about trying to bully journalists, to keep them from doing their job and from reporting unpleasant truths around world. It was about smearing journalists who risked their lives in Iraq—more than six dozen were killed there—by accusing them of collaborating with America's enemies. All while members of the fearless "101st Fighting Keyboarders" pontificated from their stateside air-conditioned offices.

Of course, if MSM players had any nerve—if they weren't afraid to call out right-wing attack dogs—they would have stood up and said so at the time. Instead, the best AP officials could muster in response to the bloggers' paranoid allegation that photographers aided terrorists was that the charge was "deeply offensive." Worse, the *New York Times* covered the bloggers' outlandish attack on the AP as if it were actual news. "Blogs Incensed Over Pulitzer Photo Award" read the the headline to the *Times* story. Who cares, should have been an editor's response before printing the silliness.

But in light of the CBS National Guard scandal, that's how the MSM treated the likes of Power Line, which robotically publishes GOP talking points, penned by attorneys and Republican activists John Hinderaker, Scott Johnson, and Paul Mirengoff. Then again, prior to Power Line, Hinderaker and Johnson had been doing that same thing for a decade, although toiling in relative obscurity as fellows with the right-wing Claremont Institution and publishing occasional pieces in the *American Experiment Quarterly*. The expanded reach of their blog, and their willingness to hatch unprovable conspiracy theories against the liberal media, turned them into high-profile commentators. Power Line's authors would no doubt argue they operate independent of any political party, but the blog's obedient allegiance to the GOP is undeniable. For instance, when GOP lobbyist Jack Abramoff pled guilty to fraud in January 2006, highlighting one of the biggest D.C. corruption scandals in decades, Power Line, trying to brush the story aside, announced Abramoff's plea agreement was of "little public interest." That same month, during a bloody four-day stretch when twenty-nine U.S. service members died in Iraq, making it one of the deadliest periods of the entire war, the Power Line bloggers posted forty items on what they considered to be the four-day span's most pressing news events. The entries covered a wide variety of topics, including a left-field obit on soul singer Lou Rawls. But none of the posts were about the fallen U.S. fighters, and neither were any of Power Line's one hundred live links posted during that four-day span. For Power Line, U.S. fatalities in Iraq were of no interest, because bad news about the war was of no real interest. The GOP certainly appreciated that blind-eye perspective and actively courted the bloggers' help on a host of issues, much the way the Republican Party co-opted talk radio during the 1990s, turning it into a mouthpiece for conservatives. For instance, during the 2006 confirmation hearing for Supreme Court nominee Samuel Alito, the RNC hand-picked right-wing bloggers, including Power Line, to cover the event from Washington, D.C., showering them with access and attention in the process, including an off-the-record interview with Karl Rove. In return the RNC was rewarded with mostly glowing, obedient coverage from bloggers in attendance. "The [Alito] sessions revived, and arguably legitimized, criticism that at least some right-leaning bloggers are tools of the GOP," noted Daniel Glover, writing for the nonpartisan *National Journal.*

Nonetheless, MSM producers at CNN, among other places, ignoring a track record of GOP sycophancy and incompetence (i.e., Schiavo memo, AP photos), regularly book the Power Line bloggers on their news shows, pretending the men are experts in something. Truth is, there's not a liberal blogger in the country who, if they floated the kind of half-baked conspiracies that Power Line did, would ever be taken seriously by the MSM. Blogging on Bush's January 31, 2006, State of the Union Address, Power Line's Hinderaker reported that antiwar protester Cindy Sheehan, present in the Capitol gallery, had been removed from the chamber "when she tried to unfurl a banner." That was plainly false, but the press, overeager to appease the right, plays dumb. The alternative, as blogger Ezra Klein put it in the wake of Power Line's phony allegations against the AP photographer, was much less appealing:

> Powerline, we must begin to understand, *has no fucking idea what they're talking about at any given moment.* They get nothing right. Their

fact-checking skills are atrocious. They neither report nor call experts, it's just whatever they invented twenty seconds ago. Arguments are created on the fly, accuracy is unimportant so long as the product accuses the "MSM" or Democrats of some cardinal sin that'll leave Powerline's sycophantic readers moaning with the exquisite pleasure that comes only from having one's biases expertly stroked. [Emphasis original.]

Indeed, the very next month the unrepentant Malkin and Power Line bloggers were peddling yet another press bias fantasy, a postscript to the Swift Boat Veterans charade from the 2004 campaign. On May 20, 2005, Senator John Kerry signed what's called a Standard Form 180, authorizing the Navy to release all of his military and medical records to, in this case, reporters at the *Boston Globe* and *Los Angeles Times*. During the Swift Boat Veterans controversy, critics had demanded Kerry release all his records, suggesting the document dump would somehow confirm their wild accusations about Kerry's fraudulent war service. Kerry, for reasons that befuddled some of his supporters, refused, waiting until the spring of 2005 to release all his military history.

On June 7, with the Navy documents finally in hand, the *Globe* and *Times* wrote up their articles, noting how none of the Swift Boat allegations were borne out by the Navy's records. It was a pretty straightforward story. But disappointed press haters who had backed the Swifties on their anti-Kerry crusade refused to accept the facts and began buzzing among themselves about possible missing documents and the likelihood of a media cover-up. So they blindly rushed into the land of make believe and promptly embarrassed themselves yet again.

Writing for Rupert Murdoch's *Daily Standard*, soxblog.com blogger Dean Barnett worked off that paranoid angle. He noted Kerry signed a privacy waiver and allowed MSM journalists to look at his records. The MSM journalists at the *Globe* and the *Los Angeles Times* reported the documents revealed little of interest. The conundrum, wrote Barnett, was should people believe the *Globe* and the *Times*—"two partial newspapers"—or were the dailies part of the Kerry cover-up, too? Of course, Barnett had zero proof to back up his paranoid what-if, and rather than concede the right-wing Swift Boat attacks on Kerry's record had been fictional, Barnett clung to the suspicion that the Navy's orchestrated document release was all an elaborate set-up. ("Stranger things have happened," he wrote.)

Actually Barnett claimed to have some proof to document the *Globe*'s liberal bias. In its story on the document release, which included Kerry's underwhelming grades from Yale University, Barnett claimed the *Globe* soft-peddled Kerry's mediocre grades by describing them as being "virtually identical" to Bush's. Not true, Barnett insisted. "Kerry's grades were demonstrably, albeit slightly, inferior to the president's." Playing gotcha, Barnett said Kerry's grades and Bush's grades were *not* "virtually identical" and that the liberal *Boston Globe*'s reporting was not credible. For the record:

Bush's cumulative grade posted at Yale: 77.
Kerry's cumulative grade posted at Yale: 76.

Joining the conspiracy, Rush Limbaugh invented his own facts two days after the *Globe* story detailed the complete and full release of Kerry's Navy records pursuant to the Standard Form 180 he signed. Limbaugh told listeners, "The records that he released only gave his grades from Yale. He still has not come forth and signed what's necessary to produce his records in the Navy, and that's what everybody's curious about." If Limbaugh had ever bothered to read it, the *first sentence* of the *Globe* article reported Kerry had "authorized the release of his full military and medical records."

Over at Power Line on June 8, the bloggers reported that a "knowledgeable reader called" to tip them off that all of Kerry's Navy records had not been released because "the Navy would not have Kerry's complete service records; according to the caller, the records are retained by the National Personnel Records Center." That needless speculation was spoiled the next day when the *New York Sun* quoted Navy spokesman Lieutenant Commander Daniel Hernandez who confirmed Kerry's records from both Navy Personnel Command in Millington, Tennessee, and the *National Personnel Records Center* in St. Louis had been released." [Emphasis added.] "It's the whole record," stressed Hernandez.

On and on it went—an orgy of (deliberate?) misinformation, all done to raise doubts about the news media's integrity. And that was over the relative minor issue of Kerry's document release. The other examples are nearly endless. For instance, over the course of two months during the summer of 2005, Malkin posted nearly forty breathless reports about liberal talk radio network Air America and how it was about to collapse from a dire lack of funding and how the biased MSM refused to cover the network's imminent demise. Yet months after Malkin launched her "Air Enron" crusade, the network was not only still broadcasting but expanding its roster of stations.

Meanwhile, the botched Republican talking points memo was not the only embarrassing misstep the overeager media watchdogs made in connection with the Schiavo story during the spring of 2005. They also tried to uncover bias in the news polls, which showed an overwhelming majority of Americans sided with Schiavo's husband Michael, and were nearly uniformly opposed to government intervention in the case. How lopsided was the "debate" over Schiavo? One CBS poll found 82 percent of Americans thought Congress and the president should not have intervened in the case. The Schiavo controversy managed to accomplish the politically impossible; it temporarily united Red and Blue America.

Desperate to explain the complete lack of popular support conservatives had on the Schiavo issue, press haters blamed the media. Specifically, they decided the real problem was that the polls measuring public opinion were biased. Bloggers latched onto one ABC poll in particular that found 63 percent of Americans sided with Michael Schiavo and labeled it bogus because of how just one of the questions was worded. Here was the offending passage:

> Schiavo suffered brain damage *and has been on life support for 15 years.* Doctors say she has no consciousness and her condition is irreversible. Her husband and her parents disagree about whether she would have wanted to be kept alive. Florida courts have sided with the husband and her feeding tube was removed on Friday. [Emphasis added.]

Using the term "life support" to describe Schiavo's medical condition telegraphed ABC's liberal, "pro-death" bias, said the online sleuths. Pivoting from her self-appointed role as photojournalism expert which she used to try to undermine the Associated Press's Iraq photos, Malkin, appointing herself a medical pro, cried foul, insisting, "Terri Schiavo is not on 'life support' and has never been on 'life support.' " She insisted it was only because ABC had misled people that so many of them sided against pro-life Republicans. Three points that Malkin and her online band of would-be medical scholars failed to take into account:

1. The phrase "life support" from the ABC polling question came straight out of court documents from an earlier appellate court decision in Florida, as in, "In this case, the undisputed facts show that the guardianship court authorized Michael [Schiavo] to proceed with the discontinuance of Theresa's life support."

2. Dr. Jay Wolfson, the court-appointed doctor who examined Schiavo for months, noted to the Washingtonpost.com that, "In Florida and elsewhere, including according to the guidelines published by the American College of Cardinals, feeding tubes are defined as 'artificial life support.' "

3. The U.S. Supreme Court has found that, legally, tube feeding was no different from other forms of life support in that it too, represents "life-sustaining treatment."

Then again, Malkin, a paid Fox News analyst, had no training in the law, politics, or academia, and her only nonpartisan journalism job had been working as a videotape librarian for a local NBC affiliate. A liberal hater by trade, Malkin disregards many boundaries of common decency. In 2005 while denigrating antiwar activist Cindy Sheehan, whose son Casey was killed in Iraq, Malkin famously took it upon herself to speak for Casey and to lecture Sheehan about how her son would not approve of war protests. Malkin also possesses a casual regard for the facts to go with her hypocritical streak. As blogger D.C. Media Girl noted, in a May 2000 syndicated column, addressing the issue of interning Japanese-Americans during World War II, Malkin wrote, "The government has apologized and provided cash compensation to victims who were forced into camps. There is no denying that what happened to Japanese-American internees was *abhorrent and wrong.*" [Emphasis added.] Just four years later, though, Malkin, the daughter of Philippine immigrants, wrote an entire book about why the internment of Japanese-

Americans was a good thing. As she told C-Span's Brian Lamb, "I look back at the past and provide evidence that that conventional view of the evacuation and relocation of ethnic Japanese, as well as the internment of 31,000 enemy aliens, had a *clear military rationale and military necessity.*" [Emphasis added.]

That kind of flip-flop became Malkin's trademark. But perhaps no single event better captured Malkin's approach, and her unusual relationship with the truth, than her much-talked about August 19, 2004, appearance on MSNBC's *Hardball* with Chris Matthews, where the topic of debate was the unfolding controversy of the Swift Boat Veterans for Truth and their anti-Kerry book *Unfit for Command*. Malkin and Matthews got into a heated argument over whether Kerry's wounds were self-inflicted and specifically whether Kerry's wounds were *intentional*. Malkin would not rule the possibility out. (Unintentional self-inflicted wounds are common during wartime. Bob Dole, for instance, suffered a self-inflicted wound during World War II; he tossed a live grenade that bounced off a tree and exploded too close to him.)

After Malkin's *Hardball* segment was over, Matthews told viewers her comments about Kerry had been "irresponsible." It was an unusually tough back-and-forth for the normally scripted TV punditry fare. (Later that evening on MSNBC, host Keith Olbermann mocked Malkin's remarks and said she'd made a "fool of herself.") The next morning, Malkin blogged on her eponymous website about the MSNBC showdown, calling Matthews a "foaming jerk." Then she appeared on C-Span's *Washington Journal* where she took calls from viewers and also talked about the TV battle the night before. In less than eighteen hours, between her appearance on *Hardball*, her blog account, and her comments on *Washington Journal*, Malkin misstated key facts nineteen separate times and seemed to do so with extraordinary ease.

The cable tête-à-tête began when a fellow MSNBC guest, former San Francisco mayor Willie Brown who was defending Kerry's war record, lashed out at the Democrat's critics: "He volunteered twice. He volunteered twice in Vietnam. He literally got shot. There's no question about any of those things. So what else is there to discuss? How much he got shot, how deep, how much shrapnel?"

Malkin, who had already questioned Kerry's courage on the show, jumped right in: "Well, yes. Why don't people ask him more specific questions about the shrapnel in his leg. They are legitimate questions about whether or not it was a self-inflicted wound."

Matthews pounced: "What do you mean by self-inflicted? Are you saying he shot himself on purpose? Is that what you're saying?"

A rapid back-and-forth followed in which Matthews tried to pin Malkin down on whether she was suggesting Kerry shot himself on purpose. The key exchange was:

Matthews: Did he shoot himself on purpose?
Malkin: Some of the soldiers have made allegations that these were self-inflicted wounds.
Matthews: No one has ever accused him of shooting himself on purpose.
Malkin: Some of the veterans say—
Matthews: No. No one has ever accused him of shooting himself on purpose.
Malkin: *Yes. Some of them say that.* [Emphasis added.]

It was quite clear; Malkin claimed that in *Unfit for Command,* some Swift Boat Veterans for Truth had alleged Kerry shot himself on purpose. It's not only obvious from that quote, but from the nearly a dozen times Matthews asked Malkin point-blank whether Kerry's self-inflicted wounds were intentional: "I want a yes or no answer." Time and again Malkin wavered. ("I'm not sure.") Clearly if she thought it was preposterous to suggest Kerry shot himself intentionally she would have said so. She did not.

The truth is the Swift Boat Veterans never alleged Kerry shot himself on purpose. Even chief John O'Neill, who during the 2004 campaign was willing to make all kinds of baseless allegations about Kerry's war record, adamantly denied Kerry ever shot himself on purpose. "Oh no. He didn't intentionally wound himself," O'Neill told PBS. "He wounded himself with his own grenade. He didn't mean to."

Malkin went on national television and slandered a presidential candidate and then, caught in the act, tried to cover her tracks with her own unique set of facts. It was the type of attack Malkin and the press haters made all the time online. The only difference was this time it was caught on tape. Here is a detailed look at Malkin's thicket of falsehoods.

1. "By the way, it's not just—not just these right wingers who have been questioning his [war] record. The *Boston Globe* isn't, aren't operatives of the Bush campaign, and they have said the same thing as the veterans did about all three incidents regarding the Purple Hearts." (Malkin on MSNBC.)

False. The Swift Boat Veterans for Truth accused Kerry of, among other things, falsifying battle reports in order to win fraudulent military honors. While the *Boston Globe* did report extensively on Kerry's war service, the paper at no time "said the same thing" that the Swifties did "regarding the Purple Hearts" Kerry was awarded.

2. "Yes. Some of them say that." (Malkin on MSNBC in response to Matthew's question on whether Kerry shot himself on purpose.)

False. The Swift Boat Veterans never alleged that Kerry "shot himself on purpose."

3. Malkin: "Patrick Runyon and William Zaldonis." (Malkin on MSNBC. That was her response to Matthews's demand that she name two Vietnam vets who claimed Kerry shot himself on purpose.)

False. Runyon and Zaldonis were Kerry *allies* from Vietnam and spent the 2004 campaign trying to help Kerry knock down the reckless Swift Boat accusations. They never suggested Kerry shot himself on purpose.

4. "I'm talking about what's in the book!" (Malkin on MSNBC.)

False. Nobody in *Unfit for Command* ever accused Kerry of shooting himself on purpose.

5. "I noted that the Boston Globe—hardly a hothouse of GOP operatives—had raised many of the same questions about Kerry's war record as the Swift Boat Vets had." (Malkin bloggin on her site, MichelleMalkin.com.)

False, see No. 1.

6, 7, 8. "Matthews . . . admitted that (a) he himself had not read the damned book, (b) he was not interested in asking Kerry about the specific doubts raised by vets about his wounds, and (c) he had not and would not question Kerry about these specific allegations." (Malkin blogging.)

False, false, and false. The first claim, that Matthews admitted on the program that he'd never even read *Unfit for Command*, is one Malkin made again and again in the aftermath of her televised meltdown. It's false. Matthews made no such comment on the program.

The second and third claims, that Matthews admitted he wasn't interested in asking Kerry about the Swifty allegations, are false. Here's the exchange Malkin was likely trying to spin to her favor:

Malkin: Have you tried to ask John Kerry these questions?
Matthews: If he shot himself on purpose. No. I have not asked him that.
Malkin: Don't you wonder?
Matthews: No, I don't. It's never occurred to me.

After the program aired, Malkin turned that exchange into the notion that Matthews wasn't interested in asking Kerry about *any* Swift Boat Veterans allegations, when during the program Matthews specifically said he wasn't interested in asking Kerry "if he shot himself on purpose."

9, 10. "Because, I said, I was talking about what was in the book, which he had admitted he hadn't read." (Malkin blogging.)

False, see No. 4, No. 6.

11. "Don't you wonder?" I asked. "No, I don't," he bellowed. "It's never occurred to me." (Malkin blogging.)

False, see No. 7.

12. "Olbermann expresses incredulity that I was simply reporting what the Swift Boat Vets' book says." (Malkin blogging.)

False, see No. 4.

13. "Olbermann, alleged journalist, is smearing me because I agreed to discuss and analyze claims made by the authors of *Unfit for Command* and actually referred to what was in the book." (Malkin blogging.)

False, see No. 4. Malkin did not refer to what was in the book.

14, 15. "All I was simply doing was being there as a journalist and as an author, and relating what I had read in the book, which he admitted he had not read." (Malkin appearing on C-Span.)

False, see No. 4, No. 6.

16. "I asked Chris Matthews if he was interested at all in asking John Kerry directly any of the questions and asking him about the allegations that were raised by the veterans, and he said no, and he said it had never occurred to him to do so." (Malkin on C-Span.)

False, see No. 7.

17. "I had no vested interest in this [Swift Boat] story." (Malkin on C-Span.)

False, as a professional right-wing pundit dedicated to the reelection of Bush and who in less than ten days in August hyped the Swift Boat affair with eight separate posts and included twenty-two links to Swift Boat stories on her website, Malkin clearly had a vested interest in promoting the story.

18. "I don't know how many shows [Matthews has] had now talking about these allegations without having cracked open the covers of the book himself." (Malkin on C-Span.)

False, see No. 6

19. C-Span's Brian Lamb: "Did [Matthews] admit that on the program last night?"
Malkin: "Yes, he did."
Lamb: "Yes, he has not read the book?"
Malkin: "Yes, he did" admit it.

False, see No. 6. Matthews made no such admission.

Malkin's malleable facts, her outlandish accusation, and hypocritical arguments would certainly doom her reputation within the MSM, right? Think again. If history is any guide, it will only be a matter of time before Malkin is toasted on the cover of *Time* magazine, which in

2005 advertised its soft spot for press and liberal haters. Specifically, *Time* lavished its love on Ann Coulter, who was on the record—*after 9/11*—as saying, "My only regret with Timothy McVeigh is he did not go to the *New York Times* Building." Coulter, who insisted Democrats wished Saddam were back in power, that liberal New Yorkers would "immediately surrender" if attacked by terrorists, and who by year's end in 2005 wrote, "I think the government should be spying on all Arabs, engaging in torture as a televised spectator sport, dropping daisy cutters [bombs] wantonly throughout the Middle East and sending liberals to Guantanamo."

Coulter wasn't merely a controversial pundit; she was a pure product of the Beltway's right-wing culture and career track. Coulter put in time clerking for Pasco Bowman II of the United States Court of Appeals for the Eighth Circuit, litigated for the Center For Individual Rights, a right-wing advocacy group, and worked as a flak for Michigan Republican Senator Spencer Abraham. She then went on to write *High Crimes and Misdemeanors: The Case Against Bill Clinton; Slander: Liberal Lies About the American Right;* and *Treason: Liberal Treachery from the Cold War to the War on Terrorism.* By design or not, *Time*'s decision to fete Coulter was also a decision by the magazine to celebrate the right wing's cottage industry of press haters.

The *Time* love-fest began in the April 18, 2005, issue when the weekly, compiling its list of the *world's* most influential people, found room alongside past and present international leaders Ariel Sharon, Bill Clinton, Nelson Mandela, and the Dalai Lama to include Coulter, a cable TV pundit. *Time*'s James Carney, who five months later was promoted to the magazine's Washington bureau chief, did the honors, typing up the Coulter valentine, headlined "Gleefully Making the Left Squirm":

"In her books, Coulter can be erudite and persuasive, as when she exposes the left's chronic softness on communism. But her signature is her gleeful willingness to taunt liberals and Democrats, to say out loud what some other conservatives dare only think—that Bill Clinton is a 'horny hick,' for example, and his wife 'pond scum.' It's what makes Coulter irresistible and influential, whether you like it or not."

Did you follow that? When Coulter labeled the freshman senator from New York "pond scum" the pundit was being "irresistible," and when she called the forty-second president of the United States a "horny hick," Coulter was being "erudite." (The odds *Time* would ever toast a left-wing flame thrower who, for instance, slurred Bush as a "recovering drunk" and fantasized about al Qaida bombing Fox News? Zero.)

The very next week *Time*'s adoring Coulter cover story arrived on newsstands. Instead of at least pretending to address how Coulter had helped drive political discourse in this country into the ground (Coulter: "American journalists commit mass murder without facing the ultimate penalty, I think they are retarded"), the magazine propped up the polemicist as a "misunderstood" "public intellectual" who "you can trust will speak from her heart." Coulter was in caring hands at *Time*. "The officialdom of punditry, so full of phonies and dullards, would suffer without her humor and fire," wrote *Time*, which insisted on taking Coulter very seriously. ("Ann Hart Coulter was born in New York City on Dec. 8, 1961 . . .") When *Time* quickly came under attack from progressives for its one-sided Coulter profile, the author, *Time*'s John Cloud, fired back, noting that nine months earlier *Time* had featured lefty Michael Moore on the cover, suggesting the magazine was simply balancing things out with Coulter.

True, both were given the cover treatment as partisan Pied Pipers for their side: Moore for the July 14, 2004 edition, Coulter for the April 25, 2005 issue. At the time of his *Time* spotlight, the pioneering filmmaker had just released the most successful documentary in history, *Fahrenheit 9/11*. At the time of her *Time* spotlight, Coulter's five-month-old book, which recycled her previous columns, had already fallen off the best-sellers list. More important, the Moore and Coulter stories themselves were not alike. Moore's profile in *Time* ran approximately 3,000 words; Coulter's was double that, at 6,000 words. On the July 14 cover, *Time* fretted over whether Moore's *Fahrenheit 9/11* was "Good for America?" On the April 25 cover, *Time* noted how Coulter "delights the right" and asked, "Is she serious or just having fun?" The Moore piece came complete with a sidebar that addressed alleged inaccuracies in *Fahrenheit 9/11*, while the Coulter piece professed to be unable to uncover any errors in her work. *Time* wondered whether Moore's charges against Bush were leveled "recklessly." The magazine never used that word to question Coulter's diatribes.

Time's Coulter profile—a whitewash, plain and simple—was an embarrassment for the weekly and illustrated just how off-kilter and unsure of itself the mainstream media had become in the wake of Bush's reelection, and how too many journalists were willing to play dumb regarding the likes of Coulter in an effort to make nice with the red-state news consumers. Despite *Time*'s loving treatment, what really elevated the feature to legendary puff status was when Cloud typed up two sentences, which his editors, and presumably *Time* fact-checkers, then signed off on:

"Coulter has a reputation for carelessness with facts, and if you Google the words 'Ann Coulter lies,' you will drown in results. But I didn't find many outright Coulter errors."

In order to print that, *Time* had to ignore not only the corrections Coulter's own publisher had to make in subsequent editions of her books, but also the tens of thousands of words posted at blogs such as the Daily Howler, Spinsanity, Mediawhoresonline, *American Prospect's* Tapped, and Scoobie Davis Online, just to name a few, that carefully chronicled the blatant misstatements by Coulter. Here are just two:

- According to Coulter, Senator Jim Jeffords (I-Vt.), "supported Clinton's tax hike, and opposed the younger Bush's tax cut." Wrong and wrong. Jeffords voted against Clinton's tax hike (as did all Republicans), and he voted for Bush's tax cut.
- In a 2004 column posted online, Coulter scolded former Vice President Al Gore for comments he made criticizing Bush for "deploying 'digital Brown Shirts' to intimidate journalists." Coulter, lambasting the liberal media, insisted, "Only one major newspaper—the *Boston Herald*—reported Gore's 'Brown Shirt' comment." Not true. News of Gore's 'Brown Shirt' quip was reported by the *Philadelphia Inquirer, Washington Post, Kansas City Star, Monterey County Herald, Chattanooga Times Free Press, Charlotte Observer, Tulsa World, Tampa Tribune,* and *Augusta Chronicle,* as well as on Fox News, CNN.com, and in Reuters, the Scripps Howard News Service, and the Cox News Service.

Rather than uncovering any blunders, which were hiding in plain sight, *Time* set out to disprove some of the "alleged mistakes" made by Coulter. In its article *Time* referred to an interview Coulter gave to the

Canadian Broadcasting Company in which she urged Canada to send troops to Iraq just as it had done during the Vietnam War: "I mean Canada sent troops to Vietnam—was Vietnam less containable and more of a threat than Saddam Hussein?" The Canadian host, Bob McKeown, corrected her, noting Canada, neutral throughout the war, never sent a fighting force to Vietnam. Again and again Coulter disagreed, insisting to McKeown that he was wrong. *Time*, scurrying through the history books, reported, "What [McKeown] didn't mention was that Canada did send *noncombat* troops to Vietnam in 1972." [Emphasis added.]

Of course, Coulter's point was that when it came to communist trouble in Southeast Asia, Canadians marched right alongside Uncle Sam. In truth, Canada sent some relief workers and peacekeepers to Vietnam around the same time the Paris Peace Accords were signed. Nonetheless, in the eyes of eager *Time* editors, Coulter deserved the benefit of the doubt for her imaginative recollection of history and how "Canada sent troops to Vietnam." (*Time*'s manic spin was all the more embarrassing considering months before the article appeared on newsstands, Coulter herself conceded "I was wrong" about the Canadian troops comment.)

For the MSM though, right-wing agitators like Coulter who made wild, reckless accusations were usually deemed off-limits from serious criticism. Take, for example, when former Senate minority leader Tom Daschle (D-S.D.), lashed out at Rush Limbaugh following the 2002 midterm elections. During a November 21 speech on the floor of the senate, Daschle bemoaned the state of America's political discourse and charged that the rhetoric from Limbaugh, and "all the Rush Limbaugh wannabes," had directly led to death threats against Daschle and his family. The next day Washingtonpost.com mocked Daschle, wondering if he had "lost a couple of screws," and professing bewilderment as to why Daschle would be so upset with Limbaugh:

"We can understand that Daschle is down, just having lost his majority leader's job and absorbed plenty of blame for this month's Democratic debacle. What we can't understand is how the South Dakotan can suggest that a mainstream conservative with a huge radio following is somehow whipping up wackos to threaten Daschle and his family," wrote Howard Kurtz. "*Has the senator listened to Rush lately? Sure, he* aggressively pokes fun at Democrats and lionizes Republicans, but mainly about policy. He's so mainstream that those right-wingers Tom Brokaw and Tim Russert had him on their Election Night coverage." [Emphasis added.]

That analysis was in line with Fred Barnes at Fox News, who dismissed Daschle's complaints, calling Limbaugh a "conventional conservative," and noting "He's not an extremist." What Kurtz, Barnes, and virtually every other journalist who covered the story failed to do was simply inform news consumers about what Limbaugh had been saying about Daschle. Here were some of the key accusations:

- "Is Tom Daschle simply another way to portray a devil?"
- "In essence, Daschle has chosen to align himself with the axis of evil."
- "You [Daschle] are seeking political advantage in the war on terrorism."
- "You now position yourself, Senator Daschle, to exploit future terrorist attacks for political gain."
- "You are worse, sir, than the ambulance-chasing tort lawyers that make up your chief contributors. You, sir, are a disgrace."
- "You are a disgrace to patriotism, you are a disgrace to this country, you are a disgrace to the Senate, and you ought to be a disgrace to the Democratic Party."
- "What do you want your nickname to be? Hanoi Tom? Tokyo Tom?"
- "You sit there and pontificate on the fact that we're not winning the war on terrorism when you and your party have done nothing but try to sabotage it."

It's clear Limbaugh's rants were not "mainly about policy," as some suggested. In fact, they were often deeply and oddly personal, dripping with a peculiar loathing for the low-key senator from South Dakota. Yet the press was *stumped* as to why Daschle was so irked by Limbaugh. Then again, the press has been playing dumb with Limbaugh for years. That is, when the press wasn't playing softball with him. Here are three of the first four questions *Time* posed to Limbaugh during a Q&A that appeared in the June 7, 2004, issue. [Emphasis added.]

- "Even Al Gore jumped on you last week. What do you make of *the New Al Gore?*"
- "As Democrats go, *how bad is John Kerry?*"
- "You're getting criticized for comparing the prison abuse in Iraq with a college prank. *Were you misinterpreted?*"

Limbaugh did, in fact, insist his prison torture comments in the wake of the Abu Ghraib scandal had been taken out of context. *Time* seemed to buy the explanation. Here are Limbaugh's comments in their original context:

- "You know, if you look at—if you, really, if you look at these pictures, I mean, I don't know if it's just me, but it looks just like anything you'd see Madonna, or Britney Spears, do onstage—maybe I'm, yeah—and get an NEA grant for something like this." (May 3, 2004)
- "You know, these [U.S. soldiers in Iraq] are being fired at every day. I'm talking about people having a good time, these people, you ever heard of emotional release? You ever heard of the need to blow some steam off?" (May 4)
- "The thing, though, that continually amazes—here we have these pictures of homoeroticism that look like standard good old American pornography, the Britney Spears or Madonna concerts or whatever." (May 6)
- "And we hear that the most humiliating thing you can do is make one Arab male disrobe in front of another. Sounds to me like it's pretty thoughtful. Maybe the people who executed this pulled off a brilliant maneuver. Nobody got hurt. Nobody got physically injured." (May 6)
- "If you take these pictures and bring them back and have them taken in an American city and put on an American Web site, they might win a video award from the pornography industry." (May 11)

Despite the controversy over Limbaugh's oddly sexual Abu Ghraib comments—at least two Republican members of Congress publicly rebuked his defense of torture—nobody should have been surprised when the Unification Church–owned *Washington Times* subsequently praised Limbaugh as "an important conservative voice," or when former

Cheney aide Mary Matalin called into Limbaugh's program that same month and gushed, "You inspired me this morning." They're all part of the same Republican noise machine that puts the party's interest far, far ahead of journalism or truth telling. If Limbaugh wants to utter wacky, indefensible assertions, then that's his choice, like suggesting the verified Downing Street memo "may be a forgery," or by mocking antiwar crusader Cindy Sheehan, whose son was slain in Iraq, by teasing, "Oh, she lost her son!' Yes, yes, yes, but (sigh) we all lose things." Then so be it.

The press scandal, and it was a hallmark through the Bush administration, was how the mainstream press treated the increasingly unhinged right-wing, press-hating pundits and their relentless struggle with the truth. Not only did Beltway insiders refuse to confront the conservative name callers, but they instead embraced the press haters, made nice with them, and pretended the right-wingers represented rational discourse. For instance, one month after Limbaugh suggested the Abu Ghraib prison tapes could win a porno award stateside, and insisting, "What's good for al-Qaida is good for the Democratic Party in this country today," the talker broke with his traditional no-guest rule and welcomed *Meet the Press* host Tim Russert on his program. Russert was too busy backslapping with Limbaugh to raise any uncomfortable questions about the pundit's puzzling torture comments. (Russert said it was "an honor" to be on the program.) In fact, at one point Russert playfully suggested nominating Limbaugh as the next host on *Meet the Press*. Limbaugh signed off the boys club chat with, "Anyway, this has been fun. I always enjoy talking to you, and I appreciate our relationship over the years." The odds Russert would ever gosh around with a radio talk show host who told listeners that what's good for Al Qaeda is good the Republican Party? Zero.

Playing dumb about Limbaugh and his outlandish and often hateful rhetoric has become a mainstream media ritual, as Beltway journalists work overtime to soften the powerful talk show host's edge and to make him seem like just another partisan. Why else would the *Washington Post* compare Limbaugh to Comedy Central's award-winning late-night satirist, Jon Stewart? Why else would the *New York Times* public editor Daniel Okrent equate Limbaugh, who literally fantasizes up facts on the air ("Nobody got hurt" at Abu Ghraib), with Media Matters for America, which documents each one of its media critiques by post-ing original transcripts as well as video and audio files online?

The almost invisible standard that the MSM hold conservative press critics to has only emboldened them to offer up often comical attempts at media analysis. For instance, in the summer of 2005, the Media Research Center (MRC), the right-wing think tank with a staff of sixty dedicated to documenting liberal media bias, teamed up with the like-minded Free Market Project to produce a content analysis report they claimed proved that network news reporters were guilty of talking down the economy and trying to convince Americans things under Bush were worse than they really were. The *Wall Street Journal*'s conser-vative editorial page trumpeted the findings: "To cite just one example, a CBS Evening News story on July 22 said that the economy is 'very tenuous. It could fall apart at any moment. One piece of bad news, one additional terrorist attack, one negative corporate earnings, and it goes right down again.' "

Was CBS really trash talking the U.S. economy? Not quite, because the quote cited did not come from a CBS reporter, as the *Journal* clearly implied, but rather from an unidentified man on the street. In other words, it was a real live American consumer who expressed anx-iety about the economy, who feared it was "very tenuous," not CBS. As another example of liberal doom-and-gloom reporting, the MRC study scolded the *CBS Evening News* for being inconsistent in its economic reporting: "On the April 26 *CBS Evening News*, Bob Schieffer said, 'Americans are getting a little concerned about where the economy is headed.' That was just before he reported that new homes were selling 'at the fastest pace on record.' "

But here's what Schieffer also said that night but that was omitted from the MRC's report on liberal bias: "A *report out today* shows that while confidence in the economy is sill relatively strong, it has now fallen for three straight months." [Emphasis added.] CBS was reporting facts—a new study—about consumer confidence, which was falling at the same time homes sales were increasing. CBS didn't manufacture the inconsistency, the network simply reported on it.

That kind of pseudo analysis—fakery, really—was par for the course among press haters, who at some point realized the timid MSM was never going to call them out for their manufactured and misleading media research. In the wake of John Roberts's 2005 nomination to the United State Supreme Court, the AP, as part of an extensive look into his background, wrote a story detailing Roberts's hometown of Long Beach, Indiana, and the fact that when he was growing up the town had banned the sales of homes to blacks and Jews. Brent Bozell, head of the MRC, claimed that with the story the AP had flaunted its "sleazy and insipid bias." Did Bozell dispute the fact Roberts grew up in Long Beach, Indiana? No. Did Bozell dispute the fact the town in the 1960s and 1970s banned blacks and Jews? No. Did Bozell object to established, albeit embarrassing, facts being reported? Yes.

And that's really what drives so much of what the conservative press critics do. Their work has everything to do with intimidation as well as advancing the conservative agenda, and too little to do with thoughtful media examination. The press haters literally do not understand how journalism works. Or least they pretend they do not. In a 2005 year-end piece, *National Review Online*'s media blogger Stephen Spruiell lambasted the MSM for the way it covered a whole host of stories, including the CIA leak investigation, Hurricane Katrina, and Tom DeLay's ethical woes. According to Spruiell, those stories were "media-manufactured scandals." When the *New York Times* finally published its 2005 exclusive about how Bush okayed the government to eavesdrop on Americans' phone calls without a proper court order, Tim Graham of the MRC demanded to know who the paper's senior anonymous sources were for the sensitive story, which was checked at the highest levels of the administration, and whether the sources weren't simply "members of MoveOn.org," the grassroots progressive organization. That's the level of logic and sophistication common among the press haters.

In October 2005, the MRC released a report that it claimed laid bare the media's liberal bias in its coverage of the war in Iraq because in its report a majority (61 percent) of network segments on Iraq that year were "negative." But that's called reporting, since the MRC itself would be hard pressed to find a single high-profile, independent military expert who thought the battle for Iraq had gone well in 2005, or that the majority of the news was "positive." The MRC seemed to think the press was supposed to make things up about Iraq if the reality on the ground wasn't comforting enough.

More? There's the time the MRC took a nasty quote about Ronald Reagan—he "couldn't tie his shoelaces if his life depended on it"—and falsely attributed it to former *New York Times* editor Howell Raines, citing it as proof of Raines's offensive "arrogance" and "liberalism." The back story: In his 1994 memoir, *Fly Fishing Through the Midlife Crisis,* Raines, out with longtime Maryland fishing guide Dick Blalock, quotes the garrulous Blalock at length—for an entire page—about fisherman presidents. During one part of his monologue Blalock announced, "Of course, I liked Carter. Charlie Fox and Ben Schley taught him a lot about fishing, and he ties a good fly. Reagan couldn't tie his shoelaces if his life depended on it." Reading the passage MRC simply took the last part of the Blalock quote and reported it came from Raines, publicly dubbing him a "Reagan-hater." The MRC liked the quip so much that it was included among the group's greatest hits when it celebrated its tenth anniversary in 1997, "The Best Notable Quotables: A Decade of Bias." And when Raines was forced to resign from the *Times* in 2003 following the Jayson Blair newsroom scandal, MRC chief Bozell resurrected the bogus quote and paraded it around on television. That's how press haters document liberal media bias.

Conservative Bernie Goldberg made good use of MRC's Raines handiwork, citing it approvingly in his 2001 best seller, *Bias: A CBS Insider Exposes How the Media Distort the News.* Goldberg used another MRC gem-of-a-quote in *Bias* to illustrate how the *New York Times,* steered by feminists (who knew?), was so anti-male. In *Bias,* Goldberg pointed disapprovingly to a story by *Times* reporter Natalie Angier that begins this way: "Women may not find this surprising, but one of the most persistent and frustrating problems in evolutionary biology is the male. Specifically . . . why doesn't he just go away?" MSM man bashing? Not quite. Angier's original *Times* piece, cited by Goldberg, was published in the newspaper's *science* section because it was an article about reproduction among *insects.* Goldberg left that information out of his book about how the liberal media "distort" the news.

Coulter, in *Slander,* her book attacking the liberal press, bemoaned the fact that while there were lots and lots of MSM stories about "the religious right" there were hardly any about "the atheist left." To prove her point, Coulter turned to Nexis and reported that the *New York Times* mentioned either "Christian conservatives" or the "religious right" 187 times during 2000. But not once did the paper refer to "atheist liberals" or "the atheist left." Not surprisingly, given the absurd context Coulter had created (the religious right represents a powerful social and political force in America; the atheist left, by comparison, does not exist), it turned out the *New York Times* was hardly alone in ignoring "the atheist left." The right-wing *Washington Times* in 2000 also turned a blind eye. As the Daily Howler chuckled, "If Coulter has sniffed out a vast left-wing plot, [*Washington Times* editor] Wes Pruden is in on it too."

Even more scholarly attempts busy "objectively quantifying" media bias have come up short. A press release for a 2005 UCLA-led quantitative study by political scientists Tim Groseclose and Jeffrey Milyo breathlessly announced the two had cracked the code of liberal bias by meticulously detailing source citations within articles and comparing them to members of Congress. For instance, if news outlets regularly cited think tanks often referenced by liberal congressmen, then the outlet had a liberal tilt. Their findings were eagerly trumpeted by conservative media outlets as long-sought-after academic proof that "almost all major media outlets tilt to the left," as the study concluded. But a closer examination of the study highlighted all sorts of problems with their methods and results. For starters, Milyo and Groseclose have enjoyed working relations with a galaxy of right-wing think tanks (American Enterprise Institute), advocacy groups (Federalist Society), and periodicals (*The American Spectator*), which raised doubts about the objectivity, and intentions, of their study. As for their odd method for cataloging bias, Media Matters for America summed it up best:

"The study rests on a presumption that can only be described as bizarre: If a member of Congress cites a think tank approvingly, and if that think tank is also cited by a news organization, then the news organization has a 'bias' making it an ideological mirror of the member of Congress who cited the think tank. This, as Groseclose and Milyo define it, is what constitutes 'media bias.' "

Basically, the two men assumed that when a reporter quotes a source, or think tank representative, the opinion expressed by that person somehow accurately reflects the reporter's own bias.

True, recent industry surveys indicate newsrooms have a slightly higher percentage of self-described liberals than does the general population. Two points about that. First, the notion that reporters purposely skew their work simply to reflect their political leanings buys into the right-wing canard that journalists have no ethics and abide by no professional code. They do. Secondly, conservative reporters are underrepresented but not because of any organized attempt to keep them out of the business, but because they simply do not apply for the jobs or, for the most part, attend journalism school. (If there were a widespread effort by editors and producers to consciously avoid hiring conservative applicants, the anecdotes would have been loudly trumpeted by right-wing activists by now.) For some reasons conservative students coming out of college do not flock to entry level journalism jobs in midsized markets where they're asked to cover Board of Education meetings or write up random slayings. That's how most reporters pay their dues, and those low-paying jobs are open to all comers. Instead, it's as if conservative press advocates want some special set-asides, a sort affirmative action program created for newsroom Republicans to make sure their side is represented, instead of simply taking the initiative to ensure their coveted "balance." Rather than joining the press corps and making it better, conservatives attack it from outside with endless allegations of bias, hoping to destroy it.

Yet reading through conservative attempts to document liberal bias, one's reminded of Casey Stengel's quip while managing the hapless 1962 New York Mets; "Can't anybody here play this game?"

In Ari Fleischer's 2005 *Taking Heat*, a look back at his time as White House spokesman, Fleischer tried unsuccessfully to substantiate charges of liberal bias. For instance, he complained that during the contested 2000 election, the press was eager to label the Supreme Court's 5–4 decision in Bush's favor to stop counting votes in Florida as "bitter" and "divided." But days earlier, when the Florida Supreme Court ruled 4–3 in Gore's favor, reporters shied away from the divisive nature of the decision, to the point where "most Americans would have thought it was a unified Florida Supreme Court that put Al Gore on the doorstep of the presidency," according to Fleischer.

But a quick check of Nexis finds the "bitter" and "deeply divided" nature of the Florida Supreme Court ruling was widely reported. (Emphasis added in all quotes.)

- "The Florida Supreme Court drops a bombshell, a *deeply divided* 4–3 opinion, a split court, but a legal shot heard around the world." (Brian Williams, MSNBC)
- "*A sharply divided* Florida Supreme Court threw the presidential election into turmoil again Friday by ordering a statewide recount of selected ballots and slashing George W. Bush's lead to 154 votes." (*Los Angeles Times*)
- "Al Gore's moribund presidential hopes were dramatically revived Friday when a *sharply divided* Florida Supreme Court ordered the immediate recount by hand of tens of thousands of disputed votes." (*The Hartford Courant*)
- "The Florida Supreme Court, [in a] *bitterly divided* 4-to-3 decision for Vice President Gore, stunned so many people, both Democrats and Republicans alike." (David Bloom, NBC)

Riding a favorite conservative hobby horse, Fleischer complained that while reporters routinely label Republicans as "conservatives," they shy away from tagging Democrats as "liberals." "Why have they largely stopped using the word 'liberal'?" Fleischer wondered. Stop using? In the twelve months prior to the publication of *Taking Heat*, the *New York Times* published 325 articles or columns that contained three or more references to "liberal," followed by the *Washington Post* (with 283 articles), *Los Angeles Times* (266), Associated Press (227), *Chicago Tribune* (165), and *USA Today* (71).

On the flip side, Fleischer didn't like the word "progressive": "I don't really know what a 'progressive' is, but I know the Democrats like the word and the press use it, particularly in their coverage of social issues." Compared to the 325 "liberal" articles in the *New York Times* over that twelve-month span, the paper generated just 39 articles that used the word "progressive" three or more times. In his analysis of the press, Fleischer argued "liberal" was underused, while "progressive" was overused. In fact, the exact opposite was true.

On the cusp of the war with Iraq, Fleischer recalled how on March 18, 2003, "someone [inside the White House] pointed out how muted the coverage was of [British Prime Minster] Tony Blair's dramatic win in Parliament authorizing the use of force against Iraq. After weeks of coverage about how much trouble Blair was in, his victory didn't get much press." First, the vote in Parliament actually represented an embarrassing setback for Blair, since 139 members of his own Labor Party deserted him on the vote, a point Fleischer ignored. Second, here is a sample of the U.S. news organizations that supposedly "muted" coverage of the Parliament vote: Associated Press, *Baltimore Sun, Boston Globe, Charleston* (S.C.) *Gazette, Charlotte Observer, Chicago Tribune* (which ran the story on the front page), CNN, South Florida *Sun-Sentinel*, Knight Ridder, *Los Angeles Times, Minneapolis Star-Tribune*, NBC, *New York Times, New York Post, Newsday, Orlando Sentinel, Philadelphia Inquirer, St. Petersburg Times, Tallahassee Democrat*, UPI, *USA Today*, Voice of America, and the *Wichita Eagle*.

Fleischer was not alone in having trouble documenting the media's liberal bias on the eve of the war. As the U.S.-led invasion unfolded on television in March 2003, the *Wall Street Journal's* Dorothy Rabinowitz ridiculed liberal commentator Roger Wilkins, appearing on PBS's *The NewsHour with Jim Lehrer*, for suggesting that the idea of embedding reporters with troops was dangerous because journalists would get too close to the military men and women who would seem to be "fellow human beings." The *Journal* highlighted the attention-getting quote, which was blown up inside a box accompanying the story: "One critic worried that reporters might come to view the military as fellow human beings." The clear implication was that, on the eve of war, liberal media commentators were anti-military.

The only problem was, as the PBS transcripts clearly showed, Wilkins never expressed any concern about soldiers coming across as "fellow human beings," or anything close to it. "The notion I would not want troops to be seen as human is absurd," said Wilkins, who served in the administration of President Lyndon B. Johnson and teaches history at George Mason University in Fairfax, Virginia. "I care about those kids over there in the desert. I teach kids who are 19, 20, 21 years old. Of course I wish them well." (At least Rabinowitz owned up to her error.)

When not embarrassing themselves with proof of media bias like that, the press haters, particularly those online, were flashing their open contempt for journalists, which often crossed over into demented loathing. When legendary ABC News anchor Peter Jennings succumbed to lung cancer during the summer of 2005, the MRC's Brent

Baker, not even waiting until Jennings's cremated ashes had been scattered by family members, went online and posted "documentation of the liberal bias from Peter Jennings." That move came off as classy compared to what press hater, and Karl Rove pal, David Horowitz did upon hearing the news of Jennings's passing. Horowitz, a fringe player whose anti-media center receives hundreds of thousands of dollars in support annually from famed Clinton hater Richard Mellon Scaife, posted comments titled, "Peter Jennings Sympathies for the Devil." Horowitz's press-hating followers online cheered the sentiment and stomped on Jennings' grave:

- "I won't be a hypocrite and shed tears at his passing. I was revulsed by him when he was alive and am indifferent to him in death."
- "I hope Lenin is giving him the business with a red hot pitchfork."
- "Mr. Jennings has dissolved into the nothingness from which all left-minded loonies sprang originally."
- "Another left wing talking head bites the dust!!"

Even when the deceased journalist was relatively unknown, press haters showed no hesitation in denigrating the dead. In early January 2006 came news that David Rosenbaum, a *New York Times* veteran of more than thirty years, had been beaten during a random Washington, D.C., mugging and subsequently died from his attackers' wounds. Press haters online at Free Republic, the high-profile conservative forum, marked Rosenbaum's brutal passing with asonishing bouts of depravity:

- "The mugging death of that Slimes presstitute is proof positive that there is a G*D, and that he has a sense of ironic humor."
- "Any other common citizen beaten to death by a street thug would be a tragedy . . . it is only human to think there is an element of blowback when the victim is a liberal reporter for the for Al-Qaeda's primary organ."
- "There's little difference between a NY Times employee and a terrorist these days."
- "No one is innocent that works for the NYT, Maybe some other paper, but I have no sympathy for the treason times or anyone who works for them."

That's not to suggest online "Freepers" or Horowitz and his minions directly influence the MSM and how they report the news on a daily basis. They do not. But they do add to the churning culture of media hatred that manifests itself in places at Power Line, MichelleMalkin.com, the Rush Limbaugh program, on Fox News, and on the *Wall Street Journal* editorial page. When it reaches those heights, newsrooms get nervous and journalists start to fear facts, and the consequences of reporting them.

CHAPTER 5

The War Over PBS

Just two months into his tenure as chairman of the Corporation for Public Broadcasting (CPB), the government-created umbrella organization that doles out tens of millions of dollars annually for public television and radio programming, Kenneth Tomlinson had an epiphany. It was a Friday night in November 2003 and Tomlinson, a round, bearded man with a honey-coated Southern drawl who breeds thoroughbred racehorses on a farm in Virginia, was watching PBS. Specifically, he was dialed into *Now with Bill Moyers*, the weekly news magazine hosted by the longtime PBS fixture.

Tomlinson, a journalist himself who spent three decades with *Reader's Digest*, ultimately becoming editor-in-chief of that Republican print bastion, did not like what he was seeing on *Now* and its special presentation, *A Question of Fairness*. Examining America's shrinking middle class and the growing disparity between rich and poor, *A Question of Fairness* focused on how the residents of small-town America, such as Tamaqua, Pennsylvania, a former coal town, had been affected by new free trade agreements, corporate fraud, and regressive tax policies.

Tomlinson, who grew up outside the tiny town of Galax, Virginia, in the Blue Ridge Mountains and knew something about small town America, considered the *Now* report to be one-sided and superficial and he decided it was his duty to take action. Right then on that Friday night, as Tomlinson later told the *Washington Post*, he resolved that it was time to bring "balance" to the public airwaves. He quickly sent a letter off to the head of PBS complaining, *Now With Bill Moyers* "does not contain anything approaching the balance the law requires for public broadcasting."

That was the genesis of what became one of public broadcasting most bruising and deeply damaging controversies. Except that Tomlinson also told a completely different version of his aha! moment story. According to the second account, which Tomlinson recounted in an op-ed column he penned for the *Washington Times* as well as told in person during a C-Span interview, his realization about PBS's liberal bias did come on a Friday night and it was in November 2003, but nothing else about the story was the same. In that telling, Tomlinson missed the weekly broadcast of *Now*, but right after the program aired he received an angry phone call from an old friend who complained about the Moyers' program and its lack of balance.

He told Tomlinson it was up to him to fix the problem and to do it for the good of public broadcasting. Or else. The old friend told Tomlinson he headed up a foundation that had recently given $300,000 to public broadcasting, but that in the light of Moyers's liberal bias the friend had ordered the foundation payments not be renewed unless Moyers's brand of liberalism was reined in.

Tomlinson, hired by Congress both to promote public broadcasting and to protect it from any outside political efforts to pressure broadcasters politically, could have told his old friend that while he appreciated his comments regarding programming concerns, heavy-handed threats of withholding funds in exchange for a crackdown on alleged media bias was not how public broadcasting operated in America, and that while it's important that all points of view be expressed on the taxpayer-funded networks, it's equally important that programmers not fear funding cuts on the basis of content. The CPB chief could have told his old friend that, but he did not. "On reflection," Tomlinson wrote in the *Washington Times*, "I decided he was right." So began Tomlinson's clumsy campaign to stomp out liberal bias at public television.

Beginning in 2003 and extending over the next two years, Tomlinson, sometimes conferring with top White House aides, including Karl Rove, spent millions of taxpayer dollars getting new conservative-friendly programs on the air, installed the former co-chairman of the Republican National Committee as CPB's president, tapped a Bush ally as head of CPB programming, created an ombudsman's office to police biased reporters, hired consultants to secretly document broadcasting bias, and demanded new journalism guidelines be implemented. All of that because out of the hundreds of hours of public broadcasting programming aired each week *one* program, *Now*, was too liberal. And for that Tomlinson was willing to risk attacking, undermining, and perhaps even crippling, public broadcasting.

The importance of the Tomlinson's smear campaign against public broadcasting was not in how the MSM covered the controversy; they, and particularly the major dailies, did a relatively good job framing the issue and chronicling Tomlinson's heavy-handed crusade and his many inconsistencies. The significance of the showdown, and how it related to the MSM's timid coverage of the Bush administration, was that it presented an unblemished look at how conservatives moved hard to throttle the press, to put reporters on notice, and to discourage them from asking too many hard questions. Tomlinson's meltdown over PBS also highlighted how rampantly dishonest the conservative debate over liberal bias often is and how it usually has little if anything to do with journalism, but everything to do with partisan politics.

Tomlinson only had authority over public broadcasting, but his complaints about "liberal advocacy journalism" and his use of code words such as "balance" in describing PBS's alleged liberal tilt mirrored the conservative talking points about the mainstream media as a whole, a debate the Bush White House did everything to encourage. The debate Tomlinson was able to spark, and the awkward position into which he placed public broadcasters who knew his conservative allies in Congress were always searching for a way to discredit—and de-fund—PBS and NPR, were the same bind conservatives wanted for all journalists: to make them fear the political consequences of their work.

"It's designed to get people's attention and warn them not to do programming that will be questioned," said David Fanning, executive producer of *Frontline*, PBS's award-winning investigative series. "We ask hard questions to people in power. That's anathema to some people in Washington these days."

The irony of Tomlinson's crusade for balance and objectivity was that as a journalist himself his background consisted of working mostly at partisan, one-sided "advocacy" journalism outlets, as he would call them. Tomlinson's reference point for fair and balanced reporting was Fox News, which is why he once suggested to the CPB board that Fox News anchor Brit Hume be invited to give pointers to public broadcasting officials about how to create balanced news programming. (Concluding a softball interview on Fox's *The O'Reilly Factor*, Tomlinson once gushed, "We love your show.")

Tomlinson may have told reporters that, "I've always been dedicated to balance," but it had been nearly forty years since he worked inside a down-the-middle news organization: the *Richmond Times-Dispatch*, which he left in 1968. Tomlinson then began a nearly three-decade affiliation with *Reader's Digest*, which conservative *National Review* magazine once described as "the quintessential magazine of 'red-state' America." Tomlinson also worked as an intern for the late, red-baiting broadcaster, Fulton Lewis, Jr., according to NewsMax.com, the conservative news outlet.

Tomlinson's *Reader's Digest* career ended with his retirement in 1996, when he left the magazine to work on the Republican presidential campaign of his friend Steve Forbes. In 2002, Bush appointed Tomlinson chairman of the Broadcasting Board of Governors (BBG), the agency that oversees the Voice of America, Radio Free Europe, and other federally funded outlets that broadcast government-sponsored news and information around the world. (Tomlinson served simultaneously as chairman of the CPB and BBG.) Under Tomlinson's supervision, VOA staffers during the Bush administration repeatedly charged that newscasts were skewed in order to make them overtly sympathetic to the White House, that reporters were told to emphasize the "good news" stories in Iraq while turning away from car bombs and terrorist attacks, and were chastised for quoting Democratic members of Congress who were critical of Bush's handling of the war on terrorism. (VOA's reporting is supposed to be neutral and professional.) "With management reportedly censoring critical stories," the *American Prospect* reported in 2004, "morale at the VOA has plummeted."

Similarly, Tomlinson's ascension to chairman of the CPB brought with it a distinct new atmosphere inside that agency. Christy Carpenter, a former Democrat-appointed member of the CPB board, recalled that with Tomlinson's 2003 arrival, "the tone of the discussion became increasingly partisan. There was an agenda being pushed to bring in more conservative voices. I have no objection if conservative voices are in the mix. But I had the impression that more was being pursued than just 'balance.'"

In retrospect, Tomlinson's objection to Moyers's work at PBS was not surprising. Movement conservatives had for years been targeting the award-winning journalist with a proud populist streak who had won more than thirty Emmy Awards over his three-decade career as a television journalist. Moyers' *Now* proved tenacious during the first Bush administration, standing out from the timid MSM pack with its consistent coverage of the unfolding landscape of media consolidation (an issue the consolidating television industry itself refused to touch), the middle-class anxiety created by big business outsourcing, as well as its unforgiving criticism of the war with Iraq, both for being ill-conceived and poorly executed.

Moyers' reporting and commentary, which often lobbed grenades at the right-wing press for being nothing more than GOP propagandists, drove some partisans to distraction. Fox News's Bill O'Reilly became so obsessed with Moyers that his name was mentioned on more than fifty *O'Reilly Factor* broadcasts between 2003 and 2005. Not surprisingly, O'Reilly's obsession wasn't always rational. Opening his January 5, 2005, telecast, O'Reilly insisted, "I have nothing against Moyers," and then minutes later labeled Moyers a "totalitarian."

Tomlinson's crusade eventually imploded in rather spectacular fashion. Tomlinson himself became the target of the CPB's inspector's general investigation, which concluded Tomlinson broke public broadcasting guidelines, abused CPB ethics, and instituted a "political test" for key hires. (Tomlinson was forced to step down from his CPB post in late 2005.) Specifically, the inspector general chided Tomlinson for hiring consultants without informing the CPB board first. One of the consultants Tomlinson hired behind the board's back was Fred Mann, a twenty-year veteran of the National Journalism Center, which was founded by the American Conservative Union to train young conservatives to break through the media's liberal bias. Ann Coulter is a proud alumna of the center. Mann was hired to chronicle the liberal bias of *Now* as well as other shows. Mann did so by documenting each guest's political leanings. Using some novel methods of tabulation, he listed guests as "anti-Bush," "anti-business," and "anti-Tom DeLay." Mann also found liberal bias in some unlikely places as his report slotted each of the following guests under the "liberal" category: former Representative Bob Barr (R-Ga.), who served as a driving force in the Clinton impeachment hearings, conservative Nebraska Republican senator Chuck Hagel, and right-wing radio host Roger Hedgecock.

Each was placed in the lefty column because they expressed opinions on *Now* that differed from official Bush administration policy. (Hedgecock was "liberal" for suggesting military personnel were underpaid.)

Tomlinson defended Mann's misleading, taxpayer-funded report, which was faxed in from a Hallmark store in Indianapolis. In fact he championed the widely ridiculed report as "irrefutable documentation" of *Now*'s bias. Tomlinson commissioned the 2004 study from Mann despite the fact the CPB itself paid for polls in both 2002 and 2003, designed specifically to measure whether Americans thought public broadcasting suffered from a liberal bias. Overwhelmingly, they did not. Tomlinson needed a report dissecting *Now* conducted by a conservative media activist like Mann because the CPB chairman had virtually no instances of unfairness—of liberal bias—to cite in order to back up his crusade. In the absence of actual infractions by PBS reporters and producers. Tomlinson insisted he was concerned by the mere *perception* of a bias. He told *Broadcasting & Cable* magazine he wanted to "broaden support for public broadcasting" while "eliminating the perception of political bias."

But the question remained, a perception of political bias by whom—Republican politicians and conservative activists, or PBS viewers and everyday Americans? If most U.S. taxpayers didn't think the programming was biased—and two national polls suggested they did not—then what was the point of Tomlinson's campaign?

Tomlinson tipped his hand in the November 17, 2003, issue of *Current* magazine, which reports on public broadcasting. In an interview he argued, "If a *significant number of conservatives* are saying public TV is not for them, we need to change that." [Emphasis added.] But what if a "significant number" of environmentalists, or libertarians or Latinos or Asians were saying public TV was not for them, would the CPB have taken drastic action to remedy that perception? And what constituted a "significant number"? According to CPB polling done in 2003, 12 percent of Americans thought PBS had a *conservative* bias. Why didn't Tomlinson address that concern as well? In truth, the CPB's crusade flipped on its head the organization's mandate which was to act as public broadcasting's "heat shield," insulating programmers from outside political pressure. By demanding programming changes to meet political concerns, Tomlinson's CPB became a heat conductor.

A longtime ideologue who said he was "strongly committed to George Bush," Tomlinson was determined to ferret out any bias in order to save public broadcasting from its liberal self. Or so Tomlinson claimed. But in a moment of candor during an interview with the conservative *Washington Times*, Tomlinson expressed mild bewilderment as to why Americans backed public broadcasting. "For whatever reason, the American people seem to support it," he said, telegraphing his own doubts about the whole endeavor. "I'm not for government getting into areas that are served by others. I do think public broadcasting is a fact of life in this country. You're not going to de-fund it." (Tomlinson's lack of enthusiasm was matched perhaps only by the interim CPB president he appointed in 2005, Kenneth Ferree, who confided to the *New York Times* that he didn't watch much public television and he listened to even less public radio.)

Many conservative activists on the far right wanted to do just that; de-fund public broadcasting and watch its independent-minded programming wither away. As Tomlinson himself noted, "A lot of my friends are against [any] taxpayer support" for PBS. Publicly, he insisted his crusade against liberal bias at PBS was supposed to help it win more funding in Congress. Not surprisingly, Tomlinson's tactics produced the opposite result—helping Republicans make small gains in their quest to turn off PBS's spigot on Capitol Hill.

Ever since America's public television system was established through the 1967 Public Broadcasting Act, it has had to dodge political bullets, nearly always fired by Republicans. Despite the consistent and high-profile presence on PBS over the years of conservatives such as William Buckley (who hosted 1,429 episodes of his public policy program *Firing Line*), John McLaughlin, Ben Wattenberg, William Bennett, Fred Barnes, Peggy Noonan, Tony Brown, and Morton Kondracke, Republicans have insisted for decades that the network suffered from a liberal bias. During the early 1970s, back when it was dubbed an "Eastern elite" bias, the Republican-controlled CPB board refused to fund news, news analysis, and political commentary programming. This, after the Nixon administration in 1972 vetoed PBS's budget.

In an April 27, 1972, memo written to Nixon by aide Clay Whitehead, head of the White House Office of Telecommunications Policy, he noted one of the administration's "long-term" goals regarding PBS was, "The elimination of the use of Federal funds for public affairs programming." Addressing attempts to fix PBS's "anti-administration bias," Whitehead pointed out to Nixon, "Our only short-run lever here is the spotlight of public attention on the widely acknowledged liberal bias of most public television commentators, and we will assure that spotlight is kept on them for the rest of this year." The ploy foreshadowed Tomlinson's 2005 strategy of constantly, and very publicly, raising doubts about the role of Moyers's *Now* and its "liberal advocacy journalism." During the Reagan era, Richard Brookhiser, then a CPB board member and a senior editor at the conservative *National Review*, proposed spending $180,000 for a two-year "content analysis" of PBS's nonfiction programming in order to detect alleged left-wing bias. (The proposal was ultimately rejected by the full CPB Board.)

Amid the Republican revolution of the 1990s the attack was full frontal, with House Speaker Newt Gingrich declaring a war on *Sesame Street*'s Big Bird and deriding PBS as "this little sandbox for the rich." He proposed to "zero-out" its federal subsidies, dismissing the network's supporters as "a small group of elitists who want to tax all the American people so they get to spend the money." The conservative offensive once again put PBS on notice, but politically it was a failure for Republicans who simply adjusted their sights. As Ken Auletta noted in the *New Yorker* in 2004, "The American right has stopped trying to get rid of PBS. Now it wants a larger voice in shaping the institution." As the magazine noted, "This year, however, the anticipated attack from the right never came. When three public-broadcasting leaders— Pat Mitchell; Kevin Klose, the head of NPR; and Robert Coonrod, the president of the C.P.B.—appeared jointly before a House subcommittee in February, no Republican members mentioned 'liberal bias.' "

In fact, throughout the first Bush term, relations between PBS and Republicans were surprisingly cordial. First Lady Laura Bush, a former librarian, spoke warmly about PBS's children's programming and embraced the Ready to Learn initiative, an effort to help prepare kids for school. And against the backdrop of Congressional hearings on indecency in the wake of Janet Jackson's Super Bowl wardrobe malfunction as well as bipartisan opposition to further media consolidation, PBS was able to stake out a unique, and largely welcomed, territory in the eyes of Congress as a refuge from what politicians saw as the increasingly obscene television landscape. PBS officials also worked hard to ingratiate themselves with Republicans, lining up Republican lobbyists to work the Hill on their behalf, and in 2003 tapped Gingrich as the keynote speaker for when PBS station managers made their annual pilgrimage to Washington to schmooze with politicians and ask for funding. (Gingrich received a standing ovation from the public broadcasting audience.) PBS president Mitchell even met with Lynne Cheney, the wife of Vice President Dick Cheney, to discuss a possible public television series based on her children's books.

Then in 2005, Tomlinson, the man charged with insuring warm relations between the public broadcasting and members of Congress, stepped into the spotlight and poisoned the relationship. Tipping logic on its head, Tomlinson insisted he needed to fix PBS's leftward tilt in order to save it from Congressional budget cuts, even though no major cuts had been proposed in years. (Congress contributes approximately 15 percent of public broadcasting's $2 billion annual budget.) Those deep cuts only surfaced *after* Tomlinson led his bias charge. Worse, the cuts seemed to take Tomlinson, public broadcasting's top steward, by complete surprise.

Taping an NPR interview that aired on June 4, 2005, Tomlinson said, "I don't think you've heard any serious call in recent years from any point on the political spectrum to do anything to significantly reduce the funding for public broadcasting." Just five days later though, a Republican-controlled House subcommittee voted to drastically reduce the federal government's financial support for public broadcasting. As news of the June 9th draconian measure spread through Washington, D.C., senior officials at the CPB urged Tomlinson to immediately release a statement condemning the Republican subcommittee vote. He balked, waiting until late in the day to issue a statement that said he was simply "concerned" about the Congressional proposal.

In the end, the full Congress, by a vote of 284 to 140, agreed to restore the deep cuts to public broadcasting, which accurately reflected the wishes of most Americans; CPB's own polling showed that just 10 percent of Americans thought the federal government was spending "too much" on public broadcasting. A separate 2005 Roper poll found that Americans believed PBS provided the second best use of tax dollars; only military defense was a better use of tax dollars.

If Tomlinson's tenure as CPB chairman was known for its partisan slant, it was also marked by his trouble with the truth, which bedeviled him throughout the controversy over PBS's liberal tilt:

• In a 2005 letter Tomlinson wrote to Senator Byron Dorgan (D-N.D.), regarding his decision to hire the consultant Fred Mann, the CPB chairman wrote that the contract had been approved and signed by CPB President, Kathleen Cox.

But a contract obtained by the *New York Times* showed Tomlinson signed off on Mann's work five months before Cox became CPB president.

• Throughout the 2005 debate about PBS, Tomlinson insisted the Bush White House never interfered with how the CPB operated and that he had no communication with the administration about how public broadcasting operated. "There is absolutely no White House involvement in what I did," he told C-Span's Brian Lamb.

However, the CPB's inspector general uncovered emails between Tomlinson and Bush's top political adviser Karl Rove discussing partisan plans for public broadcasting.

• Tomlinson told the *Washington Post* that it was the November 21, 2003, airing of *Now*'s one-sided *A Question of Fairness* special that prompted him to begin his crusade to bring "balance" to PBS. Yet, Tomlinson was already on the record in the November 17, 2003, issue of *Current* magazine openly attacking *Now* for its lack of balance.

• During an interview on C-Span, Tomlinson lashed out at the *New York Times*, insisting a probing May 2 2005, article the newspaper published about CPB had been misleading. "If you look at the original *New York Times* article, virtually every charge in there about me has either been discredited or proven false," Tomlinson sold C-Span host Brian Lamb. As Media Matters for America noted, the *New York Times* article in question contained four central charges:

First, Tomlinson hired a private consultant to monitor PBS's *Now With Bill Moyers.*

That was true.

Second, Tomlinson hired a Bush aide to do work for the CBP while she was still being paid by the White House.

That was true.

Third, Tomlinson "occasionally worked with other White House officials on public broadcasting issues."

That was true.

At the time of Tomlinson's C-Span sit-down, the only charge for which there was any doubt was the fourth one; had Tomlinson been "instrumental" in getting public broadcasting funding and distribution for the *Journal Editorial Report*, a conservative roundtable discussion show featuring the editors of the *Wall Street Journal*'s right-wing editorial page. Tomlinson insisted he was not involved. Public broadcasting guidelines forbid the CPB chairman from getting involved in programming decisions. In truth, Tomlinson personally approached Paul Gigot, editor of the *Journal*'s editorial page, and personally pitched the idea of a conservative show for PBS to balance out *Now*. "I'm *trying to pressure* [PBS president] Pat Mitchell to produce a real conservative counterpart to Moyers. Would you be available for such an effort" Tomlinson emailed Gigot on December 4, 2003. [Emphasis added.] As talks progressed between the *Journal* and PBS about the possible thirty-minute roundtable show, Tomlinson, in a February 12, 2004, email, assured Gigot, "I do not turn loose of [*sic*] CPB's money or let authorization go forward until you have a show that gets everything Moyers gets except for time." (Unabashedly partisan in his emails with fellow conservative Gigot, Tomlinson, in discussing political content on PBS, referred to the need for "our side" to get more air time. Thanking Gigot for his help in striking a political counterbalance on PBS, Tomlinson stressed on March 6, 2004, "I deeply appreciate all that you will be doing. I just want to win!")

Attacking Bill Moyers's *Now* in a December 2003 letter to the president of PBS, Tomlinson insisted the program did "not contain anything approaching the balance *the law* requires for public broadcasting." [Emphasis added.] But there had never been a standard, or "law," requiring PBS to adhere to balance within each program. Public broadcasting's fairness and balance guideline, as spelled out in 1967's Public Broadcasting Act, mandated CPB to make sure that the recipients of its funding provide maintain "strict adherence to objectivity and balance in all programs or series of programs of a controversial nature." First of all,

Now received no direct CPB funding, so Tomlinson's board had no oversight of the program. And secondly, the balance of public broadcasting's programming was always judged as a whole, over days, weeks, and months, not minute by minute.

Ironically, if strict new guidelines on fairness were applied, among the first shows that would have to be singled out for violating them would be the *Journal Editorial Report*. Unlike *Now*, which booked conservative advocates such as Ralph Reed to debate issues (and undertook actual reporting, as opposed to the *Journal's* chat-fest), the *Journal Editorial Report* made little or no pretense of airing opposing viewpoints during its weekly discussion of political events. Instead, the show offered up a "conservative view of the news," as host Gigot put it. For instance, during a discussion regarding the then-unfolding Terri Schiavo story during the spring of 2005, every panelist on the program agreed Congress had done the right thing by intervening in the right-to-die case, placing the *Journal* pundits well out of the American mainstream, which overwhelmingly objected to lawmakers' last-minute meddling in the case, according to several polls. Meanwhile, the show's December 2 group discussion about how the Bush administration could right itself politically after a difficult 2005 sounded like a bull session at the conservative Heritage Foundation. It's just not practical to think that PBS would ever air a thirty-minute prime-time show that was often exclusively about the inner workings of the Democratic Party and invited liberal, partisan journalists to sit around and discuss how party leaders could improve reelection chances for Democrats. Yet that's what the *Journal Report* often was, except that its attention was often focused solely on helping the Republican Party. (By 2006 the *Journal Editorial Report* had left PBS, having found a more suitable home on the television dial—Fox News.) The bottom line was money from CPB was used to fund the *Journal Editorial Report*, making it perhaps the first time in CPB history a new show was green lighted specifically *because* it came packaged with a political bias.

Soon after securing a slot for the *Journal Report*, Tomlinson set out to create a CPB office of the ombudsman to monitor possible biases at PBS. And in order to create an internal mechanism to make sure any taint of politics was removed from the programming, who did Tomlinson turn to for guidance? One of Karl Rove's White House aides.

(Decrying bias while tapping partisan Republicans seemed to be a favorite tactic of Tomlinson's; amid his crusade to rid PBS of any bias, Tomlinson lobbied on behalf of Patricia Harrison, a former co-chairwoman of the Republican National Committee, to become the next president of the CPB. Over the objection of PBS station managers who insisted the position should be filled by someone with a nonpartisan background, Harrison got the job.) Mary Catherine Andrews, then White House director of global communications, was chosen by Tomlinson to help create the new ombudsman office at CPB. Tomlinson "vigorously" denied the charges that Andrews was doing work for the CPB while still on the White House's payroll, but emails were unearthed by the CPB's inspector general that showed Tomlinson had instructed PBS officials to send material regarding the new ombudsman office to Andrews at her White House email address.

Additionally, Tomlinson (or perhaps Andrews, or perhaps other White House officials) decided the CPB should hire not one, but two ombudsmen; one on the left and one on the right, in the CNN *Crossfire* tradition. The dueling-ombudsmen format was unprecedented in mainstream journalism. Traditionally seen as a way to shine light on the news-gathering process and to encourage transparency between reporters and news consumers, ombudsmen, or readers' representatives as they're sometimes called at newspapers, traditionally help build a sense of trust. They function as a point person who handles journalism complaints from the public. In fact, prior to CPB's ombudsman announcement, NPR already employed its own ombudsman and PBS was actively considering hiring its own, which begged the question why would the CPB, which is largely a funding organization, get involved in critiquing programs that it did not create, schedule, nor broadcast. More disconcerting, though, was the CPB's unique decision to hire *two* ombudsmen, one from the left and one from the right, to check PBS for balance.

"It mystifies me," said Geneva Overholser, a University of Missouri journalism professor who served as the *Washington Post*'s ombudsman from 1995 to 1998. "What in the world does it mean to have two? It makes no sense." She argued that an ombudsman's responsibilities were specifically designed to be carried out by just one person as way to demonstrate that a journalist can be open-minded and listen to all sides of a dispute. By setting up a sort of left-vs.-right program, Over-holser said, the CPB model participated "in the ideological charade that journalists can't be fair." It also amplified the conservative notion behind its effort to undercut the MSM: that when it comes to reporting news stories, there are two versions, liberal and conservative.

But were Tomlinson's choices for ombudsmen, Ken Bode and William Schulz, really even "balanced"? Prior to being tapped for the CPB job, Bode, a former NBC and CNN reporter, worked as a columnist for the *Indianapolis Star* where angry red state readers often disparaged him as a liberal. But during the state's 2004 gubernatorial campaign Bode penned a strong endorsement for the Republican candidate, Mitch Daniels, who served as Bush's director of the Office of Management and Budget. The CPB's other ombudsman was William Schulz, a prominent Washington D.C., conservative and former editor at *Reader's Digest* who worked alongside Tomlinson for years at the Republican-friendly monthly. The idea that the chairman of the CPB would choose a longtime friend and colleague to act as an independent, outside observer charged with ostensibly critiquing that group's work made no sense

Like Tomlinson, one of Schulz's first jobs in journalism was working for radio talk show host and syndicated columnist Fulton Lewis, Jr., who was known for his complete lack of objectivity. At his commercial peak Lewis was heard on more than five hundred radio stations and boasted a weekly audience of 16 million listeners. An early-day Rush Limbaugh, Lewis was the master of the partisan smear who rarely strayed from GOP talking points. In 1948, *New York Herald Tribune* radio columnist John Crosby suggested that Lewis "ought to be recognized as a campaigner, not as a commentator, and his national air time be paid for and so listed by the Republican National Committee." Later, in 1987 the *Washington Post* remembered Lewis as "one of the most unprincipled journalists ever to practice the trade."

Hunting communists became a full-time job for Lewis. According to a flattering 1954 biography of the broadcaster, *Praised and Damned: The Story of Fulton Lewis, Jr.*, Lewis was "as close to Senator Joseph R. McCarthy as any other man in the national scene." *Look* magazine agreed, calling Lewis one of McCarthy's "masterminds."

To some, the idea that Fulton Lewis, Jr., alums Schulz and Tomlinson were put in charge of promoting objective journalism in public broadcasting was appalling. "It's shocking and disgraceful," said former *New York Times* columnist and reporter Anthony Lewis, who won a Pulitzer Prize for his news reporting during the McCarthy era. "If both men wrote for Fulton Lewis it means they were dedicated to an extreme-right position that should disqualify them from determining somebody's objectivity."

After working for Fulton Lewis, both men went on to long, successful careers as writers and editors at another conservative media bastion, *Reader's Digest*, a magazine once famous for its undiluted Republican voice. "The magazine spent half a century advocating a strong Republican line," said John Heidenry, who wrote the definitive history of the publication, *Theirs Was the Kingdom: Lila and DeWitt Wallace and the Story of the Reader's Digest*. He noted that during the 1950s, '60s, and '70s, *Reader's Digest*'s advocacy brand of pro-government journalism served as a dependable platform for the FBI as well as the CIA. In the 1970s, an internal attempt to broaden the magazine's political perspective away from far right sparked a civil war between the magazine's two fiefdoms—or, as Heidenry put it, a war "between the moderately conservative Pleasantville [N.Y.] office and the very right-wing, loose-cannon Washington bureau."

At the time, Schulz was running the D.C. bureau. As Heidenry described it in his book, "Though cynical about the *Digest*'s grind-it-out conservatism, [Schulz] kept an autographed photograph of Joe McCarthy in his home and claimed that the Wisconsin senator was a very misunderstood man." (During the late 1960s Schulz warned that student protesters in America "posed a major threat to the continued existence of our democratic system.") According to Heidenry, Schulz's D.C. bureau routinely tried to kill articles that strayed from the magazine's traditional right-wing agenda. Additionally, the bureau, anxious to play up Cold War fears, interviewed defectors from Russia but sometimes fabricated the details of their tales. "So the whole concept of fact checking was moot," said Heidenry. "They created their own facts. The Washington bureau certainly did not practice an objective type of journalism."

It seemed odd that Tomlinson and Schulz teamed up to show journalists at public broadcasting how to keep things fair and balanced. It's true that in the first few months after being hired as ombudsmen both Bode and Schulz wrote mostly innocuous reviews of public broadcasting's efforts and acted more as cheerleaders. ("TV at its very best.") Tomlinson and his supporters would argue that proved neither man had a partisan agenda nor was out to embarrass PBS and NPR. In truth, the ombudsmen's warm words simply confirmed—again—that there was no liberal problem in-house, that Tomlinson had gone to great lengths to fix a problem that did not exist, and in the process had inflicted serious long-term damage to the institution of public broadcasting.

For Tomlinson and administration aides who privately cheered him on, the most obvious obstacle to his public crusade against PBS's alleged liberal bias was the polling Tomlinson's CPB paid for in 2002 and 2003. Conducted jointly by respected Republican and Democratic firms that contacted 1,008 randomly selected participants from across the country, the polls showed not only that Americans held public broadcasting in extremely high regard, but the surveys also showed conclusively the vast majority of Americans—both regular public broadcasting consumers as well as those who only occasional sampled the programming—agreed the network did not have a problem with a liberal tilt.

"The overwhelming majority of adults in this country (80%) say that they have a favorable impression of PBS and NPR as a whole," wrote representatives from the polling firms The Tarrance Group and Lake Snell Perry and Associates. "Both surveys confirm the same thing: The majority of the U.S. adult population does not believe that the news and information programming on public broadcasting is biased."

In fact, 80 percent of Americans said PBS programming was "fair and balanced," 90 percent agreed PBS "provides high quality programming," and more than half said that PBS news and information is more trustworthy than CNN, Fox News Channel, ABC, and other mainstream news outlets. (In February 2005, a Roper poll, for the second consecutive year, indicated that Americans considered PBS to be the nation's most trusted institution among nationally known organizations.)

Yes, pollsters hired by CPB found that a relatively small percentage of Americans thought public broadcasting was biased in favor of the liberal perspective, but they were often self-identified conservatives who

could not cite specifics to back up their hunch about PBS, and who told
pollsters that they thought *all media* had a liberal bias. The poll results
made a farce out of Tomlinson's pronouncement about PBS and NPR,
undercutting any momentum he hoped to create in moving public
broadcasting to the right. To combat that problem Tomlinson simply
ignored the polling data, paid no attention to requests from his CPB
members who wanted the results widely promoted to the public, and
when word of the results did get out Tomlinson did his best to denigrate
the data.

"Polls are essentially meaningless in the absence of public [scrutiny],"
he told the *Washington Post*, comparing the CPB surveys to presidential
polls taken long before campaign season when people had not yet
focused on the candidates. Tomlinson's comment suggested it was his
job as the CPB chairman *to raise doubts* in people's minds about public
broadcasting, and that after his anti-PBS crusade, or campaign, was up
and running then the American people might be willing change their
minds. It was an extraordinary mind-set for someone who was
appointed to be public broadcasting's goodwill ambassador in Washington, D.C. Instead, Tomlinson, for partisan purposes and with the White
House's tacit backing, set out to undercut the institution he was charged
with protecting.

His allies in the conservative movement also did their best to dismiss
the damning CPB polling results. Writing for the conservative Opin-
ionJournal.com, Peggy Noonan, in a June 16, 2005, column, insisted
"arguing over whether PBS is and has long been politically liberal is like
arguing over whether the ocean is and has long been wet. Of course it
is, and everyone knows it." *National Review Online*'s Jonah Goldberg,
writing about PBS, declared, "It's liberal. It just is. To say it isn't is just
plain batty." Both Noonan and Goldberg simply ignored polling data,
paid for by Tomlinson's CPB, that showed even a majority of American
conservatives didn't think PBS had a liberal bias.

Appearing on MSNBC, Tim Graham, director of media analysis for
the right-wing Media Research Center, which for years has advocated
cutting federal funding for public broadcasting, insisted, "That's a
stacked poll. I mean, you take a poll where you ask them six nice questions about "Don't you like the kids' programs? Don't you like the
orchestra? Oh, and by the way, do you like PBS?" That's a biased,

paid-for poll and nobody should buy it." Graham appeared to have no idea what he was talking about or was purposefully misstating the facts regarding the polls. Rather than "six nice questions" being asked, as he suggested, pollsters conducted an exhaustive survey asking respondents fifty-plus questions, none of which were "stacked." Instead, a typical question was phrased this way, "Generally speaking, do you have a favorable or unfavorable impression of PBS?"

In fact, the polling data should have been a perfect tool for Tomlinson to help assuage fears people had about PBS's liberal bias. Again and again in 2005 Tomlinson argued that PBS was being hurt, particularly on Capitol Hill, by the *perception* of a liberal bias, and if he could correct that perception, PBS would be stronger for it. But by Tomlinson's peculiar logic, the surest way to erase the perception of a liberal bias at PBS was to unleash an unprecedented public campaign *against* PBS.

Tomlinson's polling woes began when the results from the first survey came back. It was conducted in November 2002, and undertaken specifically to measure the level of bias at PBS. "Tomlinson commissioned two polls. The first results were too good, and he didn't believe them," said one knowledgeable public broadcasting source. "After the Iraq war, the board commissioned another round of polling, and they thought they'd get worse results." But the board did not. The results from that survey, conducted during July 2003, were essentially unchanged from 2002. Asked specifically about PBS's Iraq war coverage, a miniscule 7 percent of respondents thought it was "slanted." "They couldn't use any of it" to bolster any claims of bias, said the source.

Consequently, portions of the polling data were quietly attached to a Congressional report, as well as posted on the CPB website. It was not until July 2005 when all the polling data was finally published online that it become clear how energetically Tomlinson had been willing to ignore facts, shade the truth, and obfuscate. Because in this case, the extrapolated numbers really did tell the whole story:

- Just 9 percent of Americans thought PBS's war coverage was anti-administration. (Five percent said it was pro-administration.)
- Just 9 percent said NPR's war coverage was anti-administration. (Four percent said it was pro-administration.)

- Just 3 percent thought PBS's Iraq coverage of the war was antiwar.
- Just 4 percent thought NPR's Iraq coverage of the war was antiwar.
- Just 1 percent thought PBS's Iraq war coverage was "anti-U.S." (Two percent thought it was "pro-U.S.")
- Just 1 percent though NPR's war coverage was "anti-U.S." (Two percent thought it was "pro-U.S.")

Overall, 24 percent of American adults said PBS had a liberal bias. (Twelve percent thought it had a conservative bias.) What's telling is that as the pollsters noted in their report, "58% of the total population identifies itself as conservative, while 33% identifies itself as liberal." That meant despite Tomlinson's claims to the contrary, even less than half of American conservatives thought public broadcasting leaned left.

Still, Tomlinson's CPB was determined to mine for whatever concern about bias it could find. So during the second round of polling in 2003, pollsters set up four focus groups to keep digging. Held exclusively in the Republican bastions of Utah and Kentucky, the focus groups were only open to respondents who had earlier complained to the pollsters about public broadcasting's lefty tilt. Even the focus groups were a bust though, with the pollsters reporting that most of the participants could not cite specific examples of bias, nor did they suggest how to deal with the alleged bias. More telling though, was the admission by the focus group conservatives that they thought "*all* news media has a liberal bias." [Emphasis added.] In other words, pollsters could have been asking about any major media outlets and the focus group participants would have lodged the same complaints. "There is nothing unique and/or specific about public broadcasting in this regard," wrote the pollsters.

Another point that the polls hammered home was just how few people turned to PBS specifically for news and information. Tomlinson's crusade struck such an odd note precisely because most of PBS's programming has nothing to do with left or right or politics at all. Instead, PBS is about educational programming (*Between the Lions*). It's about highbrow arts and entertainment (*Masterpiece Theater*), nifty historical documentaries (*Civil War*), and nerdy science field trips (*Nova*). Yes, there are the current events-driven *Frontline* investigations, and the nightly *NewsHour* airs every weekday. But news and information are not the engine that drives PBS, which means the debate about bias was mostly a sideshow.

Specifically, asked in the November 2002 poll, "What was the last show that you watched on PBS?" just 6 percent named a news program, the lowest response given among any of the categories offered to respondents. Asked during the July 2003, survey, "What was the last show you watched on PBS," a grand total of four Americans mentioned, unprompted, *Now with Bill Moyers*, the program that ignited Tomlinson's crusade for balance. That was a .4 percent of response rate, which placed the program right alongside PBS's *Waiting for God*, but well behind *Barney* and reruns of *Lawrence Welk*. (Ratings-wise, *Now* was always a solid performer for PBS.)

Moyers left the program at the end of 2004. But even when he hosted the show, which routinely aired critical reports about the Bush administration, *Now* wasn't exactly a lightning rod for viewers' wrath. According to an attachment to one of CPB's annual reports to Congress, CPB, eager for public feedback, created "Open to the Public," an online interactive forum in which viewers could express concerns. For 2003, the year most recent year for which statistics were publicly available before Tomlinson began his heavy-handed efforts fix PBS's fairness and balance problem, the "Open to the Public" initiative produced 1,139 emails from viewers. According to the CPB, just 24 of those—or roughly 2 percent—were angry emails about *Now*. (Drawing the most comments was *Sit and Be Fit*, an exercise program for seniors; viewers emailed asking that it be shown on more local stations.) While individual PBS stations may have logged more complaints about *Now*, CPB's own feedback mechanism barely registered any concern about the program.

There was another vital piece of polling data that Tomlinson willfully ignored as he plowed ahead with his fairness and balance reform. American adults were asked, "Do you think NPR coverage of the Middle East has a pro-Israel bias, a pro-Arab bias, no apparent bias, or do you have no opinion on this?" Just 5 percent said NPR showed a "Pro-Arab and Palestinian bias." Eight percent said it suffered from a pro-Israel bias.

Given the statistics, what did Tomlinson do? He set out to create a monitoring system to document NPR's *pro-Arab bias*, even though

Americans, polled during two time periods of extreme hostility in the Middle East and the Persian Gulf, overwhelmingly agreed that NPR had no bias. In fact, if the responses to the poll were parsed, statistically, Americans thought NPR broadcast a pro-Israel bias. But that didn't stop Tomlinson in 2005 from announcing NPR's pro-Arab tilt had already been "documented."

Just like he was convinced public broadcasting's liberal bias had been "documented."

CHAPTER 6

First Lieutenant Bush

Like a pair of convenient bookends, the saga of George Bush's service in the Texas Air National Guard during the Vietnam War was, as a media story, the tale of two news reports; a pair of detailed dispatches, one from the *Boston Globe* and one from CBS, that came four years apart. The first, a *Globe* investigation, raised serious questions about Bush's duty and honesty and was nearly uniformly ignored by the MSM in real time. The second ultimately raised serious questions about CBS's competence. That story, hyped by conservative press critics as proof of a liberal bias, was embraced by the rest of the MSM and treated as wildly significant. The way the MSM embraced one story while shunning the other said a lot about the press's priorities during the Bush years.

The *Globe* expose was published May 23, 2000, on the front page and headlined, "1-Year Gap in Bush's Guard Duty; No Record of Airman at Drills in 1972–73." After combing through 160 pages of military documents and interviewing Bush's former commanders, reporter Walter Robinson detailed how Bush's flying career came to an abrupt and unexplained end in the spring of 1972 when Bush asked to be transferred from his Texas unit to an Alabama unit. But Bush never showed up in Alabama and by most indications never returned to serve with his Texas unit either. He simply walked away from his military obligation with nearly two years still remaining.

The CBS report, as part of *60 Minutes II*, aired on September 8, 2004. It too, examined long-simmering questions about Bush's Guard service; both how he landed a coveted Guard spot and what Bush did once he joined. The key props in the report were exclusive memos that one of Bush's Guard commanders reportedly wrote to himself detailing Bush's lack of participation. Within hours of the CBS broadcast an organized army of conservative sleuths at hyperpartisan websites like Free Republic, Little Green Footballs, and Power Line began raising questions about the memos authenticity, suggesting they were fakes that could not have been written on typewriters from the era of the early 1970s and that the bogus report telegraphed CBS's anti-Bush bias. As the questions mounted, CBS, for more than a week defended its report, although with decreasing verve, until anchor Dan Rather finally conceded the news team could not authenticate the documents.

As a press story, the saga of Bush's Guard service, stretching out over two presidential campaigns, perfectly captured the MSM mind-set during the Bush era; treat serious questions about Bush, like the ones raised in the *Globe* article, with telltale timidity, while simultaneously amplifying conservative allegations that the press was too tough on Bush, as they did with the CBS report. For instance, during the 2000 campaign the *New York Times* published just two references to the *Globe* investigation into Bush's often no-show Guard service. But during the 2004 campaign the *Times* published more than forty articles or columns about controversy surrounding the CBS report on Bush's Guard service. The *Times*, like the GOP, was far more interested in detailing CBS's missteps than exploring the substance of the *Globe*'s expose.

Despite the fact the previous baby boomer candidate for president, Bill Clinton, had to withstand extraordinary press scrutiny about his military service, or lack thereof, Bush in 2000 was able to skate by with only token interest paid by pundits and reporters. (Doing a Nexis search, former Clinton aide Paul Begala said he found 13,641 stories about Clinton "dodging the draft" from the 1992 election, but just 49 stories during the 2000 campaign about Bush and the National Guard.) For the press, Bush's mysterious service in the Guard was of little interest, which was a shame because it made for a hell of a story.

The known facts: Following his graduation from Yale University in 1968, at a time when nearly 350 U.S. troops were dying each week in Vietnam, Bush managed to vault to the top of a 500-person waiting list to land a coveted spot in the Texas Air National Guard. On his application where the form asked for "background qualifications of value to the Air Force," Bush wrote, "None." Despite a complete lack of aviation or ROTC experience, despite scoring in the 25th percentile on his pilot aptitude section—the lowest allowed score for aspiring fliers—and despite already having a police record for college pranks and driving offenses, Bush was approved for an automatic commission as a second lieutenant and assigned to flight school. By every indication Bush's service between 1970 and 1972 as a fully trained pilot in the 111th Fighter Interceptor Squadron near Houston was commendable. But then came the spring of 1972 and Bush, having received $1 million worth of taxpayer-funded flight training, simply vanished. In May, he moved to Alabama to help the Senate campaign of Winton Blount, a friend of the Bush family. Bush, a fully trained pilot, was supposed to transfer to an Alabama Air National Guard unit where he could do "equivalent training." Instead, he asked to be assigned to paper-pushing duties at a postal unit that had no pilots and no airplanes. Incredibly, Bush's Houston commanders signed off on the cushy request. But officials at the Air Reserve Personnel Center in Denver eventually overruled the request, pointing out the obvious: Doing paperwork in a postal unit did not qualify as "equivalent training" for a fighter pilot.

While Bush searched for a new unit in Alabama to serve with, he took the summer off, not bothering to report for any of his mandatory monthly drills. On September 15 an issue was ordered for Bush to report to Lieutenant Colonel William Turnipseed at Dannelly Air Force base in Montgomery, Alabama, "to perform equivalent training." There's slim independent proof he ever showed up since no reliable guardsman among the approximate 600 who served in that Alabama unit ever came forward and corroborated the fact that Bush was there and that they served with the future President of the United States; a distinction that would be hard to forget. (Both Turnipseed and his personnel chief, Lieutenant Colonel Kenneth Lott, told the *Globe* Bush never showed for Guard duty. Years later Turnipseed, a self-described Bush supporter, backtracked on that statement; Lott did not.)

Meanwhile, in July of that summer, Bush's failure to take his mandatory annual physical forced the Guard to ground him. Following Blount's Alabama election loss that November, Bush returned to Houston. (Decades later Bush could recall with precision the final voter tally for Blount, yet Bush could not recall what duties he performed while serving with the Alabama Air National Guard, whose command he served under, or the name of a single guardsman he served alongside.) Bush may have returned to Houston but he did not return to his Guard duties there, at least according to his commanding officers. In May 1973, his two superior officers at Ellington Air Force Base noted on Bush's evaluation that he had not been seen during the previous year. In the comments section, Lieutenant Colonel William Harris, Jr., and Lieutenant Colonel Jerry B. Killian wrote that Bush "cleared this base on 15 May 1972, and has been performing equivalent training in a non flying role with the 187th Tac Recon Gp at Dannelly ANG Base, Alabama." Even Killian, Bush's commander and whom he called a "friend," did not know where Bush was between May 1972 and May 1973. If Bush didn't report for duty at Ellis Air Force base near Houston, as Harris and Killian insisted, and Bush didn't report for duty at the Dannelly Air Force base in Montgomery, as Turnipseed and Lott insisted, than where did Bush fulfill his monthly obligation during that twelve-month span?

Bush was finally recorded as having crammed in thirty-six active-duty credits, or make-up dates, during May, June, and July 1973, thereby meeting his minimal requirement and securing an honorable discharge. But nobody connected with the Texas unit recalled seeing Bush during his cram sessions, leading to suspicions that Bush was given credits for active duty he did not perform. Even more suspiciously, as online researcher Paul Lukasiak noted, based on the procedures in place at the time requiring that makeup dates be completed within fifteen days before or thirty days after the date of the drill missed, between half and two-thirds of the points credited to Bush for substitute training appeared to be invalid in nature. Some of the points credited to Bush were "earned" nine weeks beyond the date of the missed drill. According to Air Force policy, Bush could not have received permission for substitute training that far outside the accepted parameters. The evidence is also overwhelming that Bush failed to get authorization for substitute training in advance, suggesting the points were awarded by the Texas Air National Guard retroactively and without proper supporting paperwork. The press though, was not interested. In September 2004 the *Washington Post* threw up its hands and insisted analysis of Bush's make-up dates was "almost incomprehensible to [military] outsiders." So the paper, which had just spent the month of August meticulously tracking each allegation about Senator John Kerry's war years, didn't bother to try to solve the riddle of Bush's missing years.

Bush's potentially illegitimate make-up points are key, because without them Bush could have fallen far short of meeting his annual obligation, which meant he could have been transferred to active duty for twenty-four months and made eligible for service in Vietnam. Based on the available public records, for his final two years of service it was as if Air Force and Guard regulations simply did not apply to Lieutenant Bush who became a ghostlike figure, doing—or not doing—whatever he pleased, unsupervised and unrated by his commanders. In the military, there is a simple personnel rule; all duty is supervised and rated. Except, apparently, when it came to Lieutenant Bush. The press, ordinarily obsessed with Vietnam War service for baby boomer candidates, thought this was of little or no interest.

Not one of the key facts, all established through Bush's own military records, were altered by CBS's botched National Guard report. But the MSM, having already displayed little initiative on the story, took the 2004 CBS controversy as confirmation that they had been right in 2000 to wave off the issue of Bush's Guard duty; that there was nothing there. Spooked by the angry conservative mob assembled online and that had been taking aim at CBS and its anchor Dan Rather, the MSM in 2004 quickly sprinted away from questions about Bush's service and focused its attention solely on CBS's sins. "Everyone in the media wanted to cover CBS, not the National Guard story," wrote Mary Mapes, the CBS producer behind the so-called Memogate scandal.

Clearly the MSM were cognizant of the extraordinary toll the memo controversy took on CBS. In the months following the wreckage, Rather was gone as CBS's news anchor, several senior CBS executives were fired, and *60 Minutes II* itself was canceled. The message to the rest of the MSM was clear: Mess up on a report that's critical of Bush and you might pay with your career. (By contrast, during the Clinton years, not a single prominent journalist who consistently reported phony Whitewater allegations was ever fired or demoted for incompetence.) Unleashing decades worth of loathing for CBS, and for Rather in particular, the right-wing assault in 2004 was unprecedented. It was also unusually well organized. "I didn't know that the attack on CBS News and the story we aired was just another part of the Bush supporters' aggressive pattern of sliming anyone and everyone who raised questions about the president," wrote Mapes. "I didn't know that we were being bombarded by an army of Bush backers with different divisions, different weapons, and different techniques, but always the same agenda: Kill the messenger."

Just hours after the CBS report aired, an anonymous writer calling himself Buckhead and writing on Free Republic, posted a long analysis questioning the Killian memos. The post went into rich detail about the history of typewriters, proportionally spaced fonts, and how the memos were likely fakes. Buckhead's examination, immediately circulated among CBS's foes online, served as the opening bell in the war on the network. It turned out Buckhead was a partisan Atlanta attorney named Harry MacDougald who enjoyed strong ties to Republican causes. Affiliated with two conservative legal groups, the Southeastern Legal Foundation and the Federalist Society, MacDougald years earlier helped draft the petition that eventually won a five-year suspension of Bill Clinton's Arkansas law license after Clinton's misleading testimony in the Paula Jones sexual-harassment case. Despite an avalanche of Memogate updates and reports, the press showed virtually no interest in reporting on MacDougald and whether there was any coordinated support between the online CBS critics and the Republican Party, or specifically with the White House. (At a mock farewell party in 2005 to commemorate Rather's last night on CBS's *Evening News*, MacDougald, who called Rather the "wicked witch," was toasted by prominent Georgia Republican party officials.)

CBS opened itself to attack by rushing its National Guard story onto the air too quickly and not properly authenticating the memos. According to an independent review conducted by former Republican Attorney General Dick Thornburgh and former Associated Press president Louis Boccardi, on the night before the CBS *60 Minutes II* Wednesday night broadcast two forensic experts warned producers about the Killian memos. Mapes's associate Yvonne Miller told the independent panel that by Tuesday night "everything but the ceiling tiles" was falling down on Mapes. (Miller said she was hesitant to go over Mapes's head and inform her bosses about the growing set of concerns because it would have created a "storm" inside CBS.) The next morning Mapes thought she saw signs of hope when the White House, faced with the Killian memos for the first time, failed to raise any questions about their authenticity. CBS Washington reporter John

Roberts traveled to the White House to interview communications director Dan Bartlett about the Killian memos. Bartlett had seen them just hours before, when CBS delivered copies to the White House. When Roberts reported back that the White House did not question them—Bartlett simply stuck to time-honored GOP talking points about how Bush had fulfilled his Guard duty—higher-ups at CBS interpreted Bartlett's nonobjection as confirmation. It was a costly and mistaken assumption.

Although highly critical of CBS, the independent report could not confirm that the memos were forgeries, as most conservative critics insisted they were. The report refused to conclude that a liberal, anti-Bush bias motivated the CBS report, which also frustrated the network's right-wing critics.

Years earlier Bush and his aides sensed the press's timidity regarding the Guard story, which perhaps explained why they were casually misleading reporters about Bush's service during the early months of his first presidential run. In July 1999, a lengthy *Houston Chronicle* profile touched on Bush's now infamous transfer to Alabama in 1972. The *Chronicle* article appeared one year before the *Boston Globe* pulled back the curtain and revealed Bush's nonservice between 1972 and 1973. Going on what Bush campaign officials told the paper at the time, the *Chronicle* reported "such a transfer [to Alabama] was not unusual, and the Bush campaign says it was for the same flying job he held in Texas." That was patently false. Bush transferred to a unit that had no airplanes, which meant, of course, that Bush did not continue to fly in Alabama. The evidence suggests Bush didn't even show up at the Alabama unit.

In 2000, the *Globe* article made it clear Bush aides had misled the *Chronicle* over the most basic facts about Bush's service, that his transfer to Alabama was not "for the same flying job he held in Texas." The Houston paper, though, never went back to report on the rather glaring inconsistency. Nobody else in the national press corps bothered to pick up on the bold deception either. Time after time, attempts by Bush aides to mislead reporters on the National Guard story failed to withstand serious scrutiny, yet journalists shrugged their shoulders and looked the other way.

In Bush's 1999 autobiography, *A Charge to Keep* (ghostwritten by his aide Karen Hughes), he claimed that after completing Guard flight training in June 1970, "I continued flying with my unit for the next *several years*." [Emphasis added] In fact, Bush stopped flying with his unit just twenty-two months after completing his training. If Al Gore had ever been caught publishing that kind of self-serving exaggeration about his military service the press would have dwelled on it for weeks on end. In 1999, Bush spokeswoman Karen Hughes told reporters the GOP candidate missed his Guard physical because he was working on the Alabama campaign and had no access to the "special" doctors who performed the examinations. Wrong. Bush could have gotten an exam either at his base in Texas or at any of several Alabama Air National Guard installations in and around Montgomery.

In 2000, campaign spokesman Dan Bartlett told the *Boston Globe* that Bush failed to take a required military physical because, "As he was not flying, there was no reason for him to take a flight physical exam." Wrong. The Air Force Specialty Code required physicals be taken regardless of flight status. That in turn was reminiscent of Bartlett's flip-flop surrounding Bush's failure to locate a new Guard unit and fulfill his duty while attending Harvard Business School in 1974. In 1999, Bartlett said Bush had reported for duty at a Massachusetts Guard unit as required. Wrong. Years later Bartlett admitted he "misspoke" in the face of clear evidence that Bush made no effort whatsoever to serve out his Guard term while living in the Boston area.

On and on it went during the 2000 campaign as Bartlett and Bush seemed to simply make up answers on the spot to the occasional Guard inquiries, confident in their knowledge that reporters and pundits were never going to hold them to any sort of truth standard. And they were right. Journalists routinely showed themselves to be remarkably uncurious about Bush's military service, even though it stood in sharp contrast to the Republican credo of patriotism, honor, and service.

During the Vietnam War, Guard members were rarely called up for active duty overseas, making it a top choice among those seeking to avoid service in Southeast Asia. (On his Air Force pilot application, when asked about an overseas assignment, Bush checked "do not volunteer.") In fact, Bush's Guard unit was known as the Champagne Unit, because among its members were so many sons of prominent Texas politicians and businessmen. Yet years later when politely pressed about his decision to join the National Guard, which all but guaranteed him stateside service, Bush refused to concede that it was a logical attempt to remain stateside during the war. Instead, he insisted, as he did to the *Houston Chronicle* in 1999, that it was the chance to learn to fly that drew him to the Texas Air National Guard. "I knew I was going into the military and would have liked to come out with a skill," Bush said. "And I would have liked to make the time worthwhile." In 2000, he told the *New York Times,* "I wanted to fly, and that was the adventure I was seeking." The obvious follow-up question for any reporter should have been, if Bush simply wanted to learn how to fly while serving in the military, why didn't he join the Air Force, or the Navy, or the Marines, which were all training pilots in 1968 and sending them to fly missions over Vietnam. Instead, reporters simply typed up Bush's feel-good response about joining the Guard—that he wanted to learn to fly.

There were lots of other angles to the Guard story that the press stubbornly refused to pursue. Throughout his political career in Texas Bush adamantly denied he had received a Guard spot through preferential treatment. Then in 1999, former Texas Speaker of the House Ben Barnes confirmed that in 1968 he made a phone call to the head of the Texas Air National Guard at the request of the late Sidney Adger, a Houston oil man and longtime Bush family friend. Although a lifelong Democrat, Barnes became a well-connected lobbyist following his days in the Texas legislature and for years resisted any attempt to get dragged into a political debate about Bush's war record. It was only under threat of legal action in 1999—and only after efforts to assert "executive privilege" failed—that Barnes came forward with his statement about helping Bush. (And even then, Barnes issued it through his attorney, refusing to answer press questions.) At the time Barnes even met privately with Bush's then-campaign manager and longtime confidant Donald Evans, in order to give him a heads up about the unfolding Guard story. Bush himself sent Barnes a note thanking him "for his candor" on the matter. Bush never denied Barnes's claim about pulling strings; Bush simply insisted he never asked for the strings to be pulled and was unaware if any were.

So when the *Boston Globe* broke the story about Bush's disappearance from the National Guard in 1972 and 1973, you'd think some reporters would have picked up the string of the 1999 Barnes story; to put the two elements together to tell a more complete picture of Bush's service: that he got into the Guard because of his family connection and then, between 1972 and 1973, he essentially failed to show up for duty.

But with the exception of the *Boston Globe*, here's the grand total of U.S. newspaper, news magazine, and television reports during the 2000 campaign that examined Bush's Guard service and mentioned both the allegations of his chronic absenteeism as well as Barnes's public, albeit reluctant, confirmation about rigging the system on Bush's behalf: two—one from the Associated Press and one from *Newsweek*.

By contrast, here's the number of U.S. newspaper, news magazine, and television reports during the 2000 campaign that made reference to the phony allegation that Gore claimed to have invented the Internet: More than 4,800.

In retrospect, if the story about Bush's military service had simply been about how he used his family connections to land a slot in the Texas Air National Guard (and all indications are he did just that), it's perhaps understandable why the press failed to get worked up. That type of revelation came as big news during the 1988 campaign when Vice President Dan Quayle was dogged by questions about his entry into the Indiana National Guard. But twelve years later the idea that young men from prominent families found open slots in the National Guard was not exactly newsworthy. The real story surrounding Bush was not about how he got into the Guard. It was about how he got out. That story raised serious questions about Bush's honesty and integrity, and during the course of two presidential campaigns too many reporters refused to address it in a meaningful way.

Many reporters, but not all. The scope of Bush's no-show Guard duty was detailed by Walter Robinson in the *Globe* in 2000 and the story was met with near complete indifference by the MSM. Yet it's not hard to imagine what the MSM reaction would have been during the 2000 campaign if the same *Boston Globe* had reported on page one that Gore's discharge papers showed he rigged his Vietnam duty and orchestrated an early exit by simply refusing to report for duty during his final two years of commitment. (Fact: Gore's cousin offered to slip him into a safe slot with the National Guard in Alabama; Gore declined and volunteered for service. That flattering tidbit was mostly left unmentioned by the MSM during the 2000 campaign.)

Seven days after the *Globe* story ran, MSNBC's Chris Matthews sat down with candidate Bush for an entire hour. Forty minutes into the Q&A Matthews brought up Bush's Vietnam service. A chance for Matthews to press the candidate for answers to serious questions raised by the *Globe* story, right? Wrong.

> **Matthews:** Let me ask you about Vietnam and your service. You were in the Air National Guard. You took a lot of—and I will give you credit. It takes a lot of guts to get in a jet plane and fly it. I mean, I don't think anybody ought to knock that.
>
> **Gov Bush:** Thank you.

Matthews went on to ask Bush if, in retrospect, the draft system during Vietnam was unfair.

> **Matthews:** Do you ever feel like, damn it, what an awful system to put some guys at risk and other guys not?
>
> **Gov Bush:** No. You know what I felt? I felt like what a bad war, that we didn't fight the war to win. And the lessons from this generation ought to be not to commit troops to win a war . . .
>
> (APPLAUSE)

Despite the fact one year earlier Ben Barnes had testified under oath that he'd placed a call in 1968 in order to help get Bush a coveted slot in the Texas Air National Guard, and despite the fact that *one week* earlier the *Boston Globe* had reported that Bush's own military records showed he had fallen off the Guard's radar for months at a time between 1972 and 1973, Matthews refused to raise any uncomfortable questions for Bush about Vietnam. (It wasn't until February 2004, forty-six months after the *Boston Globe* first raised key questions, that Matthews acknowledged to MSNBC viewers that there was any kind of controversy regarding Bush's Guard service.) Matthews' allergic reaction to the story in 2000 was the norm.

In its July 17, 2000 issue, *Newsweek* at least addressed the issue of the candidate's questionable Vietnam service, but did it with a Bush-friendly spin. Right in the second sentence of its write-up *Newsweek* downplayed Bush's absenteeism, writing that the period in question only extended for "three months" during 1972, instead of the stretch of more than one year of no-show dates between April 1972 and 1973. After quickly outlining the allegations, the brief *Newsweek* article ended with word that the Bush campaign had located the candidate's former Alabama girlfriend who was insisting, twenty-eight years after the fact, that "Bush told her he had to go back to Montgomery after the [1972] election to make up some reserve requirements." Despite the loose, daisy-chain, friend-of-a-friend kind of corroboration, *Newsweek* congratulated Bush's camp on a job well done: "For the moment, at least, it seemed that Bush's damage-control team had gotten matters under control again."

Throughout the entire 2000 campaign, ABC's *Word News Tonight* made no reference—none—to Bush's questionable Guard service, according to the Daily Howler. Even during a pair of prime-time, two-hour specials hosted by anchor Peter Jennings in September 2000, *Candidates Bush and Gore*, Bush's National Guard story was politely ignored. Here's the program's *entire* reference to Bush and the war:

Jennings: "George W. had a plan. He arranged to join the Air National Guard in Texas, which meant he would not be sent to Vietnam."

Why the nonresponse from the press, which in past campaigns had dedicated hundreds, if not thousands, of working man hours trying to unravel minute details about Vietnam War service for presidential candidates? According to one prominent Texas journalist, the press passed on the story in 2000 because local reporters really, really liked Bush, and Democrats didn't make a big enough fuss about it.

Mimi Swartz, executive editor of *Texas Monthly*, an award-winning magazine that ostensibly casts a critical eye on the powerful within Texas, spelled it out for readers in an opinion piece in the *New York Times*. She wrote, "Until 2000, at least, Mr. Bush's military service was an issue in the campaign, but, again, for various reasons, the digging didn't go very deep. Why? First, George Bush was a very popular governor. . . . He wasn't the lightweight reporters had expected; he unified the Legislature, and he kept his campaign promises. His door was always open to the press—yes, he gave reporters nicknames—and many journalists were surprised that he could discuss tort reform as easily as he could talk about the Texas Rangers pitching staff."

According to Swartz, Texas reporters didn't dig into Bush's military past because he was popular, because he gave them nicknames, and because he liked to talk baseball with them. Not exactly a ringing endorsement of the Texas press corps. But why did that supposedly dogged—and supposedly liberal—national press corps essentially ignore the story throughout the 2000 campaign? According to Swartz, that was Gore's fault. "Al Gore's handlers lacked enthusiasm for this particular avenue of attack. The vice president had served in Vietnam, but he couldn't claim war hero status, and any talk of military service inevitably reminded voters of Bill Clinton, who hadn't served at all," she wrote. (*Time* magazine came to the same conclusion: the story didn't stick in 2000 because "Al Gore steered clear.")

That became a common newsroom refrain during the Bush presidency when journalists tried to explain why a story that could hurt Bush politically was not pursued. Answer: Because Democrats didn't make a fuss, and without them launching allegations, it was somehow impossible for journalists to do their jobs independently. Not only did that cop-out flip journalism on its head (the press is supposed to function independently of political parties, not wait for their signals to go track a story down), but in this case it was also dead wrong. The Gore campaign and its surrogates did push the Guard story, and they did it in real time when the *Boston Globe* article was published. One week after the *Globe* article appeared, President Clinton's veterans affairs secretary, Jesse Brown, led a conference call with reporters to question why Bush cut short his Guard service, telling reporters, "It's time that he set the record straight, let the people American people know if he was keeping his commitment during a time when over 58,000 people died in Vietnam."

Later in the 2000 campaign, Gore's surrogates, led by Senator Bob Kerry, again raised the issue of the Texas Air National Guard with reporters. By then experts said it was too late. "It's doubtful, however, Democrats will gain much ground with the move," William Lyons, a University of Tennessee political science professor, told a local reporter for the *Nashville Tennessean*. "I think if this had come out earlier and been fleshed out, it might have been an issue."

In other words, in the historically close 2000 election, the Guard story might have mattered if only it had been fleshed out earlier. Like, by the press? And specifically, by the *New York Times*, whose performance on the Guard story stands as one of the puzzling examples of no-show journalism in recent memory; an instance where the newspaper of record all but refused to cover the issue of Bush's military record in a serious manner. The significance of the *Times*'s dereliction cannot be overstated. As presidential historian Richard Shenkman observed at the time of the *Globe* expose, "It sure doesn't look good. The problem is it's in *The Boston Globe*, it's not on the front page of *The New York Times*. When it gets on the front page of *The New York Times*, then it'll be an issue and then Bush is going to have to respond." But in 2000, the Guard story never landed on page one of the agenda-setting *New York Times*. In fact, the Guard story barely even made the inside pages of the *Times*. The *Times*'s Frank Bruni who trailed Bush obsessively on the campaign trail, filing more than two hundred dispatches in 2000, never once referred in print to either the *Globe* allegations about Bush service or the fact that in 1968 an old family friend made a call on Bush's behalf in hopes of landing him a safe slot in the National Guard. For the *Times*, the story simply did not exist. In fact, in 2000 the *Times*, supposedly busy scouring the candidates' background, never reported the simple detail that Bush was grounded by his Guard superiors in 1972 for failing to take a mandatory physical.

On July 11, 2000, six weeks after the *Globe* expose, the *Times*'s Nicholas Kristof wrote a biographical feature centering on Bush's life during the Vietnam War: "The 2000 Campaign: Close to Home; Bush's Choice in War: Devoid of Passion or Anxiety." Not only did the article omit any reference to Barnes's allegation about favoritism in getting Bush into the National Guard, but the feature omitted any reference to questions about Bush's absenteeism, getting grounded, failing to take a physical, and walking away from the Guard for seasons at a time. Although Bush was the focus of the Kristof feature, the piece did find space to mock Gore's decision to *volunteer* for duty in Vietnam. That move, according to Kristof, was "political." And besides, he noted, some (unnamed) critics suggested Gore had "embellished" his service. In Kristof's eyes, Bush's decision to join the Guard and protect the Texas skies during the Vietnam War was "far more normal" than Gore's decision to actually serve in Southeast Asia. Keep in mind that during the 2000 campaign Kristof wrote twenty-four stories about Bush, twelve of which were lengthy biographical profiles that covered all aspects of his life, from his prep school days through the war years, early business ventures, and through his time as Texas governor. Collectively, Kristof wrote 50,000 words on Bush in 2000, the equivalent of a 170-page book. Kristof functioned as in-house Bush biographer for the *Times*. But Kristof, who was later promoted to *Times* columnist and fills one of the paper's "liberal" slots on the op-ed page, simply refused to report earnestly on the uncomfortable Guard issue. ("Serious questions remain about how he got into the National Guard and whether he fulfilled his obligations," Kristof wrote one week before the election; questions Kristof and the *Times* strenuously avoided addressing during the campaign.)

Kristof's July 11, 2000, profile of Bush during the war years ran the same day the *Times* unfurled a massive, 4,200-word page-one story on Gore's Vietnam experience, in which Gore sat with a *Times* reporter for "several interviews about his military experience." There was no indication that during the campaign candidate Bush ever sat with the *Times*, or was asked to sit, for several interviews about his military experience. For the *Times*, Gore's service during Vietnam, which was often mocked, was a big deal; but Bush? Not so much.

> The number of articles the *Times* published in 2000 that mentioned both "Gore" and "Vietnam" four or more times: twenty.
> The number of articles the *Times* published 2000 that mentioned both "Bush" and the "National Guard" four or more times: five.

Finally on July 22, breaking its months-long silence since the *Globe* expose, the *Times* addressed Bush's wartime experience with an article headlined, "Governor Bush's Journey; After Yale, Bush Ambled Amiably Into His Future." Certainly a piece focusing on Bush's post-Yale years in the late '60s and early '70s would offer an in-depth, albeit belated, examination of the many troubling allegations raised by the *Boston Globe*, right? Wrong. It wasn't until the sixty-third paragraph of the *Times* story that the issue was even tapped. In total, the *Times* dedicated 300 words to the controversy, giving readers just the sketchiest outlines of Bush's perplexing missing year from the Texas Air National Guard. In the end, the *Times*, in part, accepted the second-hand account of Bush's old girlfriend who assured the newspaper Bush did in fact serve in Alabama. The article's fleeting reference represented the bulk of the *Times* coverage of the Guard story for nearly the *entire* campaign.

Given the press's performance in 2000, was it any surprise when the

Guard story resurfaced unexpectedly years later that reporters and pundits appeared to be badly misinformed about the fundamental questions at the center of the story? How could they know the facts when so many reporters, editors, and producers had ignored them in 2000? In May 2003, after Bush donned a fighter flight suit and landed on the USS *Abraham Lincoln* for a premature "Mission Accomplished" photo-op in the wake of the Iraq invasion, a C-Span caller asked guest George Stephanopoulos of ABC News why, following the 2000 election, nobody in the press appeared to be perusing the story of Bush's Guard service. Host Brian Lamb then amplified the caller's question:

> **Lamb:** "My question to you is, Why is it there's a whole bunch of folk out there that think this is still a problem? And has the media given up on it because they think they've exhausted the study?"
>
> **Stephanopoulos:** "I think the trail is dead and they've exhausted the study. There may have been—and you know, I don't even again remember all the details. There may have been some questions about what happened for a couple of months, but the bottom line is that George Bush *did* serve, he *was* a pilot, he did not see active duty, but he *was* in the reserves. And you know, some people are never going to be satisfied."

It's likely Stephanopoulos couldn't quite "remember all the details" about "a couple of months" of Bush's service because ABC News completely ignored the story during the 2000 campaign.

The Guard controversy truly reignited during the winter of 2004 when filmmaker Michael Moore, appearing at a January 17 campaign rally outside Concord, New Hampshire, for Ret. General Wesley Clarke, labeled Bush as "deserter." Democratic Party chairman Terry McAuliffe quickly downgraded the allegation to the still serious charge of Bush being AWOL from the Texas Air National Guard. (An AWOL soldier, under article 86 of the Uniform Code for Military Justice, faces a maximum punishment of "a dishonorable discharge, forfeiture of all pay and allowances, and confinement at hard labor for 18 months.")

Within the context of the 2004 campaign, the issue of Bush's Guard service was even more relevant than in 2000 considering Bush had led America into a war with Iraq and literally done it on the backs of the

National Guardsmen. No longer expected to serve one weekend a month, two weeks a year, and be on duty to restore order during local natural disasters, Bush's Pentagon turned Guardsmen into full-time soldiers, sending middle-aged moms, dads, and even grandparents to fight in the sands of Iraq. For modern-day Guardsmen it was an unprecedented burden to bear, which made the question of how Bush spent his Guard years all the more telling.

Yet the MSM in 2004 seemed more interested in covering for Bush than presenting a clear look into the controversy. Columnist Michael Kinsley took euphemism to new heights when he wrote that Bush had been "lackadaisical" about fulfilling his Guard requirement. On February 1, ABC News, suggesting Democrats might turn off voters by attacking Bush's military service, reported Bush had simply "missed some weekends of training." And two days later the *New York Times* politely reported "Mr. Bush went on to miss *a number* of National Guard training sessions." [Emphasis added.] None of those descriptions, which echoed the White House's preferred narrative, came anywhere near describing the established facts at the center of the Guard controversy—that Bush skipped an entire year of duty, at least. Later in the campaign CNN's Wolf Blitzer gently tiptoed around the topic, telling viewers, "There is some question that [for] a few months [Bush] may not have necessarily done everything he technically was supposed to do." Technically? As in showing up for duty?

Appearing on *Meet the Press* in February 2004, responding to Democratic critics who renewed charges he skipped Guard duty and there was no evidence to indicate he showed up in 1972, Bush insisted, "Yeah, they're just wrong. There may be no evidence, but I did report; otherwise, I wouldn't have been honorably discharged. I got an honorable discharge, and I did show up in Alabama."

That was Bush's and the White House's mantra-like defense throughout 2004: Bush's honorable discharge, granted in October 1973, ended any debate. And for the most part it worked, as MSM reporters refused to explore the explanation. But military experts were very open about how an honorable discharge would not explain away all the gaps in a service member's record. "An honorable discharge does not indicate a flawless record," noted Grant Lattin, a military law attorney in Washington and a retired Marine Corps lieutenant colonel who served as a judge advocate, or JAG officer. "Somebody could have missed a year's worth of Guard drills and still end up with an honorable discharge. The National Guard is extremely political in the sense of who you know. And it's true to this very day. One person is handled very strictly and the next person is not. If George Bush Jr. is in your unit, you're going to bend over backward not to offend that family. It all comes down to who you know."

During that same *Meet the Press* interview, host Russert asked Bush about releasing his military records to help clear up any of the remaining confusion about his service:

> **Russert:** But would you allow pay stubs, tax records, anything to show that you were serving during that period [be released]?
> **Bush:** Yeah. If we still have them. You know, the records are kept in Colorado, as I understand, and they scoured the records.
> **Russert:** Would you authorize the release of everything to settle this?
> **Bush:** Yes, absolutely. We did so in 2000, by the way.

Russert gave no indication he understood Bush had just told a bold lie, and Russert certainly never challenged Bush's assertion that he had authorized "everything" be released in 2000. Once again, it appeared journalists who were oblivious to the key facts of the Guard story in 2000 were simply caught unaware in 2004. A search of Nexis transcripts indicates the only time Russert mentioned Bush's National Guard service on *Meet the Press* during the entire 2000 campaign was when he pressed a Democrat on whether it was out of bounds to raise questions about Bush's time in the Guard.

Sitting at home in Iowa, researcher Marty Heldt watched Russert's 2004 exchange with Bush with interest. A farmer and former railroad brakeman whose interest was piqued in 2000 about Bush's Guard service, Heldt filed a Freedom of Information request with the National Guard Bureau as well as the Air Force, seeking a detailed account of Bush's records. The chief of the National Guard Bureau's support services division wrote back, informing Heldt that parts of his Bush request were off-limits: "Social security numbers, medical records and personnel and administrative information of Mr. Bush and others have been withheld, as release of this information would be a clearly unwarranted invasion of the personal privacy of the personnel affected," wrote the chief. Indeed, according to National Archives & Records Administration guidelines, the type of information that can be released regarding military personnel include, "name, service number, rank, dates of service, awards and decorations and place of entrance and separation." (Separation refers to when a service member exits the military.)

But Bush's medical records, for instance, were never released to the general public. Nor were any disciplinary reviews, pay stubs, tax records, or personal letters, which experts said would have been the best way to document Bush's exact whereabouts in 1972–1973. According to the Freedom of Information Act and the Privacy Act, those sorts of documents remain under seal unless the military personnel in question (or the next-of-kin) authorize their release.

Had Bush authorized a complete release of his military records to the public, as he told Russert he had, Heldt would have received everything he requested. Instead, Bush pointedly refused to do that. (By contrast, during the 2004 Democratic primaries, candidate Wesley Clark actually did release all his military records, thirty-four years worth, and even invited voters to examine the papers at a room at the Manchester Hotel in New Hampshire dubbed the "Clark reading room.")

Despite the press's habit in early 2004 of downplaying the issue (the Associated Press stood out as a notable exception), the Guard story, driven mostly by online news sources, continued to percolate, in part because the White House had difficulty addressing the simplest inquiries about Bush's Guard duties and his whereabouts during 1972 and 1973. Finally, On February 13, the White House seemed to catch a break when a former Guardsman from Alabama, John "Bill" Calhoun, a proud Republican, stepped forward to announce he had seen Bush serve at Dannelly Field in Montgomery in 1972, just as the president insisted he had. The *Washington Post*, tipped off about Calhoun's story by a Bush supporter, reported, "Calhoun's claim was a rare respite for a White House that has had a difficult time locating anyone who served with Bush." Indeed, in the more than three decades since Bush supposedly served in Alabama, Calhoun was the only member of Bush's unit to come forward to say he remembered performing drills with the future president of the United States.

But when, exactly, had Calhoun seen Bush at Dannelly Field? "Cal-

houn estimated that he saw Bush sign in at the 187th Tactical Recon-
naissance Group eight to 10 times for about eight hours each from May
to October 1972. He said the two occasionally grabbed a sandwich in
the snack bar," according to the *Post*. But there was a slight problem
with Calhoun's tale of seeing Bush—of having a snack with him—
between May and October 1972. As the Daily Howler noted, Bush
wasn't even *assigned* to Dannelly until September 1972, four months
after Calhoun claimed he befriended the future commander in chief.
And even the White House claimed Bush's first Dannelly Field drills
were not until October; drills nobody else saw Bush perform.

It was telling that four years after the *Globe* first reported the correct
chronology, which the press corps ignored in 2000, neither the *Washington Post*, nor MSNBC, CNN, *The New York Times*, *Los Angeles Times*,
Associated Press, and *New York Post*, which all dutifully covered the Calhoun story, had any inkling in their initial reports that his dates did not
add up. (Credit *NBC Nightly News* and United Press International for
being among a handful of major outlets that immediately pointed out
the discrepancies in Calhoun's timeline.)

That type of lazy indifference typified the press handling of the
story in 2004, to the point where journalists didn't even report on new
developments. In late August, as the presidential campaign headed
into peak season, a video began circulating on the Web that captured
Texan Ben Barnes making comments about how "very ashamed" he was
for getting Bush into the National Guard. Speaking to a group of
Democrats, Barnes explained the remorse was prompted by his recent
visit to the Vietnam War Memorial in Washington, where he saw the
names of thousands of other young men who did not enjoy the connections of the Bush family. After years—decades—of turning down
requests from the press to talk about Bush and the Guard, Barnes's
comments represented his first, extended public statements on the
matter.

During the final weekend in August, and after having devoted
extraordinary resources to amplifying factually challenged allegations
about John Kerry's war record, the national press gave Barnes's candid
remarks only cursory coverage. The *Washington Post* ran just a brief wire
story on the same day it printed yet another exhaustive piece about allegations surrounding Kerry's war past. In a subsequent Washington-

Post.com online chat, the *Post* reporter covering the Swift Boat Veterans for Truth controversy, which was built around thirty-five-year-old war recollections, suggested Barnes's comments didn't qualify as "fresh information," and consequently the reporter wasn't interested in "simply regurgitating old controversies." The *New York Times* also ran a brief item on Barnes's statements deep inside its news section, next to yet another lengthy profile of Kerry's longtime Swift boat nemesis, John O'Neill. (Barnes was eventually interviewed by CBS and included in its botched *60 Minutes II* report.)

Days after word of the Barnes video surfaced, *Salon* published a telling exclusive that filled in some of the holes in the Bush Guard story. The online magazine's Mary Jacoby reported that in late 1972 George H. W. Bush had phoned a longtime family confidant in Alabama, Jimmy Allison, to ask if there was room on the local Red Blount campaign he was managing for Bush's troublesome son George, or "Georgie" as he was called. "The impression I had was that Georgie was raising a lot of hell in Houston, getting in trouble and embarrassing the family, and they just really wanted to get him out of Houston and under Jimmy's wing," Allison's widow, Linda, told *Salon*. "After about a month I asked Jimmy what was Georgie's job, because I couldn't figure it out. I never saw him do anything," said Allison, who for years had refused to discuss the matter and who considered herself a friend of the Bush family. Asked if she'd ever seen Bush in a uniform, Allison said: "Good lord, no. I had no idea that the National Guard was involved in his life in any way."

Allison's exclusive, firsthand account was all but ignored by the MSM, to the point where international papers paid more attention to the *Salon* story than did U.S. dailies. The *Salon* story broke on the same day Bush addressed the Republican convention at Madison Square Garden. Collectively, the all-news cable channels and the networks devoted more than twenty hours of coverage that day to the GOP confab, much of which was spent filling up time with a parade of pundits discussing the campaign. Not once, according to Nexis, during that extended talk-fest was Linda Allison's name, or her on-the-record interview, mentioned on the air. Try to imagine the level of press attention during the summer of the 2004 if a widow of John Kerry's Vietnam War buddy had come forward to discuss how her late husband used to talk about how Kerry had faked some of his war injuries in order to secure medals. Odds are, *that* would have been very widely reported.

Right after *Salon*'s scoop, the political press corps shifted out of its blanket August 2004 coverage of the Swift Boat Veterans for Truth, which significantly undermined the Kerry campaign, and soon turned its attention to the CBS's memo controversy, which significantly aided the Bush campaign.

For most news consumers CBS's high-profile bungling of its National Guard story meant the larger question about Bush's military service was irrelevant; that the CBS controversy proved that allegations of Bush being AWOL had been trumped up by Democrats. That's certainly how conservative press critics spun the story and that's how the MSM obediently handled it as well. "In other words, the allegedly 'liberal' media dropped the story like a hot rock," wrote Washington-post.com columnist Terry Neal.

In truth, the unreliable memos CBS used in its report were essentially irrelevant to the larger debate about Bush's Guard service. The memos simply added personal elements—recollections and frustrations from Bush's commander—to what was already known about Bush's final two no-show years. CBS could have told the same tale without using the memos. The facts, based on Bush's own military record and chronicled by independent researchers such as Paul Lukasiak, retired Army Colonel Gerald Lechliter, and Marty Heldt, spoke for themselves. It's just that the MSM didn't want to listen.

Here were some of the more telling, and mostly overlooked, facts:

- Upon entering the Guard, Bush agreed to fly for sixty months. After his training was complete, he owed fifty-three more months of flying.

   He flew for only twenty-two of those fifty-three months.
- On his transfer request to Alabama Bush was asked to list his "permanent address."

   He wrote down a post office box number for the campaign he was working for on a temporary basis.
- On his transfer request Bush was asked to list his Air Force specialty code.

Bush, an F-102 pilot, erroneously wrote the code for an F-89 or F-94 pilot; two planes that had been retired from the Air Force by that time. Bush, an officer, made this mistake more than once on the same form.

- On May 26, 1972, Lieutenant Colonel Reese Bricken, commander at Maxwell Air Force Base in Alabama, accepted Bush's request for a transfer to his nonflying unit but noted Bush would not be able to fulfill any of his remaining two years of flight obligation.

  Bush pressed on with his Maxwell transfer request nonetheless.

- Bush's Maxwell transfer request was eventually denied by the Air Reserve Personnel Center in Denver in the summer of 1972, which meant Bush was still obligated to attend training sessions one weekend a month with his Texas unit near Houston for the entire summer of 1972.

  In 1972 Bush failed to attend weekend drills in May, June, July, August, and September.

- According to Air Force regulations, "[a] member whose attendance record is poor must be closely monitored. When the unexcused absences reach one less than the maximum permitted he must be counseled and a record made of the counseling. If the member is unavailable he must be advised by personal letter."

  There is no record that Bush ever received such counseling, despite the fact that he missed drills for months on end.

- Bush's unit was obligated to report in writing to the Personnel Center at Randolph Air Force Base whenever a monthly review of records showed unsatisfactory participation for an officer.

  Bush's unit never reported his absenteeism to Randolph Air Force Base.

- In July 1972, Bush failed to take a mandatory Guard physical exam, which is a serious offense for a Guard pilot. The move should have prompted the formation of a Flying Evaluation Board to investigate the circumstances surrounding Bush's failure.

  No such Flying Evaluation Board was convened.

- On September 29, 1972, Bush was formally grounded for failing to take a flight physical. The letter, written by Major General Francis Greenlief, chief of the National Guard Bureau, ordered Bush to acknowledge in writing that he had received word of his grounding.

No such written acknowledgment exists.

- Each time Bush missed a monthly training session he was supposed to schedule a make-up session, or file substitute service requests. Bush's numerous substitute service requests should have formed a lengthy paper trail with the name of the officer who authorized the training in advance, the signature of the officer who supervised the training, and Bush's own signature.

  No such documents exist.

- During his last year with the Texas Air National Guard, Bush missed a majority of his mandatory monthly training sessions and supposedly made them up with substitute service. Guard regulations allowed substitute service only in circumstances that were "beyond the control" of the Guard member.

  Neither Bush nor the Texas Air National Guard ever explained what the uncontrollable circumstances were that forced him to miss so many of his assigned drills during his last year.

- On June 29, 1973, the Air Reserve Personnel Center in Denver instructed Bush's commanders to get additional information from his Alabama unit, where he had supposedly trained, in order to better evaluate Bush's duty.

  Bush's commanders ignored the request.

It's hard to imagine what further proof journalists needed to convince themselves that Bush's Guard service was newsworthy and specifically that it raised doubts about his service, along with the $1 million worth of taxpayer-supported flying lessons he received. But in 2000, Beltway journalists, playing off Republican talking points, were too busy cataloging Al Gore's alleged exaggerations. And in 2004 Beltway journalists, playing off Republican talking points, were too busy dissecting the alleged defects of John Kerry's war record. Indeed, the zeal with which the press, after ignoring the Bush Vietnam story, chased down the legend of Kerry's bogus war service was stunning.

CHAPTER 7

Attack of the Swifties

If you had to pick one whopper that John O'Neill told during the Swift Boat Veterans for Truth campaign during the 2004 presidential campaign, a single, graceless claim that captured an almost knee-jerk desire to mislead, you might turn to O'Neill's August 12 appearance on MSNBC's *Hardball* when host Chris Matthews, trying to give some context to the unfolding allegations over Senator John Kerry's combat service in Vietnam, described O'Neill as "a Republican from Texas."

Offended by the description and its partisan overtones, O'Neill shot back, "I'm not a Republican from Texas. That's just not true."

Some pertinent facts: Since O'Neill practices law in Houston, Texas, Matthews was probably on solid ground describing the guest as being "from Texas." But was O'Neill a Republican? In 1971 he was recruited by the Nixon White House to serve as pro-war advocate and to debate then-peace activist John Kerry on television. O'Neill was also invited to speak at the 1972 Republican nominating convention. He clerked for Republican-appointed William Rehnquist of the Supreme Court. O'Neill has given generously to Republican candidates. He voted in the 1998 Texas Republican state primary and turned to wealthy Republican donors to help bankroll the Swift Boat attacks, which alleged Kerry "fabricated at least two of his Purple Hearts." It's true, O'Neill told reporters he voted for Al Gore in 2000, but considering the way O'Neill told untruths with such stunning regularity on behalf of the Swift Boat brigade, only a dupe would take O'Neill at his word. Then label the press corps full of suckers, because during the summer of 2004 the media let the Swift Boat Veterans for Truth, and their leader John O'Neill, hijack the election. The Swift Boat veterans account was riddled with untruths about documents, about eyewitnesses, about their political affiliations, and even about who wrote—or didn't write—*Unfit for Command: Swift Boat Veterans Speak Out Against John Kerry.* For several crucial weeks during the campaign journalists turned away from the pile-up of Swift Boat falsehoods and contradictions, rarely daring to call the Swift Boat attack out for what it really was—a farce. An elaborate, well-choreographed, well-funded farce that not only dragged down the Kerry campaign, but played the press for fools. At every turn, military records proved the Swift Boat veterans to be untruthful. But Beltway reporters and pundits too often remained hesitant, too timid to speak up, as they propped up the veterans as serious men.

"The media, which can't get enough of Vietnam, picked up the issue and ran with it on a hundred cable finger-pointing shows—without having the slightest idea whether it was true," wrote the *Washington Post*'s media writer Howard Kurtz. "Without that echo-chamber effect, this dinky little [Swift Boat] ad would have sunk without a trace." (He was right; the irony was the *Post* itself was one of the worst MSM print offenders during the Swift Boat con.)

At the outset the Swifties landed key support from the conservative echo chamber. Writing on the *Los Angeles Times* op-ed page, Ben Wasserstein noted that the conservative press's handling—its hyping—of the Swift Boat story was a "case study in bias." The *New York Post*, Fox News, the Drudge Report, Rush Limbaugh, as well as right-wing bloggers, all dutifully amplified the Swift Boat allegations while ignoring clear contradictions in their charges. But the real scandal was that the MSM didn't function much differently. Their conduct during the manufactured Swift Boat scandal, which likely delivered Bush the cushion he needed to win in November, represented an embarrassing new benchmark for campaign season reporting. Rather than uncovering the obvious gaps in the veterans' wobbly allegations and holding the accusers accountable, the press, spooked about being tagged as too liberal, played dumb on an unprecedented scale, much to the White House's delight.

The fact that the press rushed to embrace and amplify the Swift Boat story about Kerry's Vietnam service after its long-standing allergic reaction to questions surrounding Bush's Vietnam service only highlighted the hypocrisy that unfolded during the campaign. Media Matters for America summed up the phenomenon concisely:

John Kerry, according to every available piece of documentary evidence, including official U.S. Navy records, served bravely and honorably, won five medals (including three Purple Hearts), and saved a crewmate's life. Everybody—everybody—who served on Kerry's boats during the incidents that led to his medals agrees that he deserved them and praises his distinguished service. President George W. Bush, according to the documentary evidence available, apparently didn't bother to show up for duty for a lengthy period in 1972–73—a period when, according to *USA Today*, "commanders in Texas and Alabama say they never saw him report for duty and records show no pay to Bush when he was supposed to be on duty in Alabama." In contrast with Kerry, who has shipmates who sing his praises, Bush hasn't been able to produce anyone who can credibly say they remember serving with him in the Alabama Guard.

Yet which Vietnam episode did the press dwell on? Which episode did the press suggest offered valuable insight into a candidate's character? By the time the Swift Boat story had played out, CNN, chasing after ratings leader Fox News, found time to mention the Swift Boat Veterans for Truth—hereafter, Swifties—in nearly three hundred separate news segments, while more than one hundred *New York Times* articles and columns made mention of the Swifties. And during one overheated twelve-day span in late August, the *Washington Post* mentioned the Swifties in page-one stories on August 19, 20, 21 (two separate articles), 22, 24, 25, 26, 27, 28, 29, 30, and 31. It was a media monsoon that washed away Kerry's momentum coming out of the Democratic convention.

Note that at the same time the Swifties were making their charges via cable television commercials, a group called Texans for Truth was formed and featured a former National Guardsman who questioned Bush's service. The group bought cable TV time to air its claim just as the Swifties had done. But there were two key differences between the two advocacy groups. First, the Texans for Truth allegations were based on fact (i.e., Bush's own military records). Second, Texans for Truth were nearly uniformly ignored by the MSM. Throughout the entire campaign there were just nine mentions of Texans for Truth on MSNBC, CNBC, and NBC *combined*, while the *New York Times* managed eight references, compared to the *Washington Post*'s lonely seven.

Writing about the Swifties the *New Republic Online*'s Campaign Journal, Ryan Lizza noted, "Never in a campaign has a more disreputable group of people, whose accusations have been repeatedly contradicted by official records and reliable eyewitness accounts, had their claims taken so seriously." Fox News contributing political analyst Juan Williams forcefully made the same point. "If this was a court room, this whole thing would have been thrown out a long time ago as ridiculous," he told *Fox News Sunday* viewers on August 22. "If this was Judge Judy they'd laugh at this stuff. And yet somehow, we give them all this attention and credibility, put them on network television. These people are ridiculous." Both Lizza and Williams were factually accurate, but both Lizza and Williams were among the few within the MSM to state the truth publicly.

Just as with the questions surrounding Bush and the National Guard, it's important to understand the specifics of the Swift Boat allegations in order to understand just how derelict the press was in its coverage of the scandal. The point here is not to rehash the Swift Boat allegations or re-fight the battles over Vietnam or belittle Kerry's communication aides for mishandling the campaign crisis. It's to show what kind of claims the Swifties were making and how hollow the allegations should have appeared to serious journalists interested in documenting the facts.

Specifically, it's important to understand the credibility of the men who made the Swift Boat accusations. Since they had no official documentation to support their claims, which were first made thirty-five years after the fact, all they had was their word. If contradictions and inconsistencies or clear conflicts of interest quickly emerged, the standard for campaign journalism should have dictated that the men and their charges be dismissed as not serious, or perhaps even highlighted as an example of how vicious the campaign season can get. Yet the press turned that guideline on its head—as Swift Boat contradictions and inconsistencies piled up the press seemed to give them *more* credence and prominence, which was puzzling considering the players involved and the dark tales they tried to stitch together.

Alfred French

The first person seen in the first Swift Boat ad broadcast on cable television, French made the initial televised allegation against Kerry: "I served with John Kerry. He's lying about his record."

In preparation for the ad, French, a senior deputy district attorney in Oregon and registered Republican, signed a sworn affidavit for the Swifties asserting Kerry received his Purple Heart "from negligently self-inflicted wounds in the absence of hostile fire." A fundamental requirement of any affidavit is that the person signing it must have personal knowledge of the matters involved. In fact, the affidavit French signed declared, "I do hereby swear, that all facts and statements contained in this affidavit are true and correct and within *my personal knowledge and belief.*" (Emphasis added.) But in an interview with the *Oregonian* newspaper, French freely admitted he had no firsthand knowledge of the events surrounding Kerry's medals and that his information came from secondhand accounts from "friends."

Nearly three dozen local attorneys quickly filed complaints with the Oregon Bar Association, complaining that French, a practicing prosecutor, never should have signed an affidavit about events that he knew nothing about. The country's prosecutor's office launched an investigation and French, who had publicly labeled Kerry a liar based on nothing more than secondhand gossip, was quickly reprimanded for an unrelated ethical infraction; lying to his boss years earlier when confronted about an extramarital affair with a secretary. It was an affair that would have cost French his job had he been truthful with his boss. French was then subsequently suspended without pay for two weeks for using an office computer to print out his affidavit that labeled Kerry a liar, as well as asking a legal secretary to notarize his signature on the affidavit. "French's inappropriate use of office equipment for a political document was not permitted or allowed," read a local county press release.

George Elliott

Kerry's former commanding officer, Elliott looked into the camera during the Swifty ad and said, "John Kerry has not been honest about what happened in Vietnam."

The problem was Elliott simply could not make up his mind about what actually "happened in Vietnam." Back in a December 1969, fitness report on Kerry, Elliott wrote, "In a combat environment often requiring independent, decisive action, LTJG Kerry was unsurpassed," noting Kerry was an "acknowledged leader in his peer group. His bearing and appearance are above reproach."

Years later when he campaigned *for* Kerry during the senator's reelection bid, Elliott told Massachusetts voters that Kerry's Silver Star was awarded for "an act of courage." In an April 13, 2004, article, Elliott told *USA Today* that he had no qualms about Kerry's actions that earned him the Silver Star. "This was an exemplary action," he said. "There's no question about it." For thirty-five years Elliott testified to the senator's bravery—and then, in an instant, changed his story when he signed off on the Swifty's May 4, 2004, letter delivered to the Kerry campaign documenting their allegations. In August, just as the first Swifty ad was being aired in a handful of battleground states, the *Boston Globe* reported that Elliott experienced another change of heart, confessing to their reporter, "It was a terrible mistake probably for me to sign the affidavit with those words. I'm the one in trouble here. . . . I knew it was wrong. . . . In a hurry I signed it and faxed it back. That was a mistake." And then, after conferring with the Swifties Elliott quickly denied making the statement to the *Globe* and signed a new affidavit that stood by the first. Much to the Swifty's relief no doubt, Elliott then promptly cut off all press interviews.

You'd think this double flip-flop would have undermined Elliott's, and the Swifties', credibility. But hardly anyone in the press paid attention. (The *Washington Post*, for instance, never bothered reporting on Elliott's "terrible mistake" quote.)

Dr. Louis Letson

The fourth person to appear in the first Swift Boat ad, Letson announced, "I know John Kerry is lying about his first Purple Heart, because I treated him for that injury." In another affidavit, Letson claimed Kerry's wound was too small to justify a medal. But Navy guidelines during the Vietnam War for Purple Hearts did not take into account the size of the wound when awarding the honor. Letson has also never been able to credibly answer this simple riddle: If Kerry's wounds were so insignificant, as he claimed, and if Kerry at the time was just a junior officer, then why, three and a half decades later, would a doctor who likely treated hundreds if not thousands of wartime wounds, recall the specifics of Kerry's pedestrian visit? Letson claimed he remembered Kerry's unremarkable visit because Kerry's crewmen told him that Kerry bragged that he'd be the next JFK from Massachusetts. Indeed, Kerry's medical records for that wound indicated Letson did not sign off as the "person administering treatment" on December 3, 1968. Instead, corpsman J.C. Carreon did. (Letson said Carreon, who died in 1992, signed forms on his behalf.) It certainly seemed as if Letson was commenting not just on minor wounds, but minor wounds he may not have even treated.

Additionally, Letson claimed the reason he knew Kerry was lying about his wound was because that's what Letson overheard, second-hand, from Kerry's crewmembers; that there was no enemy fire during their mission when Kerry was injured. But Letson could not name the person who allegedly told him that tale. Considering the fact that on the night in question Kerry was in the company of just *two* crewmembers, it would not be difficult to figure out that particular puzzle. But in the hazy, mazy world of the Swifties, no explanation was ever easy.

William Schachte

Schachte claims he was one of those two men with Kerry that night; the commander on the December 2, 1968, mission for which Kerry won his first Purple Heart. According to Schachte, the boat they were on did not receive enemy fire and Kerry's wound, which Letson allegedly treated, was the result of Kerry's improper use a grenade launcher.

The three U.S. servicemen who were on the boat that night don't remember seeing Schachte. Since the boat was a 14-by-15-foot skimmer, it would have been hard for him to escape notice. Besides Kerry, the other crewmembers were Bill Zaladonis and Patrick Runyon; they had told the same story for years and they insisted neither Schachte, nor anyone else, was with the three of them that night. ("Me and Bill aren't the smartest, but we can count to three," Runyon told the *New York Times*.)

But with the arrival of the Swift Boat smear campaign, Schachte conveniently stepped forward and announced he too was on the skimmer that night. He had no documentation to back up his claim. Apparently Schachte's account took the Swifties by surprise. As Media Matters for America noted, on their website the Swifties originally posted this version of events for the night in question:

"The action that led to John Kerry's first Purple Heart occurred on December 2, 1968, during the month that he was undergoing training with Coastal Division 14 at Cam Ranh Bay. While waiting to receive his own Swift boat command, Kerry volunteered for a nighttime patrol mission commanding a small, foam-filled 'skimmer' craft with *two enlisted men.*" [Emphasis added.] That was clearly a reference to Zaladonis and Runyon.

But then the Swifties were forced to quietly revise their adjustable account of history, changing the ranks of the men on the skimmer after Schachte unveiled his new version of events. Suddenly the Swifties' online description changed to this:

"The action that led to John Kerry's first Purple Heart occurred on December 2, 1968, during the month that he was undergoing training with Coastal Division 14 at Cam Ranh Bay. While waiting to receive his own Swift boat command, Kerry volunteered for a nighttime patrol mission on a small, foam-filled 'skimmer' craft *under the command of Lt. William Schachte. The two officers were accompanied by an enlisted man* who operated the outboard motor. [Emphasis added.]

Even chief Swifty John O'Neill couldn't keep the stories straight. Pressed on CNN's *Crossfire* by Lanny Davis, who asked how many men were present that night on the boat, O'Neill flinched: "There were at least three and *possibly* four men." [Emphasis added.] Apparently nervous about his tale, Schachte only granted two interviews during the entire controversy, one of which was with conservative Swifty ally, columnist Robert Novak. (Novak's son worked as director of marketing for the publisher of the Swift Boat book; a fact Novak kept quiet until others in the press called him out.) And for the record, in an interview with NBC News, Schachte said he was not technically a member of Swift Boat Veterans for Truth, only that he admired them. An attorney by training, perhaps Schachte thought twice about signing an affidavit, as all Swifties did, detailing his dubious accusations against Kerry.

Adrian Lonsdale

During the 2004 campaign Lonsdale claimed that Kerry "lacks the capacity to lead," which was odd because during Kerry's 1996 Senate

race, Lonsdale, explaining the success of the river operations during the
Vietnam War, told Massachusetts reporters, "It was because of the
bravery and the courage of the young officers that ran boats . . . the swift
boats and the Coast Guard cutters, and Senator Kerry was no exception."

Also in 1996 Lonsdale walked reporters through the citation process
for medals. Lonsdale, along with Elliott, handled the reports, he said.
Lonsdale noted awards were only approved if there was corroboration
from others. His explanation completely contradicted the Swifties'
later claim that Kerry only won his bogus awards because he was able to
write up false reports and fool his commanders.

Larry Thurlow

Another registered Republican, Thurlow commanded a Navy Swift
boat alongside Kerry's in Vietnam. And up until the election season of
2004 he had nothing bad to say about Kerry's service. Even as late as
April 2004, Thurlow told *USA Today* that Kerry "was extremely brave,
and I wouldn't argue that point."

During that summer everything changed as Thurlow's key role was
to serve as Swifties' point person on what they claimed was Kerry's disputed Bronze Star and third Purple Heart, won during a mission in Viet
Cong–controlled territory on March 13, 1969. Thurlow claimed
Kerry's award was a fraud. Thurlow signed a sworn affidavit for the
Swifties that stated Kerry was "not under fire" when he pulled Lieutenant James Rassmann out of the water. He described Kerry's Bronze
Star citation, which stated that all units involved came under "small
arms and automatic weapons fire," as "totally fabricated." Swifties also
accused Kerry of "fleeing the scene."

But then the *Washington Post* got a hold of Thurlow's own Bronze Star
citation for an honor Thurlow won that very same day for actions on a
boat that was right alongside Kerry's. The citation detailed how both his
boat and Kerry's boat faced "enemy small arms and automatic weapons
fire." Asked for a response, Thurlow still insisted there had been no
enemy fire that day. Further, based on absolutely no proof, Thurlow
claimed Kerry was responsible for the citation about enemy fire. How
Kerry, busy rescuing a crewmember out of the river, would know the
specifics of what was happening on Thurlow's boat was never explained.

But how could Thurlow have been foolish enough to sign a Swifty affidavit about there being no enemy fire that day when his own citation made reference to there being enemy fire? Thurlow had a good explanation. In fact, he had at least three of them: He alternately told patient reporters he paid little or no attention to the citation when he won the Bronze Star ("Well, I just took it home, put it away, and kind of ignored the whole thing"); that he lost the citation twenty years ago (or it was with his ex-wife; take your pick); and that no, he would not authorize the release of a copy. (The *Post* obtained a copy through a Freedom of Information request.) Nonetheless, Thurlow, who accepted a Bronze Star for bravery under fire even though he insisted there was none that day, spent the summer of 2004 accusing a man who everyone else said had displayed bravery under fire of lying. And the MSM let him.

Roy Hoffmann

According to Swifty legend, recounted over and over in the press, it was Hoffmann, the crusty retired Navy officer and Kerry's former commander, who formed the genesis of the attack campaign. Upset after reading Douglas Brinkley's *Tour of Duty*, the Kerry-friendly telling of the senator's Vietnam experience and in which veterans portrayed the commander as " 'hotheaded,' 'blood-thirsty,' and 'egomaniacal,' " Hoffmann took aim at Kerry. (Kerry himself had little negative to say about Hoffmann in the book.) "I couldn't bear that someone was betraying us and being a dastardly liar," Hoffmann told the *Washington Post*.

The fact that Hoffmann "couldn't bear" to remain silent about Kerry was odd because in 1969, Rear Admiral Roy Hoffmann congratulated Kerry on the daring Swift boat attack he led, calling it a "shining example of completely overwhelming the enemy." More recently, in 1995, Hoffmann attended a wedding party for Kerry and Teresa Heinz. In a June 2003 *Boston Globe* profile of Kerry, Hoffman was still praising the senator as he recalled the events surrounding Kerry's Silver Star: "It took guts, and I admire that." In an interview with Brinkley in March 2003, when asked about Kerry, Hoffmann said, "I am not going to say anything negative about him. He's a good man."

But after seeing his name trashed in *Tour of Duty* by his own men, Hoffmann changed his mind, and then had trouble keeping his stories straight. According to a May 6, 2004 article in the *Milwaukee Journal Sentinel,* the former commander "acknowledged he had no firsthand knowledge to discredit Kerry's claims to valor and said that although Kerry was under his command, he really didn't know Kerry much personally." The next month Hoffmann reiterated, "I did not know Kerry personally. I didn't ride the boat with him."

Fast forward to August when the first Swifty boat ad hit the airwaves, and Hoffmann suddenly updated his Vietnam memories, telling Fox News, "I knew [Kerry] well, because I operated very closely with him."

Ironically, Hoffmann's scripted line for his Swift Boat commercial was, "John Kerry has not been honest."

John O'Neill

If Hoffmann was the heart behind the Swifties, O'Neill was the brains. He served as the smooth talking attorney out front dealing with reporters, while at the same time tapping his deep-pocketed Texas Republican connections to help transform the ad-hoc attack machine into a well-oiled one. O'Neill also co-authored *Unfit for Command* with Jerome Corsi, although O'Neill later obfuscated on that simple fact. At times it was harder keeping track of the myriad of O'Neill contradictions than it was the accusations he was leveling against Kerry and his combat service.

For instance, O'Neill, like Thurlow, was emphatic that Kerry didn't deserve his March 13, 1969, Bronze Star for saving Jim Rassmann out of the Bay Hap River, because Kerry wasn't under enemy fire. As way of proof, O'Neill told Fox News, "There's not a bullet hole in any of those three boats, not one." There was, "not a bullet-hole anywhere," O'Neill also assured ABC News. In fact, a report on the battle damage done to a boat that motored upriver alongside Kerry's on March 13, made reference to "three 30 cal bullet holes about super structure."

During an August 11 appearance on CNN, O'Neill insisted, "[T]he people in our organization have no partisan ties." Nine days later the Swifties unveiled a new ad which featured Vietnam veteran Ken Cordier who at the time served as a member of the Bush-Cheney '04 National

Veterans Steering Committee. Cordier had also been selected to serve on the Bush administration's POW Advisory Committee. So much for no partisan ties.

During another appearance on CNN on August 12, O'Neill said there "are more than 60 people that served with John Kerry that contributed to this book." Perhaps, but only one man who served on Kerry's boat, Stephen Gardner, contributed to the book. (Gardner, a Rush Limbaugh devotee, told author Brinkley that while in Vietnam he "had no trouble shooting gooks.")

That same August 12 day, O'Neill was busy dissembling on MSNBC's *Hardball*, where host Chris Matthews was trying to establish how long Kerry served in Vietnam. John Hurley, the national director of Veterans for Kerry, explained that Kerry had served two tours; one four-month run as a swift boat commander, and an earlier stint aboard the USS *Gridley*, off the coast of Vietnam. Those facts were clearly spelled out in Kerry's military records. But O'Neill objected.

> **O'Neill:** The USS *Gridley* was not a tour in Vietnam. It was a ship way off the coast of Vietnam.
>
> **Matthews:** But my brother was on one of those ships that was off the shore. And that was considered combat.
>
> **O'Neill:** [Kerry] was there for five weeks on the *Gridley* off the coast.
>
> **Matthews:** But was that recorded as combat theater duty?
>
> **O'Neill:** Absolutely.
>
> **Matthews:** Was [Kerry] given credit by the Navy for serving in Vietnam?
>
> **O'Neill:** Yes. But it would never have been considered a tour in Vietnam by the Navy or anybody else.
>
> **Matthews:** Well, why was he given credit for it?
>
> **O'Neill:** Well, he was given credit for exactly what he did, which was being on the *Gridley* off the coast.

For a moment there on national television, O'Neill literally argued out of both sides of his mouth insisting that yes, Kerry was "absolutely" given combat duty credit by the Navy for serving on the USS *Gridley* and that no, Kerry's time on the USS *Gridley* did not qualify as combat duty. On and on it went, yet the press continued to take O'Neill's peculiar logic seriously.

The somewhat simplistic overview detailed above merely limns the main Swifty players and some of their most outlandish buffooneries. Let's just pick out a few of the more obvious contradictions offered up as the Swifties made their stand against Kerry:

1. Larry Thurlow's own Bronze Star citation contradicting his claim about Kerry not taking on enemy fire.

2. Al French signing an affidavit asserting he had "personal knowledge" about Kerry's war wounds, but then admitting he had heard everything secondhand.

3. George Elliott's flurry of flip-flops during the month of August.

4. The Swifties having to alter their allegations about the events of December 2, 1968, after William Schachte emerged with a whole new set of anti-Kerry facts.

5. John O'Neill telling reporters there were no bullet holes in any of Kerry's flotilla following a disputed firefight, despite the fact Navy that records reported the opposite.

All those clumsy missteps were in the public record during August, 2004, but reporters covering the story and talking it to death on television did their best to avoid addressing the specifics.

- The number of MSM newspaper, magazine, and television reports during the entire Swift Boat campaign (and judging by Nexis, there were nearly two thousand of substance to choose from), that made mention of all five of those obvious Swifty blunders: zero.
- The number that made mention of four of the five: zero.
- The number that made mention of three of the five: one; a single guest column in the Durham, North Carolina, *Herald-Sun* written by Caroline Usher.

The missteps didn't really matter though, since the press corps remained committed to the story no matter how many times the Swifties revealed themselves to be hopelessly confused. Embraced by the Republican's far right media noise machine, led by Fox News, the Drudge Report, Rush Limbaugh, and the *New York Post*, the mainstream media refused to stand up to those forces. Instead, the press played along, letting the right wing set the media agenda, and pretend-

ing the media's primary duty was to accurately record the Swifty allegations, call the Kerry camp for comment, and then proclaim the story
too tangled to figure out. *USA Today*, for instance, threw up its hands,
declaring, "A clear picture of what John Kerry did or did not do in Vietnam 35 years ago may never emerge, given the fog of war, the passage
of time and the intense partisan sentiments of the players." A headline
on August 27 for Hotline, the daily D.C. media tip sheet announced,
"VIETNAM: JUST LIKE THE WAR ITSELF, THIS STORY'S NOW A QUAGMIRE."

In a detailed August 17 Swifty report, the *Los Angeles Times* noted
three key findings: that contemporaneous military documents supported Kerry's version of the events surrounding his medals, that the
men who actually served directly with Kerry on his swift boat strenuously supported Kerry's claims, and that some of the Swift Boat critics
had been caught changing their stories and giving conflicting accounts.
Three strikes and you're out? Nope. The *Times* came to this timid conclusion: "What actually happened . . . 35 years ago along the remote
southern coast of Vietnam remains murky," suggesting the controversy was an impossible-to-solve he-said/he-said dispute.

In *Time*, the magazine offered up a one-page scorecard, "Kerry in
Combat: Setting the Record Straight." In each account of Kerry's
medals, the magazine accurately reported how the Swift Boat charges
failed to hold up under any sort of factual scrutiny. Yet *Time* dutifully
restrained itself from coming to the obvious conclusion: The Swift
Boat charges were a campaign hoax. And after poring over the facts,
ABC News concluded, "thirty-five years later, we may never know the
exact truth."

But was the story really that hard for journalists to decipher? As Fairness and Accuracy in Reporting suggested in 2004, what if the situation
had been reversed and the shoddy Vietnam-era attacks targeted Bush's
war service? What if all the available documents showed that George
Bush had fully completed his obligation in the Air National Guard with
flying colors? What if virtually every member of his unit said he had
been there the whole time, and had done a great job? And then suppose
a group of fiercely partisan Democrats who never actually served in
Bush's Guard unit came forward to claim for the first time—after
thirty-five years of silence—that Guard documents and the firsthand
accounts were wrong, and that Bush really hadn't been present for his

Guard service. Would the MSM really have had a hard time figuring out who was telling the truth, and would the MSM really have showered the accusers with weeks worth of free media coverage?

But playing dumb about the Swifties had become epidemic among journalists who must have known better. At one point, NBC's Tim Russert asked a guest, "If the substance of many of the charges [from] *Unfit for Command*, aren't holding up . . . why is it resonating so much?" Like so many other journalists, Russert refused to acknowledge the media's integral role in turning the Swifty story into a news phenomenon. Why was it "resonating so much" Russert wondered out loud. Maybe because in the month of August, 2004, NBC network news alone covered the Swift Boat story on August 8, 15, 19, 20, 22, 23, 25, 26, and 29. CBS covered the story August 8, 22, 23, 24, 25, 26, and 30, while ABC devoted airtime to it on August 6, 8, 9, 19, 20, 21, 22, 23, 25, and 26. Some of the networks, using different morning and evening news programs, returned to the topic several times in one day. For instance on August 23, CBS reported on the Swifty controversy four different times, which of course, represented four more times than the CBS News division reported on questions surrounding Bush's Guard service during the *entire* 2000 campaign.

Reporters had the power the knock the phony Swift Boat story down fast and reveal it for the dirty trick it was, but too many chose not to. As early as May 2004, *Salon*'s Joe Conason detailed the close association the supposedly nonpartisan Swifties enjoyed with longtime Republican activists, such as the group's communications advisor Merrie Spaeth, the former director of media relations in the Reagan White House. During the 1990s Spaeth helped Kenneth Starr prepare for his testimony urging the impeachment of President Clinton before the House Judiciary Committee. Later it was learned that Bob Perry, the longtime Bush family fundraiser, had bankrolled the Swifty ads and that Benjamin Ginsberg, a prominent attorney working for the Bush reelection campaign, had provided legal advice to the Swifties. But for the most part the MSM, and particularly cable news, glossed over the GOP ties and gladly accepted the Swifties' tortured insistence that they were politically independent.

Relatively early on in the August coverage, ABC's *Nightline* devoted an entire episode to the allegations and reported, "The Kerry campaign calls the charges wrong, offensive and politically motivated. And points to Naval records that *seemingly* contradict the charges." (Emphasis added.) Seemingly? A more accurate phrasing would have been that Navy records "completely" or "thoroughly" contradicted the Swifties. In late August, CNN's scrawl across the bottom of the screen read, "Several Vietnam veterans are backing Kerry's version of events." Again, a more factual phrasing would have been "Crewmembers have always backed Kerry's version of events." But that would have meant not only having to stand up to a well-funded Republican campaign attack machine, but also casting doubt on television news' hottest political story of the summer.

When the discussion did occasionally turn to the facts behind the Swift Boat allegations, reporters and pundits seemed too spooked to address the obvious—that the charges made no sense and there was little credible evidence to support them. To George Stephanopoulos's credit, during an appearance on ABC's *World News Tonight Sunday*, he tried to steer the debate towards the facts, telling anchor Terry Moran, "The question for the Swift Boat Veterans is, are their charges accurate?" Moran wasn't interested. Instead, he wanted to know about the effects of the attack campaign: "Is there any sense that you have that it's sticking?"

Substituting as host of *Meet the Press*, Andrea Mitchell on August 15 pressed *Boston Globe* reporter Anne Kornblut about the facts surrounding Kerry's combat service: "Well, Anne, you've covered him for many years, John Kerry. What is the truth of his record?" Instead of mentioning some of the glaring inconsistencies in the Swifties' allegation, such as George Elliott's and Adrian Lonsdale's embarrassing flip-flops, Kornblut ducked the question, suggesting the truth was "subjective": "The truth of his record, the criticism that's coming from the Swift Boat ads, is that he betrayed his fellow veterans. Well, that's a subjective question, that he came back from the war and then protested it. So, I mean, that is truly something that's subjective." Ten days later Kornblut scored a sit-down interview with O'Neill. In her 1,200-word story she politely declined to press O'Neill about a single factual inconsistency surrounding the Swifties' allegations, thereby keeping her *Globe* readers in the dark about the Swift Boat farce. (It was not until Bush was safely reelected that Kornblut, appearing on MSNBC, conceded the Swift Boast ads were clearly inaccurate.)

Hosting an August 28 discussion on CNBC with *Newsweek*'s Jon Meacham and *Time*'s Jay Carney, NBC's Tim Russert finally, after weeks of overheated Swifty coverage, got around to asking *the* pertinent question: "Based on everything you have heard, seen, reported, in terms of the actual charges, the content of the book, is there any validity to any of it?" Carney conceded the charges did not have any validity, but did it oh, so gently: "I think it's hard to say that any one of them, by any standard that we measure these things, has been substantiated." Apparently Carney forgot to pass the word along to editors at *Time* magazine, which is digested by significantly more news consumers than Russert's weekly cable chat show on CNBC. Because it wasn't until its September 20, 2004 issue, well after the Swift Boat controversy had peaked, that the *Time* news team managed enough courage to tentatively announce that the charges levied against Kerry and his combat service were "reckless and unfair." (Better late than never; *Time*'s competitor *Newsweek* waited until *after* the election to conclude that the Swift Boat charges were "misleading," but "very effective.") But even then, *Time* didn't hold the Swifties responsible for their "reckless and unfair" charges. Instead, *Time* celebrated them. Typing up an election postscript in November, *Time* toasted the Swift Boat's O'Neill as one of the campaign's "Winners," while remaining dutifully silent about the group's fraudulent charges.

That kind of Beltway media group self-censorship was evident throughout the Swift Boat story, as the perimeters of acceptable reporting were quickly established. Witness the MSM reaction to Wayne Langhofer, Jim Russell, and Robert Lambert. All three men served with Kerry in Vietnam and all three men were witnesses to the disputed March 13, 1969, event in which Kerry rescued Green Beret Jim Rassmann, winning a Bronze Star and his third Purple Heart. The Swifties, after thirty-five years of silence, insisted Kerry did nothing special that day, and that he certainly did not come under enemy fire when he plucked Rassmann out of the drink. Therefore, Kerry did not deserve his honors.

It's true every person on Kerry's boat, along with the thankful Rassmann, insisted they were under fire, and so did the official Navy citation for Kerry's Bronze Star. Still, the Swifties held to their unlikely story, and the press pretended to be confused about the standoff. Then during the last week in August three more eyewitnesses, all backing the

Navy's version of events that there had been hostile gun fire, stepped forward. They were Langhofer, Russell, and Lambert.

Russell wrote an indignant letter to his local *Telluride Daily Planet* to dispute the Swifties' claim: "Forever pictured in my mind since that day over 30 years ago [is] John Kerry bending over his boat picking up one of the rangers that we were ferrying from out of the water. All the time we were taking small arms fire from the beach; although because of our fusillade into the jungle, I don't think it was very accurate, thank God. Anyone who doesn't think that we were being fired upon must have been on a different river."

The number of times Russell was subsequently mentioned on CNN: one. On Fox News: one. MSNBC: zero. ABC: one. On CBS: zero. On NBC: zero.

Like Russell, Langhofer also remembered strong enemy gunfire that day. An August 22 article in the *Washington Post* laid out the details: "Until now, eyewitness evidence supporting Kerry's version had come only from his own crewmen. But yesterday, The Post independently contacted a participant who has not spoken out so far in favor of either camp who remembers coming under enemy fire. 'There was a lot of firing going on, and it came from both sides of the river,' said Wayne D. Langhofer, who manned a machine gun aboard PCF-43, the boat that was directly behind Kerry's. Langhofer said he distinctly remembered the 'clack, clack, clack' of enemy AK-47s, as well as muzzle flashes from the riverbanks." (For some strange reason the *Post* buried its Langhofer scoop in the fiftieth paragraph of the story.)

The number of times Langhofer was subsequently mentioned on CNN: zero. On Fox News: zero. On MSNBC: zero. On ABC: zero. CBS: zero. NBC: zero.

As for Lambert, *The Nation* magazine uncovered the official citation for the Bronze Star he won that same day and it too reported the flotilla of five U.S. boats "came under small-arms and automatic weapons fire from the river banks."

The number of times Lambert was mentioned on. On Fox News: one. On CNN: zero. On MSNBC: zero. ABC: one. On CBS: zero. On NBC: zero.

Additionally, the *Washington Post*'s Michael Dobbs, who served as the paper's point person on the Swifty scandal, was asked during an August 30, 2004, online chat with readers why the paper hadn't reported more aggressively on the public statements of Langhofer, Russell, and Lambert. Dobbs insisted, "I hope to return to this subject at some point to update readers." But he never did. *Post* readers, who were deluged with Swifty reporting, received just the sketchiest of facts about Langhofer, Russell, and Lambert.

If that doesn't represent a concerted effort by the press to look the other way, than what does? The Swift Boat scandal was littered with similarly wrongheaded decisions by the media, which time and again aided the phony accusers. For instance, why didn't major newspapers review *Unfit for Command* in a timely manner? The book was released in August, dominated the news for a month, and was obviously being taken seriously by the press corps. Shouldn't editors have pressed for a timely review of the thin book to help put the unfolding story in some perspective? You'd think. But then that would have meant drawing the curtain back on the entire charade. Because, as the Daily Howler wrote, "When John O'Neill and Jerome Corsi published *Unfit for Command*, it was clear—to anyone who read it—that the pair were deeply kooky themselves. The book self-contradicts on page after page, and its gonzo chapter on Kerry-the-commie was straight from a mid-50s fever swamp. Any sensible person who read it would have known that its authors had emerged from those corner bars and were now engaging in 'crackpot theorizing' and 'ill-informed rumor-mongering' right out in public!"

Instead, newspaper editors looked away, careful not to let news consumers in on the secret that the book at the center of the election controversy was a barely readable mess. According to a search of Nexis, just a handful of major newspapers saw fit to hand the book over a critic, including the *New York Times*, the *Philadelphia Inquirer* and the *Los Angeles Times*, whose reviewer concluded, "This book is not journalism. The authors feel no need to be factual, accurate, truthful, fair or, finally, compassionate, all of which we tell journalism students they should be. It's more like pro wrestling—a dirty hold, an eye gouge, a knee to the groin are all good, for they will draw cheers from the fans." Good news for the Kerry camp. The bad news? The *Los Angeles Times* waited until *ten weeks* after *Unfit for Command* was published—and five weeks after it had exited the center stage—to call the book a farce.

Aside from actually reading the book at the center of an election-year controversy, a typical way journalists judge accusers is to examine the people lobbying the charges. For instance, *Unfit for Command* was coauthored by O'Neill and Corsi. Or was it? The Swifties couldn't decide. Corsi's name clearly appeared on the book jacket as a coauthor. The book's publisher, Regnery, referenced Corsi as the coauthor in marketing materials. The book's acknowledgment section was written in the plural—"We particularly appreciate . . ."; "We recognize that . . ."; "We, as so many others, are indebted . . ." So Corsi cowrote the book with O'Neill, right? Not according to O'Neill, who explained with a straight face on television that Corsi was more of an editor than a writer. "He simply helped us in editing the book," he told CNN's Wolf Blitzer.

The reason O'Neill had to suddenly announce that Corsi didn't coauthor the book was because Media Matters for America discovered that Corsi had a long history of posting wild-eyed rants online at the notorious, liberal-hating right-wing forum, FreeRepublic.com, where Corsi denigrated Catholics, Jews, Muslims, and Democrats. Appearing on MSNBC, O'Neill lied about that too; he said the Corsi controversy was about "his e-mails where he made stupid statements," when in fact they were public postings that Corsi had made online. Here were some of Corsi's more notable bon mots.

On the Pope:

—"So this is what the last days of the Catholic Church are going to look like. Buggering boys undermines the moral base and the lawyers rip the gold off the Vatican altars. We may get one more Pope, when this senile one dies, but that's probably about it."

On Islam:

—"Islam is like a virus—it is a cancer that destroys the body it infects."

On Kerry:

—"Kerry has a long history of Communist supporters."
—"Kerry offers a clear choice. Anti-American hatred."

On Al Gore:

—"He is growing his regulation length Bin Laden beard. Mullah Ali'Gore-ah, as he now wishes to be called, is focused on his new career

as a pilot. 'Want to fly like bird,' he says after his stint as a professor at
Columbia. 'No need to learn take-off or landing, just soar like bird and
look at buildings.' "

On President Clinton:
     —"When is this guy going to admit he's simply an anti-American
communist? Won't he and his leftist wife simply go away???? Enough
already."

On Senator Hillary Rodham Clinton:
     —"Let the FAT HOG run!!!" (Regarding a possible presidential bid.)
     —"Anybody ask why HELLary couldn't keep BJ Bill satisfied? Not
lesbo or anything, is she?"

Of course, Corsi was free to express his hatred. But when he cowrote a
book that aspired to be journalism and lobbed explosive charges during
the height of a presidential campaign, shouldn't the press have paid
attention to his past work? What are the odds that an anti-Bush book
coauthored by someone who made fanatical slurs online against Jews
and compared Bush, for instance, to a terrorist, would ever have been
taken seriously by CNN producers? And when Corsi's right-wing rants
were noted and O'Neill threw him overboard, insisting that Corsi only
helped with the *editing*, shouldn't that have raised a red flag for reporters
who were basing weeks worth of news coverage on his work? Apparently not. The Associated Press appears to have been the only major
news organization to have done a stand-alone news brief about Corsi's
offensive postings. (He told the AP they were meant to be humorous.)
As for Corsi's strange demotion from coauthor to research assistant
after *Unfit for Command* arrived in bookstores, the press ignored the
whole charade.
     During the month-long controversy there was much the press
politely ignored or downplayed. Take the small but telling incident
regarding Kerry's initials. One of the Swifties' elaborate explanations for
Kerry's Bronze Star for rescuing Rassmann, which Swifties insist he did
not deserve, was that Kerry falsified the after-action report, thereby
ensuring himself a medal he never should have won. Over and over
Swifties referred to "Kerry's report." How did the Swifties know Kerry

wrote the allegedly phony account? His initials were on it, they insisted. Of course when reporters got copies of the report, Kerry's initials of "JFK" were not on it. Instead it was emblazoned with "KJW." *The Washington Post* asked O'Neill about the discrepancy and O'Neill simply continued to lie, telling the paper the initials of "KJW" "identified" Kerry as the author. *The New York Times* reported, "Several veterans insist that Mr. Kerry wrote his own reports, pointing to the initials K. J. W. on one of the reports and saying *they are Mr. Kerry's.*" [Emphasis added.]

Kerry's initials are JFK and the after-action report initials are KJW, yet neither the *Post* nor the *Times*, dutifully noting the conflict, raised the obvious possibility that the Swifties were just making stuff up as they went along. Then again, at least the *Times* and *Post* devoted a couple of sentences to the telling Keystone Kops episode regarding the mismatched initials. The embarrassing hiccup was mostly ignored by other mainstream players.

Meanwhile, note how that standard changed—was completely inverted in fact—just weeks later when an accuser stepped forward to question Bush's Vietnam War service. The vehicle was CBS's story on Bush and the National Guard which aired on *60 Minutes II*, and relied on memos, reportedly from Bush's former commanders, which CBS executives could not authenticate when confronted by critics after the segment aired.

Note how dramatically different the media's reaction to the CBS story and the Swift Boat story were. When the Swifties first came forward with spurious allegations against Kerry's combat service in May 2004 with a press conference that predated the airing of the Swifty television attack ads in August, reporters waited three months before making a concerted, albeit halfhearted, effort to untangle the truth about their charges. But when CBS came forward with allegations, based on questionable documents, against Bush and his Vietnam service, it was all hands on deck in newsrooms around the country as armies of reporters were dispatched—*within hours* of the CBS telecast—to try to untangle the truth about the memos.

As for the central players involved in the two stories, they were O'Neill, who accused Kerry of fabricating portions of his military service, and Bill Burkett, who supplied CBS with the memos in question and who accused Bush of shirking his duty during the Vietnam War. The MSM created two entirely different standards by which to judge the accusers. For example, on ABC, newsman Chris Bury described Burkett as "a retired official in the Texas National Guard, [who] apparently had an ax to grind. He has a long history of political antagonism toward George W. Bush."

An accuser with "an ax to grind" and "a long history of . . . antagonism" toward one of the candidates? That certainly could have described O'Neill, who sparred bitterly with Kerry over the war during a 1971 a televised debate and who returned thirty-five years later to try to derail Kerry's presidential bid. (The *Los Angeles Times* once reported that O'Neill "loathed" Kerry.) But for some reason ABC News never described O'Neill as having an "ax to grind." The same double standard was advertised at the *Washington Post*, which described Burkett as "an anti-Bush zealot," and "an embittered, Bush-hating Texas cattle rancher." But the *Post* never labeled O'Neill an embittered, anti-Kerry zealot. To the MSM, O'Neill was a respectable truth-teller; Burkett a fraud.

In a sense, O'Neill was smarter than Burkett because O'Neill didn't bother with dubious documents to try to back up his claims about a presidential candidate's Vietnam military service. O'Neill and the Swifties had no documentation at all. In fact most of their allegations against Kerry were knocked down based solely on the Navy's own record keeping. Yet that did not stop cable and network television producers from extending a month's worth of invitations to O'Neill to come on their shows and detail, yet again, his charges about how Kerry lied bout his duty and smeared Vietnam veterans by opposing the war. As for Burkett, he was largely portrayed in the press as a crackpot.

If you took just a few of the Swifties' public stumbles and put them together—O'Neill caught fibbing about who coauthored the book with him, O'Neill caught fibbing about Kerry's initials, and the Swifties caught changing their stories about Kerry—it's perplexing how any reporter took anything the Swifties said seriously. But they did. Incredibly, faced with an elaborate campaign charade, most in the press didn't set their sights on the Swifties or the Bush campaign, which refused to denounce the lies. Instead, the punditocracy, echoing Republican spin, collectively agreed that the smear campaign was really Kerry's fault. "In

some ways you can certainly say that John Kerry brought this on himself," insisted *Time* magazine's Carney. "He should have known that this
was coming because he has experienced it in previous campaigns. He
knows that John O'Neill is out there."

ABC's Bury made the same point: "Because it's [Kerry's military ser-
vice] the central tenet of John Kerry's campaign. . . . And once that
issue is open, it's fair game."

In a sense they were right, it was fair game—just as questions about
Bush's military service were fair game. But the Swifties never played
fair—they couldn't even keep their stories straight. As their dishonesty
become obvious, journalists never adjusted their coverage. Instead,
pundits and reporters diverted their eyes from the porous, poorly con-
structed smear campaign and focused the blame on the Kerry campaign.
That saved reporters the trouble of labeling Vietnam veterans as liars
(not to mention Bush's father, wife, and political advisor Karl Rove, who
all publicly supported the Swifty campaign), which in turn would have
unleashed the fury of right-wing press critics. It also kept the Swift Boat
storyline on familiar ground, one of tactics and process—were Kerry's
consultants too slow in responding? Was there coordination between
the Swifties and the Bush campaign? And so on. All of that should have
been secondary to the central and pressing question—Were any of
these allegations true?

Time concluded Kerry's slow-footedness—his faulty political
instinct—was *"almost worse"* than the Swift Boat charges themselves,
which *Times* conceded were "reckless and unfair." [Emphasis added.] In
the eyes of the D.C. media elite, not successfully knocking down
libelous charges was "almost worse" than lobbing them. For reporters
(like Republicans), the whole controversy was born at the Democratic
convention when Kerry, they said, went overboard with his Vietnam
references. "Fifty percent of the convention, or more, was about [Viet-
nam], and his speech was about that," insisted *New York Times* reporter
Adam Nagourney. With all that nostalgia, "There was not, I think it's
fair to say, that much talk about what [Kerry] would do as president."

Fact: During his nearly sixty-minute convention address, Kerry
made fewer than five references to his military service. By comparison,
he devoted nineteen paragraphs of his speech to buttressing national
security, nine paragraphs to improving the economy, and six to address-

ing health insurance woes. But just one month later, journalists, echoing the talking points of Republicans, insisted the convention was all
about Vietnam, which then somehow made it okay for partisans who
had remained quiet for thirty-five years to suddenly question Kerry's
medal-winning service.

And so what if the Kerry campaign highlighted his distinguished
combat service? He's hardly the first presidential candidate to do that.
The notion that because Kerry talked about his war record he opened
the door to false accusations was certainly a novel theory for the press
to peddle. During the 1996 campaign Republican nominee Senator Bob
Dole was featured in television ads that showed him recovering from his
World War II injury. Dole also talked about his service during his convention acceptance speech, ("The 10th Mountain Division, in which I
served in Italy, and the Black troops of the 92nd Division who fought
nearby were the proof for me once again of the truth I'm here trying to
convey.") Does anybody really think that if a group of disgruntled
fringe activists had bought TV time in 1996 to smear Dole's war record
with bogus charges, that reporters and pundits would have tsk-tsked
Dole's handlers for opening the door to such allegations by relying too
much on his biography? The blame-the-victim standard in 2004 was
created out of whole cloth by Republicans and warmly adopted by the
journalists. It allowed them to pretend there was nothing unseemly
about the whole charade.

To a degree, journalists and commentators were right about the
Kerry campaign because it did make a colossal blunder—it expected the
press to quickly ferret out the lies, the gaps, the plain contradictions of
the Swift Boat brigade and their secondhand accusations. It appeared
the Kerry camp thought the *New York Times* and the *Washington Post*
and PBS and *Nightline* and *Newsweek* and CNN would do due diligence
and out the Swifties for the tricksters they were. Once exposed, the
Kerry camp probably thought their candidate would not only be in the
clear but that Bush and his camp would pay a price for (a) being so
closely allied with the accusers and (b) refusing to do the decent thing
by denouncing a freelance hit job that so obviously disregarded the
truth about a Vietnam veteran's service.

Kerry was sorely disappointed on both accounts. Some have argued
that Kerry's aides didn't understand that the media landscape had

changed, that with the lower journalism standards found on cable television and parts of the Internet, attack ads didn't necessarily have to be
true, they simply had to generate heat in order to be treated seriously,
and it was up to the Kerry camp to forcefully rebut them. And that may
be true. But what Kerry aides really didn't understand was that the political press corps had decided to walk away from its traditional duties—
particularly during national campaigns—of being truth tellers, unofficial
referees, to hold campaigns responsible for scurrilous allegations, for
cheap shots, and for peddling lies. Perhaps exhausted from hearing
complaints from Republican partisans on the sidelines about the liberal
media, the MSM opted to collectively hand in their referee whistle.

Asked about the press's role during a campaign marked with attacks,
USA Today White House reporter Richard Benedetto articulated the
new credo, saying he didn't know "where the whole concept of we, the
media, as referees came from. I'm not sure it's one of our primary
roles. It's more incumbent on the campaigns to defend themselves
against scurrilous charges than for us to do it."

Commenting in 2004 on his paper's coverage of the Swift Boat story,
Washington Post executive editor Leonard Downie Jr. insisted, "We are
not judging the credibility of Kerry or the (Swift Boat) Veterans, we just
print the facts."

But why did the *Post* not judge the credibility of the Swift Boat Veterans? It's probably the paper's most important role when unknown
accusers step forward during a presidential campaign to levy explosive
charges of fraud and cowardice. The *Post* may have printed the facts, as
Downie claimed, but the paper did so with amazing timidity and in a
way that was careful to avoid raising the obvious, albeit uncomfortable,
question of whether the Swifties were just flat out lying. In fact, despite
two strong reporting efforts by the *Post*'s Michael Dobbs—one on
August 18 and one on August 22—that highlighted the deficiencies of
the Swift Boat claims, the *Post*'s Swift Boat coverage, as a whole, was
among the worst of the major media players as it habitually glossed over
the glaring gaps in the Swift Boat allegations:

On August 24, the *Post* ran a page-one article about the Swift Boat
controversy and made no mention of the glaring gaps in the allegations
against Kerry.

On August 25, the *Post* ran a page-one story about the Swift Boat controversy and made no mention of the glaring gaps in the allegations against Kerry.

On August 26, the *Post* ran a pillow-soft profile on the cover of its Style section about the Swifties, suggesting their crusade was wrapped in "honor." ("The Swifties say they feel their sense of dishonor deeply, abidingly.") The article made no mention of the glaring gaps in the allegations against Kerry.

On August 27, the *Post* ran a page-one story about the Swift Boat controversy and made no mention of the glaring gaps in the allegations against Kerry.

On August 28, the *Post* ran a page-one story about the Swift Boat controversy (a 2,800-word feature on John O'Neill) and made no mention of the glaring gaps in the allegations against Kerry.

On September 2, the *Post* ran a page-one story about the Swift Boat controversy and made no mention of the glaring gaps in the allegations against Kerry.

The *Post* was not alone. That was the media *rule*. The examples were boundless.

On August 20, PBS's *Washington Week in Review* hosted a detailed roundtable discussion about the Swifties, featuring editors and reporters from the *Wall Street Journal, Houston Chronicle, Los Angeles Times*, and *USA Today*. There was no mention of the glaring gaps in the Swift Boat allegations.

On August 23, the *New York Times* ran a page-one story on the Swift Boat controversy and made no mention of the glaring gaps in the allegations against Kerry.

On August 24, a *Boston Globe* page-one article on the Swift Boat controversy made no mention about the glaring gaps in the allegations against Kerry.

On September 12, the *Philadelphia Inquirer*, in a page-one, 2,000-word article on the Swifty phenomenon made no mention of the glaring gaps in their allegations.

The fact that the allegations didn't hold up was of little or no interest to the campaign press corps. The correct journalistic approach was not all that hard to figure out: just report the facts and give news consumers some context. For instance, *The Los Angeles Times* did the right thing in an August 28 Swifty report, by stating clearly in the sixth paragraph that, "Numerous questions have been raised about the group's honesty and credibility." The fact that so often reporters could not even muster that minimum level of disclosure when dealing with a group as dishonest and conflicted as the Swifties was startling. Journalists simply abdicated their responsibility for fact-finding and let Republicans change the dynamics of the campaign.

A postscript. During the campaign the Swifties regularly demanded that Kerry release his complete military records which, they said, would clear up once and for all any confusion about his medals. The Swifties clearly implied there was embarrassing information buried in Kerry's Vietnam file; information that would confirm their wild claims about bogus medals. On May 20, 2005, Kerry belatedly did what the Swifties asked. (The puzzling delay angered some of his supporters.) He executed a Standard Form 180, okaying the Navy Personnel Command to release his "complete military service record and medical record." (Despite questions about Bush's Vietnam service surfacing over the course of two different presidential campaigns, Bush never executed a Standard Form 180.)

The records, which included glowing commodations from Swifties who later turned on Kerry, once again vindicated Kerry's combat service and represented just the latest wave of proof that the Swift Boat allegations leveled against him were baseless. So, given one final chance to set the record straight about the Swifties and highlight their hollow allegations, did the press make amends for abysmal performance in 2004? No.

On June 7, the *Boston Globe* published a modest article on page seven, noting the lack of evidence found in the files to substantiate any of the Swifty allegations. Yet the *Globe* emphasized in the third sentence that the documents actually raised questions about *Kerry*, asking why he didn't authorize the release earlier, not about his accusers who were once again revealed as untruthful. (It was the old it's-Kerry's-fault approach.)

That same day the *Boston Globe*, using information cobbled together from the same just-released Kerry documents, published another article about what poor grades Kerry received while attending Yale University in the 1960s. That story, an utterly trivial pursuit, ran on page one of the newspaper. And it was that angle that news outlets across the country picked up, while they essentially ignored the news that the documents which the Swifties had demanded be released in 2004 simply contradicted their claims, yet again.

Another major newspaper, the *Los Angeles Times*, covered the release of Kerry's military records, reporting, "Kerry provided access to his complete records. The long-awaited documents contained no bombshells, and his enemies still were not satisfied." Note how interested the *Times* was in playing up what Kerry's "enemies," and how the enemies were not satisfied. Indeed, the *Times* dutifully dialed up head Swifty John O'Neill and let him dissemble at will, never once asking him about the latest round of Swifties discrepancies. And when O'Neill complained that Kerry still hadn't met the Swifties' demands in terms of releasing military documents ("We asked him to universally release his entire file," he said), the *Times* played dumb. The truth is, in an August 27, 2004, op-ed published in the *Wall Street Journal*, O'Neill specifically requested that Kerry "execute Standard Form 180 so the American people can see your complete military record." When Kerry did just that, O'Neill said he didn't, and the press corps had no clue what the facts were.

It was just like old times.

CHAPTER 8

'This Is Scripted'

Thirteen days before he announced United States–led coalition forces had begun the war to "disarm Iraq, to free its people and to defend the world from grave danger," President Bush on the evening of March 6, 2003, strolled into the East Room of the White House at 8:02 p.m. for a rare press conference—just his eighth since taking office. With war looming, the evening was clouded in a strange dynamic. Perhaps trying to shake off allegations of being a cowboy charging towards war, Bush appeared oddly sedate throughout the prime-time appearance, talking slowly and in a pronounced hush. His low-key approach was mirrored by the ninety-four equally somnambulant reporters assembled that night in the East Room who meekly walked through the motions with Bush.

If anxious viewers at home were hoping for some last-minute insight from Bush to help ease their doubts about the imminent war, why it had to be fought now, and why so many of the United States' longtime allies around the world refused to support it, those viewers were likely disappointed as the president stuck to his well-worn talking points ("Saddam Hussein has had twelve years to disarm. He is deceiving people"). And for any viewers who held out hope that members of the assembled MSM would firmly, yet respectfully, press Bush for answers to tough questions about the pending invasion, they could have turned their TVs off at 8:05 p.m.

The press corps's barely-there performance that night, as reporters quietly melted into the scenery, coming at such a crucial moment in time remains an industry-wide embarrassment. Laying out the reasons for war, Bush that night mentioned al-Qaida and the terrorist attacks of September 11 thirteen times in less than an hour, yet not a single journalist challenged the presumed connection Bush was making

205

between Al Qaeda and Iraq, despite the fact that intelligence sources had publicly questioned any such association. And during the Q&A session, nobody bothered to ask Bush about the elusive Osama bin Laden, the terrorist mastermind whom Bush had vowed to capture. Follow-up questions were nonexistent, which only encouraged Bush to give answers to questions he was not asked.

At one point while making his way through the press questioners, Bush awkwardly referred to a list of reporters whom he was instructed to call on. "This is scripted," he joked. The press laughed. But Bush meant it was scripted, literally. White House spokesman Ari Fleischer later admitted he compiled Bush's cheat sheet, which made sure he did not call on reporters from some prominent outlets like *Time*, *Newsweek*, *USA Today*, or the *Washington Post*. Yet even after Bush announced the event was "scripted," reporters, either embarrassed for Bush or embarrassed for themselves, continued to play the part of eager participants at a spontaneous news conference, shooting their hands up in the air in hopes of getting Bush's attention. For TV viewers it certainly looked like an actual press event.

That was not the night's only oddly scripted moment. Before the cameras went live, White House handlers, in a highly unusual move, marched veteran reporters to their seats in the East Room, two-by-two, like school children being led onto the stage for the annual holiday pageant. The White House was taking no chances with the choreography. Looking back on the night, *New York Times* White House correspondent Elizabeth Bumiller defended the press corps' timid behavior: "I think we were very deferential because . . . it's live, it's very intense, it's frightening to stand up there. Think about it, you're standing up on prime-time live TV asking the president of the United States a question when the country's about to go to war," she told students at Towson University in Maryland. "There was a very serious, somber tone that evening, and no one wanted to get into an argument with the president at this very serious time."

It's unlikely viewers expected "an argument" that night in the East Room. But what about simply asking pointed questions and firmly requesting a direct response? On March 6, even that was beyond the media's grasp. The entire press conference performance was a farce— the staging, the seating, the questions, the order, and the answers.

Nothing about it was real or truly informative. It was, nonetheless, unintentionally revealing. Not revealing about the war, Bush's rationale, or about the bloody, sustained conflict that was about to be unleashed inside Iraq. Reporters helped shed virtually no light on those key issues. Instead, the calculated kabuki press conference, stage-managed by the White House employing the nation's most elite reporters as high-profile extras, did reveal what viewers needed to know about the mind-set of the MSM on the eve of war.

And for viewers that night who didn't get a strong enough sense of just how obediently in-step the press corps was with the White House, there was the televised post-press conference analysis. On MSNBC, for instance, *Hardball*'s Chris Matthews hosted a full hour of discussion. In order to get a wide array of opinion, he invited a pro-war Republican senator (Saxby Chambliss, from Georgia), a pro-war former Secretary of State (Lawrence Eagleburger), a pro-war retired Army general (Montgomery Meigs), pro-war retired Air Force general (Buster Glosson), a pro-war Republican pollster (Frank Luntz), as well as, for the sake of balance, somebody who, twenty-five years earlier, once worked in Jimmy Carter's White House (Pat Caddell).

Battered by accusations of a liberal bias and determined to prove their conservative critics wrong, the press during the run-up to the war—timid, deferential, unsure, cautious, and often intentionally unthinking—came as close as possible to abdicating its reason for existing in the first place, which is to accurately inform citizens, particularly during times of great national interest. Indeed, the MSM's failings were all the more important because of the unusually influential role they played in advance of the war-of-choice with Iraq. "When America has been attacked—at Pearl Harbor, or as on September 11—the government needed merely to tell the people that it was our duty to respond, and the people rightly conferred their authority," noted Harold Meyerson in the *American Prospect* magazine. "But a war of choice is a different matter entirely. In that circumstance, the people will ask why. The people will need to be convinced that their sons and daughters and husbands and wives should go halfway around the world to fight a nemesis that they didn't really know was a nemesis."

It's not fair to suggest the MSM alone convinced Americans to send some sons and daughter to fight. But the press went out of its way to tell a pleasing, administration-friendly tale about the pending war. In truth, Bush never could have ordered the invasion of Iraq—never could have sold the idea at home—if it weren't for the help he received from the MSM, and particularly the stamp of approval he received from so-called liberal media institutions such as the *Washington Post*, which in February of 2003 alone, editorialized in favor of war nine times. (Between September 2002 and February 2003, the paper editorialized *twenty-six times* in favor of the war.) The *Post* had plenty of company from the liberal East Coast media cabal, with high profile columnists and editors—the newfound liberal hawks—at the *New Yorker, Newsweek, Time,* the *New York Times*, the *New Republic* and elsewhere all signing on for a war of preemption. By the time the invasion began, the de facto position among the Beltway chattering class was clearly one that backed Bush and favored war. Years later the *New York Times Magazine* wrote that most "journalists in Washington found it almost inconceivable, even during the period before a fiercely contested midterm election [in 2002], that the intelligence used to justify the war might simply be invented." Hollywood peace activists could conceive it, but serious Beltway journalists could not? That's hard to believe. More likely journalists could conceive it but, understanding the MSM unspoken guidelines—both social and political—were too timid to express it at the time of war.

To oppose the invasion vocally was to be outside the media mainstream and to invite scorn. Like some nervous Democratic members of Congress right before the war, MSM journalists and pundits seemed to scramble for political cover so as to not subject themselves to conservative catcalls. One year later, a pro-war writer for *Slate* conceded he was "embarrassed" by his support for the ill-fated invasion but he insisted, "you've got to take risks." But supporting the war posed no professional risk. The only MSM risks taken at the time of the invasion were by pundits who staked out an unambiguous position in opposing the war.

Bush's rationale for war—Saddam Hussein, sitting on a swelling stockpile of weapons of mass destruction, posing a grave and imminent threat to America—turned out to be untrue. And for that, the press must shoulder some blame. Because the MSM not only failed to ask pressing questions, or raise serious doubts about the White House's controversial WMD assertion, but in some high-profile instances, such as with Judith Miller's reporting for the *New York Times*, the MSM were responsible for spreading the White House deceptions about Saddam's alleged stockpile; they were guilty of "incestuous amplification," as former Florida senator Senator Bob Graham called it. Being meek and timid and dictating administration spin amidst a wartime culture is one thing. But to be actively engaged in the spin, to give it a louder and more hysterical voice, is something else all together. In fact, the compliant press repeated almost every administration claim about the threat posed to America by Saddam. The fact that virtually every one those claims turned out to be false only added to the media's malpractice.

And when not playing up the threat of WMDs in 2002 and 2003, the press was busy playing down the significance of peace activists and war doubters, as the MSM instead handed over the press platform at times exclusively to pro-war drum beaters and government talking heads. The White House could not have asked for more. Of course, by March 2003, the White House had already become accustomed to having a compliant press diligently detail each and every one of the administration's War on Terror warnings, warnings that played to Bush's political strength by casting him as a wartime leader and warnings that almost always fell into the less-than-meets-the-eye category. The often overblown MSM reporting on terror threats, fed directly from the White House, segued right into the overblown reporting on Saddam's deadly arsenal, also fed directly from the White House. The latter would not have been possible without the former. The press's timid War on Terror coverage foreshadowed its timid WMD coverage.

As *Washington Post* ombudsman Michael Getler later wrote, the MSM's performance in 2002 and 2003—its inability and refusal to demand sharp answers to difficult questions about prewar intelligence—likely represented their most crucial newsroom failing in nearly half a century. "How did a country on the leading edge of the information age get this so wrong and express so little skepticism and challenge?" asked Getler. "How did an entire system of government and a free press set out on a search for something and fail to notice, or even warn us in a timely or prominent way, that it wasn't or might not be there?" The single word answer is, timidity.

Looking back, bigfoot journalists conceded they failed to do their jobs during the run-up to war. ABC's Ted Koppel admitted, "If anything, what we've been criticized for, and probably more justifiably, is that we were too timid before the war." Dan Rather agreed: "We did not do our job of pressing and asking enough questions often enough." They weren't the only ones disappointed. A majority of Americans thought the news media could have done a better job informing the public about Iraq and the stakes involved in going to war, according to an August 2005 survey conducted by the McCormick Tribune Foundation in Chicago.

While some journalists admitted their mistakes, most refused to admit it was political pressure from the right and a fear of being labeled unpatriotic that fueled the timidity. Instead, journalists offered up head-scratching explanations for their timorous prewar performance. PBS's Jim Leher's suggested journalists just weren't smart enough to have foreseen all the troubles that would plague Iraq following the invasion. Appearing on MSNBC's *Hardball*, Lehrer was asked by host Matthews about the press's wartime performance. Matthews noted, "During [the] course of the war, there was a lot of snap-to-it coverage. We're at war. We have to root for the country to some extent. You're not supposed to be too aggressively critical of a country at combat, especially when it's your own." Matthews asked Lehrer if he thought the press had failed to provide "critical analysis" in the months before the war.

> **Lehrer:** I do. The word "occupation," keep in mind, Chris, was never mentioned in the run-up to the war. It was "liberation." So as a consequence, those of us in journalism never even looked at the issue of occupation.
> **Matthews:** Because?
> **Lehrer:** Because it just didn't occur to us. We weren't smart enough to do it. I agree. I think it was a dereliction of our—in retrospective.

It never occurred to journalists that the United States might have to effectively occupy Iraq in the wake of the invasion? That's just not believable. It's far more likely journalists were too anxious to express their doubts during the drum-beating of early 2003. Lehrer later returned to the topic, suggesting even if journalists had been smart enough to figure out the occupation angle, it still would have been hard to report it out:

Lehrer: It would have been difficult to have had debates about that going in, when the president and the government of the—it's not talking about "occupation." They're talking about—it would have been—it would have taken some—you'd have had to have gone against the grain.

"Could 'courage' be the word Lehrer sought?" asked the Daily Howler. "Did he want to say: 'It would have taken some *courage*' " for the nation's press to have gone against the grain.

Equally odd, *Washington Post* columnist David Ignatius, looking back on the press's failings with regards to Iraq, suggested "The media were victims of their own professionalism. Because there was little criticism of the war from prominent Democrats and foreign policy analysts, journalistic rules meant we shouldn't create a debate on our own."

Little criticism of the war from prominent Democrats? In a sense, Ignatius was right and for *Post* readers that statement may have had a ring of truth to it simply because the *Post* seem to do such a masterful job of *ignoring* prewar criticism from prominent Democrats, like party stalwart Senator Ted Kennedy. In September 2002 he made a passionate, provocative, and newsworthy speech raising all sorts of doubts about the war. It garnered exactly one sentence—thirty-six words total—of coverage from the *Post*, which in 2002 printed more than a thousand articles and columns, totaling perhaps 1 million words about Iraq, but only set aside thirty-six words for Kennedy's antiwar cry. As for Ignatius's suggestions that journalists were supposed wait to be signaled by the political parties before leaping into action—that reporters and pundits couldn't raise doubts about the war because Democrats, supposedly, were not—that represented an entirely new standard for news gathering. Or did Bob Woodward and Carl Bernstein wait for Democrats to raise doubts about Watergate before the duo started making calls?

When the *Post* was not downplaying criticism from Democrats, it was downplaying the warnings from respected foreign policy analysts, and even decorated generals. On October 10, 2002, retired Marine General Anthony Zinni, the former head of Central Command for U.S. forces in the Middle East, delivered a keynote address at a Washington think tank where he outlined his grave concerns about the Bush administration's war with Iraq. Among the key points made by Zinni, who endorsed Bush during the 2000 campaign and whom Bush then hand-picked to serve as the United States' envoy to the Middle East, was that war with Iraq should not be the United States's top priority. "I'm not convinced we need to do this now," said Zinni. "I believe that [Saddam] can be deterred and is containable at this moment." How did the *Post* play the antiwar speech by one of the administration's own senior officials? It set aside 336 words, which were tucked away on page 16. (One year later Zinni spoke before the U.S. Naval Institute and the Marine Corps Association, undressed the administration for its bungled handling of the war, and famously described its misguided preemptive war effort as "a brain fart of an idea." The *Washington Post* declined to cover those remarks.)

Zinni was hardly alone in getting snubbed. A survey conducted by the liberal media watchdog group Fairness and Accuracy in Reporting focused on the first two weeks of February, 2003, when the debate about the war should have been raging on the public airwaves. The survey found that of 393 people interviewed on-camera for network news reports about the war, just 6 percent were people who expressed skepticism about the looming invasion. Keep in mind, at that time a majority of Americans—61 percent according to one national poll—expressed some skepticism over the war; specifically favoring diplomacy over invasion. But on television, the narrative was quite different. Additionally, according to Media Matters for America, 23 percent of U.S. senators voted to oppose the war in the fall of 2002, but only 11 percent of the senators invited to appear on the Sunday morning talk shows prior to the invasion were antiwar.

Then again it should not have been surprising that most guests invited by MSM producers to discuss the war on television were in favor of it, since so many of the experts were on the government payroll themselves. According to figures from media analyst Andrew Tyndall, of the 414 Iraq stories broadcast on NBC, ABC, and CBS from September 2002 until February 2003, almost all the stories could be traced back to sources from the White House, the Pentagon, or the State Department. Only 34 stories, or just 8 percent, were of independent origin.

Independence did not seem to be a trait held in particularly high regard by the MSM at the time. Prior to the invasion of Iraq, CNN's then-news chief Eason Jordan took the extraordinary step of making sure he received a personal okay from Pentagon officials regarding the retired military officers CNN planned to use as on-air commentators for its war coverage. As Jordan explained it, "I went to the Pentagon myself several times before the war started and met with important people there and said, for instance, at CNN, 'Here are the generals we're thinking of retaining to advise us on the air and off about the war.' And we got a big thumbs-up on all of them. That was important."

MSNBC was so nervous about employing an on-air liberal host opposing Bush's ordered invasion that it fired Phil Donahue preemptively in 2003, after an internal memo pointed out the legendary talk show host presented "a difficult public face for NBC in a time of war." MSNBC executives would not confirm—nor deny—the existence of the report, which stressed the corporate discomfort Donahue's show might present if it opposed the war while "at the same time our competitors are waving the flag at every opportunity." By canning Donahue, MSNBC made sure that cable viewers had no place to turn for a nightly opinion program whose host forcefully questioned the invasion. The irony was that at the time of Donahue's firing one month before bombs started falling on Baghdad, MSNBC officials cited the host's weak ratings as the reason for the change. In truth, Donahue was beating out Chris Matthews as MSNBC's highest-rated host.

Newspapers played it safe, too. In 2003 the *Columbia Journalism Review* called around to letters-page editors to gauge reader response to the looming war in Iraq and was told that at *The Tennessean* in Nashville letters were running 70 percent against the war, but that the newspaper was trying to run as many pro-war letters as possible in order to avoid accusations of bias.

Indeed, between the time Bush first included Iraq as part of the "axis of evil" in January 2002, and the time the invasion commenced in March 2003, the MSM didn't seem to know how to cover those who opposed the war. The press just wanted the protesters to go away. Maybe because, as influential broadcast news consulting firm Frank N. Magid Associates informed its clients, covering antiwar protesters turned off news consumers, according to its survey. On October 26, 2004, antiwar protesters staged a massive rally in Washington, D.C., drawing more than 100,000 people from across the country. The next day in a small piece on page 8 that was accompanied by a photo larger than the article itself, the *New York Times* reported falsely that "fewer people attended than organizers had said they hoped for." Two days later, scrambling to fix the article's obvious error, yet at the same time refusing to run an actual correction, the *Times* published a second, sort of do-over article about the rally. As historian Todd Gitlin noted, "the *Times* ran a rare nonapology apology story under the peculiarly passive headline, "Rally in Washington Is Said to Invigorate the Antiwar Movement," stating that the demonstration had drawn "100,000 by police estimates and 200,000 by organizers" this time declaring that the numbers "startled even organizers."

Meanwhile, editors at the *Washington Post* seemed similarly unsure with how to handle the October 2004 outpouring of antiwar sentiment in its backyard, as the newspaper dramatically downplayed the story. The *Post*'s ombudsman Michael Getler was not impressed. "Last Saturday, some 100,000 people, and possibly more, gathered in downtown Washington to protest against possible U.S. military action against Iraq," he wrote. "The *Post* did not put the story on the front page Sunday. It put it halfway down the front page of the Metro section, with a couple of ho-hum photographs that captured the protest's fringe elements." Months later Getler detailed the *Post*'s laundry list of misses when it came to covering the antiwar movement or even noteworthy displays of war doubt. The list is worth reading in full, while keeping in mind the extraordinary resources the *Post* devoted to covering the war story, albeit only certain parts of the war story:

> The [missed opportunities] started last August with the failure to record promptly the doubts of then-House Majority Leader Richard K. Armey (R-Tex.) and of Brent Scowcroft, the first President Bush's national security adviser. The first public hearings on the implications of war, held by the Senate Foreign Relations Committee, got just a few paragraphs at the end of stories. In September, there was no spot coverage of the testimony of three retired four-star generals before the Senate Armed Services Committee warning against an attack without exhausting diplomatic options and gaining United Nations backing. Soon after, a widely reported speech by Sen. Edward M. Kennedy

(D-Mass.) got one line in The Post, and large antiwar rallies in London and Rome went unreported the next day. In October, when more than 100,000 people gathered in Washington to protest war, the paper put the story in the Metro section. Then came complaints that a major speech by Sen. Robert C. Byrd (D-W.Va.), one of the few senators who has taken a strong antiwar position, was missed and that the story about the most recent bin Laden audiotape failed to point out bin Laden's description of Iraqi leaders as "infidels." An overflow town meeting on war policy in Alexandria was missed. A rare story last month estimating the cost of the war, which was front-page news elsewhere, ran on Page A19. The congressional testimony the following day of Deputy Defense Secretary Paul D. Wolfowitz, who discounted those cost estimates and who described as "wildly off the mark" previous testimony by the Army chief of staff that hundreds of thousands of troops might be needed for occupation duty, was not reported.

The MSM's awkward look-the-other-way approach to peace activists extended for years. In August 2005 Cindy Sheehan, a mother from Vacaville, California, whose son Casey was killed while serving in Iraq, set up a bring-the-troops-home vigil in Crawford, Texas, as Bush relaxed during his five-week vacation. On August 8, and one week into her campaign, the *New York Times* profiled Sheehan, reporting that much to the White House's chagrin, she and her antiwar protest had been "transformed into a news media phenomenon."

But had she really? The story certainly seemed compelling; an angry mom camped out on the side of the road in the 100 degree Texas heat waiting out a reluctant president who refused to meet with her but whose caravan of Secret Service SUVs actually sped past her in a cloud of dust on the way to a GOP fundraiser. Yes, reporters took an early interest. But as had become customary since 2003 when dealing with any antiwar protest story, the press proceeded with extreme caution.

Between August 5 and August 8, the time frame during which the *Times* called Sheehan a "phenomenon," here's how many times "Cindy Sheehan" was mentioned on CNN: eight.

Between August 5 and August 8, here's how many times "Britney Spears" was mentioned on CNN: eighteen.

During the second and third weeks of August the MSM did increase its coverage of Sheehan's protest, as her antiwar camp quickly swelled in size to include hundreds of fellow demontrators. (*USA Today* correctly described it as a "headline-grabbing national movement.") But there were still some notable MSM holdouts. For three weeks, as the protest story continued to mushroom, ABC's *Nightline* refused to touch it. (*Nightline* finally addressed the Sheehan story on August 19, giving it just seven minutes of air time.) The omission was telling because, despite the uptick in print coverage, the Sheehan story still had not crossed over into phenomenon territory for most television producers, and certainly not at network news outlets. For instance, between August 8 and August 18, ABC News aired more than fifty hours of morning and evening national news programming, but nentioned "Cindy Sheehan" just twenty-six times.

Compare that to the 2005 springtime news craze when Terri Schiavo's parents, who like Sheehan, staged a very public, and political, vigil for their child. The Schiavo story, cherished by conservatives, dominated the networks night after night. During the peak ten-day period of that saga, from March 20 to March 30, here's how many times ABC News mentioned "Terri Schiavo": 189. During that same stretch *Nightline* devoted four entire programs to the story. The message was clear: Schiavo, a right-to-life martyr (for some) was very big big news, but Sheehan, an antiwar martyr (for some), was not.

As Sheehan's star rose through August, so did the right-wing attacks. As nervous Bush supporters watched the president's approval rating slide, they unleashed their wrath on Sheehan, labeling the mourning mom a "crazy," "anti-Semite," "left-wing moonbat," "crackpot" whose behavior bordered on "treasonous" and who was nothing more than a "hysterical noncombatant." They also charged that Sheehan was a creation of the radical left, that she was being exploited, and she did not represent mainstream Americans. That kind of organized attack was to be expected from the conservative operatives. What was not expected was how easily some in the MSM absorbed those talking points for themselves. On MSNBC, Norah O'Donnell referred to the "left-wing supporters" behind Sheehan. Later she asked a guest if Sheehan had become "a tool of the left," while pressing another on whether it was wise for Sheehan to be associated with "antiwar extremists" camped out in Crawford. (At no point during the 2005 Schiavo story did an MSNBC anchor ever suggest the pro-life parents had become "tools of the right.")

The *Washington Post*'s Dana Milbank wondered out loud if Sheehan would be remembered as a modern-day Lyndon LaRouche, the fringe political figure who's been accused of being a cult leader and fascist, and who served a prison sentence for mail fraud and tax code violations. Later that month, Milbank gave prominent display in the *Post* to a right-wing activist who accused Sheehan of being a communist. Meanwhile, Milbank's *Post* colleague Mike Allen, appearing on CBS's *Face the Nation* on August 21, belittled the Crawford protesters by highlighting what he considered to be the camp's fringe elements: "Right now it's PETA, hippies, Naderites." Allen conveniently left out the fact that also in attendance at the Sheehan camp were military parents whose children had also been killed while serving in Iraq.

The *Atlanta Journal-Constitution* printed an opinion column in which a critic of Sheehan asserted "Cindy Sheehan evidently thinks little of her deceased son." Asked if that was appropriate, even in an opinion column, to suggest a mother "thinks little" of her dead son, the *Journal-Constitution*'s op-ed page editor David Beasley insisted the attack on Sheehan was fair game. Yet it's hard to imagine that if a prominent Georgia politician's son was killed in the line of duty the *Journal-Constitution* op-ed page would allow a columnist to assert that the politician thought little of his or her dead son.

At the same time several corporate-owned television stations refused to broadcast antiwar ads that Sheehan appeared in. In one ad Sheehan pleaded with Bush for a meeting and accused him of lying to the American people about Iraq's development of weapons of mass destruction and its connection to Al Qaeda. An ABC affiliate in Utah owned by Clear Channel Communications informed backers their ad was an "inappropriate commercial advertisement for Salt Lake City." A CBS affiliates in Boise, Idaho, also refused to air the ad, insisting its claim that Bush lied about Iraq's WMDs was not provable. The station's action was highly unusual. As the Associated Press noted in a 2004 article about political advertising, "Stations rarely reject commercials" over a concern about accuracy.

The following month, on September 24, Sheehan helped lead a

massive antiwar rally in Washington, D.C., which drew between 100,000 and 200,000 participants, making it the largest United States demonstration since the war began. Nonetheless, the event was effectively boycotted by television news outlets. Instead, CNN, Fox, and MSNBC were obsessed with providing wildly overexcited coverage of Hurricane Rita, which delivered less-than-expected damage as it came ashore in the marshlands along the Texas and Louisiana borders. Unlike Hurricane Katrina, the monster storm that decapitated New Orleans just weeks before, television news outlets struggled to find compelling images of real Rita-related devastation to justify their breathless, around-the-clock coverage, while at the same time they all but refused to even acknowledge the historic antiwar rally.

Question: If between 100,000 and 200,000 *pro-war* demonstrators had assembled in the nation's capital on that same September 2005 weekend and cheered Bush outside the White House, would the MSM have given them just cursory coverage, Rita or no Rita?

The night of the antiwar protest, NBC *Nightly News* at least managed to mention the rally on the air. Anchor Brian Williams, though, was careful to give one sentence to the antiwar protesters and one sentence to a small group of pro-war demonstrators who also gathered in Washington, D.C., that day. Antiwar forces absolutely dwarfed their pro-war counterparts but NBC news executives thought both groups deserved the same amount of coverage, with the subtext being dueling war demonstrators facing off against each other. That was a common MSM theme. CNN reported it "was a weekend of protests and counter-protests in Washington."

The MSM's ingrained timidity regarding war protesters, even in 2005, was telling because on the eve of the Sheehan-led rally, a CNN/*USA Today* poll revealed 67 percent of Americans disapproved of Bush's handling of the war in Iraq and 59 percent said sending troops to invade Iraq was a mistake. Both numbers represented public opinion high-water marks since the war began. Yet the press, still spooked about charges it was not being sufficiently pro-administration during a time of war, treated antiwar demonstrators with an overabundance of caution.

On Monday, September 26, when Sheehan along with 370 war protesters were arrested outside the White House, NBC's *Nightly News* ignored the arrests. Both the CBS and ABC nightly newscasts gave the arrests one sentence, downplaying the numbers involved. CBS reported Sheehan was arrested along with "dozens" of others. (As in, thirty-dozen?) The next morning CNN, ignoring the fact that nearly four hundred people chose to be arrested in order to protest the war, reported "Sheehan and *several others* were arrested." [Emphasis added.]

The MSM's signature 2002–2003 timidity during the run-up to war though, was most clearly visible in their reporting on weapons of mass destruction and the overblown prewar estimates about Iraq's firepower. The topic was absolutely essential. If the White House could prove, or at least convince most Americans, that Saddam posed an imminent danger, then the war of choice with Iraq would be easier to sell. Easier for Bush to announce, one month before the invasion, "My job is to protect the American people from further harm. I believe that Saddam Hussein is a threat to the American people." Any lingering, why-a-war-now doubts would hinder that sales pitch. In the fall of 2002 the White House needed to paint a picture of Saddam's Iraq as a country flooded with illegal chemical and biological warfare agents. The MSM was more than willing to help with the task.

A telling and comprehensive media study of the WMD coverage conducted by Center for International and Security Studies at Maryland (CISSM) and the University of Maryland and released in March 2004 concluded too many press stories simply repeated the "official line" on WMD regarding the Iraq war, and that most journalist accepted the Bush administration's linking of the War on Terror with WMDs, while at the same time failing to note that there was no precedent of terror organizations demonstrating the capacity to use WMDs. Simply put, "The American media did not play the role of checking and balancing the exercise of power that the standard theory of democracy requires," according to CISSM, which monitored WMD coverage between October 2002 and May 2003 from seven U.S. news outlets: *Christian Science Monitor, Los Angeles Times, New York Times, Washington Post, Newsweek, US News & World Report*, as well as NPR's *Morning Edition* and *All Things Considered.*

In retrospect, NBC's Brian Williams argued the MSM had no choice but to simply repeat what administration officials were saying about Saddam's alleged WMD arsenal. "We had no independent testing

authority," Williams told CNN. "We had to go with [what] the government experts and witnesses [were saying], including our own secretary
of state before the United Nations." Williams's predecessor Tom
Brokaw agreed, insisting "A lot of what happened during the lead-up to
[war] was unknowable." In truth, there was a long list of distinguished
military and political experts who were ready and willing—before the
war began—to illuminate NBC's viewers about the gaping holes in
Bush's justification for war and what the colossal hurdles would be
post-invasion. NBC anchors, though, were not overly interested in
hearing from them and yet years later insisted there was no way to have
known the war had been poorly thought out.

As the MSM watched Fox News post big rating numbers with its
openly conservative broadcasts while at the same time journalists were
being dogged by accusations of being too liberal, out of touch, and
unpatriotic in a time of national crisis, pressure mounted to prove they
could play nice with a Republican administration and forcefully back a
war. That seemed to be particularly true at the *New York Times*, which
knee-jerk conservatives had singled out as being too pro-peace in its
reporting. Executive editor Howell Raines wanted to show his right-
wing critics wrong. "According to half a dozen sources within the
Times, Raines wanted to prove once and for all that he wasn't editing the
paper in a way that betrayed his liberal beliefs," wrote Seth Mnookin in
his 2004 *Times* expose, *Hard News*. Mnookin quoted Doug Frantz, the
former investigative editor of the *Times*, who recalled how "Howell
Raines was eager to have articles that supported the war-mongering out
of Washington. He discouraged pieces that were at odds with the
administration's position on Iraq's supposed weapons of mass destruction and alleged links of Al Qaeda." The *New York Observer* later
reported, "One senior Washington bureau staffer said that as the Bush
administration edged closer to invasion, the editorial climate inside *The
Times* shifted from questioning the rationale for military action to putting the paper on a proper war footing. 'Everyone could see the war
coming. *The Times* wanted to be out front on the biggest story,' the
staffer said. 'It became the plan of attack.' "

For the administration, one cornerstone of its plan of attack was built
around Iraqi defectors who told reporters wild tales about Saddam's
WMDs. Shepherded to the press by Ahmad Chalabi, the unreliable,

glad-handing Iraqi defector who, much to the White House's delight, conned reporters with tales of Saddam's fearsome arsenal, the defectors were greeted as truth tellers. And perhaps nowhere were their tales told more excitedly than on the front pages of the *New York Times*, and most often told by the sympathetic Judith Miller who stood out as the paper's go-to person for anonymous heavy security scoops and who had risen to the top of the *Times*'s newsroom star system. Miller may have won the admiration of the *Times* leadership, but years prior to the war in Iraq at least one reporter with the paper voiced his distaste for Miller's unique style of pro-government reporting. According to the *Washington Post*, Craig Pyes, a former contract writer for the *Times* who teamed up with Miller for a series on Al Qaeda, complained about her in a December 2000 memo to *Times* editors and asked that his byline not appear on one piece:

> I'm not willing to work further on this project with Judy Miller. I do not trust her work, her judgment, or her conduct. She is an advocate, and her actions threaten the integrity of the enterprise, and of everyone who works with her. . . . She has turned in a draft of a story of a collective enterprise that is little more than dictation from government sources over several days, filled with unproven assertions and factual inaccuracies.

One of the *Times*'s first high-profile, post-9/11 defector stories came on December 20, 2001, when neoconservatives inside the White House were first pressing their case for an invasion of Iraq. The article was headlined, "An Iraqi Defector Tells of Work on at Least 20 Hidden Weaponsites." Written by Miller, the story wove the startling tale of Adnan Ihsan Saeed al-Haideri, a forty-three-year-old Iraqi who had fled his homeland in Kurdistan and who, according to Miller, "said he personally worked on renovations of secret facilities for biological, chemical, and nuclear weapons in underground wells, private villas, and under the Saddam Hussein Hospital in Baghdad as recently as a year ago." If verified, she noted, "his allegations would provide ammunition to officials within the Bush administration who have been arguing that Mr. Hussein should be driven from power partly because of his unwillingness to stop making weapons of mass destruction, despite his pledges to do so."

As James Bamford later detailed in *Rolling Stone*, al-Haideri was lying about his claims about Saddam. CIA officials, who had strapped al-Haideri up to polygraph tests for hours at a time, knew he was lying long before Miller ever wrote her ominous sounding article. (The CIA did not peddle the fake al-Haideri story to Miller, Chalabi did.) Regardless of its authenticity, al-Haideri's fanciful tale, trumpeted by the *Times*, proved to be invaluable to the White House. Wrote Bamford:

> For months, hawks inside and outside the administration had been pressing for a preemptive attack on Iraq. Now, thanks to Miller's story, they could point to "proof" of Saddam's "nuclear threat." The story was soon being trumpeted by the White House and repeated by newspapers and television networks around the world. It was the first in a long line of hyped and fraudulent stories that would eventually propel the U.S. into a war with Iraq—the first war based almost entirely on a covert propaganda campaign targeting the media.

The administration's war architects had set up a simple, yet foolproof way to disseminate pro-war propaganda through the *Times*; foolproof as long as *Times* reporters and editors played along. Here's how one former CIA analyst described the scheme to James Moore, writing in *Salon:*

> The White House had a perfect deal with Miller. Chalabi is providing the Bush people with the [Saddam] information they need to support their political objectives with Iraq, and he is supplying the same material to Judy Miller. Chalabi tips her on something and then she goes to the White House, which has already heard the same thing from Chalabi, and she gets it corroborated by some insider she always describes as a "senior administration official."

Round and round it went. Of course there were scores of senior intelligence officials within the administration, and specifically within the CIA, who refuted Chalabi's intelligence, but they never received the same type of airing in Miller's articles. In retrospect, Miller's Iraq reporting was in desperate need of balance, not to mention professional skepticism. Two page-one stories in particular stand out not only for being extraordinarily helpful to the White House's war efforts—in fact, the articles appear to have been spoon-fed by government officials—but also for being untrue.

The first arrived September 8, 2002, and was co-written with Michael Gordon. The duo were investigating the state of Iraq's arsenal and discovered that Saddam had made a bold initiative in hopes of reconstituting his nuclear weapons program. Two weeks earlier Vice President Dick Cheney announced in an August 26 speech, that "Many of us are convinced that Saddam Hussein will acquire nuclear weapons fairly soon . . . and subject the United States and any other nation to nuclear blackmail." Few independent arms experts signed off on Cheney's Armageddon warning. But that's where the *Times* September 8 expose came in. Keep in mind that the *Times* article surfaced after Bush's chief of staff and former General Motors executive Andy Card had famously explained that the administration held off from trying to publicly make the case for war during the summer months of 2002 because, "From a marketing point of view, you don't introduce new products in August."

So think of the *Times* September 8 article as the launch commercial in the war marketing effort. And what more could the White House have asked for than the so-called liberal *New York Times* trumpeting on its front page a Holy Shit-type exclusive that forcefully reported, "More than a decade after Saddam Hussein agreed to give up weapons of mass destruction, Iraq has stepped up its quest for nuclear weapons and has embarked on a worldwide hunt for materials to make an atomic bomb, Bush administration officials said today." Specifically, the article relayed on administration claims that Saddam had been trying to import thousands of high-strength aluminum tubes used for rotors in centrifuges to enrich uranium, a key step in producing an atomic bomb. None of the tubes ever reached Iraq. The article came complete with colorful quotes from administration officials who feared a "mushroom cloud" if Saddam's mad arms march was not stopped.

At times it was difficult for readers to discern where White House spin ended and the *Times* reporting began. Adopting the administration rhetoric with astonishing ease, Miller and Gordon wrote, "Mr. Hussein's *dogged insistence on pursuing his nuclear ambitions,* along with what defectors described in interviews as Iraq's push to improve and expand Baghdad's chemical and biological arsenals, have brought Iraq and the United States to the brink of war." [Emphasis added.] Of course, arms inspectors later determined that allegations about Saddam's "nuclear ambitions" were erroneous.

The tubes article, which was later discredited, appeared on a Sunday. That morning administration officials, the same who ones who likely leaked the story in the first place, hyped the *Times* exclusive on the morning talk shows. On CNN's *Late Edition*, National Security Adviser Condoleezza Rice insisted the tubes "are only really suited for nuclear weapons programs, centrifuge programs." She added: "We don't want the smoking gun to be a mushroom cloud," using the exact same language as one of the off-the-record administration sources featured in the *Times* exclusive. The synergy between the White House and the *Times* was stunning, even to other members of the MSM. "You leak a story to the *New York Times* and the *New York Times* prints it, and then you go on the Sunday shows quoting the *New York Times* and corroborating your own information," noted CBS reporter Bob Simon. "You've got to hand it to them. That takes, as we say here in New York, chutzpah."

As Michael Massing wrote in the *New York Review of Books*, "The September 8 story on the aluminum tubes was especially significant. Not only did it put the *Times'* imprimatur on one of the administration's chief claims, but it also established a position at the paper that apparently discouraged further investigation into this and related topics." In other words, Miller, a star reporter, had publicly and forcefully staked out her, and the paper's, position regarding Saddam's WMD. Unfortunately for both, it was the wrong position.

The *Times* tubes article immediately raised doubts among scientists and other independent experts who did not believe the tubes in question would have been used for making nuclear weapons. At least one, David Albright, director of the Institute for Science and International Security, contacted Miller after the article ran and spoke with her at length, relaying the skepticism he and others had. A follow-up to the tubes story was imminent and the *Times* had two choices. It could step back and emphasize the doubts being raised regarding the story being told by the White House, thereby deflating some of the original article's hyperbole, or the paper could stick close to the president and forge ahead with the Saddam-might-have-nukes narrative. Miller opted for the latter. Said Albright after reading the *Times* follow-up tubes article, "I thought for sure she'd quote me or some people in the government who didn't agree. It just wasn't there."

Fast forward to Iraq, April 2003, and Miller was embedded with U.S. forces, hunting for WMDs, sporting a military uniform, and boasting top-secret security clearance no other reporter—let alone *Times* editor—could match. (Secretary of Defense Donald Rumsfeld reportedly signed off on Miller's unique arrangement.) It seemed clear Miller, rewarded for her bellicose prewar WMD reporting, had landed a unique role in the search for WMDs, although one that would be hard to describe as a journalist. Instead, she seemed to be more of quasi government agent who happened to file dispatches on deadline. As the *Washington Post*'s Howard Kurtz reported, "More than a half-dozen military officers said that Miller acted as a middleman between the Army unit with which she was embedded and Iraqi National Congress leader Ahmed Chalabi, on one occasion accompanying Army officers to Chalabi's headquarters, where they took custody of Saddam Hussein's son-in-law. She also sat in on the initial debriefing of the son-in-law, these sources say. Since interrogating Iraqis was not the mission of the unit, these officials said, it became a "Judith Miller team," in the words of one officer close to the situation. Kurtz also quoted an anonymous senior staff officer complaining, "It's impossible to exaggerate the impact she had on the mission of this unit, and not for the better."

Miller was embedded with the high-profile WMD military search team, Mobile Exploitation Team (MET) Alpha, which was combing Iraq looking for the same weapons Miller had spent so much of 2002 hyping. Being embedded with MET Alpha—the best seat in the house—and being the first reporter to break the worldwide news when MET Alpha found the WMDs was going to be Miller's victory lap, and likely lock up her second Pulitzer Prize award in three years. And on April 21, it all seemed to come together when Miller filed her biggest post-invasion scoop: "Illicit Arms Kept Till Eve of War, an Iraqi Scientist Is Said to Assert." In it, she reported MET Alpha had hit the trifecta in the sands of Iraq when it located a scientist who said he worked in Iraq's chemical weapons program for more than a decade and that: (a)

He'd "led Americans to a supply of material that proved to be the building blocks of illegal weapons." (b) He insisted Saddam had destroyed chemical weapons and biological warfare equipment just days before the war began. (c) And Saddam had also ferried lots of WMDs into Syria for safekeeping, which explained why U.S. forces couldn't find them. In case readers missed the implications, Miller reported that the scientist's allegation "supports the Bush administration's charges that Iraq continued to develop those weapons and lied to the United Nations about it." Indeed, the scientist represented the answer to anxious White House prayers.

But when readers delved deeper into the story, Miller's account became more peculiar as she revealed that she had no independent confirmation on any of the information; it was all relayed to her by MET Alpha commanders. That's because Miller was never told the scientist's name, she could not confirm he was a scientist, she was not allowed to interview him, and she was not allowed to visit his home. She was, however, allowed to look at him, from a distance, and watch as he "pointed to several spots in the sand where he said chemical precursors and other weapons material were buried." Additionally, Miller agreed not to write about the scientist and his claims for three days while military officials read over her story and okayed it for publication. In other words, military officials provided Miller with a string of exclusive and extraordinary WMD revelations via the scientist. Miller then typed the information up and military officials double-checked it to make sure she got everything right. The next day, appearing on PBS, Miller hyped the scientist's story even harder, suggesting he was better than a "smoking gun" of Saddam's WMD arsenal. To Miller, the alleged scientist was "a silver bullet in the form of a person." (Reporter James Moore noted that during the same PBS appearance Miller referred to scientists, plural, whom the MET Alpha team had found; her article referred only to a single mysterious scientist.)

Like Bush's infamous March 6 press conference, Miller's MET Alpha article should be studied and dissected in journalism schools for years to come. The fact that it was printed as-is, with no independent verification of any kind, on the front page of the *New York Times* was stunning. But in retrospect, the "wacky-assed piece," as one anonymous *Times*man famously dubbed it, served a very useful purpose—it illustrated just how dramatically the wartime mind-set among top *Times* editors had shifted, to the point where they thought that kind of trust-me brand journalism was acceptable. (It's ironic: During the Clinton years, high-profile reporters at the *Times* cut journalism corners writing dubious Whitewater stories that embarrassed the White House. But during the Bush years, *Times* reporters cut journalism corners writing dubious WMD stories that aided the White House.)

Needless to say, the scientist's claims championed by Miller were never verified, and the United States' handpicked weapons inspector—and war supporter—David Kay, concluded the WMDs were nowhere to be found. Or as Kay put it, "There were no stockpiles of weapons of mass destruction at the time of the war." In 2005 Miller did concede her WMD articles failed to hold up, but Miller insisted everyone else got it wrong, too: "W.M.D.—I got it totally wrong. The analysts, the experts and the journalists who covered them—we were all wrong. If your sources are wrong, you are wrong."

But other reporters found the right sources prior to the war. Knight Ridder's Warren Strobel and Jonathan Landay wrote in October 2002 about a "bitter feud over secret intelligence" that was unfolding between the CIA and Bush administration appointees at the Pentagon who were pushing for the war rationale. "The dispute," they wrote "pits hardliners long distrustful of the U.S. intelligence community, against professional military and intelligence officers who fear the hawks are shaping intelligence analyses to support their case for invading Iraq." Another Knight Ridder piece quoted an anonymous official who said "analysts at the working level in the intelligence community are feeling very strong pressure from the Pentagon to cook the intelligence books." Miller never wrote those kinds of stories during the run-up to war. Instead of sparking debate over intelligence, she, along with the White House, seemed intent on snubbing it out.

Walter Pincus, the veteran national security reporter for the *Washington Post*, was another notable example. Prior to the war Pincus wrote a string of insightful articles about the type of intelligence the administration was leaning on to justify a preemptive war. Those stories included "Bush Clings To Dubious Allegations About Iraq," "U.S. Lacks Specifics on Banned Arms," "Alleged Al Qaeda Ties Questioned; Experts Scrutinize Details of Accusations Against Iraqi Government," and "Making the Case Against Baghdad; Officials: Evidence Strong, Not Conclusive."

The only problem was, prior to the war Pincus's prophetic dispatches were routinely buried by his editors inside the *Post*'s A section, on page 13, 16, 18, or 21. It wasn't until three months after the invasion when the elusive weapons of mass destruction could not be found that *Post* editors began to regularly feature Pincus's Iraq exposes on the front page. "[They] went through a whole phase in which they didn't put things on the front page that would make a difference," Pincus complained.

The same mind-set was on display at the *New York Times;* breathless scoops about Saddam's mighty arsenal were paraded on page 1, while insightful examinations about doubts surrounding prewar intelligence got buried. For instance, the *Times*'s James Risen completed "C.I.A. Aides Feel Pressure in Preparing Iraqi Reports" days before the invasion began. Yet editors held the article for a week before finally publishing it on page B10.

Given that reticence, it was not surprising that MSM outlets were so slow in admitting their prewar shortcomings. As early as July 2003, *Slate* media critic Jack Shafer, looking back on Miller's overexcited reporting, labeled it "wretched." The *Times* leadership, though, did nothing. Nine months later, in March 2004, the paper's public editor, badgered by readers asking that the paper hold itself accountable for its fraudulent reporting, asked executive editor Keller about the issue. In a dismissive response, he insisted there was no need to recant Miller's reporting, that she was a "fearless" journalist, that her critics basically didn't know what they were talking about, and that an internal review would simply "consume more of my attention than I was willing to invest." (During the run-up to war in 2002 and 2003 Keller worked as a *Times* columnist and wrote for the Sunday *Times Magazine*, where he supported the war and wrote glowingly of Paul Wolfowitz, then-deputy defense secretary and chief architect of the Iraq invasion.)

On May 26, 2004, the *Times*, without mentioning Miller by name, finally addressed the paper's faulty WMD reporting. In its "From the Editors" note, *Times* leaders conceded the reporting was "not as rigorous as it should have been." Keller though, remained in a defensive crouch. "I don't see this as an apology," he told the *Boston Globe* the day the editors' note was published. "I see this as an explanation. It's not a note that's going to satisfy our most bloodthirsty critics." He stressed that while there may be a "small lynch mob of people who want to see someone strung up," it was time for the *Times*, "to move on" from the debate; to get past the annoying "distraction" of the paper's faulty WMD reporting. It was telling that the *Times*'s "mini-culpa," as Shafer dubbed it, only appeared after the *Times* public editor tipped off the paper's leadership that he was going to investigate, and write about, the *Times*'s prewar reporting. (He later called it "very bad journalism.")

Another year later, and now nearly thirty months after the invasion, the *Times* was still wrestling with the ghost of Miller's war reporting after she got dragged into court as part of the ongoing criminal investigation into which Bush White House insider leaked the identity of CIA operative Valerie Plame, the wife of a prominent Bush administration war critic. Miller stood her ground and served eighty-five days in jail rather than cooperate with prosecutors, a move the *Times* cheered from its editorial page. But when Miller emerged from prison only to announce she couldn't remember who leaked her the sensitive information (it was not Cheney's top aid, Scooter Libby, she insisted), nor could she recall why she had scribbled the name "Valerie Flame" in a notebook she brought back from a July 2003 meeting with Libby at the time Plame's name was being leaked by the White House, the notion that Miller had swapped her allegiance from the *Times* to the White House became impossible to ignore. Amid the unfolding scandal, which did deep damage to the newspaper's reputation, Keller addressed the staff in an October 21 memo and was forced, yet again, to circle back to the paper's faulty prewar reporting. "I wish we had dealt with the controversy over our coverage of WMD as soon as I became executive editor [in July 2003]. At the time, we thought we had compelling reasons for kicking the issue down the road," Keller explained. "The paper had just been through a major trauma, the Jayson Blair episode, and needed to regain its equilibrium. It felt somehow unsavory to begin a tenure by attacking our predecessors." (Blair was a young reporter who had duped *Times* editors into publishing scores of his fictitious news reports.) "I was trying to get my arms around a huge new job, appoint my team, get the paper fully back to normal, and I feared the WMD issue could become a crippling distraction."

That's a plausible explanation. But there was likely another, unspoken, element in play—Keller in 2003 simply didn't feel like he had to deal with the WMD controversy because the criticism mostly came from the left (i.e., the "small lynch mob"), and from the MSM perspective in 2003, antiwar critics did not have to be engaged, which was part of the larger media mind-set during the Bush years of ignoring their liberal critics.

But try to imagine a parallel universe where the WMD facts had been reversed. Imagine that Miller, playing up tips from Democrats and progressives, had been aggressively skeptical in her prewar reporting about administration claims about Saddam's WMDs, and that time and again her editors gave Miller's pro-peace-flavored dispatches page-one placement. But then months after the invasion, U.S. troops uncovered WMD stockpiles bigger and deadlier than even the administration officials had claimed. At that point right-wing press critics like Rush Limbaugh, Michelle Malkin, and the team at *Weekly Standard* would have declared war on the *Times*, accusing the paper of undermining the president, putting the nation at risk, and being driven by a blind liberal bias. The notion that, beset with those kinds of outside political attacks, editor Keller would have kicked the Miller controversy down the road for a year or more because it would have been too messy to deal with is just not believable. Instead, following an immediate internal review, Miller likely would have been quietly relieved from the paper within six months of the invasion. In reality though, *Times* leadership, for nearly two years, did not treat criticism of Miller's reporting seriously. In fact, if it hadn't been for the subpoena power of Fitzgerald, whose investigation cast the spotlight on the *Times*'s regrettable prewar performance, it's doubtful the paper, based on its halfhearted effort at self-examination in 2004, would have ever come clean.

The *Times* WMD embarrassment was not an isolated incident. In fact, it fit into a larger pattern that the paper's leaders refused to address, let alone fix. Just as with its dishonest Whitewater coverage in the 1990s and its misleading coverage of Wen Ho Lee, the scientist inside the Los Alamos National Laboratory who was wrongly charged with espionage, a charge the *Times* hyped relentlessly, the paper continued to let itself be used by partisan Republicans who were planting and pushing phony stories for political advantage. During the Clinton years the fantastic tales—Whitewater and Wen Ho Lee—were designed to embarrass a Democratic president. During the Bush years the fantastic tale about WMDs was designed to help start a war. In each case the *Times*, anxious to shed its "liberal media" tag, fell for the ploy, promoted the false stories, and did severe damage to the newspaper's reputation in the process.

Both the press and the White House were guilty of hyping the WMDs' existence, and both often avoided taking a serious look back. Unless, of course, it was to look back and have a good laugh together about the administration's fruitless hunt. The backslapping occurred on March 24, 2004, at the annual black-tie dinner of the Radio and Television Correspondents Association, held at the Washington Hilton. The eagerly anticipated social event attracted a media-saturated crowd of approximately 1,500 people who were treated to a tongue-in-cheek address from Bush. Tradition held that sitting presidents took the opportunity at the Correspondents dinner to poke fun at the press as well as themselves. Bush did just that during his ten-minute, professionally written monologue, delivering some topical zingers: *"Queer Eye for the Straight Guy.* My Cabinet could take some pointers from watching that show. In fact, I'm going to have the Fab Five do a makeover on [Attorney General John] Ashcroft."

Then Bush turned to the "White House Election-Year Album," as photos flashed on the screen behind his podium. One showed Bush gazing out an oval office window as he provided the narration: "Those weapons of mass destruction must be somewhere!" The audience laughed. Then came a picture of Bush on his hands and knees peering under White House furniture. "Nope, no weapons over there!" The MSM audience laughed harder. And then came a snapshot of Bush searching behind the drapes. "Maybe under here?" The audience roared in approval—Bush couldn't find the WMDs!

The next morning, newspaper reporters who laughed out loud themselves at the Correspondents dinner dutifully typed up the jokes. It wasn't until some Democratic members of Congress, along with parents whose children had been killed in Iraq, expressed their disgust that it dawned on some members of the MSM that Bush's jokes might be considered offensive. Even after objections were raised the MSM rallied around Bush arguing the jokes were no big deal. In fact, it was telling

how the MSM were reading off the exact same talking points as the
Bush supporters in the right-wing press. Their mutual message was
simple—lighten up! On *National Review Online*, conservative talk show
host Michael Graham, who attended the Correspondents dinner,
mocked the critics: "Somehow, over the past 30 years, liberalism has
mutated into something akin to an anti-comedy vaccine. The more
you're Left, the less you laugh."

The supposedly liberal *Los Angles Times* completely agreed. In an
unsigned editorial, the paper belittled Democrats and anyone else who
had the nerve to question Bush's sense of wartime humor, or daring to
question Beltway tradition: "The truly serious thing about what's known
as Washington's 'Silly Season' is whether presidents rise to the challenge." On Fox News, there was heated agreement between *Sunday
News* anchor Chris Wallace and the network's Washington bureau
managing editor, Brit Hume, that Bush's WMD jokes were perfectly
acceptable.

Wallace: "I still think it's funny."
Hume: "I thought it was a good-natured performance."

But what about Fox liberal Juan Williams? He also had no patience
for the Bush critics upset about the jokes: "I think people are petty in
the situation."

Washington Post news reporter and Fox panelist Ceci Connelly concurred: "The pictures were funny. I laughed at the photos."

To his credit, MSNBC's Chris Matthews was among the few Beltway
celebrity pundits who separated from the pack and expressed real
resentment over the poor taste displayed by Bush and his press apolo-
gists: "I wonder if they're spending a day at Walter Reed Hospital
with all the guys who had limbs amputated and brain injuries and
things like that, how funny they think it is that the reason they were
given for fighting this war is now the butt of humor by their commander in chief."

The MSM's meek performance prior to the war did not spring out of
a vacuum—the WMD charade, the mad rush to quote government
sources, and the knee-jerk attempt to undermine and ignore administra-

tion critics. It was all telegraphed in the wake of 9/11 and through the early stages of the press's deferential War on Terror coverage, which worked full-time to portray Bush as a savvy wartime president. Those efforts didn't come any more devoted than *Washington Post*'s 2002 eight-piece series, "10 Days in September: Inside the War Cabinet," in which reporters Bob Woodward and Dan Balz were given extraordinary access to the White House and in exchange explained away lingering questions about Bush's response to 9/11, like why he spent that day flying around the country instead of returning to the capitol, and why it was his flak Karen Hughes who first addressed the nation and took questions that traumatic day, not Bush or Cheney. The duo also covered up for the White House regarding its phony cover story that a coded message had come in on 9/11 indicating Air Force One was a terrorist target.

Conservative pundits cheered the series, suggesting it was a Pulitzer Prize must-win. Raves from the right were understandable. To say the series presented the administration, and Bush in particular, in a favorable light would be an understatement. Readers saw Bush utterly sure of himself, operating on gut instincts, leading roundtable discussions, formulating complex strategies, asking pointed questions, building international coalitions, demanding results, poring over speeches, and seeking last-minute phrase changes.

The portrait was so contrary to the public's previous perception of the president that it was reminiscent of the classic *Saturday Night Live* sketch that ran at the height of the Iran-Contra scandal and featured an outwardly jolly and oblivious Ronald Reagan, who in private Oval Office meetings revealed himself as a mastermind of the complicated arms-for-hostage operation, barking out orders to befuddled cabinet members. In the same way, but without satire, the *Post* series suggested that a president often depicted prior to 9/11 as a genial delegator of duties, who ducked the Vietnam War with a stateside post in the Texas Air National Guard, was in fact a natural, hands-on commander in chief of the War on Terror.

From the ubiquitous flag pin lapels for anchor men and women and the stirring news team theme music to the permanent terror alert logos sketched into the corner of television screens, the MSM broadcast their allegiance. It was CBS anchor Dan Rather, on September 17,

2002, declaring, "George Bush is the president, he makes the decisions. Wherever he wants me to line up, just tell me where. And he'll make the call."

Twenty months after announcing he'd take orders from Bush, Rather, as the war in Iraq unfolded, made another public proclamation: "Look, I'm an American. And when my country is at war, I want my country to win, whatever the definition of 'win' may be. Now, I can't and don't argue that that is coverage without a prejudice. About that I am prejudiced." NBC's Brian Williams called it "the 9/11 syndrome," or "guilty of settling in to too comfortable a journalistic pattern." Some outside the MSM likely preferred the phrase "dictation." It was the kind of pronounced and prolonged presidential press reverence likely not seen in this country in half a century.

ABC News's White House correspondent Terry Moran claimed he was offended when he overheard two print reporters talking inside the briefing room in January 2002, as they awaited spokesman Ari Fleischer's arrival to face mounting questions about the administration's role in the burgeoning Enron business scandal. "I heard people saying, 'All right, we're back, to hell with the war [in Afghanistan],' as if chasing the shadows and ghosts of potential appearances or possible conflicts of interest [regarding Enron] was more important than the war the country had been thrust into," Moran told *American Journalism Review*. "I was shocked . . . I'm not sure that lower Manhattan had actually stopped smoldering." Four months after the attacks of 9/11, Moran thought it was still inappropriate for reporters to pose tough questions to the White House.

That was the prevailing MSM attitude as 2002 unfolded. Then halfway through the year the administration doubled down and secured another round of free passes when it signaled its interest in invading Iraq. Between the War on Terror and the war with Iraq, the Bush White House all but guaranteed itself a timid press corps that emphasized its megaphone function. The MSM coverage of the War on Terror and their reporting during the run-up to the invasion of Iraq were inexorably linked. By the time the invasion was launched in March of 2003, the press was so comfortable having spent the previous year lying down for the White House and its foreboding War on Terror, that it could not muster enough energy to get up off the floor.

What was telling, and often ignored by the MSM, was how the White House's choreographed terror alerts so often coincided with crass political maneuvering; jockeying the MSM refused to acknowledge. For instance, the first noticeable wave of terror scares came in early 2002, in the weeks surrounding Bush's hawkish "Axis of Evil" State of the Union Address, in which the first seeds for an invasion of Iraq were publicly planted. In his speech Bush warned about "thousands of dangerous killers" who had spread throughout the world "like ticking time bombs set to go off without warning." Later, White House communications director Karen Hughes told reporters 100,000 men had been trained in Al Qaeda camps and were now scattered in sixty countries.

The same week, FBI Director Robert Mueller warned Americans that undetected Al Qaeda sleeper cells may still be operating on American soil. Secretary of Defense Donald Rumsfeld warned Americans to prepare for other attacks that "could grow vastly more deadly than those we suffered" September 11. And CIA Director George Tenet sent a report to Congress indicating agents found crude diagrams of nuclear weapons in a suspected Al Qaeda safe house in Afghanistan. Maybe the scariest scenario of all was an alleged terrorist plot to fly a commercial airliner into an American nuclear power plant.

The bad news came so fast and furious that it was hard to get a handle on what was more upsetting; that the Bush administration, which had previously maintained absolute secrecy about its domestic antiterror operations, was suddenly so talkative, or that the media reported the thinly documented terror threats so breathlessly and uncritically. This was the same administration, after all, that refused to identify hundreds of mostly Middle Eastern immigrants jailed in the United States in the wake of September 11, that ordered many routine immigration hearings closed to the public and mandated records of the proceedings not be released to anyone. It also refused to release the identities of Al Qaeda fighters held at Guantánamo Bay, Cuba, and proposed that accused terrorists be tried in secret military tribunals. Yet when it came to suggestive and potentially deadly terrorist scenarios, the White House opened the spigots for the press.

Of course, for careful news consumers who read deep into news stories and searched out lots of different perspectives, they soon realized the dire warnings coming from the White House were not all that they appeared to be. Those 100,000 Al Qaeda-trained terrorists roaming the world? One week after the allegation was made by the White House, *Newsweek* reported that intelligence officials thought the number was inflated . . . by 90,000.

The White House alone controlled virtually all the information about the war on terrorism and it alone decided how that information was disseminated. The press, anxious for access, eagerly played along. That snug relationship was on stark display on January 17, 2002, just weeks before Bush's State of the Union Address. That's when Attorney General John Ashcroft and FBI Director Mueller held a hurried press conference, carried live on CNN, to unveil five videotapes found in the rubble of a home near Kabul, Afghanistan owned by Muhammad Atef, a top aide of bin Laden's. Five men seen on the tapes were identified as deadly terrorists, who, in the words of Ashcroft, "may be trained and prepared to commit future suicide terrorist attacks."

What made the discovery so unsettling, Ashcroft said, was the fact that "the videotapes depict young men delivering what appear to be martyrdom messages from suicide terrorists." The nation's top crime fighter added that the seriousness of the threat demanded the information be released immediately. The names and pictures of the five Al Qaeda members were distributed to the press as a sort of worldwide version of the TV show *America's Most Wanted*, as Ashcroft asked for tips from concerned world citizens in helping track the men down.

The press eagerly complied. The *New York Times* played the story on page 1, where it also ran color head shots of the men. The *Washington Post* also printed the story on its front page, reporting excitedly that "five al-Qaeda members . . . may be on the loose and planning suicide attacks against Western targets." (Then again, they "may" not.) Meanwhile, CNN reported extensively about the "extraordinary videotape." In fact, there wasn't a television news operation in the country that didn't display the government's most-wanted poster of the five Al Qaeda members. It was the best War on Terror prop producers had had in weeks.

Naturally it's newsworthy when government officials lay out those sorts of terror warnings, and nobody's suggesting they should be ignored. But it's also the press's job to seek context and perspective, and pry additional information from officials to determine just how dire the threats might be. Because there was something odd about Ashcroft's breathless news bulletin. For instance, pressed further at the press conference, Ashcroft seemed to back away from his original, already tentative description of the taped utterances, suggesting, "We believe that these could be, and likely appear to be, sort of, martyrdom messages from suicide terrorists." Sort of? Either the statements were martyrdom messages or they were not. Even the overworked Arabic translators inside the government should have been able to make that simple distinction.

Meanwhile, what exactly did the men say on the tapes? Journalists were never told, because before being shown snippets of the tapes, the government stripped all the sound off and refused to provide a printed transcript. Reporters instead were reduced to describing the men's silent gesticulations in an effort to wring out any meaning. There was even less to the story than that. Ashcroft and Mueller did not know, or would not say, if the men planned any imminent attacks, when the tapes were made, when the tapes were found, who found the tapes, what the nationalities of the five men were, if they were in America, or even if they were dead or alive.

No matter. The tapes were universally treated as very big news. Two weeks later though, in a brief, 235-word aside, the *Washington Post* revealed intelligence officials had determined the martyrdom tapes had actually been made more than two years earlier, raising doubts about the fear of "imminent" suicide attacks. Would the *Post* or the *New York Times* have originally played that story on page 1 if Ashcroft had forthrightly announced the so-called suicide tapes had been made in 1999? Probably not. But that's how the War on Terror press game was played; Ashcroft garnered huge headlines with frightening allegations about terrorist threats, and then when the stories petered out the MSM obediently looked away.

On February 20, 2003, when Ashcroft personally announced the terrorist indictment of Sami Al-Arian, a former University of South Florida professor, the news conference was carried live on on CNN (Ashcroft tagged Al-Arian the North American leader of the Palestinian Islamic Jihad) and the story generated a wave of excited media attention. Al-Arian's case never had anything to do with bin Laden or Saddam, but Bush's Justice Department, which indicted Al-Arian just one month before the invasion of Iraq, made sure to leave the impression that the crucial terror case would keep America safe. That night, ABC's *World News Tonight* led its newscast with the Al-Arian indictment. Both NBC and CBS also gave the story prominent play that evening. But fast forward to December 2005 when, in an embarrassing blow to prosecutors, Al-Arian was acquitted by a conservative Tampa, Florida, jury. Big news, right? Nope. That night, neither ABC, CBS, nor NBC led with the terror case on their evening newscasts. None of them slotted it second or third either. In fact, none of networks reported the acquittal *at all*. The odds that the networks would have ignored the conclusion of the Al-Arian trial if the jury had returned a guilty verdict in a case that the government had called a centerpiece to its War on Terror? Zero.

By early 2003, with the war in Iraq only weeks away, the MSM, and particularly the cable news outlets, had taken their unique brand of "Fear Factor" programming to new extremes (remember the duct tape scare?), never pausing to ask whether the red-hot terror rhetoric streaming out of the administration was intended to accomplish anything besides whip up hysteria about Arab terrorists and placing the country on a firm war setting for the Iraq invasion.

"With terrorists out there somewhere, how scared should you be?" asked CNN one month before the invasion. Terror experts displayed the hottest models of gas masks on television, the way toy gurus usually run down the must-have gifts during the Christmas buying season; endless what-if chatter about possible terrorist attacks replaced the kind of hype that usually comes with the arrival of a category-four hurricane. ABC News, trotting out its *Good Morning America* home-improvement editor, showed viewers how to turn a laundry room into a fallout shelter with duct tape and drop cloths.

Solid reporting could have helped relieve some of the anxiety surrounding terror threats, instead of heightening it. For instance, the Pentagon's decision to deploy Avenger surface-to-air missile launchers around Washington, D.C., at the time clearly ratcheted up the panic level. The New York *Daily News* simply reported they were there to "protect prime targets—the White House, Congress and the Pentagon—from an aerial attack."

But an aerial attack from whom? The newspaper never asked. Neither Saddam nor bin Laden had planes or missiles that could reach America. Of course, Al Qaeda successfully turned commercial jets into missiles. But if seventeen months after 9/11 the government was placing surface-to-air missile launchers to shoot down hijacked planes as a last defense before crashing into U.S. targets, what did that say about the country's national defense? The press was entirely uninterested in that debate.

There's no question that the White House, teaming up with the MSM in early 2003, succeeded in scaring the hell out of Americans, with an amazing 82 percent of those interviewed by CBS/*New York Times* pollsters saying they expected America to be hit by a terrorist attack in the next few months. For the White House, the scare offense made for great politics. First, the anxiety level helped boost support for the war in Iraq since Bush—falsely—assured Americans an invasion would help eliminate Islamic terrorists. And second, Americans routinely gave the Bush presidency its highest marks for his handling of terrorist threats. (By early 2006, polls indicated that battling terror was virtually the only issue Bush scored well in.)

The media's obedient brand of terror scare reporting extended all the way into 2005, as the MSM dutifully played up the White House's selected theme for Bush's second inauguration: Terror. The MSM's signature timidity was on full display as it detailed the massive, unprecedented, and largely unexplained security blanket that turned the nation's capital into something akin to an armed fortress. Snipers were positioned on rooftops, bombers flew overhead, Humvee-mounted antiaircraft missiles dotted the city, manholes were cemented shut, and news racks swept off the streets. Specialists in chemical, biological, and radiological terrorism prevention mingled with the spooked inauguration crowds. Armed Coast Guard boats patrolled the Potomac River. And there was even an emergency engineering unit on standby to deal with any collapsed buildings.

The MSM, though, were too afraid to ask the simple question, why? Why were tens of millions of taxpayer dollars being spent—nearly 9,000 police officers and military personnel were deployed—to transform a public celebration of democracy into a show of foreboding military force? And was it all simply a political ploy for a White House that thrived on the issue of national security? Keep in mind, the military clampdown came despite the fact an assessment compiled at the time by the departments of Defense, Homeland Security, and Justice declared, "There is no credible information indicating that domestic or international terrorist groups are targeting the inaugura-tion." Indeed, Homeland secretary Tom Ridge refused the raise the ter-ror alert level, announcing on the eve of Bush's second swearing-in, "There is nothing that we've seen that gives us any reason to even con-sider [it]."

Another way cable news outlets boosted Bush's War on Terror was by simply handing over huge chunks of airtime to the president for him to use however he wanted. By the spring of 2002, Bush's afternoon stump speeches from cereal factories, elementary schools, and chambers of commerce had become a staple on the cable news networks. CNN officials insisted the coverage reflected the unique war on terrorism being waged. "CNN, like all news organizations, makes decisions about its coverage based on the stories of the day. In covering a war at home and military action overseas, it is necessary to cover the administration making the decisions, regardless of political party," said a network spokesperson.

The high-minded protestations of the news channels notwith-standing, the fact was that the majority of the Bush events the cable outlets rushed to cover had nothing whatsoever to do with the war on terrorism. Viewers who regularly watched CNN in 2002 saw it break away from programming to show Bush delivering prepared, extended remarks in front of friendly, partisan crowds about faith-based charities, defense modernization, education reform and tax cuts, education, simplifying tax codes for small business, strengthening Social Security, protecting the rights of investors, welfare reform, and on and on and on.

The irony was that in May of 1999, CNN's high-profile anchor Lou Dobbs got into an on-air tiff with then CNN chief Rick Kaplan. A noted friend of the Clintons, Kaplan demanded that producers cut away from Dobbs' program in order to show Clinton addressing a ceremony honoring the victims of the shooting at Columbine High

School. Dobbs, a firm Republican, was incensed. As the *New York Post* reported, "Dobbs, who didn't consider the staged event breaking news, was absolutely livid." But no one at CNN seemed mildly concerned—let alone absolutely livid—about the countless staged events CNN aired for Bush. Once again, the MSM came up with new, more convenient rules for the wartime president.

CHAPTER 9

Lost on Downing Street

"Let me turn to the now-famous Downing Street memo," announced Tim Russert, hosting NBC's *Meet the Press* on June 5, 2005. It was halfway through the broadcast and Russert had already quizzed his Republican guest about a laundry list of newsworthy topics; stem cell research, gay marriage, Social Security, Democrats, and the war on terror. While setting up his twenty-second question to Republican National Committee chairman Ken Mehlman, Russert shifted the focus to a top-level British government memorandum. Consisting of minutes from a secret, July 2002, meeting attended by Prime Minister Tony Blair and his closest advisors, the memo revealed their impression that the Bush administration, eight months before the start of the Iraq war, had already decided to launch an invasion, that intelligence was being "fixed" to support the invasion, the U.S. justification for war was "thin," and that the administration seemed more concerned with selling a war than preventing one. Dubbed the Downing Street memo, named after Blair's London residency, the document was leaked to the *Sunday Times* of London, which printed an exclusive on May 1. Coming as it did on the eve of Blair's reelection, the story generated headlines throughout Britain. Five weeks after it was first published, Russert referred to the document as the "now-famous" memo.

It was an interesting choice of words because the Downing Street memo would have been "famous" in America if the D.C. press corps had functioned the way it was supposed to; reporting the news without fear or favor. Instead, Russert's belated June 5, reference represented the first time NBC News had even mentioned the document or the controversy surrounding it. In fact, Russert's query was the first time *any* of the network news divisions addressed the issue in a serious manner. In an age of instant communication, the slow-footed MSM took an exceed-

ingly long time—as if news of the memo had traveled by vessel across
the Atlantic Ocean—to report on the leaked document. And even then
the MSM were careful not to dwell on the memo's troubling implications—namely, that President Bush lied to the American people and
Congress during the fall of 2002 when he insisted over and over that
war was his administration's last option and that no decision to invade
had yet been made.

Worse, the MSM's hesitant reaction to the Downing Street memo in
2005 came after several major news outlets, including the *New York
Times* and the *Washington Post*, had already conceded their timorous
reporting during the prewar stages was not what it should have been.
With mea culpas in print, those news outlets might have chosen to bore
into the Downing Street memo story as a way to atone for their previous shortcomings. Instead, they simply avoided the story, falling right
back into the same cautious mind-set that produced insecure journalism
in late 2002 and early 2003 that was later apologized for. The story of
the Downing Street memo and the MSM's puzzling indifference offers
perhaps one of the best case studies in how, during the Bush years, the
press was afraid of the facts and how the phobia affected virtually every
major news outlet.

And yet, as Russert's belated inquiry illustrated, the story of the
"now-famous" Downing Street memo also refused to fade away despite
the MSM's initial near total blackout. Championed by progressive
activists, media advocates, more than 100 Democratic members of
Congress, liberal radio hosts, bloggers, newspaper ombudsmen, a handful of columnists and an army of newspaper readers who flooded editors
with letters demanding that the story be reported, the British memo
enjoyed a peculiar media afterlife. One retired Air Force lieutenant
colonel even held a sidewalk vigil outside a Tampa, Florida, television
station demanding that it "Air the truth!" about the memo. The Downing Street memo not only came to symbolize the administration's
wartime deceptions, but it became prime example of the media's
extraordinary timidity in refusing to confront that dishonesty.

Like a newborn placed in a roomful of bachelors, the Downing
Street memo was greeted with befuddled stares; a hard-to-figure puzzle that was better left for somebody else to solve. And that's what was
so striking—how uniform the MSM response was. Why, in the face of

the clearly newsworthy memo did senior editors and producers at virtually *every* major American news outlets fail to do the most rudimentary reporting—the who, what, where, why, and how of the Downing Street memo? Instead, journalists looked at the document and instinctively knew it was not a news story. Journalists didn't simply fail to embrace or investigate the Downing Street memo story, they actively ignored it.

The Downing Street memo itself represented the minutes from a meeting of Blair's senior policy advisers which took place on July 23, eight months before the war with Iraq began. The meeting brought together Britain's prime minister, defense secretary, foreign secretary, attorney general, the head of the Joint Intelligence Committee, which advises Blair, the head of the MI6, Britain's equivalent of the CIA, the national security adviser, Blair's chief of staff, Blair's senior communications and political adviser, and the director of government relations. The two main players within the text of the Downing Street memo were Jack Straw, the foreign secretary, and Sir Richard Dearlove, head of MI6, and who was referred to in the memo simply as "C." Dearlove had just returned from a trip to Washington, D.C., where he discussed war plans with CIA chief George Tenet and National Security Adviser Condoleezza Rice.

The Downing Street memo was written by Blair's aide Matthew Rycroft, who prefaced the memo by noting, "This record is extremely sensitive. No further copies should be made. It should be shown only to those with a genuine need to know its contents." The Downing Street memo was first disclosed by the *Sunday Times* of London on May 1, 2005. The British government did not contradict any of the points in the memo or question its authenticity and a former senior U.S. official later confirmed for the Knight Ridder Newspaper Service that the memo was "an absolutely accurate description of what transpired" during Dearlove's visit to Washington.

According to Andrew Bacevich, a war analyst at Boston University and retired Army colonel, the importance of the Downing Street memo was instantly obvious: "The memo is significant because it was written by our closest ally, and when it comes to writing minutes on foreign policy and security matters, the British are professionals," he noted in 2005. "We can conclude that the memo means precisely what it says. It says that Bush had already made the decision for war even while he was insisting publicly, and for many months thereafter, that war was the last resort. This is no longer a suspicion or accusation. The memo is an authoritative piece of information, at the highest level."

Among the most intriguing passages of the Downing Street memo was this one: "C [Dearlove] reported on his recent talks in Washington. There was a perceptible shift in attitude. Military action was now seen as inevitable. Bush wanted to remove Saddam, through military action, justified by the conjunction of terrorism and WMD. But the intelligence and facts were being fixed around the policy. The NSC [National Security Council] had no patience with the U.N. route. . . . There was little discussion in Washington of the aftermath after military action."

That more reporters, editors, and producers didn't grasp the significance of the memo remains baffling. As Mark Danner spelled out in the *New York Review of Books*, the memo helped establish five key facts in understanding how the war in Iraq unfolded:

1. By mid-July 2002, eight months before the war began, President Bush had decided to invade and occupy Iraq.
2. Bush had decided to "justify" the war "by the conjunction of terrorism and WMD."
3. Already, "the intelligence and facts were being fixed around the policy."
4. Many at the top of the [U.S.] administration did not want to seek approval from the United Nations (going "the U.N. route").
5. Few in Washington seemed much interested in the aftermath of the war.

If that weren't enough to set off alarm bells inside newsrooms, there was also this from the Downing Street memo:

The Foreign Secretary said he would discuss [the timing of the war] with Colin Powell this week. It seemed clear that Bush had made up his mind to take military action, even if the timing was not yet decided. But the case was thin. Saddam was not threatening his neighbors, and his WMD capability was less than that of Libya, North Korea or Iran.

The issue of the United Nations was also addressed. In the United States, Bush administration officials prior to the war had always stressed that they went to the U.N. in effort to avoid a war with Iraq; a narrative the press faithfully followed during the run-up to the invasion. But according to the Downing Street memo, the U.N. was used as a mechanism to *trigger* the desired invasion. In the Downing Street memo, Straw mentioned, "We should work up a plan for an ultimatum to Saddam to allow back in the UN weapons inspectors. This would also help with the legal justification for the use of force."

At that point, the Downing Street memo noted, "The Prime Minister said that it would make a big difference politically and legally if Saddam refused to allow in the UN inspectors. Regime change and WMD were linked in the sense that it was the regime that was producing the WMD . . . If the political context were right, people would support regime change. The two key issues were whether the military plan worked and whether we had the political strategy to give the military plan the space to work."

In other words, by using the U.N. weapons inspectors as bait for an ultimatum which they hoped Saddam would refuse, Blair and Bush would use the U.N. to create the missing *casus belli*—to prompt a war, not to prevent one.

In total, the remarkable Downing Street Memo offered intriguing, "extremely sensitive" insights into the timing of the war, the use of U.S. intelligence estimates, the "thin" rationale behind the invasion, the lack of postwar planning, and the cynical use of the United Nations to trigger a preemptive war. A treasure trove of information, the Downing Street memo revelations created an electronic stampede to the *Sunday Times* of London website, where the exclusive was still attracting a large online readership one month after the newspaper published it. Additionally, the memo prompted more than one hundred Democratic members of Congress to write to the White House, asking for answers to questions raised by the memo.

Despite all that, the early reaction from the American media, with a few noticeable exceptions, came in the form of a collective yawn.

As the *Chicago Tribune* noted two weeks after the memo's publication overseas, the Downing Street memo's "potentially explosive revelation has proven to be something of a dud the United States." The newspaper reported, "The White House has denied the premise of the memo, the American media have reacted slowly to it and the *public generally seems indifferent to the issue* or unwilling to rehash the bitter prewar debate over the reasons for the war." [Emphasis added.]

But where was the proof the general public was indifferent, particularly when the newspaper conceded the Downing Street memo had essentially been ignored by the American press? How could news consumers be indifferent to something they did not know existed? On May 31, Bush held his first press conference since the Downing Street memo had been published and since Democratic members of Congress had written to the White House demanding answers. Bush fielded almost two dozen questions over a sixty-minute span. As Tim Grieve at *Salon* noted, reporters not only asked Bush about the day's obvious topics, such as the situation in Iraq and naming a new Supreme Court justice, but they covered every conceivable news angle. They pressed Bush for his thoughts on the sentencing of the former head of Russia's oil company, about the decision to let Iran apply for World Trade Organization status, and about his commitment to making his tax cuts permanent. They pressed Bush about his relations with Congress, about the way America is viewed in the world, and about how often he disagreed with his wife. What nobody asked Bush though, was about the Downing Street memo and the widely held feeling among senior British officials that eight months before the invasion of Iraq Bush had decided to go to war, that during 2002 intelligence was being "fixed" to justify the invasion, and that United Nations was used as a way to trigger war, not prevent it.

Between May 1 and June 7, White House spokesman Scott McClellan held nineteen press briefings, at which he fielded approximately 940 questions from reporters, according to the White House's online archives. Exactly two of those questions were about the Downing Street memo and the administration's reported effort to fix prewar intelligence. For an entire month the Associated Press wire service, which serves as the international eyes and ears for many regional American newspapers, was silent about the Downing Street memo; not a single dispatch was filed. ("There is no question AP dropped the ball in not picking up on the Downing Street memo sooner," AP's international editor Deborah Seward later conceded.) On May 20 the *New York*

Times published a belated follow-up article but it ran fewer than eight hundred words and despite a headline that read "British Memo on U.S. Plans for Iraq War Fuels Critics," the *Times* reporter did not quote a single war critic about the memo or its implications.

The issue of the Downing Street memo was barely discussed on television, and when it did pop up at the prompting of a guest, hosts appeared to have no interest. For example, here's the May 25 exchange between actor and activist Tim Robbins and Chris Matthews on MSNBC's *Hardball*.

> **Robbins:** I think there should be more discussion about the Downing Street memo . . . I think that that story seemed to be buried. And there seems to be a lot of questions that the Downing Street memo raises.
>
> **Matthews:** Tell me about that.
>
> **Robbins:** Well, it suggests that the administration knew full well they were being duplicitous and were operating with weak intelligence.
>
> **Matthews:** Well, they—well, they did tell us at the time, Tim, that the best argument for getting the Europeans to join us in the war was using the WMD argument, but it wasn't their primary purpose. The primary purpose apparently was democratization in the Middle East, nation building.
>
> **Robbins:** And I think they didn't mention that until much later, Chris. I think that the original—original reason was that [Saddam] was an imminent threat.
>
> **Matthews:** Let me ask you about Hollywood. . . .

Between May 1 and June 6, the Downing Street memo story received approximately twenty mentions on CNN, Fox News, MSNBC, ABC, CBS, NBC, and PBS *combined*, according to TVEyes, an around-the-clock television monitoring service. By contrast, during the same five-week period, the same outlets found time for more than 260 mentions of the silly tabloid controversy that erupted when a prison photograph of Saddam Hussein in his underwear was leaked to the British press.

Asked why NBC took a month to even mention the Downing Street memo, Russert told the *Washington Post* the document had to be checked out first: "One thing I've learned is when you see something from the British press, you have to vet it." That's wise advice—the British print press has been notoriously breathless with its post-9/11, wartime scoops. But if the Downing Street memo had been bogus when it was published during the final days of the British campaign, the Blair government would have forcefully challenged it. Blair did not, which begged the question, why did Russert's NBC need more than a month to verify the document?

Meanwhile, the online crusade to keep the Downing Street memo alive, powered in part by Downingstreetmemo.org and Media Matters for America, not only resulted in some belated MSM coverage for the story, but it also ticked off journalists who clearly resented being told how to do their jobs. On his blog, NBC *Nightly News* anchor Brian Williams pushed back against online activists, writing on June 9, "One more note to those of you who are part of the mass e-mail project on the so-called Downing Street Memo: That's enough, we get it . . . We're well aware of the story, *we've covered it*, and likely will again." [Emphasis added.]

But as of June 9, had NBC "covered" the Downing Street memo story, as Williams insisted? The *Nightly News* made a passing, two-sentence reference to it on the June 7 broadcast. NBC viewers though, were hard-pressed from that single mention to put the Downing Street memo in any kind of perspective. The first significant memo report on *Nightly News* did not air until June 16, six weeks after the memo was first published in London and weeks after activists began their emailing campaign.

The truth is it would have been very easy for the networks, the cable channels, the news weeklies, and the nation's newspapers to cover the release of the Downing Street memo. The Knight Ridder Newspaper Service showed how on May 6, with a straightforward dispatch that reported, "A highly classified British memo, leaked during Britain's just-concluded election campaign, claims President Bush decided by summer 2002 to overthrow Iraqi President Saddam Hussein and was determined to ensure that U.S. intelligence data supported his policy." (Early on, the *New York Times* and *Washington Post* both published brief articles on the memo; the *Times* focused exclusively on the implications for the Blair government, while the *Post* buried its dispatch on page 18.) Instead of covering the obvious news event, most Beltway journalists, guilty of overthinking the story, went to unusual lengths to convince themselves that the many points raised in the British document did not represent news. For instance, on May 20 the *New York Times* public editor, or ombudsman, Byron Calame echoed readers' complaints that the paper's Downing Street memo coverage had "languished," which in turn "left Times readers pretty much in the dark." Calame pressed the newspaper's Washington bureau chief Phil Taubman about the Downing Street memo's assertion that the Bush administration had manipulated intelligence estimates during the run-up to war. Calame wondered why that was not worth a news article. Taubman's response is worth reading in full. Note the detailed deliberations that apparently went into the decision not to publish a simple follow-up story about the Downing Street memo. And keep in mind that the question from Calame wasn't why did the *Times* keep Downing Street memo stories off page 1, or why didn't the *Times* assign an in-depth investigation. The simple question was, why didn't the *Times* cover the Downing Street memo as stateside news, period? According to Taubman:

> As I read the minutes, they described the impressions of the head of MI6, who had recently returned from Washington, where he had met with George Tenet. It is mighty suggestive that Lord Dearlove, the chief of MI6, came home with the impression, or interpretation, that "the intelligence and facts were being fixed around the policy." However, that's several steps removed from evidence that such was the case. The minutes did not say that Mr. Tenet had told that to Lord Dearlove or that Lord Dearlove had seen specific examples of that. The minutes, in my estimation, were not a smoking gun that proved that Bush, Tenet and others were distorting intelligence to support the case for war. All these considerations were factored into the decision that the bureau did not have to jump on the story immediately after *The London Times* account appeared.

Through May and June of 2005, as the press corps made plain its lack of interest in the DSM, an aggressive Internet-based campaign rose up and pressed journalists to simply do their job and report the news, even if that meant embarrassing the White House. The MSM then backed off its insistence that the Downing Street memo was not news and embraced a more nuanced position that the memo was simply "old news." Specifically, journalists—setting aside the memo's suggestion that the case for war was "thin," that intelligence was being "fixed," and the United Nations might be used as a way to trigger the invasion—cherry-picked the issue of the war's timing and insisted the Downing Street memo was about planning, and that everyone in 2002 knew the United States was preparing for war, so what was the big deal?

That "old news" angle would have made sense if Britain's top spy, after having met with Bush's head of the CIA and director of National Security, had reported back to Blair in the summer of 2002 that the United States was *preparing* for war. That was old news because everyone knew war planning was underway. Congress held hearings on the topic in 2002. But that's not what the Downing Street memo implied. It suggested "Military action was now seen as inevitable," and that "Bush had made up his mind to take military action." Yet the MSM kept assuring news consumers the Downing Street memo was simply about war "planning."

- The *Wall Street Journal*'s news team, which took eight weeks to finally do in-depth reporting on the Downing Street memo, assured readers "The documents don't reflect much new; at the time they were produced, U.S. news outlets were speculating that Mr. Bush *might be heading toward* conflict in Iraq, which is why they garnered little attention here when reported earlier." [Emphasis added.]
- CNN erroneously summarized the Downing Street memo contents as "suggesting that the Bush administration was *preparing* for military action in Iraq in the summer of 2002. [Emphasis added.]
- In his response to the public editor's query, the *Times*'s Taubman told Calame, "Given what has been reported about war *planning* in Washington, the revelations about the Downing Street meeting did not seem like a bolt from the blue." [Emphasis added.]
- The hawkish *Washington Post* editorial page, which forcefully supported the invasion of Iraq, belittled the Downing Street memo, insisting it was irrelevant because during the summer of 2002 "the pages of this and other newspapers were filled with reports about military *planning* for war to remove Saddam Hussein." [Emphasis added.]

Did Beltway journalists really think people pushing for action on the Downing Street memo were so ill-informed that they thought it was news that the Pentagon was preparing for war in 2002? Did journalists really think administration critics did not understand Congressional hearings were held during the summer of 2002 about that very topic? Doubtful. It's more likely they deliberately tried to obscure the facts and manufactured an excuse—it's old news!—for their negligence. It was telling that the MSM's mantra that the Downing Street memo represented old news was the exact same point partisan conservatives were making at the time. Writing for *National Review Online*, James Robbins, appearing under the headline, "Downing Street Memo Is Old News," waved off the budding story, insisting "As smoking guns go, it is not high caliber." Republicans and Beltway reporters were in lock step on that point.

Definitive proof that the Downing Street memo revelations were not "old news" for news consumers arrived in the form of a poll conducted by ABC News in late June 2005. As part of its ongoing survey, ABC pollsters regularly asked Americans whether, on the eve of war, the administration had intentionally exaggerated evidence about Iraq's WMD program. In the wake of the Downing Street memo, after the press was finally shamed into covering the memo's contents, and specifically the British impression that intelligence was being "fixed" around the war policy, a record high 57 percent of voters suddenly agreed that Bush had intentionally exaggerated the need to go to war. Rather than being old news, for most Americans the Downing Street memo disclosures came as a shocking revelation.

Meanwhile, the press also ignored the clear contradictions between what Bush was saying publicly prior to the war and what the Downing Street memo suggested he was saying privately, that "Bush had made up his mind to take military action." That was plainly newsworthy because, despite his countless public proclamations during the fall of 2002 and winter of 2003 about how the United States was determined to avoid war, Bush and his top allies seemed to have privately determined, nearly one year before the invasions, that the preemptive war was going to happen and their main job was to justify, or sell the war. Yet Bush and his operatives were adamant in their public pronouncements about both his resolve to circumvent war, and the fact no decision had been made about an invasion:

- "I think that that presumes there's some kind of imminent war plan. As I said, I have no timetable." (Bush, August 10, 2002)
- "The President has not made a decision about the use of military action vis-à-vis Iraq." (White House spokesman Ari Fleischer, August 27, 2002)
- "Our goal is to fully and finally remove a real threat to world peace and to America. Hopefully this can be done peacefully." (Bush, October 16, 2002)
- "War is not my first choice . . . it's my last choice." (Bush, November 7, 2002)
- "The President continues to seek a peaceful resolution. War is a last resort." (White House spokesman Scott McClellan, November 12, 2002)
- "You said we're headed to war in Iraq—I don't know why you say that. I hope we're not headed to war in Iraq. I'm the person who gets to decide, not you. I hope this can be done peacefully." (Bush, December 31, 2002)
- "I've not made up our mind about military action. Hopefully, this can be done peacefully." (Bush, March 6, 2003)
- "We are doing everything we can to avoid war in Iraq." (March 8, 2003)

In the wake of the Downing Street memo's appearance, and the clear contradiction it offered to Bush's previous public statements, the media's implied position seemed to be that, yes, Bush used give-peace-a-chance rhetoric, but nobody really believed him, and that plugged-in journalists all knew war was coming. As *New York Times* reporter Todd Purdum put it during a public radio interview on June 16, 2005, arguing that the Downing Street memo was old news, "You'd have to be a moron [in the summer of 2002] to think we were not headed to war."

But if everyone in the summer of 2002 knew Bush was going to war and yet for months he took nearly every public opportunity to insist he'd not decided to go to war—and that he didn't *want* to go to war—than why didn't the press call him out on that? Where were the stories, in real time, that suggested nobody inside the Beltway believed Bush when he insisted a peaceful solution was possible? Those stories and those televised pundit panels, by and large, do not exist. But when the Downing Street memo arrived in 2005, reporters pretended it was all old news because everyone knew war had been inevitable. It was nice that MSM journalists were in the know regarding the White House's apparently disingenuous reassurances about a possibly peaceful solution, but it might have been helpful if they had informed their readers, viewers, and listeners in 2002 and 2003, allowing them to make informed decisions about an impending war.

Discussing the media's mostly allergic reaction to the story, Jefferson Morley, who covered the Downing Street memo as a staff writer for Washingtonpost.com (which maintains editorial independence from the *Post*'s more Beltway Establishment–friendly print version), suggested reporters didn't really want to know the answers to the questions being posed. "The Downing Street Memo invites the thought that maybe . . . people in the Bush administration were having meetings dedicated to figuring how to, as Richard Dearlove said, "fix the facts and the intelligence." "I think it's hard [for] journalists born and bred in the ways of Washington to contemplate the implications," said Morley during a Washingtonpost.com chat session with readers.

Playing catch-up on the Downing Street memo story during the month of June produced some awkward moments for reporters, like when NBC's Russert on the June 4 telecast of *Meet the Press* referred to the Downing Street memo as "the now-famous" document. On June 10th, busy promoting the news channel's twenty-fifth anniversary, CNN chief Jon Klein lavished praise on his own news organization. "We're rollicking, aggressive pursuers of facts," Klein cheered. "We're the only ones who go out and report the news. Our editorial chops are alive and well. We're kicking butt every day. The American people want serious news—and they're not getting enough of it from cable." The irony was that Klein's rah-rahing about CNN's hunger for "serious news" came in the wake of the news channel's nearly month-long boycott of the Downing Street memo story.

And even after Blair and Bush were quizzed about the memo at a Washington, D.C., press briefing on June 7, CNN continued with its allergic reaction to the touchy story. From the time the memo was published in London until June 10, the day of Klein's "kicking butt" comment, the news network had aired approximately 900 hours of programming in the United States, during which time the Downing Street memo was mentioned thirteen times. By contrast, when word got out that a young American woman vacationing in Aruba had gone missing, it was all hands on deck at CNN. During just one seven-day stretch in June of 2005, CNN anchors, reporters, and guests mentioned "Aruba" more than 190 times.

The MSM's across-the-board obliviousness was what likely triggered such a passionate response among media activists, as well as everyday news consumers, who demanded the Downing Street memo be taken seriously by the press. Timid Beltway reporters, pundits, and producers might have convinced themselves the memo was not news, but around the country—outside the Beltway—letters-to-the-editor pages began to fill up with strident requests for media attention. The letters appeared in the *Sunday Oregonian* (Portland), *Los Angeles Times*, *Raleigh News and Observer*, *Arizona Republic*, *South Florida Sun-Sentinel*, *Anchorage Daily News*, *Ithaca Journal* (New York), *Berkshire Eagle* (Pittsfield, Mass.), *Allentown Morning Call* (Pennsylvania), *Dubuque Telegraph Herald* (Iowa), *Bangor Daily News* (Maine), *Springfield State Journal-Register* (Illinois), *Modesto Bee* (California), and *Tulsa World*, among others. (The published correspondence did not appear to be form letters, or so-called Astroturf letters, designed by activists to mimic grassroots support for a particular political issue.)

By mid-June the MSM began to reluctantly cover the Downing Street memo, but journalists did not go without a fight. The *New York Times* on June 14, with an unusually dismissive tone for a news report, noted the Downing Street memo was not "the Dead Sea Scrolls," as if that were suddenly the paper's standard for reporting on leaked government documents. Appearing on *Meet the Press* on June 12, longtime *Washington Post* columnist David Broder was asked to respond to an accusation made by Senator Hillary Rodham Clinton who, in the wake of the Downing Street memo controversy, chastised the press for its timidity. Broder, perfectly capturing the media establishment's knee-jerk defensive crouch, dismissed the accusation. In fact, he pointed to that day's *Washington Post* as proof of why Clinton was wrong about the MSM going easy on Bush—the *Post* had run a page-one piece about the

Downing Street memo! Forget the fact that it took six weeks for the story to travel from the front page of the *Sunday Times* of London to the *Post*'s front page, or that it had been four weeks since the *Post*'s ombudsmen had publicly scolded the paper for ignoring the memo story. In Broder's eyes, the slow-motion news gathering process was proof positive that the press was tough on Bush.

Other key mainstream media figures, such as syndicated columnist Michael Kinsley, not only dismissed the Downing Street memo story, but openly mocked those who considered it worth covering. Kinsley, a political iconoclast whose normally sharp timing betrayed him on the Downing Street memo issue, came close to comparing the memo to a UFO, or at least suggesting that progressives urging the media give the Downing Street memo more attention were akin to paranoid conspiracy buffs and on "the very edge of national respectability." Kinsley wrote that six weeks after it had been published in London and generated international headlines, "I decided to read" "something called the Downing Street Memo." He announced, "I don't buy the fuss."

Why didn't Kinsley buy the fuss? Because everybody in 2002 knew Bush was *planning* for war. Not convinced by the Downing Street memo's reference that war was "now seen as inevitable" by "Washington," Kinsley suggested that because the memo made no mention of specific administration officials, perhaps Britain's top spy Dearlove simply repeated information he picked up from the "usual Washington chatterboxes." Kinsley, who once edited the *New Republic* magazine, seemed to suggest that the head of British intelligence was reporting back to the British prime minister and his war cabinet about a factfinding mission with the most senior members of the United State government—Rice and Tenet—yet was basing his information on what he read in the *Washington Post* or overheard at embassy cocktail parties.

Kinsley's condescension was matched perhaps only by the *Washington Post*'s Dana Milbank, who unloaded on Downing Street memo supporters twice in ten days, suggested Democrats in Congress who embraced the memos were delusional, and that liberal activists who backed the memo were "anti-Semitic" "wing nuts." The first putdown came in a June 8 column when Milbank noted Bush, appearing with Blair at the June 7 press conference, had finally been asked about the Downing Street Memo. Milbank noted, "Earlier in the day, Democrats.com, a group of left-wing activists, sent out an e-mail offering a 'reward' to anyone who could get an answer from Bush about" the memo. Milbank reported the Reuters reporter who asked Bush the question had no idea about the slightly tongue-in-cheek $1,000 bounty (which the reporter refused), and didn't pose the question in order to "satisfy the wing nuts," as Milbank referred to members of Democrats.com, a mainstream group of partisan activists.

What's curious about Milbank's outburst is that throughout Bush's time in office, when right-wing press critics regularly derided journalists as traitors and terrorist sympathizers, neither Milbank nor anyone else at the *Post* thought those people should be called out as "wing nuts." But when activists on the left suggested the mainstream media pay attention to authentic British documents which exposed parts of the White House's misinformation campaign on the eve of the Iraq war, they were the ones mocked in the pages of the *Post* as crackpots.

In fact, the Daily Howler researched the *Post*'s use of "wing nuts" during the previous four years and found the phrase was published sparingly and used mainly to describe members of fringe organizations like the Symbionese Liberation Army, the group that kidnapped Patricia Hearst thirty years earlier. As the Howler noted, "In short, it's essentially impossible to find *Post* writers using this term to attack someone else. But all that changed on June 8, when Dana Milbank had heard enough. Some Americans citizens wanted to know if their president had lied their country into war. To Milbank, this concern made them 'wing nuts.' "

Milbank's "wing nuts" attack only served as a warm-up to the centerpiece of his scornful coverage; a hearing Congressional Democrats held on June 16 to publicize the Downing Street memo. Because they're in the minority and didn't have the power to issue subpoenas or gavel actual hearings, Democrats held an unofficial forum in a crowded basement room on Capitol Hill, which was attended by more than a dozen members of Congress. Representative John Conyers, a Democrat from Michigan, oversaw the forum. Milbank's contemptuous dispatch mocked Conyers and "his hearty band of playmates" at the hearing for playing "make-believe"; for conducting a "fantasy" "dress-up game." Keep in mind Milbank's name-calling column was the only coverage the *Post* offered readers of the Conyers hearings. (It's curious that Milbank, already on record as mocking Downing Street memo supporters as "wing nuts," was allowed to cover Conyers' hearing.)

The overall lack of coverage on the Downing Street memo story only highlighted the contempt Beltway journalists had for Democrats, their concerns, and the complaints they lodged against the Bush administration. Instead of being embraced and amplified by the press the way the opposition party's allegations were during the Clinton years, Democrats and their misgivings were summarily dismissed by the press. One of the arguments journalists made during the Bush years, in trying to explain their timidity as compared to their extraordinary pursuits during the Clinton years, was to emphasize that Democrats didn't scream and yell as loud as Republicans did, and that if Democrats weren't making a big deal about a particular story, the press couldn't either. "There's no denying that we give more coverage to stories when someone is shouting," wrote the *Washington Post*'s John Harris in a May 2001 article addressing early complaints that the Beltway press corps was going easy on Bush. Instead, what the Downing Street memo episode graphically illustrated was how often the Beltway press uniformly ignored the issues, no matter how loudly Democrats were shouting about the administration's misconduct.

The truth is Democratic members of Congress, as well as their staffs, worked furiously for weeks to try to convince the press to pay attention to the Downing Street memo story, and used the Democrats' letter to the White House, signed by more than one hundred members, as a news hook. It was a losing cause. "We worked that letter with Washington bureaus of AP, *New York Times* and every single other Washington contacts you can think of (CNN, MSNBC, etc.) as hard as you can work anything," insisted one Democratic Hill staffer.

Five weeks after the Downing Street memo story broke in London, Conyers arrived at the gates of the White House on June 16 for a compelling photo-op where he was met by guards as he tried to deliver a petition signed by 560,000 Americans seeking answers to the questions raised by the memo. Once again the press shrugged. None of the network news broadcasts reported on the event that night. Among the three all-news cable channels, Conyers's White House showdown garnered just sixteen mentions, total.

The blackout extended to that Sunday's talk shows as well. In the wake of the Democrats' Downing Street memo hearing and Conyers's White House showdown, that week's *Meet the Press, Face the Nation, This Week,* and *Fox News Sunday* all ignored the DSM story.

In fact, CBS's *Face the Nation* made it through both May and June 2005 without ever discussing the document—nine broadcasts featuring thirty-one guests and not a single mention of the Downing Street memo.

CHAPTER 10

The MSM Goes to War

Ronald Schulz died from a bullet to the back of his head. After his blindfolded and bound body hit the dirt ground, he was shot several more times from close range with a semiautomatic weapon. On December 19, 2005, insurgents from the Islamic Army of Iraq posted an ultra-violent video on the Internet showing their cold-blooded execution of Schulz, an American forty-year-old industrial electrician and former Halliburton employee, who had been abducted in Iraq weeks earlier. The shocking act of terror was barbaric as well as newsworthy. Any time an innocent American citizen gets abducted in a foreign country and executed, on-camera no less, for purely political purposes, that qualifies as news. Except, apparently, when it happens in Iraq and when the MSM seems so intent on sanitizing war coverage that atrocities like Schulz's murder are quietly set aside.

On December 19, NBC's *Nightly News* paid no attention to the bloody story of Ronald Schulz's execution, neither did CBS's *Evening News*. On cable television, word of the chilling video received just a handful of mentions from Fox News and MSNBC, while CNN took no notice of the story, which was odd considering twenty-four hours earlier when a German hostage was set free by her Iraqi captures, CNN reported the story nearly a dozen times throughout the day. But when a U.S. hostage was executed by his Iraqi captures, CNN's team went mute.

Given the backdrop of an ongoing war which had claimed the lives of more than 2,000 U.S. troops and the fact that, sadly, Schulz was not the first U.S. hostage to be killed while insurgents' cameras rolled, word of his death might not have qualified as a major event. But the idea that it did not, according to CNN and NBC, rise to the level of news *at all* and his murder did not deserve a single on-air reference? That benchmark

261

was hard to comprehend, although the White House likely appreciated the MSM's hushed reponse considering news of the Schulz execution came just hours after Bush announced, during a prime-time address, that the United States was "winning the war in Iraq."

Just as the press coverage during the run-up to the war played a unique role as the administration rolled out its marketing plan to sell, through the press, an invasion of choice, coverage of the war itself and its chaotic aftermath proved to be just as important—and helpful—for the Bush White House. And just as Bush's presidency is inexorably linked to the events in Iraq, so too is the MSM when it comes to grading them on their Bush era coverage. From the moment Operation Iraqi Freedom was announced on March 19, 2003, no other story was as important as Iraq.

There's no question that lots of heroic and insightful MSM reporting was produced inside Iraq from journalists who deserve much admiration. But in general, the war coverage, as directed by stateside editors and producers, was marked by its early cheerleading, its sanitary presentation, and how the press, particularly television, for months at a time collectively lost interest in the story as the occupation became increasingly bogged down. For instance, in 2003, the ABC, NBC, and CBS nightly newscasts, on average, devoted 388 minutes each month to covering Iraq, according to media researcher Andrew Tyndall. By 2005 that monthly tally had decreased by more than 50 percent—to 166 minutes each month—despite the fact that the number of U.S. troops killed in Iraq increased nearly 80 percent between 2003 and 2005. In other words, as more Americans died in Iraq, the war became less newsworthy for the MSM. (For historical context, in 1972, *seven years* after U.S. Marines first arrived in Vietnam, the three network newscasts were still airing approximately 250 minutes per-month of coverage.)

"It's almost as if the media fears the public thinking of them as being too negative if they go with too much war coverage," noted Charles Peña, director of defense policy studies at the Cato Institute, a libertarian think tank in Washington, D.C. "Enough of the media doesn't want to cross some imaginary line where they're going to be accused of politicizing the news and going after the administration." As the invasion unfolded in 2003 there was little chance of the MSM crossing that imaginary line.

"We're extremely happy with the coverage," announced Captain Stewart Upton, a public affairs officer with the U.S. Central Command in Qatar, less than forty-eight hours after President Bush ordered the attack on Iraq. Like the coverage of the WMD debate during the run-up to war, it's hard to imagine how the White House, in general, could not have scripted better press play than the kind they played out for American news consumers during March 2003.

Of course, the Iraq war was supposed to be the first full-access invasion for journalists, as the Pentagon swung open its doors and invited reporters to come along for the ride of their lives. By attaching some six hundred print, radio, and TV reporters with coalition forces, the Pentagon gave reporters unprecedented access to the battlefield, allowing them to file, theoretically, uncensored views and updates in real time. In terms of entrée, the embedding initiative represented a sizable improvement from the first Gulf War in 1991 when the Pentagon used a heavy hand and limited journalists' ability to report. The concern some skeptics had with the embedding process in 2003 was that it would turn reporters from objective observers into cheerleaders for the U.S. armed forces. Ironically, the overwhelming problem with the deferential, Bush-friendly war journalism surrounding the first month of the war did not come from the embedded journalists. It came from the reporters working back in United States, and specifically those inside the Beltway, who succumbed to the forced, flag-waving patriotism that blanketed the coverage.

For instance, embedded reporters had little to do with the most famous example of overly excited wartime reporting—the harrowing, Hollywood-like saga of Private Jessica Lynch. It was stateside reporters who fell hard for the administration's gratifying spin about Lynch, the one-hundred-pound supply clerk and aspiring kindergarten teacher from Palestine, West Virginia, who was riding in a terribly lost convoy on March 23, 2003, that made yet another wrong turn and drove into a deadly ambush in Nasiriyah. Injured and knocked unconscious when the Humvee she was riding in smashed into a jackknifed U.S. truck, Lynch was taken prisoner and held for nine days at Nasiriyah's Saddam Hussein hospital.

On the night of April 1, U.S. Special Forces stormed the building and rescued her in dramatic fashion and with overpowering force.

News of the midnight raid—Saving Private Lynch—became the MSM's hottest human drama of the invasion. The headlines also helped beat back a week's worth of bad news. By the end of March, U.S. troops were facing fiercer-than-expected fighting in Iraq, early criticism was being voiced about the Pentagon trying to invade Iraq on the cheap with too few troops, and the all-important weapons of mass destruction were still missing. Saturation coverage of the meticulously stage-managed Lynch rescue helped the White House turn the page.

On April 3, the *Washington Post*, in a front-page exclusive teeming with pleasing facts, filled in the details of the Lynch story. With the aid of anonymous "U.S. officials," the paper painted the portrait of a Rambo-like warrior who battled through the ambush. That morning, network wake-up news programs quickly amplified the *Post*'s cinematic account. More than a week after the rescue CNN's Anderson Cooper was still extolling its virtues: "To many, Private Lynch, her daring rescue, and her return have come to symbolize the qualities the US military holds highest: loyalty, endurance and daring." The Lynch chatter was all-consuming. In truth, the *Post*'s depiction of Lynch was riddled with errors. The story's opening sentences contained no fewer than six factual inaccuracies:

> Pfc. Jessica Lynch, rescued Tuesday from an Iraqi hospital, fought fiercely and shot several enemy soldiers firing her weapon until she ran out of ammunition, U.S. officials said yesterday. Lynch, a 19-year-old supply clerk continued firing at the Iraqis even after she sustained multiple gunshot wounds "She was fighting to the death," the official said. "She did not want to be taken alive." Lynch was also stabbed when Iraqi forces closed in on her position, the official said.

The problem was:

1. Lynch did not fight fiercely. (She was immediately knocked unconscious by the vehicle collision.)
2. She did not shoot any enemy soldiers.
3. She did not fire her weapon. (It jammed.)
4. She did not sustain any gunshot wounds.
5. She was not fighting to the death.
6. She was not stabbed.

Lynch never claimed she did any of those things. It was the admin-istration that was spinning the false tale.

Months later, after the actual facts about Lynch and her rescue had been revealed, the MSM had another chance to return to the topic and finally pose some critical questions about the Pentagon's manufactured tale of heroism. But the press demurred. On July 21, Lynch was awarded the Bronze Star. Lynch herself seemed embarrassed, claiming she was no hero, but the Pentagon insisted on presenting the award, complete with a citation that read: "For exemplary courage under fire during combat operations to liberate Iraq, in support of Operation Iraqi Freedom. Private First Class Lynch's bravery and heart persevered while *surviving in the ambush* and captivity in An Nasiriya." [Emphasis added.]

The award caught the attention of some combat veterans who decried it as a cheap publicity stunt that degraded the honor. The late syndicated columnist and retired Army Colonel David Hackworth pointed out in 2003 that Lynch, "was injured and knocked uncon-scious in a vehicle that crashed as it was hauling butt to try to escape an enemy ambush. It was probably the first time that an American soldier was awarded the country's fourth-highest ground-fighting combat award for being conked out and 'off the air' throughout the fight."

Hackworth was not alone. Writing to the *Navy Times*, a Marine gunnery sergeant complained, "Isn't the Bronze Star given to someone who has demonstrated heroic or meritorious achievement? I never realized surviving was heroic or meritorious. Why not give it to all the soldiers, sailors, airmen and Marines who fought in the war?"

A Marine veteran from the Korean War wrote to the *News Journal* in Wilmington, Delaware, to, "raise my voice along with others criticizing the award of the Bronze Star medal to former Army prisoner of war Jes-sica Lynch."

A Vietnam veteran wrote to the *San Antonio Express-News:* "My brother and I served in Vietnam and witnessed more heroism daily then [*sic*] described in the Jessica Lynch incident. Many of our friends died with little or no recognition."

And one Marine back from serving in Iraq, wrote to his college newspaper at the University of California–Riverside, to take issue with the Pentagon's decision to award Lynch the Medal: "Lynch got a Bronze Star as a publicity stunt for the U.S. Army."

The MSM, though, remained dutifully silent, refusing to pick up on the obvious news story and refusing to raise any uncomfortable questions about the Pentagon's myth-making machine that had forcefully attached itself to Lynch.

Then again, in the spring and summer of 2003 the MSM wasn't posing many uncomfortable questions to anyone in power. NBC anchor Tom Brokaw certainly shied away from any awkward inquiries during the April special he hosted, *Commander in Chief: Inside the White House at War*, which featured the first lengthy, post-invasion interview with Bush. Brokaw spent the first ten minutes of the program walking Bush through the decision to launch an opportunity strike against Saddam Hussein on March 19 before the scheduled start of the attack. The last minute audible was called after the Pentagon received intelligence that Saddam was inside a Baghdad bunker. NBC's prime-time special with Bush portrayed the strike as a victory of American intelligence and military ingenuity, never acknowledging to viewers that the consensus among analysts at the time was that the attack was a failure because Saddam was either not in the bunker or that he managed to survive.

In fact, two weeks *before* the *Commander in Chief* aired, NBC itself had reported the Pentagon had launched its second assassination attempt on Saddam, which meant military officials, busy hunting for Saddam in April, assumed correctly that the first strike on Saddam in March was a bust. But Brokaw pretended not to know the facts. Later in the NBC special Brokaw gently pressed Bush about the fact that a month after the invasion the WMDs, the pivotal justification for the war, had still not been found.

> **Brokaw:** But it is important to find the weapons of mass destruction, or the evidence that he had a massive program underway, isn't it?
> **Bush:** Yes, I think we will. I'm pretty confident we will.

Fourteen months later Brokaw again sat down with Bush for an extended interview. By then it was obvious that the WMDs were not going to be found and it was likely Saddam hadn't had them for years, if ever. As part of this sixteenth question to the president, Brokaw inserted just a passing reference to the WMDs and never asked Bush to explain their startling absence.

That second Brokaw interview aired on June 6, 2004. Three weeks later a correspondent for RTE, Ireland's national broadcasting service, showed the flip side to the American media's rampant timidity. Interviewing Bush, Carole Coleman pressed him hard on the increasingly violent situation in Iraq. Not used to pointed, persistent questions, even about war, Bush snapped back.

Coleman: The world is a more dangerous place today. I don't know whether you can see that or not.
Bush: Why do you say that?
Coleman: There are terrorist bombings every single day. It's now a daily event. It wasn't like that two years ago.
Bush: What was it like on September 11, 2001? It was a . . . there was relative calm, we . . .
Coleman: But it's your response to Iraq that's considered—
Bush: Let me finish. Let me finish. Please. You ask the questions and I'll answer them, if you don't mind.

After the interview an indignant Bush aide called Coleman to inform her that her previously scheduled interview with Laura Bush had been canceled, that her access to the White House would be curbed, and that an official complaint was going to be lodged with the Irish embassy in Washington. "You were more vicious than any of the White House press corps," the aide said. Instead of "vicious," the aide could have used the word "diligent"—"You were more diligent than any of the White House press corps"—which would have been more accurate.

As for American correspondents, there was one who, during the height of the pro-war frenzy in the spring of 2003, stood up and asked serious questions about the MSM war coverage. And for that, her career came to a screeching halt. On April 24, 2003, Ashleigh Banfield gave a speech at Kansas State University addressing the state of cable TV journalism. In the wake of September 11, Banfield had emerged as one of the most well-known correspondents for MSNBC and its parent company NBC, filing reports in Afghanistan as well as Iraq. In her campus address, Banfield bemoaned television's unrealistically soft coverage of the Iraq invasion:

So was this journalism or was this coverage? There is a grand difference between journalism and coverage, and getting access does not
mean you're getting the story, it just means you're getting one more
arm or leg of the story. And that's what we got, and it was a glorious,
wonderful picture that had a lot of people watching and a lot of advertisers excited about cable news. But it wasn't journalism, because I'm
not so sure that we in America are hesitant to do this again, to fight
another war, because it looked like a glorious and courageous and so
successful terrific endeavor, and we got rid of a horrible leader: We got
rid of a dictator, we got rid of a monster, but we didn't see what it took
to do that.

The repercussion for Banfield was swift—she was "taken to the
woodshed" by her bosses and her NBC career effectively ended.

By contrast, Brokaw, by adopting a more informal, cushioned
approach to interviewing Bush and dealing with the war, was simply
playing by the MSM's new wartime rules, which seemed to stress timidity as it turned away from uncomfortable stories and embraced administration sources to tell the war story. Of the 319 on-camera sources
who appeared in nightly network new stories about Iraq during October 2003, 76 percent were current or former government and military
officials, according to a study by Fairness and Accuracy in Reporting, a
liberal advocacy group.

At the outset of the war and for the first few months that followed, it
was not just the American flag pins news anchors proudly wore on
their lapels, or the White House–penned "Operation Iraqi Freedom"
logos that were tattooed to the bottom corner of cable channel screens
that confirmed the MSM's firm allegiance. It extended well into the
news-gathering process, as well. Less than one week into the war on
March 23, Middle East broadcaster Al Jazeera aired disturbing images
of American GIs who had been captured, held as POWs, and questioned
by Iraqis. Also included in the clips were images of several dead U.S. soldiers on the ground, some with apparent bullet wounds to their heads.
(They were captured in the same ambush that had knocked Private
Lynch unconscious.) For the White House, the tapes represented the
worse batch of news since the war had begun, and for the MSM, the
tapes represented their first real test as to how independent the wartime
news gathering was going to be. The quick answer was, not very inde-

pendent at all. At a U.S. Central Command briefing, Lieutenant General John Abizaid immediately put the press on notice: "I regard the showing of those pictures as absolutely unacceptable." News organizations dutifully fell into line. Instead of treating the pictures of the still-living captured soldiers as breaking news, most U.S. television news organizations acquiesced to the Pentagon, at least temporarily, which wanted to first contact the soldiers' families before the clips were aired. As for the portion of the tape that showed dead U.S. troops, ABC News president David Westin vowed never to air those kinds of pictures because they were not "newsworthy" and because they would be "troubling to many people." ABC anchorman Charlie Gibson completely agreed: "Any time that you show bodies, it is simply disrespectful, in my opinion." For ABC, wartime reporting apparently meant avoiding "troubling" and "disrespectful" dispatches. Meanwhile, CBS officials at the time also vowed not to air any images of the dead U.S. troops.

That represented a dramatic departure from the standard used just ten years earlier during President Clinton's first term, when major American television outlets aired a grotesque news clip of the bloated corpse of a U.S. soldier being dragged through the dusty streets of Mogadishu, Somalia, after rebels there shot down American helicopters and killed a dozen soldiers. The incident became the basis for the book and movie, *Black Hawk Down*. In 1993 the MSM saw clear news value in the brutal images, and what they suggested about the failure of U.S. foreign policy, and gave them prominent play. Several major dailies ran the close-up Mogadishu photo on page one while both *Time* and *Newsweek* gave the image big play inside. The MSM did not wait for the soldier's family to be notified. They simply reported the event as news, which it was.

CNN was counted among them. At the time, the channel's executive vice president for news gathering, Ed Turner, was adamant about putting the disturbing images on the air. "We are in the job of reporting. You hate to distress people, but it sort of goes with the territory," said Turner, who suggested that trying to censor wartime images was a losing battle, given the rapid improvement in high-speed communications. "We're not going to have less of this kind of an issue. We're going to have more of it," he said in 1993.

He was right about advancing technology. By the time of the 2003 Iraq invasion new technology like digital cameras and video phones allowed embedded correspondents to relay, in real time, any image they wanted. In theory, coverage of the Iraq war should have been the most unvarnished in history. But the images were not always relayed directly to the American people. First, stateside MSM gatekeepers had to okay footage, and in 2003, afraid of appearing confrontational, negative, or unpatriotic, many in the media were reluctant to offer up images that showed U.S. servicemen and women in trouble. It was that type of media self-censorship that CNN's Turner likely never foresaw in 1993 when he discussed the Mogadishu images. Turner also failed to see the MSM's coming hypocrisy in war coverage.

For example, when the video of American POWs was aired on Al Jazeera in March 2003, CBS News president Andrew Heyward warned against showing unnecessarily gruesome pictures or anything that could be used for propaganda purposes. Three months later when news broke that Saddam's sons, Uday and Qusay Hussein, had been killed in a shoot-out with coalition forces, CBS, like every other American television news outlet, went on the air to broadcast government-issued photos of the men's bloated, bullet-ridden bodies. "I don't see how we could meet our journalistic responsibility and meet the competitive aspects of what we do and not put them on," CBS anchor Dan Rather said at the time. CBS's earlier concern for wartime propaganda seemed to evaporate when it was the Pentagon supplying the photos of dead bodies. (The killing of Uday and Qusay, and the hyping of the story, had clear political implication for Bush at home as administration officials—falsely, it turned out—suggested the men's capture would weaken the insurgency.)

One year later, on March 31, 2004, another set of macabre images captured in Iraq did cause editors and producers to examine their wartime guidelines. This time they came from the insurgent city of Fallujah and included a charred body being beaten by a man wielding a metal pole, part of a body being dragged behind a car, and two bodies dangling from the steelwork of a bridge over the Euphrates River. The bodies were of four American contractors who were attacked and mutilated in front of a cheering Iraqi crowd. Unlike the corpse photos of Uday and Qusay, American broadcasters either blurred the images from Fallujah or refused to air the most graphic portions, while several newspapers included editors' notes to explain their decision to publish the pictures at all. "A lot of that came across as apologizing for having to show readers the images, and that's not appropriate," said Janet Weaver, dean of faculty at the Poynter Institute, a journalism training institute in Florida. "There were real contortions over the Fallujah pictures, and it showed how very uncomfortable the press remains with graphic images of war violence."

Wrestling with how best to use the disturbing Fallujah photographs, MaryAnne Golon, picture editor at *Time*, went back to see how the magazine had handled the bloody Mogadishu crisis. She and her colleagues were stunned at how graphic the images were that the magazine published in 1993. "We couldn't believe the things we ran then—a full-page image of a dead U.S. soldier being dragged through the streets. It's shocking," she said. "There's a completely different mind-set today. It's a reflection of the culture and the fact that the country has become more conservative." *Time* wasn't the only major outlet, between the Clinton and Bush years, to radically alter its policy of showing grave images of dead U.S. troops. In 1993, CBS's nightly newscast broadcast the gruesome clips of the dead American solider being dragged through the streets of Mogadishu. In fact, CBS aired the most graphic clips of all the three networks; footage of three Somalis standing over the body of a U.S. soldier jamming the muzzle of his rifle into the soldier's backside. But in 2004, the CBS's *Evening News*, suddenly sensitive to White House wishes, opted to electronically blur the Fallujah videotape, since it was too upsetting for viewers.

In an American culture increasingly drenched in violence, it seemed odd that war imagery, of all things, was treated so timidly. The European mainstream press, for instance, routinely offered up graphic depictions from Iraq. "I certainly think we've seen an extremely sanitized version of the war," said Peter Howe, author of *Shooting Under Fire: The World of the War Photographer.* "If war is divorced from daily life, as a video game is, we can't make judgments, and we find ourselves mired in something we did not expect." American news consumers, particularly during the first months of the war, had little idea of what happens when the world's mightiest military power unleashes sustained attacks on an impoverished, despot-ruled nation, or what happens when that regime, fighting for its life, answers in kind.

Howe noted that unlike the first Gulf War, when battlefield images were tightly controlled—even censored—by the U.S. military, photographers in Iraq for the second Gulf War had complete freedom to shoot whatever they wanted. Whether those images ever reached news consumers was another issue. "There's censorship being applied, but by the media itself," said Howe in 2004. "Everybody is running scared." One year later, Jeff Fager, executive producer for *60 Minutes*, concurred: "We tend to err on the side of sanitizing news to keep people from the realities of a war. We do a lot of self-censorship. Usually we don't see enough of what's really going on in Iraq." For photojournalist Kael Alford, working in Baghdad as the bombs from the 2003 air raids pounded the city and killed thousands of locals, her instructions from a weary editor were explicit: "Please don't send any more wounded civilian pictures."

Images of wounded or dead Americans were even less welcome stateside. One 2005 survey of media professionals found that 42 percent said they were discouraged from showing images of dead Americans—17 percent were prohibited from doing so. That same year the *Los Angeles Times* reviewed six prominent U.S. newspapers (*Atlanta Journal-Constitution*, *Los Angeles Times*, *New York Times*, *St. Louis Post-Dispatch*, and *Washington Post*), along with *Time* and *Newsweek*, and reported that during a six-month period from late 2004 into 2005, it "found almost no pictures from the war zone of Americans killed in action." Several of the publications were reluctant to even print images of *wounded* Americans in Iraq. That, despite the fact that during the six-month period monitored, 559 Americans and coalition forces were killed and thousands more injured in Iraq.

Uneasy images weren't the only things kept under wraps a year after the war. So were inconvenient facts, like why the war was waged in the first place. Appearing on C-Span in late January 2004 was former senior weapons inspector Scott Ritter who prior to the war repeatedly warned that Saddam did not have the WMD stockpile Bush said he did and that the administration's rationale for war was thin. A C-Span caller that January day phoned in to ask why he rarely saw Ritter on the television anymore, particularly since Ritter's assessment of Iraq's WMDs turned out to be accurate. Ritter's response, which perfectly captured the MSM's postwar predicament, is worth reading in full:

Well, it's probably a question best posed to the producers and the bookers at the various television shows and radio talk shows. I've always been confident that I'm saying things that are factually sound, based upon the truth, that I'm not spinning them for anyone's benefit. Unfortunately, I don't believe the mainstream media acted responsibly in regard to Iraq. Back in the fall of 2002, I was belittled, I was called a traitor, I was called crazy—Paula Zahn of CNN accused me of drinking Saddam Hussein's Kool-Aid for making accurate statements in response to aluminum tubes and uranium allegedly coming from Niger. I think we have a problem here in that the media is culpable for the misleading of the American public. They bought into the Bush administration's rhetoric and war fervor, they sold the war to the American public, and now they have to deal with the fact that they're the ones that were out there beating the war drums and you have this guy, Scott Ritter, who was saying something different and—maybe they just don't know how to deal with me.

The media's boycott of Ritter was indeed widespread. During the six months prior to his C-Span interview, the guy who got the facts right about the WMDs appeared on just three national news shows. By comparison, during the same post-invasion time span, right-wing war supporter Frank Gaffney, who insisted Saddam was connected with the 9/11 attacks, appeared on nearly two dozen television programs to discuss Iraq. During one of Ritter's three appearances, on CNBC, host Gloria Bulger insulted him on the air by referring to him as "the last man in America to defend Saddam Hussein." Of course Ritter never "defended" Saddam—he actually called him "a pathetic old, brutal dictator." But Ritter did oppose the war and did question the Bush administration's justifications for it. And for that and for being right, in the wake of the botched occupation he was either shunned by the MSM or called a Saddam apologist.

Meanwhile, nearly thirty months after the invasion of Iraq the *New York Times Magazine* got around to conceding that liberal antiwar activists, and specifically the Hollywood variety, had been vindicated by the deadly aftermath of the invasions. But the *Times* spent paragraph after paragraph mocking the "rich and beautiful" for their "Pollyannaish politics" and their "self-righteous" way. Like Ritter, the people who got it right about the war were the ones being ridiculed by the MSM. (Imagine the press contempt if the liberals had been wrong about the war?) Also, compare that caustic coverage to the *Times's* warm embrace of the *Weekly Standard*, Rupert Murdoch's Republican-friendly magazine and neoconservative hotbed that served as the loudest cheerleader for the war. (The magazine began calling for Saddam's removal in 1997.) In March 2003, one week before the war, the *Times* toasted the wonky magazine for its Beltway influence—"White House Listens When Weekly Speaks," read the fawning headline. At the time that certainly passed as a smart assignment. Yet months and years later when it became clear that almost everything the *Weekly Standard* had predicted about the war had been wrong, the *Times* politely refused to go back and ask tough questions to *Weekly Standard* editors who urged the nation, and helped convince the administration, to go to war. The *Times* was hardly alone; *Weekly Standard* editor Bill Kristol waltzed in and out of television studios all over Washington, D.C. and rarely had to fend off tough, sustained questioning about the botched Iraq war. There seemed to be a sort of a MSM gentleman's agreement not to make the war backers in the press feel uncomfortable. Comedy Central's Jon Stewart proved to be an exception, albeit in his unique way. From Kristol's October 24, 2005 appearance on *The Daily Show:* "I think, and if you go back and you read the essays certainly about what you were saying about Saddam Hussein in 1997, you were wrong about Iraq way before anyone else, and I just want to say that I have to give you credit." (The audience roared.)

As the troubled occupation of Iraq stretched into the U.S. election year of 2004, the urgency assigned to the story by the MSM clearly declined and coverage waned, much to the delight of the White House. In fact, the fade could be pinpointed to a specific date: June 28, 2004, the day U.S. officials handed over sovereignty to the Iraqis. The administration heralded the event as yet another positive turning point for Iraq and that's certainly how the MSM played it. That night CNN devoted its entire prime-time lineup to analyzing the brief, fifteen-minute ceremony in Baghdad. (The official transfer was moved up, unannounced, out of fear of violence.) Fox News cheered it as "a day that will go down in history." Newspapers the next morning were clogged with reports from Iraq and speculation about what the transfer of political power would mean for the rebuilding of Iraq, as well as for the 140,000 U.S. troops serving there.

The administration's hopes for a new day in Iraq, though, were quickly squashed as the violence inside Iraq simply escalated in the wake of the sovereignty transfer. Kidnappings by insurgents multiplied, as did assassinations, while electricity remained in short supply. Iraq's national conference—critical to the eventual implementation of free elections—was postponed, and U.S. soldiers continued to die at a predictable clip. The one element that did change however was the U.S. press coverage, particularly on television. Buying into the administration's hopeful spin that an important page had been turned on June 28, the MSM pulled back and, consciously or subconsciously, decided the story was winding down. "Clearly the volume in press coverage has gone way down," noted Steven Cook during the summer of 2004. A fellow at the Council on Foreign Relations, Cook observed that "sleepy" is a good word to describe it. "The coverage doesn't compare with anything we'd seen during the previous 12 months from Iraq. The drop-off has been noticeable." From the media's perspective in 2004, the Iraq occupation had at times become the new Korean War—the Forgotten War. The Center of Media and Public Affairs tracked the media withdrawal from Iraq; TV reports declined 25 percent in 2004.

The MSM's attention in 2004 shifted from Iraq to the unfolding presidential campaign and the press had trouble paying attention to both big stories at the same time. During the Democrats' national convention in Boston, where pundits and producers spent much time bemoaning how little actual news there was to report, here's a small sampling of what happened in Iraq that same week, little of which was deemed newsworthy enough to seriously interrupt the endless, repetitive cable TV discussion about swing voters:

- July 26: Attackers shot and killed Iraq's senior Interior Ministry official and two of his bodyguards in a drive-by shooting.
- July 26: A suicide bomber detonated a car filled with explosives, mortars, and rockets near the gates of a U.S. base in Mosul, killing three.
- July 27: The dead body of a kidnapped Turkish truck driver was found.

- July 27: One Iraqi was killed and fourteen coalition soldiers were injured when a mortar hit a Baghdad residential district.
- July 28: A suicide car bomb exploded on a busy boulevard in Baquba, killing sixty-eight people and wounding nearly one hundred, making it the deadliest insurgent strike since the U.S. occupation began one year earlier.
- July 28: Seven Iraqi soldiers and thirty-five insurgents were killed during a firefight in Suwariyah.
- July 29: Reeling from the violence and a wave of kidnappings, Iraqi officials once again postponed a three-day national conference to choose an interim assembly in preparation for the country's first elections.

That week was typical of the chaos that transpired in Iraq that summer, with or without the spotlight of the U.S. press shining on the region. The MSM indifference to Iraq was a blessing for the Bush campaign, which was anxious to downplay the endemic violence in the war torn country. Instead of a summer of tenacious coverage from Baghdad, Bush was blessed with a cable news agenda that focused on endless hurricane updates, Martha Stewart's legal woes, and the tawdry Laci Peterson trial. As pollster Peter Hart suggested, any day between August 15 and October 15 that Iraq was *not* making headlines in the American media was a good day for the Bush campaign. Conversely, lots of Iraq headlines likely boosted the political fortunes for the John Kerry campaign. Once again, the White House agenda and the MSM's were in perfect sync.

In fact, a summer of 2004 survey by the Pew Research Center for People and the Press found a direct link between reporting on Iraq and Bush's political fortunes. During the month of June, just 39 percent of Americans paid very close attention to the news coming out of Iraq, the lowest rate for all of 2004. During that same month, the survey found Americans' opinion of Bush, as well as of the situation in Iraq, improved noticeably. In other words, slow news from Iraq was good news for Bush.

If that weren't enough, some within the MSM tried to manufacture good news out of Iraq during the crucial summer of 2004. A July 21, *New York Times* campaign dispatch noted a key factor that could work in

Bush's favor come November: "In Iraq, the transfer of sovereignty has led to some reduction in American casualties." Not true. The number of fatalities among U.S. service members serving in Iraq actually increased by 30 percent in the month following the transfer of sovereignty. Yet four days after the *Times*'s pro-administration error, *Washington Post* columnist Jim Hoagland made the same point: "[N]o one can express unhappiness about the overall decline in U.S. military casualties that has followed the change in tactics and the June 28 transfer of political responsibility." Again, that was plainly false. But for casual news consumers in the summer of 2004, with the presidential election looming just months away, it certainly *seemed* like the situation in Iraq was more secure, or at least less deadly.

The diminished attention paid to Iraq created an odd media disconnect because while most pundits agreed the war would be *the* key issue in the November election, Americans were being exposed to less reporting and analysis about the war. Despite the clear increase in violence and casualties in 2004, TV outlets continued to treat the situation with a strange detachment. For instance, at 8 a.m. on September 5 came news that seven Marines had been killed by a suicide car bomber as they patrolled the outskirts of Fallujah, marking one of the deadliest attacks of the entire summer. Yet at 10 a.m. during their top-of-the-hour news reports, CNN, Fox News, and MSNBC made just cursory mention of the mass killings. The channels instead were entrenched in hurricane mode, covering Hurricane Frances nearly nonstop, for the fourth straight day.

And just look at how on September 29, a group of military families whose relatives had died serving in Iraq unveiled plans to target Bush with new television ads to be aired before the election. The group was called RealVoices and seemed to offer reporters an intriguing news angle. But in the forty-eight hours following its September 29 press conference, here's how many times the group was referenced on CNN: zero; on CNN Headline News: one; on MSNBC: zero; on Fox News: zero. On ABC: zero. On NBC: zero. On CBS: three. Incredibly, one of CBS's three RealVoices mentions came during a *CBS Evening News* report that singled out political attack ads that were "breaking new ground on the low road." The antiwar ads from RealVoices were depicted as among the worst offenders. The *New York Times* took the same path. In a tsk-tsk article, the newspaper counted a RealVoices commercial among the "grim," and "confrontational" campaign ads that were "pushing the boundaries of emotion."

For the record, the RealVoices ads that MSM pundits and reporters found so offensive featured emotional parents and siblings recalling the pain of losing loved ones in Iraq and posing critical questions about the war directed to Bush. There was nothing in the ads that could have been remotely construed as "breaking new ground on the low road," yet that's how the MSM portrayed the ads, when they bothered to reference them at all. And incredibly, neither the CBS report nor the *Times* article about "grim" attack ads from the campaign season that took the "low road" included any mention of the untruthful and Republican-funded, Swift Boat Veterans for Truth.

By September, in the wake of a leaked CIA assessment that could not rule out a full-scale civil war in Iraq, as well as a fresh round of extraordinary and indiscriminate violence in Iraq, the MSM reporting, noticeably on television, did regain some urgency. But even then, the press never elevated Iraq to a top domestic priority. Instead, during the crucial campaign month of September, the MSM was obsessed with CBS's botched report on Bush and the National Guard, which aired on *60 Minutes II.* During one three-day period in late September when disturbing news broke that two more Americans had been beheaded by insurgents while the killers' cameras rolled, CNN, MSNBC, and Fox combined made approximately 220 mentions of the beheadings, according to TVEyes. During that same period, though, they made more than 1,000 references to the CBS report. The White House couldn't have been happier with the MSM's news judgment.

In the end it was a private email of all things that in September pierced the everyday MSM war coverage and delivered perhaps the most graphic and telling report about where Iraq stood eighteen months after the ordered invasion. Written by *Wall Street Journal* reporter Famaz Fassihi and intended only for friends and family members to give them an insider's view of the situation on the ground in Iraq, the dispatch quickly bounced around the Internet and caused much commotion. According to Fassihi's report, security inside Iraq was an unmitigated disaster, which made her job as a journalist almost impossible:

I can't go grocery shopping any more, can't eat in restaurants, can't strike a conversation with strangers, can't look for stories, can't drive in any thing but a full armored car, can't go to scenes of breaking news stories, can't be stuck in traffic, can't speak English outside, can't take a road trip, can't say I'm an American, can't linger at checkpoints, can't be curious about what people are saying, doing, feeling. And can't and can't.

Despite thousands of dispatches filed from Iraq, and hundreds of hours of broadcast time over the previous year and a half, Fassihi's informal yet riveting account, stripped of the usual MSM varnish, painted a disturbing portrait of Iraq that had only been hinted at in most of the other American news reports—that the occupation, in every way measurable, stood as a colossal failure. "The genie of terrorism, chaos and mayhem has been unleashed onto this country as a result of American mistakes and it can't be put back into a bottle," she wrote, a description that looked more prophetic with each passing month. (Sixteen months later, Fassihi's frustrations were privately confirmed by fellow American journalists in Iraq who "off the record," according to Defensetech.org, "describe a place where fear and frustration make their jobs almost impossible.")

Under attack from conservatives who charged Fassihi's personal opinions clouded her judgment and betrayed her objectivity, the *Journal* soon announced she was going to take a previously scheduled vacation from Iraq which would keep her from writing anything more about it until after the U.S. presidential election. Question: If Fassihi's email had extolled the virtues of the invasion, suggesting the "good news" in Iraq was going underreported, would *Journal* editors have located a previously scheduled vacation to remove her from Iraq?

And that's not a rhetorical question. The U.S. press corps working in Iraq was made up of some self-identified war cheerleaders. Upon leaving his post as *Newsweek*'s Baghdad bureau chief in 2005, Rod Nordland revealed that he had arrived in Iraq two years earlier, "as an unabashed believer in toppling Saddam Hussein." Of course, the odds of *Newsweek* in 2003 assigning a Baghdad bureau chief who was "an unabashed opponent" of the war were nonexistent. As war loomed, vocal war critics were largely banned from the upper echelons of the MSM. "Unabashed" war supporters though, landed key assignments.

Fassihi's Iraq truth-telling was, in a sense, accidental. One MSM reporter who did it on purpose was the *Philadelphia Inquirer*'s Ken Dilanian, who experienced a profound change of heart on the topic. In April 2004, fresh from reporting inside Iraq, an optimistic Dilanian wrote in the *Inquirer* that the press too often ignored improvements in Iraq and underplayed the chance for a real turnaround. His optimistic essay was passed around online by conservatives who toasted Dilanian as a rare MSM truth teller. That summer Dilanian returned to Baghdad to cover the sovereignty handover only to be shocked at the deteriorating conditions. "The situation in Iraq right now is not as bad as the news media are portraying it to be. It's worse," Dilanian announced on August 1. "Most Iraqis aren't seeing the improvements they had hoped for, and they're not blaming the guerrillas—they're blaming the Americans. Sovereignty seems to have had zero effect on this equation."

That was the story so many American news outlets missed during the summer of 2004. And it just so happens that was the story the Bush White House did not want to have told.

Even two years after the invasion the press was still stepping gingerly around the topic of Iraq and its Beltway ramifications. Writing up a March 2005 survey about how Americans felt the war was going, the *Washington Post* reported, "Fifty-three percent of Americans said the war was not worth fighting, 57 percent said they disapprove of the president's handling of Iraq, and 70 percent said the number of U.S. casualties, including more than 1,500 deaths, is an unacceptable price. The *mixed assessment* of the situation in Iraq comes near the second anniversary of the U.S. invasion." [Emphasis added.] A clear majority agreed the war was not worth fighting, that too many Americans were dying, and Bush wasn't handling the conflict well, yet the *Post* deemed that to be a "mixed assessment"?

In June, the *Post*, returning to the topic of public opinion, noted that, "To a surprising degree, given the strength of the insurgency in Iraq, Bush has maintained support for the broad goals of his Iraq policy and for a continued military presence there." Maintained support? Maybe among Beltway editors and producers. But at the time the *Post* article was published a clear majority of Americans had already decided that sending troops to Iraq was "a mistake," according to a CNN/*USA Today*/Gallup poll.

On August 3, a roadside bombing near Haditha, the the deadliest single attack on U.S. forces of the entire war, claimed the lives of fourteen Marines and forced the war back to the forefront for the MSM, although just barely. Incredibly, news of the Marine slaughter ran neck-and-neck with the second-day, everyone's-fine coverage of Air France Flight 358, which skidded off the runway in Toronto and came to a safe stop. In the twenty-four hours immediately following the troubled Air France touchdown, CNN mentioned "Toronto" 115 times. By comparison, in the twenty-four hours immediately following the deadly roadside bombing in Iraq, CNN mentioned "Marines" just 62 times on the air. CNN was not alone. Each cable news outlet and each of the three networks paid significantly more attention to Air France's bumpy landing than they did to the fourteen Marines killed in Iraq.

Cable news outlets sometimes showed so little interest in Iraq that their counterparts in Europe were actually giving it more coverage. During the randomly selected seven-day period between September 7 and September 13, 2005, CNN referenced "Iraq" 153 times, compared to CNN Europe which mentined "Iraq" 221 times. So despite the fact that roughly 90 percent of the coalition casualties in Iraq were being suffered by Americans, and at least 90 percent of the costs were being shouldered by Americans, CNN viewers in Europe were often getting more coverage about the war than CNN viewers in America.

And even when the MSM did focus on Iraq and asked the appropriately tough questions, it was woefully late. In the September 26, 2005, issue of *Time*, Joe Klein penned an exhaustive and damning look at how the war in Iraq was being lost. Citing interviews with scores of senior military officials, Klein noted, "They voiced their growing frustration with a war that they feel was not properly anticipated by the Bush Administration, a war fought with insufficient resources, a war that almost all of them now believe is not winnable militarily." Tough talk for sure. But did it really take a MSM institution like *Time* more than twenty months and nearly two thousand dead U.S. servicemen to arrive at that rather obvious conclusion? The pronouncement certainly would have carried more authority if *Time* hadn't patiently waited until a majority of Americans told pollsters the war was a mistake. The press, bogged down by its own timidity, often seemed to be working off a calendar that lagged twelve months behind the facts on the ground in Iraq.

Indeed, the disconnect between the MSM and the public could not have been any more dramatic. Even after a majority of Americans concluded the war in Iraq was a mistake, the MSM clung to its signature timidity. Sitting for a *GQ* interview on the eve of his November 2005, departure as the longtime anchor on ABC's *Nightline*, Ted Koppel conceded the war had been "one fiasco after another," that war planners had "miscalculated the consequences," had concocted "phony" or "inadequate cases" for the invasion, and that the Bush White House had not been "honest with the American public" about the war.

But it's telling *when* Koppel made his comments, waiting until Bush's job approval rating had plummeted and waiting for his time at ABC to be up. It's telling because the criticisms Koppel raised—the Pentagon not sending enough troops, not leveling with the American people about the need for war, not asking the whole country to share the burden of war—were issues that had been on public display for years. Nightline did tackle those issues over time. But it was only when Koppel began his farewell tour from *Nightline* that the famous anchor himself talked tough about Iraq. And he did it in a monthly magazine, not on network television where he appeared several nights each week and where his comments would have had a larger impact. Koppel could have followed in the footsteps of Walter Cronkite who, at the conclusion of the February 27, 1968, CBS *Evening News* famously announced victory in Vietnam was no longer realistic. ("To say that we are mired in stalemate seems the only realistic, yet unsatisfactory, conclusion.") Cronkite's pronouncement struck the political landscape like a thunderbolt. "If I've lost Cronkite," President Lyndon Johnson told his aides, "I've lost Middle America." Koppel didn't carry that cultural mantle like Cronkite did, but Koppel could have plainly stated his points about the war being "one fiasco after another," about war planners who had concocted "phony" or "inadequate cases" for the invasion, and about how the White House had not been "honest with the American public" about the war. Instead, Koppel said his peace about Iraq during a Q&A with a men's fashion magazine.

And it's telling what else Koppel said. One of network news's most respected anchors told *GQ* he felt "every once in a while" administration war planners "deserve to be challenged" about Iraq. Every once in a while? The war had claimed more than two thousand U.S. lives, produced tens of thousands of Iraqi civilian causalities, cost the U.S. Treasury more than $300 billion, and had sparked a worldwide increase in terrorist attacks. It's hard to imagine what issue would have been troubling enough to prompt Koppel to call for *regular* challenges of the Bush White House.

CHAPTER 11

Still Afraid of the Facts

Hurricane Katrina was supposed to change the press, awaken it from its four-year slumber, and help it reestablish a purpose. At least that's what some journalists suggested in the wake of the deadly storm and the government's negligent rescue response. "Amidst the horror, American broadcast journalism just might have grown its spine back, thanks to Katrina," the BBC observed. Hope for change grew out of suddenly tough-talking correspondents covering the Big Easy calamity and who publicly challenged and chastised the administration, determined to showcase the chasm between what government officials were saying and what was actually happening on the ground. The poignant TV outbursts were noted, and in some cases toasted, by the *New York Times*, *Los Angeles Times*, *Washington Post*, and *Slate* as signs of renewed media vigor. Perhaps, thought some, the natural catastrophe would double as a larger wakeup call for the MSM, pushing them to return to the topic of Iraq with renewed vigor, to stop nervously dancing around the issue of prewar intelligence the way it did with the Downing Street memo, to refrain from obediently repeating administration terror threats without first asking tough questions, and to finally stand up to the press-hating bullies. In short, perhaps the MSM would get back to their primary responsibility of informing the public and asking tough questions of people in power without fear or favor. As *USA Today* suggested, "Katrina's media legacy may be a return to a post-Watergate-like era of tougher scrutiny of the federal government and public policy issues."

No such luck.

Ultimately the killer storm had little long-term effect on the press and the way it covered the Bush White House. Despite the fact the president emerged from the storm politically battered and by late 2005 and early 2006 had established himself as the most unpopular two-term president since Richard Nixon, managing to lose more than *50 points* off his job approval rating since 2001, for months and months most of the D.C. press crops steadfastly refused to alter its preferred narrative about Bush being a firm leader surrounded by a group of super savvy strategists who routinely outmaneuver hapless Democrats.

In fact, even before most of the Katrina homeless victims had found refuge, the press was retreating to its old habit of sheltering Bush from bad news. Three weeks after the storm *Los Angeles Times* Washington bureau chief Doyle McManus claimed Bush received a "bump in the polls" following his nationally televised speech regarding the rebuilding efforts planned for New Orleans. But no such bump existed. When Bush's job approval rating fell further into the 30s in early November, Fox News's Chris Wallace, perhaps the network's straightest shooter, likely spoke for lots of high-profile journalists when he conceded on-air, "I was genuinely surprised to see these poll numbers." The president had been in a slow and steady decline throughout 2005, yet confirmation still caught the MSM by surprise. After Iraq and even after Katrina, two large-scale debacles that would have toppled most presidents in the eyes of the Beltway press corps, given any kind of opening cautious journalists were still eager to cut Bush and the Republicans all sorts of slack.

In January 2006, when *Newsweek* wrote up the indictments of Jack Abramoff, the GOP kingpin lobbyist, the magazine's headline read "A Washington Tidal Wave: Members of Congress rushed to give back money," suggesting the influence-peddling scandal was a bipartisan "Washington" problem. The *Newsweek* article stressed the public would likely "remain appropriately skeptical of *both parties.*" [Emphasis added.] *Time* used the same kid glove approach: "Jack Abramoff built a power network using the rich and naive. *Washington* may pay the price." [Emphasis added.] The *Washington Post* falsely reported Abramoff had "made substantial campaign contributions to both major parties," and NBC's Katie Couric insisted, "Democrats took money . . . from Jack Abramoff, too." All four MSM organizations dutifully mouthed GOP spin about a bipartisan scandal and ignored the plain fact that not one Democrat had accepted tainted contributions from Abramoff, not one Democrat had been indicted, and not one Democrat was under investigation for accepting Abramoff money.

In the wake of Abramoff's guilty plea, some press outlets did their best, belatedly, to explain the crooked lobbying empire Abramoff had built with the help of the Republican leadership. And specifically, some news outlets addressed the K Street Project, the Republicans' well-oiled money machine guidelines that required lobbyists who wanted access to GOP lawmakers not only to be registered Republicans themselves, but also to give donations exclusively to Republican candidates. Congressional leaders kept an updated dossier handy to make sure which lobbyists were abiding by the GOP's K Street Project pay-to-play rules. But even following the Ambramoff guilty plea, the media's descriptions of the pivotal K Street Project seemed half-hearted at best. Appearing on the Don Imus radio show, *Newsweek*'s Evan Thomas mentioned, "this thing called the K Street Project," as if he'd just heard about it the day before over lunch at The Palm.

In truth, there was not a serious reporter in Washington, D.C., who for the previous three years did not know exactly what the K Street Project was, in part because GOP leaders openly boasted about it. The K Street Project was, hands down, the most important behind-the-scenes development in terms of how power/legislation was bought and sold inside the Beltway and represented an epic story with endless angles for journalists to pursue. And yet for years those same serious MSM reporters participated in a virtual boycott of the K Street Project story. (Curious, because during the Clinton years the press couldn't *stop* writing about alleged Democratic funny money scandals that rarely materialized into criminal wrongdoing.)

And yes, boycott is the proper word to describe the MSM's don't-ask/don't-tell policy regarding the K Street Project. It's true that on June 10, 2002, the *Washington Post* and the *New York Times* both published articles detailing the creation of the K Street Project. (Again, GOP leaders were practically advertising it.) But then the cones of silence went up. Between June 10, 2002, and January 3, 2006 when Abramoff pled guilty, the *Times* D.C. bureau produced just four articles that even mentioned the K Street Project. The number of articles that mentioned the K Street Project three or more times? Zero. During that same time frame, here's how many *Los Angeles Times* articles mentioned the K Street Project three or more times: zero. *USA Today*: zero. Associated Press: zero. *Miami Herald*: zero. *Chicago Tribune*: zero.

Boston Globe: zero. *Newsweek:* zero. Even the *Washington Post,* which is supposed to meticulously detail the legislative and lobby culture of D.C., published just three news articles that contained three or more references to the K Street Project.

As for television news, the boycott was nearly universal. Here's how many references ABC News made to the K Street Project between June 2002 and Jan. 3, 2006: one. CBS: zero. NBC: one. MSNBC: one. Fox News: zero. CNN: five. CNN never aired a reported piece explaining what the K Street Project was, although interestingly CNN International (seen mostly outside the United States) did. When the story of K Street Project finally began to get some traction in early 2006, some within the MSM belittled Democrats for trying to score points talking about it, suggesting the inside-the-Beltway topic went over the heads of most Americans. Writing on his ABC News blog, correspondent Jack Tapper noted, "While the brainy readers of this blog might be able to understand the terms and significance of terms such as 'K Street Project,' I don't see such tactics as coming close to the resonant language and communications brilliance of Team Gingrich a dozen years ago."

Maybe he was right. Then again if MSM reporters, producers, and anchors hadn't spent the previous three years consciously ignoring the K Street Project story, perhaps the phrase would have resonated a bit more with Americans.

Meanwhile, in February 2006, Bush, hoping to move public dialogue back to the issue of terror threats, suddenly shared vivid details—five years after the fact—of a plot by al-Qaida to fly airplanes into the Liberty Tower, the largest building on the West Coast. Bush announced the deadly plan had been "thwarted." But scores of U.S. senior national security officials disagreed, insisting that al-Qaida's scheme never got past the planning stages. Nonetheless, lots of MSM outlets, including CNN and *CBS Evening News,* falling right back into their dutiful post-9/11 War on Terror mode, simply repeated White House spin and reported that the plot had been busted up.

Bush's top political aide Karl Rove also spent the winter talking up terror threats. Revealing that the Republican election strategy for 2006 would again revolve around national security, Rove suggested during a January 20, 2006, speech that Democrats were too soft to defend America. Specifically, Rove, defending the administration's controversial wiretapping initiative, announced, "Let me be as clear as I can: President Bush believes if Al Qaeda is calling somebody in America, it is in our national security interest to know who they're calling and why. Some important Democrats clearly disagree."

Rove did not say who the "important Democrats" were who opposed spying on Al Qaeda, most likely because there were no "important Democrats" who opposed spying on Al Qaeda. Instead, what they, along with a significant number of important Republicans, objected to was the administration's decision to allow the National Security Agency to listen in on Americans' phone calls without first getting a special court order as required by law. Nonetheless, reporters for CNN, the *New York Times*, and the *Los Angeles Times*, who covered Rove's speech simply repeated his incendiary line about "important Democrats" without informing news consumers it was completely untrue.

The story of U.S. wiretapping itself represented a paradox that neatly captured the MSM during the Bush years. On the one hand the story only came to the public's attention thanks to stand-out investigative journalism by the *New York Times*'s James Risen. And for the two months following the scoop the *Times*, as well as the *Washington Post*, helped advance the story by uncovering key new details through admirable legwork. Proof that the press, post-Katrina, had broken free of its entrenched timidity, right? No quite. Because just as with dozens of other controversial Bush administration initiatives that the press helped bring to light (torturing war prisoners, paying pundits, outing a CIA operative, lying about outing a CIA operative, etc.), once the central facts were known most news organizations dutifully reported the story and rounded up appropriate expert quotes, but few MSM outlets seemed to have their heart in the pursuit. That was particularly true of television news outlets which, for better or worse, have come to define political journalism today. Outside of the badgering that took place inside the White House briefing room, which most Americans never saw, reporters, for most of Bush's first five years in office, rarely pressed the administration hard and they certainly never whipped up the type of sustained frenzy that was common during the Clinton administration for affairs less pressing then the warrantless wiretapping of thousands of Americans.

For instance, in the wake of the *Times*'s December 2005 wiretapping scoop, all the major news outlets had access to a Bush quote captured on tape from 2004 when he reassured Americans, "any time you hear the United States government talking about wiretap, it requires . . . a court order." That assurance certainly seemed to contradict the facts of the secret surveillance program. Yet CNN, for instance, aired the clip of that Bush "wiretap" quote just four times between December 2005 and February 2006. By contrast, during that same two months span, CNN found time to air thirty-five mentions of actress Angelina Jolie.

In the nearly two months after the wiretapping story broke, the administration was unable to produce even a handful of independent legal scholars to vouch for the fact the wiretapping program was legal, that it did not violate the 1978 Foreign Intelligence Surveillance Act which specifically required government officials receive a special warrant before tapping the phone lines of Americans; warrants that are granted approximately 99 percent of the time. Yet for news consumers the press continued to couch the wiretap story as a legal standoff, as if there were deep-seeded disagreement over whether the warrantless surveillance was legal. The only debate, per se, was that administration officials insisted the program was legal, and virtually every serious, nonpartisan legal scholar insisted it was not.

In truth, both Democrats *and* Republicans were raising serious questions about the surveillance initiative. Yet some within the MSM, feeding off White House spin, seemed anxious to place the controversy safely behind the president. For instance, Michael Duffy at *Time* magazine in late January 2006 insisted Bush had effectively put the wiretap story "to bed." In other words, Bush had answered his critics, won over Americans, and silenced the debate. It's more likely Bush had put the wiretap story "to bed" only among certain media elites because just one week later an Associated Press poll found that just as many Americans *opposed* the wiretapping program as who supported it. The following week a Gallup poll revealed 49 percent of Americans, including 58 percent of independents, believed Bush "broke the law" with the warrantless wiretaps.

Interestingly, also in January while eager to promote the notion that Bush was enjoying a political rebound, *Time* announced the president had "found his voice" amid the wiretapping debate and that relieved

White House aides "were smiling again" following a turbulent 2005, punctuated by the woes of New Orleans. Fact: A *Time* poll from that very same January 2006 issue showed Bush's job approval rating to be just 41 percent, or the lowest level recorded by *Time* since Bush's reelection. (And 20 points below the job approval rating Bill Clinton enjoyed at the dawn of his sixth year in office.) *Time* though, simply dismissed its own polling data in order to boost GOP spin that Bush had "found his voice." (A month later, Bush had gone nowhere but down in the polls.)

On the flip side, the *New York Times* was also busy obfuscating polling data, but in order to suggest Democrats were on the decline. (Bush up, Democrats down; the narrative had become ironclad for the MSM.) The *Times* published a page-one piece on February 7, 2006, quoting Democratic leaders as being anxious about their chances come November. The article, which painted a very bleak picture for Democrats, carefully avoided mentioning any recent polling results which would have helped put the issue in context. Perhaps that's because at the time, surveys indicated the Democratic Party was enjoying a renaissance of sorts among voters, with more Americans viewing the party in a positive light than at any time in the previous decade. Asked which party voters intended to support in November, Democrats had opened up, in some national polls, a 15–16-point lead over Republicans (the party's best showing in nearly twenty years), while approval for the Republican-controlled Congress had dropped to record lows. For some reason, the *Times* left all that relevant—and easily accessible— data out of its article about the Democrats' shaky prospects at the ballot box in 2006.

Over at ABC's The Note, the Beltway bellwether continued its robotic cheerleading for the Bush White House. In January, The Note suggested Bush's newfound rhetorical flourishes would help get his "approval rating back over 53% any day now." They did not. When news broke in February that Vice President Dick Cheney had shot a man in the face during a hunting trip and then waited nearly twenty-four hours before informing the public, which created a furor in the White House press room, The Note obediently announced it didn't see what the fuss was all about. It was only after a string of Republicans, including two former White House spokesmen—Ari Fleischer and

Marlin Fitzwater—criticized the administration for obviously mishandling the incident, that The Note adjusted its dismissive tone.

As for the war, which creaked on in Iraq, most elite MSM players shied away from discussing the chaos in candid terms. Some even tried to sugarcoat Bush's fateful miscue. Appearing on NBC's *Meet the Press* in December 2005, retired network anchormen Ted Koppel and Tom Brokaw, busy portraying the U.S.–led invasion of Iraq as *inevitable*, insisted President Clinton would have ordered the same, unprecedented, preemptive attack against Saddam Hussein.

> **Koppel:** If 9/11 had happened on Bill Clinton's watch, he would have gone into Iraq.
> **Brokaw:** Yeah. Yeah.

Separately, CBS anchor Bob Schieffer agreed, insisting "there was no other choice for the president to make," but to invade Iraq. No other choice.

Meanwhile, when the Pentagon announced on January 6, 2006, that eleven U.S. service members had died the previous day in Iraq, the MSM, bored of reporting bad news from Iraq, turned away. That night, the *CBS Evening News* set aside fifty-four words for the double-digit death toll, ABC's *World News Tonight* reported the eleven deaths in thirty-eight words, and NBC's *Nightly News* ignored the story all together.

By 2006 it was obvious that the MSM's tilt to the right was institutional, the imbalance codified. It's simply not plausible to suggest it was a coincidence the way the mainstream press treated prominent Democrats such as Bill Clinton, Al Gore, and John Kerry—the way Clinton was hounded virtually from the day he announced his candidacy for president in 1991 until the day he left office in 2001, the way Gore was ridiculed in 1999 and 2000 and depicted by the press as a liar and a fraud, and the way the MSM did the White House's bidding in 2004, portraying Kerry as a flip-flopper who may have lied about his war record. At the same time, during nearly seven years on the national stage Bush never had to deal with the kind of sustained, dishonest, and personally hostile press coverage that key Democrats were subjected to.

And while the point of *Lapdogs* is to document the press's failings and not necessarily to offer Democrats communication or campaign strategies, it does seem obvious that if Democrats have to battle both entrenched Republicans as well as a MSM that refuses to give the party out of power a fair shake, then Democrats are going to continue to have trouble winning elections. As blogger Peter Daou noted, "It's simple: if your core values and beliefs and positions, no matter how reasonable, how mainstream, how correct, how ethical, are filtered to the public through the lens of a media that has inoculated the public against your message, and if the media is the public's primary source of information, then NOTHING you say is going to break through and change that dynamic."

But Democratic candidates aren't the only ones who suffer from the press's timidity. So do everyday citizens trying to stay informed about matters of the day. Take for instance the serious issue of judicial picks, and specifically Supreme Court nominees. Most interested Americans don't go searching through legal stacks, reading old opinions to educate themselves about nominees. They rely on the MSM to learn more about the would-be justices. In the summer of 2005 Bush had a chance to appoint the first new Supreme Court Justice in more than a decade and selected John Roberts for the job.

The Roberts pick certainly qualified as big news at both *Time* and *Newsweek*, which delivered all-hands-on-deck profiles for the issues following his nomination. (In all, twenty reporters contributed to the two articles.) Fawning, glowing, congratulatory, adulatory, sycophantic. Take your pick, the stories were over the top. It's doubtful that the White House itself could have topped *Newsweek*'s portrait of Roberts as a too-good-to-be-true "centrist" who's "enormously self-confident" but "not arrogant or showy." An "unpretentious" "regular guy" with a "wicked wit" who "mows his own lawn." (*Newsweek* conveniently omitted the name of the high school John "Regular Guy" Roberts attended: La Lumiere.) According to the weekly, Roberts was loyal to church, family, school, and "most importantly" . . . "to the law."

There's nothing wrong with the press toasting a man's life accomplishments, and certainly Roberts had had many. But *Time* and *Newsweek* were supposed to be *news* magazine, helping to put events in context. At the time of his nomination there was quick and vocal opposition voiced by liberal activists. *Time* and *Newsweek* were oblivious, though. Combined, the two magazine features ran 6,390 words, with over twenty-four people quoted. The number of quotes from people even politely questioning the Roberts nomination? Zero.

On July 26 the *Washington Post* detailed the White House's decision to keep some of Roberts's previous federal government writings under wraps during the confirmation process. In a peculiar move, the Democratic side of the debate was not represented in the *Post* article though, because, as part of a deal struck, in exchange for the scoop the *Post* was not allowed to contact Democrats for comment. Even the *Post*'s own media reporter, Howard Kurtz, claiming the administration had reached "new heights of audacity," highlighted the absurdity of the agreement: "Now they're dictating when the story can run and who can be called for comment? Incredible." Unfortunately, the *Post* played along.

That was typical of the MSM's coverage regarding the larger issue of judicial appointments that raged during the spring and summer of 2005. Prior to Roberts's nomination the White House had been leaning on Senate Republicans to force a showdown; to demand up-or-down votes for a handful Bush's judicial nominees that were still languishing. If Democrats balked, if they used a procedural motion to effectively filibuster a nominee's final vote by extending the Senate debate indefinitely, Senate Majority Leader Bill Frist, on orders from the White House, was to take extraordinary action and change the Standing Rules of the Senate. That would mean that in order for a final vote to take place, Frist would need just fifty-one votes, as opposed to the sixty needed under the old rules. Under that scenario the minority party would likely be unable to stop any vote from taking place. Not just regarding judges, but on any matter before the Senate.

The pending filibuster showdown revolved around what became known as the "nuclear option," a term coined by Trent Lott, the Republican senator from Mississippi, as a way to describe the politically explosive nature of the maneuver. (If Republicans went through with the Senate rule change, Democrats, through other procedural tactics, threatened to effectively shut the chamber down for months—to go nuclear.) When the issue began to come to a head in April of 2005, though, Republicans disowned the phrase "nuclear option," uncomfortable with its imagery, as well as being associated with what sounded like a radical undertaking. (Frist preferred "constitutional option" instead.)

But for some reason many in the MSM started attributing the "nuclear option" term to Democrats and suggesting *they* were the ones—not Republicans—threatening to flip the switch on a wild partisan Beltway fight. As Media Matters for America reported, NPR, *Chicago Tribune*, *Newsweek*, CNN, *New York Times*, *Los Angeles Times*, and *Slate* were among the many major media outlets that erroneously assigned "nuclear option" to Democrats. At one point, CBSNews.com posted an Associated Press filibuster article and a CBSNews.com staffer actually inserted right into the AP text the erroneous assertion that a possible showdown would be what "Democrats term the 'nuclear option.' " The misinformation campaign was not just sloppy, because polls at the time showed a majority of Americans were not closely following the filibuster debate, news consumers were likely being misled by the MSM's mischaracterization. (Moderates from both parties were able to craft a last-minute compromise on the filibuster issue.)

At the time of the judicial jockeying, one nominee at the center of the looming filibuster debate was Priscilla Owen. Her nomination to the federal bench had been effectively blocked by Democrats who rejected her as an ideologue who tried to create law from the bench. Considering 90 percent of Bush's judicial nominees had previously been confirmed, there must have been something about Owen's record that raised serious concerns. But for *Los Angeles Times* readers who picked up the paper on May 19, 2005, and read the 1,600-word feature on Owen, it was impossible to understand what the fuss was about since the article (headline: "Judge Seen as Conservative, Fair") failed to quote *a single* person who opposed her nomination.

The *New York Times* adopted an equally odd way of educating readers about another controversial Bush nominee to the federal bench, Janice Rogers Brown. Rather than inform readers about Brown's judicial record and her streak of inflammatory remarks while the larger debate over her nomination was unfolding, the *Times* waited until one day *after* Brown was confirmed—after the coast was clear—to finally report that Brown "often invokes slavery in describing what she sees as the perils of liberalism." As the Daily Howler noted, "With these day-after profiles, the Times announces a fact; the paper has officially stood down from traditional journalistic duties. The paper will hide from the day's leading issues; it will only lay out a few facts after the issue is settled."

By March 2006, President Bush's job approval ratings had plunged back into the 30s, right where they landed after the natural disaster in New Orleans six months earlier. Swamped by waves of bad news, such as Vice President Cheney shooting a 78-year-old man, the administration badly bungling the homeland issue of port security, fresh evidence that the government had completely botched the Hurricane Katrina rescue effort, and continued runaway violence inside Iraq, Bush's presidency appeared to be unraveling, with even loyal Republicans telling pollsters they had lost faith in the president. In fact, according to an *Indianapolis Star* survey published March 5, which quizzed residents of that Republican bastion (Bush won the Hoosier state by 21 percentage points during the 2004 election), the president's job approval had fallen to 37 percent statewide; down 18 points in one year's time.

It was an astonishing finding. It would have been the equivalent of President Clinton plummeting to a 37 percent approval rating in Massachusetts, the electoral backbone of the Democratic Party. Of course Clinton never fell to those lows, but if he ever had you can be sure the MSM would have quickly, and emphatically, declared his presidency all but over. With its signature timidity, though, the MSM carefully steered clear of that kind of talk in early 2006. Yes, some Beltway reporters and pundits toughened up, but in light of the administration's well-advertised stumbles, particularly in 2005 and 2006, did journalists really have any choice? In truth, more and more Americans were suggesting Bush was in over his head, yet the press begged off announcing that verdict. Afraid of the facts and the consequences of reporting them, the MSM still had not found their bearings during the Bush years.

Notes

Introduction. Afraid of the Facts

1 "disgraceful": *Washington Post*, Nov. 22, 2005.
1 "junkyard prosecutor": *Washington Post*, Nov. 22, 2005.
2 "This is Watergate in reverse . . .": CNN's *Reliable Sources*, Nov. 25, 2005.
4 "whining": *Reliable Sources*, Feb. 18, 2006.
5 "aggressive reporting mode . . .": CNN's *Larry King Live*, Nov. 21, 2005.
5 "whoa": Larry King Live, Nov. 21, 2005.
7 "put something in the . . .": *Larry King Live*, Nov. 21, 2005.
7 "casual offhand remark": *Larry King Live*, Nov. 21, 2005.
8 "5:10 p.m.": *Washington Post*, Nov. 16, 2005
8 "mid-June": *Washington Post*, Nov. 16, 2005.
8 "This is the guy . . .": Americablog, Nov. 21, 2005 (http://americablog.blogspot
.com/2005/11/this-is-guy-who-brought-down-nixon.html).
9 "We'll keep chipping at . . .": *Larry King Live*, Nov. 21, 2005.
9 "one of the toughest, . . . ": Ari Fleischer, *Taking Heat: The President, The Press,
and My Years in the White House* (New York: William Morrow, 2005).
9 "Conflict is juicy, . . . ": *Taking Heat*, p. 61.
10 "The Failed Clinton Presidency": *Washington Post*, May 27, 1993.
11 "I think it would be a mistake for us to go on to Baghdad . . .": CBS's *Face the
Nation*, Aug. 27, 2000.
11 "Under what journalistic . . .": Huffington Post (http://www.huffingtonpost
.com/jane-hamsher/time-magazine-spikes-the-_b_15279.html), Feb. 8, 2006.
12 "not a serious option": Washingtonpost.com, Dec. 20, 2005 (http://www
.washingtonpost.com/wpdyn/content/discussion/2005/12/19/DI2005121900972
.html).
12 "Accommodating passivity": Mark Hertsgaard, *On Bended Knee: The Press and the
Reagan Presidency* (New York: Schocken Books, 1988).
12 "A lot of the Teflon . . .": *On Bended Knee*.
12 "The general rolling over . . .": The Media Giraffe, Feb. 14, 2006
(http://www.mediagiraffe.org/arman/publish/printer_438.shtml).
13 "In the 2000 elections . . .": MSNBC's *Hardball*, Nov. 18, 2002.
13 "Everybody sort of likes the president, . . ." MSNBC's *Hardball*, Nov. 28, 2005.
14 "Why is the national media easy on Bush . . .": Washingtonpost.com, April 13,
2005 (http://www.washingtonpost.com/wp-dyn/articles/A35213-2005
Apr7.html).

14 "their ears cocked to the right": *American Prospect*, April 1, 2005.

14 "is the liberal media taking up the defense . . .": Fox News, Dec. 22, 2005.

14 "feel they have to go to war . . .": *Boston Globe*, July 26, 2004.

14 "I hear more about conservative concerns . . .": *Boston Globe*, July 26, 2004.

14 "all over your telephones, . . . ": *The Nation*, Nov. 1, 2004.

15 "any detectable bias on Lehrer's part . . .": The Daily Standard (http://www.weeklystandard.com/Content/Public/Articles/000/000/004/698zkz up.asp), Sept. 30, 2004.

15 "You have to be prepared before . . .": author interview.

15 "This particular anti-press campaign . . .": *Washington Post*, May 27, 2005.

15 "miserable, carping retromingent vigilante.": *New Yorker*, Feb. 14, 2005.

16 "It used to be we, as the press . . .": *Salon*, Sept. 1, 2004.

16 "I am completely exasperated by this approach to the news": *New York Review of Books*, Dec. 15, 2005.

16 "I always have a good time talking to him": ABC's *Good Morning America*, Jan. 12, 2006.

17 "not confrontational": *Variety*, Jan. 17, 2006.

17 "I'm wondering if I could kill him myself . . .": *Glenn Beck Show*, May 17, 2005.

17 "scumbags": *Glen Beck Show*, Sept. 9, 2005.

17 "pretty big prostitute.": *Glenn Beck Show*, Jan. 10, 2006.

17 "When I covered the White House I had . . .": author interview.

17 "Let's be frank: the Bush administration . . .": *New York Times*, Oct. 14, 2005.

Chapter One. From the Big Apple to the Big Easy

19 "The tough-talking . . .": *Boston Herald*, Sept. 3, 2004.

19 "lofty": *Washington Post*, Sept. 3, 2004.

19 "powerful": *Chicago Tribune*, Sept. 3, 2004.

19 "Republican strategists have succeeded . . .": *New York Times*, Sept. 3, 2004.

20 "Bush's most memorable phrase": Reuters, Dec. 30, 2005.

20 "The news media have been operating . . .": *Los Angeles Times*, Sept. 17, 2005.

20 "halo over the presidency": *New York Times*, Sept. 21.

21 "Try as they might, . . . ": *National Review*, Nov. 19, 2004.

21 "More than half of all Bush stories . . .": Project for Excellence in Journalism, "How the Press Covered the Pivotal Period of the 2004 Presidential Campaign" (http://www.journalism.org/resources/research/reports/debateeffect/default.asp).

23 "Cheney, Edwards Stretch Facts, Figures to Make Points" Knight Ridder Washington Bureau, Oct. 6, 2004.

23 "Misleading Assertions Cover Iraq War and Voting Records" *Washington Post*, Oct. 6, 2004.

23 "When Points Weren't Personal, Liberties Were Taken With the Truth" *New York Times*, Oct. 6, 2004.

23 "slapped": MSNBC's *Hardball*, Oct. 5, 2004.

23 "liberal press": *Hardball*, Oct. 5, 2004.

24 "It turns out that the vice president . . .": NBC's *Today*, Oct. 6, 2004.

24 "I thought that John Edwards . . .": *Today*, Oct. 6, 2004.

24 "a thunderous blow against . . .": *Hardball*, Oct. 6, 2004.

25 "badly tailored suit": *Boston Herald*, Oct. 14, 2004, p. 9.

25 "poorly tailored shirt": ABC's *Good Morning America*, Oct. 26, 2004.

26 "Sorry to have been a source of disappointment . . ." FAIR *Extra!* Jan/Feb. 2005 (http://www.fair.org/index.php?page=2012).

26 "In the end, nobody, including . . .": *Extra!* Jan/Feb. 2005.

27 "another attack by the media . . .": *Rush Limbaugh Show*, Oct. 26, 2004.

27 "long litany of complaints.": *The New Yorker*, Feb. 14, 2005.

27 "I am willing to stake my scientific reputation . . .": *Salon*, Oct. 29, 2004.

28 "conspiracy freaks": *The Hill*, Nov. 4, 2004.

28 "inappropriate to broadcast . . .": *New York Times*, Sept. 23, 2004.

28 "Time editors were concerned . . .": *Los Angeles Times*, Aug. 25, 2005.

29 "We would have been here . . .": *New York Times*, Aug. 29, 2005.

29 "In Iraq, the American forces . . .": *NBC News Special Report*, Nov. 4, 2004.

29 "What about other strategic . . .": *NBC News Special Report*, Nov. 4, 2004.

29 "U.S. military officials have said . . .": *NBC News Special Report*, Nov. 4, 2004.

30 "was compelling enough and interesting . . .": *Salon*, Oct. 6, 2004 (http://www.salon.com/politics/war_room/archive.html).

31 "President Bush won reelection . . .": *Columbus Dispatch*, Nov. 4, 2004.

31 "the polarized atmosphere . . .": *Washington Post*, Nov. 5, 2004.

31 "President Bush also had . . .": *Editor & Publisher*, Nov. 5, 2004.

31 "a narrow but unmistakable mandate": *Washington Post*, Nov. 3, 2004.

31 "going to say he's got a mandate . . .": CNN Breaking News, Nov. 3, 2004.

31 "a clear mandate to advance a conservative . . .": *Boston Globe*, Nov. 4, 2004.

31 "Clear Mandate Will Boost Bush's Authority, Reach": *USA Today*, Nov. 4, 2004.

31 "I think he does have a mandate": NBC's *Today Show*, Nov. 4, 2004.

31 "Bush can claim a solid mandate . . .": *Los Angeles Times*, Nov. 4, 2004.

31 "But Mr. Bush no longer . . .": *New York Times*, Nov. 5, 2004.

32 "There was no ringing mandate . . .": *New York Times*, Nov. 7, 1996.

32 "Mr. Bush overestimated his postelection capital . . .": *Wall Street Journal*, Oct. 20, 2005.

32 "discipline, secrecy and nerve": *Time*, Dec. 27, 2004.

32 "hands-on, [is] detail-oriented . . .": *Newsweek*, Jan. 24, 2005.

33 "And if you're a younger worker . . .": Associated Press, April 29, 2005.

33 "If nothing happens, at your age . . .": *Desert Morning News*, Jan. 12, 2005.

33 "If you're twenty years old, in . . .": Associated Press, Jan. 11, 2005.

33 "We will not be able to look at . . .": *New York Times*, Jan. 13, 2005.

34 "the current system is heading for an iceberg": Cox News Service, Jan. 6, 2005.

34 "At the White House today, . . . ": *ABC World News Tonight*, Jan. 11, 2005.

36 "published regularly": Associated Press, Feb. 10, 2005.

36 "existed": *Philadelphia Inquirer*, Feb. 28, 2005.

37 "the talk of Washington": *NBC Nightly News*, Feb. 17, 2005.

37 "valuable and necessary": *Vanity Fair*, June 2005.

37 "super naïve": *Vanity Fair*, June 2005.

38 "articles in the past seven days . . .": Media Matters for America, March 25, 2005 (http://mediamatters.org/items/200503250008#1).

41 "Strong divided opinions across this country": CNN's *Live Today*, March 24, 2005.

41 "These images [of Schiavo] have sparked . . .": CBS's *The Early Show*, March 21, 2005.

41 "a huge national debate over Terri Schiavo": ABC's *Good Morning America*, March 27, 2005.

41 "Terri Schiavo [is] at the center of . . .": NBC's *Sunday Today*, March 27, 2005.

41 "Schiavo Debate Grips Nation": *Chicago Tribune*, March 22, 2005.

41 "an Agency operative on weapons . . .": *Chicago Sun-Times*, July 14, 2003.

42 "boondoggle": *Washington Post*, Oct. 12, 2003.

42 "For two years, it's been unknown . . .": ABC's *Nightline*, July 12, 2005.

43 "reporters should at least . . .": *Salon*, Jan. 22, 2004.

43 "totally ridiculous": White House press briefing, Sept. 16, 2003 (http://www.whitehouse.gov/news/releases/2003/09/20030916-6.html).

43 "we'll find out who the leaker is": President Meets with Cabinet, Discusses National and Economic Security, Oct. 7, 2003 (http://www.whitehouse.gov/news/releases/2003/10/20031007-2.html).

44 "exaggerate": *New York Times*, Oct. 25, 2005.

44 "The best thing Patrick Fitzgerald . . .": *Washington Post*, Oct. 12, 2005.

44 "creative crap charges": *Slate*, Oct. 18, 2005.

47 "Their testimony *seems* to . . .": *Washington Post*, Oct. 2, 2005.

47 "It is much more likely they . . .": *Newsweek*, Nov. 7, 2005.

48 "Who Is Scooter Libby?": *Slate*, Oct. 21, 2005.

48 "a heroic, romantic sense . . .": *Newsweek*, Nov. 7, 2005.

48 "audacious novelist": *Washington Post*, Oct. 23, 2005.

48 "a self-effacing public servant . . .": *Washington Post*, Oct. 31, 2005.

49 "pretty good July.": *New York Times*, July 29, 2005.

49 "Summer slump": *Newsweek*, June 27, 2005.

49 "How could the president . . .": NBC's *Meet the Press*," Sept. 4, 2005.

50 "So far, the federal government's . . .": *Washington Post*, Sept. 1, 2005.

51 "an advantageous setting": *Washington Post*, Sept. 4, 2005.

51 "wildly off target": *Washington Post*, Dec. 29, 2003.

Chapter Two. Watching the White House Play Hardball

53 "The possibility of that group . . .": *Washington Post*, Dec. 17, 2003.

53 "rare interview": NPR's *Morning Edition*, Dec. 18, 2003.

54 "opportunist": *Center for Media and Democracy*, May 11, 2005 (http://www.prwatch.org/node/3632).

54 "The single worst interview . . .": *Salon*, Jan. 12, 2005.

55 "Secretly paying Iraqi newspapers . . .": *Los Angeles Times*, Nov. 30, 2005.

56 "noted in the building": *Washington Post*, May 14, 2001.

56 "did a story on a senior figure . . .": *The New Yorker*, Jan. 19, 2004.

56 "the reality-based community": *New York Times Magazine*, Oct. 17, 2004.

57 "I believe the press is in awe . . .": *Salon*, July 1, 2003.

57 "Republicans have a clear, agreed-upon . . .": *Salon*, March 2, 2005.

57 "high-level laughingstock": *Slate*, Nov. 18, 2002.

58 "At this point the Democrats are a party . . .": *Chris Matthews Show*, June 12, 2005.

58 "The party chairman, Howard Dean . . .": Time.com, Dec. 10, 2005.

58 "The idea that we are going . . .": CNN's *Anderson Cooper 360 Degrees*, Dec. 5, 2005.

58 "small but cheesy bit . . .": Time.com, Jan. 8, 2006.

59 "You're out of time, Congressman": ABC's *Nightline Vote 2004: The New Hampshire Democratic Debates*, Dec. 9, 2003.

59 "And to all of you, if I may make the observation . . .": *Nightline Vote 2004*.

59 "To begin this kind of a forum with a question . . .": *Nightline Vote 2004*.

59 "Ambassador Braun, Reverend Sharpton . . .": *Nightline Vote 2004*.

59 "I want the American people to see where the media . . .": *Nightline Vote 2004*.

59 "You're not doing terrific in the polls, either.": *Nightline Vote* 2004.

60 "highly selective": *Washington Post*, June 23, 2003.

60 "Can you honestly go . . .": NBC's *Meet the Press*, June 22, 2003.

60 "As commander in chief . . .": *Meet the Press*, June 22, 2003.

60 "Mr. Dean's *Meet the Press* performance . . .": *Washington Post*, June 28, 2003.

60 "Can kids avoid sex?": *Meet the Press*, Nov. 21, 1999.

61 "get to know the governor of Texas": Tim Russert, *Big Russ and Me* (New York: Miramax Books, 2004), p. 205.

61 "I can't remember the exact number": *Meet The Press*, Nov. 21, 1999.

61 "politicization of the government": *New York Times*, Nov. 20, 2005.

62 "When we go on television . . .": www.nytco.com/pdf/assuring-our-credibility.pdf.

65 "Just say no": *Washington Post*, September 20, 2005.

65 "We are lucky to have had you": *International Herald Tribune*, Oct. 23, 2004.

66 "Every couple of years, Ted will come by . . .": *Washington Post*, Oct. 16, 2004.

66 "I can only say that he persuaded me . . .": *Washington Post*, Feb. 6, 2003.

67 was "a litany of Iraqi deception, evasion, brutality, and noncompliance": *Nightline*, Feb. 5, 2003.

67 "I'm the one who presented it to the world . . .": Associated Press, Sept. 8, 2005.

68 "a balanced presentation." *Nightine*, Jan. 7, 2004.

68 "a difficult balancing act": Andrea Mitchell, *Talking Back . . . To Presidents, Dictators, and Assorted Scoundrels* (New York: Viking, 2005), p. 331.

68 "At the Rumsfelds' . . .": Mitchell's *Talking Back*, p. 367.

68 "His response was beautiful": Russert's *Big Russ and Me*, p. 122.

69 "This just isn't a guy who's . . .": *Meet the Press*, Feb. 6, 2003.

69 "an excellent cook": The Daily Howler, Aug. 11, 2003.

70 "cover to cover a couple of times": The Daily Howler, Aug. 11, 2003.

71 "I told them all no": *Fort Worth Star-Telegram*, Aug. 14, 1996.

71 "I thought it was one of the best interviews . . .": Bob Schieffer, *Face the Nation: My Favorite Stories from the First 50 Year of the Award-Winning News Broadcast* (New York: Simon & Schuster, 2004), p. 126.

71 "The White House doesn't hate . . .": *Philadelphia Inquirer*, July 22, 2005.

72 "the election of a Republican administration . . .": *Newsweek*, Oct. 4, 2004.

72   "Republican problem": CBS's *Face the Nation*, Oct. 2, 2005.
72   "still give them the benefit of the doubt": *The Imus in the Morning Show*, Dec. 1, 2005.
72   "Bob Schieffer will have an . . .": CBS.com, Jan. 23, 2006.

Chapter Three. Noted at ABC

73   "reminds people of Whitewater": CNN's *Inside Politics*, May 10, 2005.
74   "The opening and closing . . .": The Note, May 10, 2005.
74   "The Justice Department case against . . .": *New York Post*, May 10, 2005.
74   "Waiting for the Rosen verdict . . .": The Note, May 26, 2005.
74   "must-read efforts from Saturday through Monday . . .": The Note, May 31, 2005.
75   "Skull and Bones for the political . . .": *The New Yorker*, Oct. 25, 2004.
75   "For everyone else in Washington . . .": *The New Yorker*, Oct. 25, 2004.
75   "We try to channel . . .": *The New Yorker*, Oct. 25, 2004.
76   "Cliché-Meister": The Note, Jan. 18, 2006.
76   "To read ABC News's 'The Note' . . .": *The Nation*, May 9, 2005.
76   "Who wrote (and edited) . . .": The Note, July 15, 2005.
76   "Hats off to the White House . . .": *The New Yorker*, Oct. 25, 2004.
77   "Judd did not say who her sources . . .": *Los Angeles Times*, Aug. 5, 19989.
77   "After Murray Waas and I . . .": *Salon*, June 22, 1998.
78   "Undermining ONE of the . . .": The Note, Aug. 23, 2004.
78   "read more like something from . . .": The Note, Aug. 20, 2004.
78   "The Republican leadership seems . . .": The Note, March 21, 2005.
79   "some public opposition.": The Note, March 21, 2005.
79   "perhaps the beginning of a *media* . . . ": The Note, March 23, 2005.
79   "what exactly accounts . . .": The Note, March 38, 2005.
80   "There is an iron triangle . . .": The Note, April 14, 2005.
81   "Mr. Bush still hasn't found . . .": The Note, Sept. 8, 2005.
81   "living with [approval] ratings . . .": The Note, Sept. 13, 2005.
82   "will probably bear fruit": The Note, Feb. 15, 2005.
82   "all of the Republican Party's problems": The Note, Dec. 6, 2005.
83   "disastrous and defensive": The Note, Jan. 24, 2006.
84   "apocalyptic and apoplectic": The Note, July 15, 2005.
84   "Like it or not . . .": The Note, Dec. 10, 2004.
84   "a window into what anti-Bush liberals . . .": The Note, Sept. 13, 2005.
84   "the best columnist today writing . . .": The Note, Sept. 22, 2005.
85   "Will New York Times management . . .": The Note, Jan. 4, 2006.
85   "one of the greatest political . . .": The Note, May 3, 2005.
85   "successful and dashing": The Note, April 19, 2005.
85   "brilliance, elan, and grace": The Note, Oct. 12, 2005.
85   "indescribably delicious": The Note, Sept. 12, 2005.
85   "super savvy and smart": The Note, June 24, 2005.
85   "Jim Kelly is more powerful . . .": The Note. Oct. 9, 2005.
85   "is the arbiter of who . . .": *The Washington*, July, 2002.

85 "sets out concepts for stories . . .": *The New York Sun*, July 29, 2002.
85 "Reporters really like to see . . .": *Washington Life*, September, 2004.
86 "slobber[ing] so effusively on . . .": The Note, Aug. 2, 2005.
86 "just as the DNC would want.": The Note, Oct. 19, 2005.
86 "Halperin's head should roll.": *The New Yorker*, Oct. 25, 2004.
86 "expression of partisanship . . .": *USA Today*, Oct. 11, 2004.
87 "Mark Halperin's idea of what . . .": *Front Page Magazine*, Oct. 14, 2004.
87 "The last thing we want . . .": The Note, Aug. 11, 2004.
87 "Note to Rush Limbaugh: out of professional courtesy . . .": The Note, Sept. 15, 2004.
88 "Twelve o'clock for a normal . . .": *The New Yorker*, Oct. 25, 2004.
88 "Judge John Roberts is by all . . .": The Note, July 20, 2005.
88 "the Bush campaign is counting . . .": The Note, July 13, 2004.
89 "hands down the biggest story . . .": The Note, May 12, 2005.
90 "A growing number of senior . . .": *The Philadelphia Inquirer*, June 13, 2005.
90 "The nation is at war and . . .": The Note, June 28, 2005.
92 "was intentionally misleading . . .": The *Washington Post*, Nov. 6, 2005.

Chapter Four. The Press Haters

95 "investigation": CNBC's *Kudlow & Company*, March 24, 2005.
96 "political dirty trick": Newsmax.com, March 31, 2005.
96 "Schiavo-Quiddick": Ankle Biting Pundits, March 24, 2005.
97 "The news media consistently use language": *Los Angeles Times*, July 1, 1990.
98 "I certainly hope that this is so": Power Line, Sept. 20, 2005.
98 "to harass and hector any journalist who . . .": Associated Press, Oct. 6, 2005.
98 "Which side is the NYTimes on?": MichelleMalkin.com, Dec. 14, 2005.
99 "The managements of the networks may . . .": *Washington Post*, June 29, 2005.
99 "God has called me to proclaim truth": *USA Today*, April 22, 2004.
100 "Thanks to their tireless efforts, the American people . . .": Center for American Progress, May 26, 2005.
100 "within a few yards": Power Line, Dec. 25, 2004.
101 "something happened on Haifa Street": Associated Press, April 5, 2005.
101 "its stunning series of photographs . . .": *New York Times*, April 5, 2005.
101 "Pulitzer Prize for felony murder": Power Line, April 5, 2005.
101 "The media establishment puts their thumb . . .": Little Green Footballs, April 4, 2005.
101 "the assassination picture has all . . .": Power Line, April 10, 2005.
101 "If you're going to serve up a conspiracy . . .": Power Line, July 6, 2005.
102 "101st Fighting Keyboarders": Term first coined by blogger Tbogg to describe online pro-war pundits who studiously avoid military service themselves.
102 "deeply offensive": *Editor & Publisher*, April 6, 2005.
102 "Blogs Incensed Over Pulitzer Photo Award": *New York Times*, April 11, 2005.
102 "little public interest": Power Line, Jan. 4, 2006.
103 "The [Alito] sessions revived . . .": *National Journal*, Jan. 16, 2006.
103 "when she tried to unfurl a banner": Power Line, Jan. 31, 2006.

103 "Powerline, we must begin to understand . . .": Tomorrow's Media Conspiracy
     Today, April 8, 2005.
104 "two partial newspapers": Daily Standard, June 14, 2005.
105 "Stranger things have happened.": Daily Standard, June 14, 2005.
105 "virtually identical": Daily Standard, June 14, 2005.
105 "The records that he released only . . .": *Rush Limbaugh Show*, June 9, 2005.
105 "authorized the release of his full . . .": *Boston Globe*, June 7, 2005.
106 "Schiavo suffered brain damage . . .": *St. Petersburg Times*, March 18, 2005.
107 "Terri Schiavo is not on 'life support' and . . .": *Kansas City Star*, March 25, 2005.
107 "In this case, the undisputed facts . . .": *Jeb Bush v. Michael Schiavo*.
107 "In Florida and elsewhere, including . . .": Washingtonpost.com, March 23,
     2005.
107 "life-sustaining treatment": *Cruzan v. Director*.
107 "The government has apologized and . . .": *Jewish World Review*, May 26, 2000.
108 "I look back at the past and provide . . .": C-Span's *Washington Journal*, Aug. 20,
     2004.
109 "Oh no. He didn't . . .": PBS's *NewsHour with Jim Lehrer*, Aug. 19, 2004.
113 "My only regret with Timothy McVeigh . . .": *New York Observer*, Aug. 26,
     2002.
113 "immediately surrender": Fox News' *Hannity & Colmes*, Aug. 25, 2005.
113 "I think the government should be . . .": *Augusta Chronicle*, Dec. 23, 2005.
113 "In her books, Coulter can . . .": *Time*, April 18, 2005.
114 "American journalists commit mass murder . . .": *New York Observer*, Aug. 26,
     2002.
114 "misunderstood" "public intellectual": *Time*, April 25, 2005.
116 "I was wrong": C-Span's *Washington Journal*, Feb. 18, 2005 (http://www
     .cbcwatch.ca/?q=node/view/936).
116 "all the Rush Limbaugh wannabes": NBC's *Nightly News*, Nov. 20, 2002.
116 "lost a couple of screws": Washingtonpost.com, Nov. 21, 2002.
117 "conventional conservative": Fox News' *Special Report*, Nov. 20, 2002.
117 "Is Tom Daschle simply another way to portray a devil?": *Rush Limbaugh Show*,
     July 20, 2002.
117 "In essence, Daschle has chosen to align himself with the axis of evil": *Rush Lim-
     baugh Show*, Feb. 11, 2002.
117 "are seeking political advantage in the war on terrorism": *Rush Limbaugh Show*,
     Nov. 15, 2002.
117 "to exploit future terrorist attacks for political gain": *Rush Limbaugh Show*, Nov.
     15, 2002.
117 "You are worse, sir, than the ambulance-chasing tort lawyers": *Rush Limbaugh
     Show*, Nov. 15, 2002.
117 "You are a disgrace to patriotism": *Rush Limbaugh Show*, Nov. 15, 2002.
117 "What do you want your nickname to be? Hanoi Tom . . .": *Rush Limbaugh
     Show*, Nov. 15, 2002.
117 "You sit there and pontificate on the fact that we're not winning . . .": *Rush Lim-
     baugh Show*, Nov. 15, 2002.
118 "an important conservative voice": *Washington Times*, May 9, 2004.
119 "You inspired me this morning": *Rush Limbaugh Show*, May 21, 2004.

119 "may be a forgery": *Rush Limbaugh Show*, June 20, 2005.

119 "Oh, she lost her son! . . .": *Chicago Sun-Times*, Aug., 18, 2005.

119 "What's good for al-Qaida is good for the . . .": *Rush Limbaugh Show*, March 15, 2004.

119 "Anyway, this has been fun": *Rush Limbaugh Show*, June 10, 2004.

119 "Nobody got hurt": *Rush Limbaugh Show*, May 6, 2004.

120 "To cite just one example . . .": *Wall Street Journal*, Aug. 19, 2005.

120 "A *report out today* shows . . .": *CBS Evening News*, April 25, 2005.

121 "sleazy and insipid bias": Media Research Center, Aug. 18, 2005.

121 "media-manufactured scandals": National Review Online's Media Blog, Dec. 20, 2005.

121 "members of MoveOn.org.": National Review Online's The Corner, Jan. 3, 2006.

122 "Of course, I liked Carter . . .": Howell Raines, *Fly Fishing Through the Midlife Crisis (New York: William Morrow, 1993)*.

122 "Reagan-hater": Media Research Center, May 22, 2001.

122 "a story by *Times* reporter Natalie Angier . . .": Bernie Goldberg, *Bias: A CBS Insider Exposes How the Media Distort the News* (Washington, D.C., Regnery, 2001), p. 134.

122 "the atheist left": Anne Coulter, *Slander: Liberal Lies About the American Right* (New York: Three Rivers Press, 2003), p. 167.

123 "If Coulter has sniffed out . . .": The Daily Howler, July 9, 2002.

123 "objectively quantifying": UCLA press release, Dec. 14, 2005 (http://www.news room.ucla.edu/page.asp?RelNum=6664).

123 "almost all major media outlets tilt to the left": http://www.newsroom.ucla .edu/page.asp?RelNum=6664.

123 "The study rests on a presumption . . .": Media Matters for America, Dec. 21, 2005.

124 "most Americans would have thought it was . . .": Ari Fleischer, *Taking Heat: The President, The Press, and My Years in the White House* (New York: HarperCollins, 2005), p. 14.

125 "The Florida Supreme Court drops . . .": MSNBC's *The News with Brian Williams*, Dec. 8, 2000.

125 "*A sharply divided* Florida Supreme . . .": *Los Angeles Times*, Dec. 9, 2000.

125 "Al Gore's moribund presidential hopes . . .": *Hartford Courant*, Dec. 9, 2000.

125 "The Florida Supreme Court . . .": NBC's *Saturday Today*, Dec. 9, 2000.

125 "Why have they largely stopped . . .": *Taking Heat*, p. 88.

125 "I don't really know what a 'progressive' is . . .": *Taking Heat*, p. 86.

125 "someone [inside the White House] pointed out how muted . . .": *Taking Heat*, p. 327.

126 "One critic worried that . . .": *Wall Street Journal*, March 28, 2003.

126 "The notion I would not want troops to . . .": *Salon*, April 1, 2003.

127 "documentation of the liberal . . .": Media Research Center, Aug. 8, 2005.

127 "Peter Jennings Sympathies for the Devil": Moon Bat Central, Aug. 8, 2005.

127 "I won't be a hypocrite . . .": Moon Bat Central, Aug. 8, 2005.

127 "I hope Lenin is giving . . .": Moon Bat Central, Aug. 8, 2005.

127 "Another left wing talking . . .": Moon Bat Central, Aug. 9, 2005.

127 "The mugging death of that Slimes . . .": Free Republic, Jan. 8, 2006.

127 "There's little difference between a NY Times . . .": Free Republic, Jan. 8, 2006.

127 "No one is innocent that works . . .": Free Republic, Jan. 8, 2006.

Chapter Five. The War Over PBS

129 "does not contain anything approaching . . .": *New York Times*, May 2, 2005.

130 "On reflection": *Washington Times*, May 10, 2005.

131 "liberal advocacy journalism": *Washington Post*, May 20, 2005.

131 "It's designed to get people's . . .": *Salon*, May 10, 2005.

132 "We love your show": Fox News' *The O'Reilly Factor*, May 12, 2005.

132 "I've always been dedicated to balance": C-Span, July 27, 2005.

132 "the quintessential magazine . . .": *National Review*, Feb. 11, 2002.

132 "morale at the VOA has plummeted": American Prospect Online, Aug. 15, 2005.

132 "the tone of the discussion became increasingly partisan . . .": *Salon*, May 10, 2005.

133 "I have nothing against Moyers": *The O'Reilly Factor*, Jan. 5, 2005.

133 "political test": Office of Inspector General Review of Alleged Actions Violating The Public Broadcasting Act of 1967, No. 15, 2005.

133 "anti-Bush," "anti-business," and "anti-Tom DeLay": *New York Times*, May 1, 2005.

134 "irrefutable documentation": *Washington Times*, May 10, 2005.

134 "broaden support for public broadcasting": *Broadcasting & Cable*, May 2, 2005.

134 "Eliminating the perception of political bias": Tomlinson statement, released May 2, 2005.

134 "If a *significant number of conservatives* are . . .": *Current*, Nov. 17, 2003.

135 "strongly committed to George Bush": C-Span, July 27, 2005.

135 "For whatever reason . . .": *Washington Times*, July 28, 2005.

135 "A lot of my friends are against . . .": *Washington Post*, May 20, 2005.

136 "The elimination of the use of . . .": Public Broadcasting PolicyBase (http://www.current.org/pbpb/nixon/nixon72.html).

136 "content analysis": *Los Angeles Times*, July 8, 1986.

136 "this little sandbox for the rich": *Daily Variety*, Jan. 3, 1995.

136 "a small group of elitists who . . .": *Washington Times*, Jan. 8, 1995.

136 "The American right has stopped . . .": *The New Yorker*, Jan. 7, 2004.

137 "concerned": *New York Times*, June 16, 2005.

139 "occasionally worked with . . .": *New York Times*, May 2, 2005.

139 "I'm *trying to pressure*": http://www.freepress.net/docs/tomlinsonpbs.pdf

139 "not contain anything approaching . . .": *New York Times*, May 2, 2005.

139 "strict adherence to objectivity . . .": Associated Press, Oct. 30, 1986.

140 "conservative view of the news": *The Journal Editorial Report* Dec. 5, 2005 (http://www.pbs.org/wnet/journaleditorialreport/120205/leadstory.html#).

141 "vigorously": *Washington Post*, May 20, 2005.

141 "It mystifies me": *Salon*, May 17, 2005.

142 "ought to be recognized as a campaigner . . .": *Salon*, May 26, 2005.

142 "one of the most . . .": *Washington Post*, May 6, 1987.

143 "It's shocking and disgraceful": *Salon*, May 26, 2005.

143 "The magazine spent half a century . . .": *Salon*, May 26, 2005.

143 "posed a major threat to the continued . . .": *Reader's Digest*, Oct. 1969.

143 "So the whole concept of fact checking . . .": *Salon*, May 26, 2005.

144 " 'TV at its very best.' ": CPB Ombudsman Report, July 6, 2005 (http://www.cpb.org/ombudsmen/050706shulz.html).

144 "The overwhelming majority . . .": CPB-Commissioned National Opinion Polls, Dec. 2003 (http://www.cpb.org/aboutcpb/goals/objectivity/poll summary.html).

145 "Polls are essentially meaningless . . .": *Washington Post*, May 20, 2005.

145 "arguing over whether PBS . . .": OpinionJournal, June 16, 2005.

145 "It's liberal. It just is . . .": National Review, July 1, 2005.

145 "That's a stacked poll . . .": MSNBC's *Coast-to-Coast*, June 22, 2005.

146 "Tomlinson commissioned two polls.": *Salon*, May 10, 2005.

146 "They couldn't use . . .": *Salon*, May 10, 2005.

147 "58% of the": Executive Summary: National Survey of Adults Regarding Public Broadcasting.

149 "documented": NPR's *Diane Rehm Show*, May 18, 2005.

Chapter Six. First Lieutenant Bush

152 "background qualifications of value . . .": *Austin American-Statesman*, July 17, 1999.

153 "to perform equivalent training": *Boston Globe*, May 23, 2000.

154 "cleared this base on . . .": *Boston Globe*, May 23, 2000.

154 "almost incomprehensible to": *Washington Post*, Sept. 12, 2004.

155 "Everyone in the media wanted . . .": Mary Mapes, *Truth and Duty: The Press, the President, and the Privilege of Power.* (New York: St. Martin's Press, 2005).

155 "I didn't know that the attack on CBS News . . .": *Truth and Duty*.

156 "wicked witch": *Atlanta Journal-Constitution*, March 10, 2005.

156 "but the ceiling tiles": *Los Angeles Times*, Jan. 16, 2005.

157 "such a transfer . . .": *Austin American-Statesman*, July 17, 1999.

158 " 'Special' doctors": *St. Louis Post-Dispatch*, June 5, 1999.

158 "As he was not flying . . ." *Sunday Times* of London, June 18, 2000.

158 "misspoke": *Boston Globe*, Sept. 8, 2004.

159 "I knew I was going into the military . . .": *Austin American-Statesman*, July 17, 1999.

159 "I wanted to fly, and that was the . . .": *New York Times*, July 11, 2000.

159 "for his candor": Associated Press, Sept. 27, 1999.

161 "Let me ask you about . . .": MSNBC's *Hardball*, May 31, 2000.

162 "Bush told her he had . . .": *Newsweek*, July 17, 2000.

162 "George W. had a plan": *ABC's Family Business; Backgrounds of George W. Bush and Al Gore*, Sept. 14, 2000.

162 "Until 2000, at least . . .": *New York Times*, Feb. 27, 2004.

163 "Al Gore's handlers . . .": *New York Times*, Feb. 27, 2004.

163 "Al Gore steered clear": Time.com, Feb. 8, 2004.

163 "It's time that he set the . . .": CNN's *Crossfire*, June 3, 2000.

163 "It's doubtful, however, Democrats . . .": *The Tennessean*, Nov. 3, 2000.

164 "It sure doesn't look good . . .": CNN's *Spin Room*, Nov. 1, 2000.

165 "Serious questions remain . . .": *New York Times*, Oct. 29, 2000.

166 "My question to you is . . .": C-Span's *Washington Journal*, May 2, 2003.

166 "deserter": Associated Press, Jan. 17, 2004.

167 "lackadaisical": *Washington Post*, Dec. 5, 2003.

167 "missed some weekends of training": ABC's *World News Tonight Sunday*, Feb. 1, 2004.

167 "Mr. Bush went on to . . .": *New York Times*, Feb. 3, 2004.

167 "There is some question that . . .": CNN's *Wolf Blitzer Reports*, Sept. 10, 2004.

167 "Yeah, they're just wrong . . .": NBC's Meet the Press, Feb. 8, 2004.

167 "An honorable discharge . . .": *Salon*, Feb. 5, 2004.

169 "Clark reading room": *Arkansas Democrat-Gazette*, Jan. 17, 2004.

169 "Calhoun's claim was a rare respite . . .": *Washington Post*, Feb. 13, 2005.

170 "very ashamed": Cox News Service, Aug. 27, 2004.

171 "simply regurgitating old controversies": Washingtonpost.com, Aug. 30, 2004.

171 "The impression I had was that Georgie . . .": *Salon*, Sept. 2, 2004.

171 "After about a month I asked . . .": *Salon*, Sept. 2, 2004.

172 "In other words . . .": Washingtonpost.com, May 23, 2005.

Chapter Seven. Attack of the Swifties

175 "a Republican from Texas": MSNBC's *Hardball*, Aug. 12, 2004.

175 "I'm not a Republican from . . .": *Hardball*, Aug. 12, 2004.

175 "fabricated at least two . . .": *Hardball*, Aug. 12, 2004.

176 "The media, which can't get enough . . .": Washingtonpost.com, Aug. 24, 2004.

176 "case study in bias": *Los Angeles Times*, Aug. 24, 2004.

177 "John Kerry, according to every . . .": Media Matters for America, Aug. 26, 2004.

178 "Never in a campaign . . .": *New Republic*, Sept. 6, 2004.

178 "If this was a court room . . .": *Fox News Sunday*, Aug. 22, 2004.

178 "If this was Judge Judy . . .": *Fox News Sunday*, Aug. 22, 2004.

179 "from negligently self-inflicted . . .": Associated Press, Aug. 25, 2004.

179 "I do hereby swear . . .": Associated Press, Aug. 23, 2004.

179 "friends": *The Oregonian*, Aug. 20, 2004.

179 "French's inappropriate use . . .": *The Oregonian*, Sept. 25, 2004.

180 "In a combat environment . . .": *The Marine Corps Times*, Sept. 27, 2004.

180 "This was an exemplary action . . .": *USA Today*, April 13, 2004.

180 "It was a terrible mistake probably for . . .": *Boston Globe*, Aug. 6, 2004.

181 "person administering treatment": *New York Times*, Aug. 20, 2004.

181 "Me and Bill aren't the smartest . . .": *New York Times*, Aug. 20, 2004.

182 "The action that led to . . .": Media Matters for America, Sept. 3, 2004.

182 "There were at least three and . . .": CNN's *Crossfire*, Aug. 12, 2004.

182 "lacks the capacity to lead": *Richmond Times Dispatch*. Aug. 15, 2004.

183 "It was because of the bravery and the courage . . .": *Marine Corps Times*, Sept. 27, 2004.

183 "was extremely brave . . .": *USA Today*, April 13, 2004.

183 "totally fabricated": *Washington Post*, Aug. 19, 2004.

184 "Well, I just took it home . . .": Fox News' *The O'Reilly Factor*, Aug. 19, 2004.

184 " 'hotheaded,' 'blood-thirsty,' ": Doug Brinkley's *Tour of Duty* (New York: William Morrow, 2004).

184 "I couldn't bear that someone . . .": *Washington Post*, Oct. 3, 2004.

184 "It took guts, and I admire that": *New York Times*, Aug. 20, 2004.

185 "acknowledged he had no . . .": *Milwaukee Journal Sentinel*, May 6, 2004.

185 "I did not know Kerry personally": Fox News' *Hannity & Colmes*, May 28, 2004.

185 "well, because I operated very . . .": ABC Radio's *Sean Hannity Show*, Aug. 5, 2004.

185 "There's not a bullet hole . . .": *Hannity & Colmes*, Aug. Aug. 19, 2004.

185 "three 30 cal bullet . . .": *Los Angeles Times*, Aug. 20, 2004.

185 "[T]he people in our organization . . .": CNN's *Wolf Blitzer Reports*, Aug. 11, 2004.

186 "are more than 60 people . . .": CNN's *Crossfire*, Aug. 12, 2004.

188 "A clear picture of what John Kerry . . .": *USA Today*, Aug. 21, 2004.

188 "Kerry in Combat: Setting . . .": *Time*, Aug. 30, 2004.

188 "thirty-five years later . . .": ABC's *World News Tonight*, Aug. 19, 2004.

189 "If the substance of many . . .": CNBC's *Tim Russert Show*, Aug. 28, 2004.

189 "The Kerry campaign calls the charges . . .": ABC's *Nightline*, Aug. 9, 2004.

190 "The question for the . . .": ABC's *World News Tonight Sunday*, Aug. 22, 2004.

191 "misleading," but "very effective": *Newsweek*, Nov. 15, 2004.

191 "Winners": *Time*, Nov. 15, 2004.

192 "Forever pictured in my mind . . .": *Telluride Daily Plane*, Aug. 20, 2004.

192 "Until now, eyewitness evidence . . .": *Washington Post*, Aug. 22, 2004.

192 "came under small-arms . . .": *The Nation*, Aug. 23, 2004.

193 "I hope to return to this . . .": Washingtonpost.com, Aug. 30, 2004.

193 "When John O'Neill and Jerome . . .": The Daily Howler, Jan. 3, 2005.

193 "This book is not journalism.": *Los Angeles Times*, Oct. 31, 2004.

194 "We, as so many others . . .": Media Matters for America, Aug. 12, 2004.

194 "He simply helped us . . .": CNN's *Wolf Blitzer Reports*, Aug. 11, 2004.

194 "his e-mails where he made . . .": MSNBC's *Scarborough Report*, Aug. 10, 2004.

194 "So this is what the last days . . .": Free Republic, Dec. 16, 2002.

194 "Islam is like a virus": Free Republic, Nov. 26, 2002.

194 "Kerry has a long history . . .": Free Republic, March 12, 2004.

194 "Kerry offers a clear choice.": Free Republic, Feb. 8, 2004.

194 "He is growing his regulation . . .": Free Republic, Dec. 15, 2001.

195 "When is this guy going . . .": Free Republic, Feb. 24, 2004.

195 "Let the FAT HOG run!!!": Free Republic, Aug. 30, 2003.

195 "Anybody ask why . . .": Free Republic, June 8, 2003.

195 "Kerry's report": ABC's *World News Tonight*, Aug., 19, 2004.

196 "Several veterans insist . . .": *New York Times*, Aug. 20, 2004.

197 "a retired official in the Texas National Guard . . .": ABC's *Nightline*, Sept, 20, 2004.
197 "loathed": *Los Angeles Times*, Aug. 28, 2004.
197 "an anti-Bush zealot": *Washington Post*, May 23, 2005.
197 "an embittered, Bush-hating Texas cattle . . .": *Washington Post*, Nov. 9, 2004.
197 "In some ways you can certainly say . . .": CNBC's *Tim Russert Show*, Aug. 28, 2004.
198 "the central tenet of John Kerry's campaign . . .": CNN's *Reliable Sources*, Aug. 29, 2004.
198 "*almost worse*": *Time*, Sept. 20, 2004.
198 "Fifty percent of the . . .": PBS's *Charlie Rose Show*, Aug. 2, 2004.
199 "The 10th Mountain Division . . .": CNN, Aug. 15, 1996.
200 "where the whole concept of we . . .": *Hartford Courant*, Nov. 12, 2004.
200 "We are not judging the credibility . . .": *Editor & Publisher*, Aug. 24, 2004.
203 "Kerry provided access to his complete records . . .": *Los Angeles Times*, June 8, 2005.
203 "execute Standard Form 180 . . .": *Wall Street Journal*, Aug. 27, 2004.

Chapter Eight. This Is Scripted

205 "disarm Iraq, to free its . . .": *USA Today*, March 20, 2003.
205 "Saddam Hussein has had twelve years . . .": NBC News *Special Report*, March 6, 2003.
206 "This is scripted": NBC News *Special Report*, March 6, 2003.
206 "I think we were very deferential . . .": *Baltimore Sun*, April 14, 2004.
207 "When America has been attacked . . .": *American Prospect*, Sept., 2005.
208 "journalists in Washington . . .": *New York Times Magazine*, Nov. 13, 2005.
208 "you've got to take risks": *Slate*, May 3, 2004.
209 "incestuous amplification": Bob Graham, *Intelligence Matters: The CIA, the FBI, Saudi Arabia, and the Failure of America's War on Terror* (New York: Random House, 2004).
209 "How did a country . . .": *Washington Post*, Oct. 9, 2005.
209 "If anything, what we've been criticized for . . .": *Newark Star-Ledger*, July 14, 2004.
210 "We did not do our job . . .": PoynterOnline, July 27, 2004 (*http://www.poynter.org/column.asp?id=54&aid=69110*).
210 "there was a lot of snap-to-it coverage": MSNBC's *Hardball*, May 12, 2004.
211 "Did he want to say . . .": The Daily Howler, May 17, 2004.
211 "The media were victims . . .": *Washington Post*, April 27, 2004.
212 "I'm not convinced we need to do this now": *Salon*, Oct. 17, 2002.
212 "a brain fart of an idea": *The Nation*, Sept. 26, 2003.
213 "I went to the Pentagon myself . . .": CNN's *Reliable Sources*, April 20, 2003.
213 "a difficult public face for NBC . . .": All Your TV, Feb. 25, 2003 (*http://www.allyourtv.com/0203season/news/02252003donahue.html*).
214 "fewer people attended . . .": *New York Times*, Oct. 27, 2002.
214 "the *Times* ran a rare nonapology . . .": *American Prospect*, March 2003.

214 "Last Saturday, some 100,000 people . . .": *Washington Post*, Nov. 3, 2002.

214 "started last August with the failure . . .": *Washington Post*, March 16, 2003.

216 "headline-grabbing national movement": *USA Today*, Aug. 16, 2005.

216 "crazy": Michelle Malkin, Aug. 8, 2005.

216 "anti-Semite": Israpundit, Aug. 13, 2005.

216 "left-wing moonbat": Conservative Dialysis, Aug. 8, 2005.

216 "crackpot": Michelle Malkin, Aug. 8, 2005.

216 "treasonous": Fox News' *The O'Reilly Factor*, Aug. 9, 2005.

216 "hysterical noncombatant": *Slate*, Aug. 15, 2005.

216 "exploited": The Anchoress, Aug. 8, 2005.

216 "left-wing supporters": *Hardball*, Aug. 17, 2005.

216 "a tool of the left": *Hardball*, Aug. 17, 2005.

217 "Cindy Sheehan evidently thinks . . .": *Atlanta Journal-Constitution*, Aug. 11, 2005.

217 "inappropriate commercial advertisement . . .": Associated Press, Aug. 22, 2005.

217 "Stations rarely reject commercials . . .": Associated Press, Aug. 24, 2004.

218 "was a weekend of protests . . .": CNN's *Sunday Morning*, Sept. 25, 2005.

219 "Sheehan and *several others* . . . ": CNN's *Daybreak*, Sept. 27, 2005.

219 "My job is to protect the American . . .": CNN's *Breaking News*, Feb. 10, 2003.

219 "The American media did not . . .": *Media Coverage of Weapons of Mass Destruction*, Phillip Merrill College of Journalism, University of Maryland, College Park, March 9, 2004.

219 "We had no independent testing authority . . .": CNN's *Reliable Sources*, Dec. 4, 2005.

220 "A lot of what happened . . .": NBC's *Meet the press*, Dec. 25, 2005.

220 "According to half a dozen . . .": Seth Mnoonkin, *Hard News: The Scandals at The New York Times and Their Meaning for American Media* (New York: Random House, 2004), p. 242.

220 "One senior Washington bureau staffer . . .": *New York Observer*, Nov. 23, 2005.

221 "I'm not willing to work further . . .": *Washington Post*, Oct. 17, 2005.

222 "For months, hawks inside and . . .": Rollingstone.com, Nov. 17, 2005.

222 "The White House had a perfect deal . . .": *Salon*, May 27, 2004.

223 "Many of us are convinced . . .": NBC's *Nightly News*, Aug. 26, 2002.

223 "From a marketing point of view . . .": *New York Times*, Sept. 7, 2002.

224 "are only really suited for nuclear . . .": CNN's *Late Edition*, Sept. 8, 2002.

224 "You've got to hand it to them": *American Journalism Review*, August/September, 2003.

224 "The September 8 story on the aluminum . . .": *New York Review of Book*, Jan. 29, 2004.

225 "I thought for sure she'd quote . . .": *New York Review of Books*, Jan. 29, 2004.

225 "More than a half-dozen military officers . . .": *Washington Post*, June 25, 2003.

226 "a silver bullet in the form of a person": PBS's *NewsHour with Jim Lehrer*, April 22, 2003.

226 "wacky-assed piece": *New York Obserer*, April 28, 2003.

227 "There were no stockpiles of . . .": *The Guardian*, March 3, 2004.

227 "W.M.D.-I got it totally wrong": *New York Times*, Oct. 16, 2005.

227 "bitter feud over secret intelligence . . .": *Charlotte Observer,* Oct. 25, 2005.

227 "analysts at the working level . . .": *Miami Herald,* Oct. 8, 2002.

227 "Bush Clings To Dubious . . .": *Washington Post,* March 18, 2003.

227 "U.S. Lacks Specifics on Banned Arms": *Washington Post,* March 16, 2003

227 "Alleged Al Qaeda Ties . . .": *Washington Post,* Feb. 7, 2003

228 "Making The Case Against . . .": *Washington Post,* Jan. 30, 2003.

228 "went through a whole phase . . .": *New York Review of Books,* Jan. 29, 2004.

228 "C.I.A. Aides Feel Pressure in Preparing Iraqi Reports": *New York Times,* May 30, 2004.

228 "wretched": *Slate,* July 25, 2003.

228 "consume more of my attention . . .": http://forums.nytimes.com/top/opinion/readersopinions/forums/thepubliceditor/danielokrent/index.html, March 25, 2004.

228 "I see this as an explanation": *Boston Globe,* May 27, 2004.

229 "very bad journalism": *Salon,* May 12, 2005.

229 "I wish we had dealt with . . .": Associated Press, Oct. 21, 2005.

231 "My Cabinet could take . . .": *Washington Post,* March 25, 2004.

231 "Those weapons of mass destruction . . .": *Washington Post,* March 25, 2004.

232 "Somehow, over the past 30 years . . .": National Review Online, March 26, 2004.

232 "The truly serious thing about . . .": *Los Angeles Times,* March 27, 2004.

232 "I thought it was a good-natured . . .": *Fox News Sunday,* March 38, 2004.

232 "I wonder if they're spending . . .": *Hardball,* March 25, 2004.

233 "10 Days in September: Inside . . .": *Washington Post,* Jan. 27, 2002.

234 "George Bush is the president . . .": *Chicago Sun-Times,* Sept. 19, 2001.

234 "Look, I'm an American": CNN's *Larry King Live,* April 14, 2003.

234 "I heard people saying, 'All right . . . ' ": *American Journalism Review,* October/November 2003.

236 "the videotapes depict young . . .": CNN's *Breaking News,* Jan. 17, 2002.

236 "may be on the loose and . . .": *Washington Post,* Jan. 18, 2002.

236 "extraordinary videotape": CNN's *Breaking News,* Jan. 17, 2002.

238 "With terrorists out there somewhere . . .": CNN's *Crossfire,* Feb. 14, 2003.

239 "protect prime targets . . .": *New York Daily News,* Feb. 13, 2003.

240 "There is no credible . . .": *Washington Post,* Jan. 18, 2005.

240 "CNN, like all news organizations . . .": *Salon,* April 18, 2002.

241 "Dobbs, who didn't consider . . .": *New York Post,* May 25, 1999.

Chapter Nine. Lost on Downing Street

243 "Let me turn to the . . .": NBC's *Meet the Press,* June 5, 2005.

244 "Air the truth!": *St. Petersburg Times,* June 3, 2005.

245 "This record is extremely sensitive": *Sunday Times* of London, May 1, 2005. (http://www.timesonline.co.uk/article/0,2087-1593607,00.html).

245 "an absolutely accurate . . .": *Charlotte Observer,* May 6, 2005.

245 "The memo is significant because . . .": *Philadelphia Inquirer,* June 12, 2005.

246 "reported on his recent talks . . .": *Sunday Times* of London, May 1, 2005.

246 "By mid-July 2002 . . .": *New York Review of Books*, June 9, 2005.

246 "The Foreign Secretary said . . .": *Sunday Times* of London, May 1, 2005.

247 "potentially explosive revelation has . . .": *Chicago Tribune*, May 17, 2005.

248 "There is no question AP dropped the ball": *Salon*, June 14, 2005.

249 "British Memo on U.S. Plans . . .": *New York Times*, May 20, 2005.

249 "I think there should . . .": MSNBC's *Hardball*, May 25, 2005.

249 "One thing I've learned is . . .": *Washington Post*, June 16, 2005.

250 "One more note to those . . .": MSNBC.com's The Daily Nightly, June 9, 2005 (http://www.msnbc.msn.com/id/8119083/#050609).

250 "A highly classified British memo . . .": *Seattle Times*, May 6, 2005.

251 "languished": http://forums.nytimes.com/top/opinion/readersopinions/forums/thepubliceditor/danielokrent/index.html, May 20, 2005.

251 "As I read the minutes . . .": http://forums.nytimes.com/top/opinion/reader-sopinions/forums/thepubliceditor/danielokrent/index.html, May 20, 2005.

252 "The documents don't reflect . . .": *Wall Street Journal*, June 28, 2005.

252 "suggesting that the Bush . . .": CNN's *Inside Politics*, May 12, 2005.

252 "Given what has been reported . . .": http://forums.nytimes.com/top/opinion/readersopinions/forums/thepubliceditor/danielokrent/index.html, May 20, 2005.

252 "the pages of this and . . .": *Washington Post*, June 15, 2005.

253 "As smoking guns go, it is not high . . .": National Review Online, June 6, 2005.

253 "Bush had made up his mind": *Sunday Times* of London, May 1, 2005.

254 "I think that that presumes . . .": Associated Press, Aug. 10, 2002.

254 "The President has not made . . .": White House Press Release, Aug. 27, 2002.

254 "Our goal is to fully . . .": Agence France, Oct. 16, 2002.

254 "War is not my first choice . . .": NBC News *Special Report*, Nov. 7, 2002.

254 "I've not made up our . . .": NBC News *Special Report*, March 6, 2003.

254 "We are doing everything . . .": Associated Press, March 8, 2002.

254 "You'd have to be a moron . . .": WBUR's *Here and Now*, June 16, 2005.

255 "The Downing Street Memo invites . . .": Washingtonpost.com, June 7, 2005.

255 "We're rollicking, aggressive . . .": CBS Market Watch, June 9, 2005.

256 "the Dead Sea Scrolls": *New York Times*, June 14, 2005.

257 "the very edge of national respectability": *Washington Post*, June 12, 2005.

257 "usual Washington chatterboxes": *Washington Post*, June 12, 2005.

257 "anti-Semitic": *Washington Post*, June 19, 2005.

257 "wing nuts": *Washington Post*, June 8, 2005.

258 "In short, it's essentially impossible . . .": The Daily Howler, June 20, 2005.

258 "his hearty band of playmates": *Washington Post*, June 17, 2005.

259 "There's no denying that we . . .": *Washington Post*, May 6, 2001.

259 "We worked that letter with . . .": Author interview.

Chapter Ten. The MSM Goes to War

262 "winning the war in Iraq": CNN's Live Event, Dec. 18, 2005.

262 "It's almost as if the media . . .": *Salon*, Sept. 24, 2004.

262 "Enough of the media . . .": *Salon*, Sept. 24, 2004.

263 "We're extremely happy . . .": *New York Times*, March 22, 2003.

264 "U.S. officials": *Washington Post*, April 3, 2003.

264 "Pfc. Jessica Lynch, rescued . . .": *Washington Post*, April 3, 2003.

265 "For exemplary courage under . . .": *Long Beach Press-Telegram*, Aug. 27, 2003.

265 "was injured and knocked . . .": *Long Beach Press-Telegram*, Aug. 27, 2003.

265 "Isn't the Bronze Star given . . .": *Navy Times*, Aug. 11, 2003.

265 "raise my voice along with . . .": The Wilmington *News Journal*, Aug. 20, 2003.

265 "My brother and I served . . .": *San Antonio Express-News*, Sept. 4, 2003.

265 "Lynch got a Bronze Star . . .": University Wire, Dec. 17, 2003.

266 "But it is important to find . . .": NBC's *Commander in Chief*, April 25, 2003.

267 "The world is a more dangerous . . .": *Sunday Times* of London, Oct. 9, 2005.

267 "You were more vicious . . .": *Sunday Times* of London, Oct. 9, 2005.

268 "So was this journalism . . . ' ": Common Dreams, Sept. 22, 2005.

268 "taken to the woodshed": *Newsday*, May 11, 2003.

269 "troubling to many people.": *Baltimore Sun*, March 24, 2003.

269 " 'Any time that you show bodies . . .": *Baltimore Sun*, March 24, 2003.

269 " 'hate to distress to people . . .": CNN's *Reliable Sources*, Oct. 10, 1993.

270 "I don't see how we could . . .": *Washington Post*, July 25, 2003.

271 "A lot of that came across . . .": *Salon*, May 6, 2004.

271 "We couldn't believe the things . . .": *Salon*, May 6, 2004.

271 "I certainly think we've seen an . . .": *Salon*, May 6, 2004.

272 "We tend to err on the side . . .": CBSNews.com, Sept. 26, 2005 (http://www.cbsnews.com/blogs/2005/09/26/publiceye/entry885006.shtml).

272 "Please don't send any more . . .": Reality Frame, Nov. 15, 2005 (http://realityframe.blogspot.com/2005/11/inconvenient-photographs.html).

272 "found almost no pictures . . .": Los Angles Times, May 21, 2005.

273 "Well, it's probably a question . . .": C-Span's *Washington Journal*, Jan. 30, 2004.

273 "the last man in America . . .": CNBC's *Capital Report*, Sept. 30, 2003.

273 "rich and beautiful": *New York Times Magazine*, Nov. 13, 2005.

274 "White House Listens When Weekly Speaks": *New York Times*, March 11, 2003.

274 "I think, and if you go back . . .": Comedy Central's *The Daily Show*, Oct. 24, 2005.

275 "Clearly the volume in press coverage . . .": *Salon*, Aug. 12, 2004.

277 "in Iraq, the transfer of sovereignty . . .": *New York Times*, July 1, 2004.

277 "[N]o one can express unhappiness about . . .": *Washington Post*, July 25, 2004.

277 "breaking new ground on the . . .": *CBS Evening News*, Sept. 29, 2004.

278 "pushing the boundaries . . .": *New York Times*, Oct. 17, 2004.

279 "I can't go grocery shopping . . .": Poynter Online, Sept. 29, 2004 (http://www.poynter.org/column.asp?id=45&aid=72659).

279 "The genie of terrorism . . .": Poynter Online, Sept. 29, 2004 (http://www.poynter.org/column.asp?id=45&aid=72659).

279 "describe a place where fear . . .": Defense Tech, Jan. 18, 2006 (http://www.defensetech.org/archives/002093.html).

279 "as an unabashed believer . . .": *Newsweek*, June 13, 2005.

280 "The situation in Iraq right now . . .": *Philadelphia Inquirer*, Aug. 1, 2004.

280 "Fifty-three percent of . . .": *Washington Post*, March 16, 2005.

280 "To a surprising degree, given the strength . . .": *Washington Post*, June 29, 2005.

281 "They voiced their growing frustration . . .": *Time*, Sept. 18, 2005.

282 "one fiasco after another": *GQ* (http://men.style.com/gq/features/landing?id=content 4019).

282 "miscalculated the consequences": *GQ* (http://men.style.com/gq/features/landing?id=content 4019).

282 "phony" or "inadequate cases": *GQ* (http://men.style.com/gq/features/landing?id=content 4019).

282 "honest with the American public": *GQ* (http://men.style.com/gq/features/landing?id=content 4019).

282 "To say that we are . . .": *New York Observer*, Nov. 13, 2005.

282 "every once in a while . . .": *GQ* (http://men.style.com/gq/features/landing?id=content 4019).

Chapter Eleven. Still Afraid of the Facts

285 "Amidst the horror": BBC News, Sept. 5, 2005 (http://news.bbc.co.uk/2/hi/americas/4214516.stm).

285 "Katrina's media legacy . . .": *USA Today*, Sept. 5, 2005.

286 "bump in the polls": PBS's *Washington Week*, Sept. 23, 2005.

286 "I was genuinely surprised . . .": *Fox News Sunday*, Nov. 6, 2005.

286 "A Washington Tidal Wave": *Newsweek*, Jan. 16, 2006.

286 "Jack Abramoff built a . . .": *Time*, Jan. 16, 2006.

286 "Democrats took money . . .": NBC's *Today*, Jan. 26, 2006.

287 "this thing called the K Street Project": *Don Imus Show*, Jan. 9, 2006.

288 "While the brainy readers of this blog . . .": Down and Dirty, Jan. 17, 2006 (http://blogs.abcnews.com/downanddirty/2006/01/something tepid.html).

289 "Let me be as clear as I can": *Washington Times*, Jan. 21, 2006.

290 "any time you hear the United States government . . .": White House press release, April 20, 2004.

290 "to bed": *The Chris Matthews Show*, Jan. 29, 2006.

290 "found his voice": *Time*, Feb. 6, 2006.

291 "approval rating back over 53% . . .": ABC's The Note, Jan. 24, 2006.

292 "If 9/11 had happened on Bill Clinton's watch . . .": NBC's *Meet the Press*, Dec. 25, 2005.

292 "there was no . . .": *Imus in the Morning*, Dec. 1, 2005.

293 "It's simple: If your core values . . .": The Daou Report, Jan. 25, 2006 (http://daoureport.salon.com/synopsis.aspx?synopsisId=59f92c44-e7ec-48c4-91c7-b51768df79a3).

293 "centrist" who's "enormously self-confident": *Newsweek*, Aug. 1, 2005.

294 "Now they're dictating . . .": Washingtonpost.com, July 27, 2005 (http://www.washingtonpost.com/wp-dyn/content/blog/2005/07/27/BL2005 072700846 pf.html).

295 "Judge Seen as Conservative, Fair": *Los Angeles Times*, May 15, 2005.

295 "often invokes slavery . . .": *New York Times*, June 9, 2003.

295 "With these day-after profiles . . .": The Daily Howler, June 9, 2003.

Index

About the Author

ERIC BOEHLERT, an award-winning journalist who has written extensively about media, politics, and pop culture, is a contributing editor to *Rolling Stone*, writes frequently for The Huffington Post, and is a former senior writer for *Salon*. He lives with his wife and two children in Montclair, New Jersey.